THOMAS HOBBES

THOMAS HOBBES

Radical in the Service of Reaction

B Y

ARNOLD A. ROGOW

In the writings of some historians "there be subtle
conjectures at the secret aims and inward cogita-
tions of such as fall under their pen; which is
also none of the least virtues in a history, where
conjecture is thoroughly grounded, not forced to
serve the purpose of the writer in adorning his
style, or manifesting his subtlety in conjecturing."

—THOMAS HOBBES
"To the Reader," *Thucydides* (1629)

W · W · NORTON & COMPANY · *NEW YORK · LONDON*

FRONTISPIECE PHOTOGRAPH: Portrait of Thomas Hobbes in 1654, when he was sixty-six years old.

Copyright © 1986 by Arnold A. Rogow. *All rights reserved.* Published simultaneously in Canada by Penguin Books Canada Ltd, 2801 John Street, Markham, Ontario L3R 1B4. Printed in the United States of America.

FIRST EDITION

The text of this book is composed in Aster, with display type set in Weiss Initials Series I. Composition and manufacturing by the Maple-Vail Book Manufacturing Group. Book design by Marjorie J. Flock.

Library of Congress Cataloging in Publication Data
Rogow, Arnold A.
  Thomas Hobbes: radical in the service of reaction.

  Bibliography: p.
  1. Hobbes, Thomas, 1588–1679. 2. Philosophers—
Great Britain—Biography. I. Title.
  B1246.R66 1986   192 [B]   85-15592

ISBN 0-393-02288-9

W. W. Norton & Company, Inc., 500 Fifth Avenue, New York, N. Y. 10110
W. W. Norton & Company Ltd., 37 Great Russell Street, London WC1B 3NU

1 2 3 4 5 6 7 8 9 0

*For Joan Pyle Dufault
and for my children
Jennifer W. Rogow
Jeanne L. Rogow
Sarah Wolf
with love and gratitude*

CONTENTS

PREFACE

THE YEAR 1988 marks the four hundredth anniversary of the birth of Thomas Hobbes (1588–1679), perhaps the greatest, certainly the most original, of the British political philosophers. Unlike other philosophers of his time, Hobbes developed political ideas that have become more rather than less relevant in the twentieth century; indeed, today many of these ideas command greater respect, even among those who disagree, than ever before. Certainly, Hobbes was the most original of the theorists in basing political authority not on God's will or popular consent but on sheer necessity. Without such authority, as he put it in the most famous phrase of his greatest work, *Leviathan* (1651), the life of man is "solitary, poor, nasty, brutish, and short." In an age whose ruling classes—and many well below that level—still believed in the divine right of kings, Hobbes had grave doubts about the existence of a Supreme Being, and little use for the notion of rights, divine or otherwise. But equally, in an era when the concept of the social contract was beginning to take form, Hobbes in a sense looked backward to an age when absolute sovereignty was accepted absolutely. Thomas Hobbes, in short, who lived and wrote in a world that had more than its fair share of civil wars and rebellions, was the most radical thinker of his time, but he was a "radical," as someone once shrewdly observed, "in the service of reaction."[1]

He also was one of the most colorful personages of the seventeenth century. Already a student at Oxford when the long reign of Queen Elizabeth came to an end in 1603, Hobbes's life of ninety-one years witnessed the accession to the throne of three British monarchs, beginning with the first Stuart, James I; the Civil War and the execution of Charles I in 1649; the establishment and dissolution of Cromwell's Protectorate; and the Restoration of 1660. Indeed, his death in 1679 was only ten years short of England's second revolution, the so-called Glorious Revolution of 1688–89. He knew or was acquainted with, among others, Charles II, Galileo, Descartes, Bacon, Clarendon, Selden, Harvey, and, in France, Mersenne and Gassendi. Author of a dozen major works of philosophy, ethics, and political theory, many of them written in a vigorous prose style that ever since has commanded attention and even praise from literary critics, Hobbes early in his career composed a lengthy poem in Latin celebrating a geological oddity in Derbyshire known locally as the Devil's Arse, and toward the end of his life he compiled a book of bawdy epigrams.

Hobbes's originality, moreover, was not confined to politics or to his much less important writings, dealing with physics, mathematics, and optics. His extraordinary longevity (average life expectancy in seventeenth-century England was barely forty years) may have been the result of a self-imposed regimen that was centuries ahead of its time. Believing that "old men were drowned inwardly by their own moisture," Hobbes exercised strenuously to induce perspiration. Somehow aware that the quantity of air one was able to breathe diminished with age—an awareness that perhaps owed something to discussions with Harvey—Hobbes sang songs aloud as a way of expanding his lungs. When he was a young man, he developed the detoxifying habit of vomiting after an evening of heavy drinking, and from his sixtieth birthday on he drank little or no wine. He also, after sixty, preferred eating fish to eating meat and apparently curtailed his pipe smoking.

Despite his importance, Hobbes has never been the subject of a full-length biography. For almost three centuries the major source of information about his life has been John Aubrey's *Brief Lives*, a collection of biographical sketches first published in 1813, in which Hobbes is given more space than any other person.[2] Aubrey (1626–1697), the Wiltshire antiquarian and historian whose home was not far from Hobbes's birthplace in Malmesbury, met Hobbes when Aubrey was a child of eight and Hobbes was forty-six. But Aubrey did not become a friend until after Hobbes returned from France in 1651. Hence Aubrey's knowledge of Hobbes's formative period and the years that culminated in *Leviathan* is, at best, second-hand and, in addition to being sparse, often inaccurate or misleading. A tireless collector of gossip and anecdotes about the celebrities of his day, Aubrey usually left the task of verification to others. According to the *Encyclopaedia Britannica*, "he had little time for systematic work. . . . He constantly leaves blanks for dates and facts, and many queries. . . . He made some distinction between hearsay and authentic information, but had no pretence to accuracy, his retentive memory being the chief authority."[3] Nevertheless, and as frequent references to *Brief Lives* in the present work demonstrate, Aubrey's pages are indispensable to anyone interested in Hobbes's life. Although Aubrey's account should not constitute the only source of information, no writer on Hobbes, insofar as he makes any mention of Hobbes's personal history, does more than repeat Aubrey.

The reliance on Aubrey is not difficult to explain. Hobbes was a somewhat secretive man who rarely confided in others, and apparently never discussed with anyone his early years in Malmesbury and at Oxford. Unlike Pepys and Evelyn, whose lives overlapped his own, Hobbes left behind no diary; to make matters even more arduous for a biographer, only a small number of his letters survive, none of them written before he was forty. While he composed, toward the end of his life, a short autobiography in Latin verse, his *Vita* is almost wholly confined to intellectual development and achievements, brief mentions of travels, and equally brief references to certain friends of his mature years. Neither the *Autobiography* nor any other writing of Hobbes's provides much information about his family; were it not for his having been named after his father, we would probably be ignorant of his father's given name, as we are of his mother's.

As a consequence of the near silence of Hobbes, and of his contemporaries other than Aubrey, about the first twenty years of his life, most who have written about Hobbes have assumed that biographical data apart from *Brief Lives* and the sparse details contained in certain letters do not exist. In fact, as the present author was to discover, Aubrey's diligent and conscientious effort to write a complete life of Hobbes had not made use of all possible sources of information. This new knowledge of Hobbes's life, presented in the pages that follow, suggests that the Hobbes of reality was far more complex than the Hobbes described by Aubrey, and therefore not identical with the portrait we are given in *Brief Lives*.

The principal purpose of these pages, however, is not to correct the invaluable Aubrey but to argue the thesis that Hobbes's great contribution to political philosophy cannot be fully explained or understood without references to the vicissitudes of his life, beginning with the early years in Malmesbury and at Oxford. Hobbes's thought is usually said to flow from the turmoil and insecurities of his time or to be related to discoveries in science and philosophy that were influencing all men of ideas. But the relevance of his personal history has not gone entirely unnoticed. George Croom Robertson and Leo Strauss, among others, have observed that the main lines of Hobbes's political thought were fixed some years before he became a "systematic philosopher," that, in Robertson's words, "more than other philosophers, it can be said of Hobbes that the key to a right understanding of his thought is to be found in his personal circumstances and the events of his time."[4] Robertson, however, related Hobbes's philosophy to his early observations "of men and manners," whereas the interpretation advanced here stresses that Hobbes's conception of human nature, upon which his political theory rested, derived less from observations of others than from self-observation. A timid, fearful, competitive, and inordinately ambitious man himself, Hobbes assumed that timidity and fear, together with envy, greed, and ambition, were basic components of the human condition, whose evil consequences could be avoided only in an all-powerful state. Leaving aside the question whether Hobbes was right or wrong about human nature, we can infer that Hobbes's emphasis on the sovereign as protector and the state as enforcer of law and order derived, in significant part, from his own character structure and the demands it generated. Moreover, Hobbes's own need for security and his somewhat complicated view of religion cannot be wholly separated from his childhood experience of his father as a failed minor clergyman. When Hobbes was hardly more than adolescent, his father fled from Malmesbury to London, where he disappeared into obscurity. Clearly, the early years of Hobbes, like the early years of many others, were not without their traumas, and these traumas, we shall attempt to demonstrate in the chapters that follow, were not without their long-term effects.

But in making any connection between the known facts of a life and their consequences for thought and behavior, one must exercise extreme caution. Of no biography is this more true than the present work. If knowledge of Hobbes's life does not lend itself to a names-dates-places-events biography of the conventional type, even less does such knowledge support a psychoanalytic interpretation or what sometimes is called, often loosely, a psychobiography, and this study does not purport to be one. Although it makes use of psychological insights, it does so in an effort to fuse Hobbes's biography and his intellectual history. The aim is to promote a better understanding of both his life and his thought.

To the extent the effort is successful—and the best judge, as Aristotle remarked of feasts, is the guest rather than the cook—it should illuminate some origins or determinants of Hobbes's thought, clarify certain of his meanings, and perhaps, in the end, expand his continuing importance in political thought. The work at hand, however, is less a study of Hobbes's ideas than a study of his life; as the Select Bibliography suggests, many competent, even distinguished, books have been written about Hobbes's philosophy. The present author saw no need to produce still another one. Biographical studies, on the other hand, have been few. The guests, in short, in judging the feast, should bear in mind that they are being served one entrée rather than another.

ACKNOWLEDGMENTS

I AM VERY GRATEFUL TO His Grace the Duke of Devonshire for permission to examine Hobbes's papers and manuscripts at Chatsworth. Not least among the satisfactions of writing this book have been the hours spent at Chatsworth, one of the great and most beautiful houses in England. I also wish to thank Mr. Peter Day and Mr. Michael Pearman, archivists and librarians at Chatsworth, for their guidance, occasional assistance, and unfailing courtesy at all times. Mr. Pearman was particularly helpful, and I hope he is not displeased with the result. The staff of the British Library, in which whole days of effort seemed to pass in minutes, were always generous of their time in searching for, and invariably finding, the elusive book, manuscript, or letter, and I tender them my most sincere appreciation. As at Chatsworth, one of the pleasures of the research was the setting in which it could be conducted; where else but the British Library, when wishing to escape briefly from the demands of scholarship, can a fugitive from note taking stroll among Egyptian, Greek, and Roman antiquities? Would that the New York Public Library and the Metropolitan Museum of Art were housed in one building!

I have been aided and abetted by a veritable platoon of research assistants: Madeleine Wicks Argyle, Alexander Bagley, Ronald Hayduk, Eileen Koerner, Andrew Kolin, Barbara Lyon, John May, Annie Meyer, Ken Rogers, Kathleen Wilkins, and Sarah Wolf. They should not be held accountable, of course, for the uses I have made of their investigations, transcriptions, and translations. Nor is Anne Whitman, translator *sans peur and sans reproche* of some of Hobbes's more difficult Greek and Latin pages, responsible for the interpretations I have attached to them. I am grateful to her, in any case, for rendering into English what would otherwise, given my ignorance of Greek and Latin, have been unavailable.

Finally, I cannot praise too much, or thank enough, Mrs. Helen Rogers, who, among other merits, has the distinction of living in Silverthorne's House, Wiltshire. No document however obscure and buried in dust, or letter however blurred and unreadable, was beyond her ability to locate and, once located, to transcribe into intelligible English. Had I been deprived of her services, this book about Hobbes, assuming it is of interest, would have been much less worth reading.

Research and writing time were provided by a variety of institutions: the City University of New York, Tel-Aviv University, and the Rockefeller Foundation's Villa Serbelloni in Bellagio, Italy, where, in 1980, a month passed all too quickly. Certain themes discussed in the following pages were first developed before faculty seminars at the University of Sussex, Tel-Aviv University, and the Villa Serbelloni, and I am grateful to those who were present for comments and criticisms, whether or not they are reflected in the book.

The manuscript was typed by the incomparable Annette Phillips, formerly of Kenilworth, England. She, too, is free of blame for any errors of fact or interpretation.

ARNOLD A. ROGOW

January 21, 1986

THOMAS HOBBES

A Note on Sources

Unless otherwise indicated, all references to Hobbes's writings are to *The English Works of Thomas Hobbes of Malmesbury*, collected and edited by Sir William Molesworth, 11 vols. (London: Bohn, 1839–45); the Molesworth edition is cited as *E.W.*, followed by the volume and page number.

References to Aubrey's life of Hobbes, and all of his statements quoted, unless other sources are mentioned, are to *"Brief Lives," Chiefly of Contemporaries, Set Down by John Aubrey, between the Years 1669 and 1696*, edited from the author's MSS by Andrew Clark, 2 vols. (Oxford: Clarendon Press, 1898). Pages 321–403 of vol. 1 are devoted to Hobbes. I have not thought it necessary to give page references.

For the sake of convenience I have cited the Latin rather than the English titles of certain works by Hobbes, such as *De Cive*, because the Latin titles are better known. All references, however, are to editions in English, whether written in English or translated. In most instances, I have retained the original spelling and punctuation.

Within quotations, material inserted by authors or editors is indicated by parentheses; material I have added is indicated by brackets.

MALMESBURY

THE BIRTH OF THE HERO, according to many legends, often is accompanied by momentous and miraculous happenings, such as earthquakes, volcanic eruptions, or falling stars. While the event heralding Thomas Hobbes's birth in Malmesbury, Wiltshire, on April 5, 1588, was man-made rather than natural, it could hardly have been more momentous for the future of England and Europe. In his brief *Autobiography*, written in Latin verse when he was eighty-four years old, Hobbes implied that he was born prematurely as a consequence of rumors concerning the Spanish Armada. "The little worm that is myself," he declared, did not enter the world alone. Reports that the Armada "was bringing the day of doom to our race" occasioned such fear in his mother that "she brought twins to birth, myself and fear at the same time."[1]

The images in these opening lines of the *Autobiography* are as startling as they are original, and I shall return to them in due course. Let me first observe, however, that there are certain difficulties in taking Hobbes's word for it that his own appearance in this world was connected with the rumored appearance of the Armada off the English coast. The Spanish fleet did not initially sail until May 18–19, and at that time the winds blew it south, not north. On the second attempt, beginning July 11, the Armada encountered adverse weather in the English Channel, but it was within sight of The Lizard, on the southwest coast, on July 19–20. By August 2, not quite two weeks later, the Armada had been defeated.*[2]

More than one month *before* Philip's ships left Belem, at the mouth of the Tagus, on their first abortive effort to sail for England, could

---

*Some effects of the storms that battered the Spanish fleet were felt in Malmesbury. According to A. L. Rowse, in "the stormy summer of Armada year, 1588, the Avon [which flows through Malmesbury] rose so high three men [in Stratford] were marooned on a bridge." *Shakespeare the Man* (London: Paladin Books, 1976; first published 1973), 32.

Hobbes's mother have been so frightened by rumors that she was, in her son's words, "big with . . . fear"? In December 1587 some inhabitants of English coastal towns had fled at reports the Armada was in the Channel, and there may have been similar reports all through the early months of 1588. Malmesbury, however, is about thirty miles from the Bristol Channel, and almost three times that distance from the south coast. Clearly, the Spanish galleons, had they reached the English Channel as early as April 1588, would not have posed an immediate threat to inland Malmesbury.[3]

Hobbes did not mention in his *Autobiography* a prediction concerning 1588 that may have had a special significance for his mother. More than a century earlier, certain eminent Europeans were saying that 1588 would be a year of unprecedented sorrows and disasters. Basing themselves on numerologies of the Old and New Testaments, or on astronomical tables, these prophets of doom forecast, in the words of the German mathematician and astronomer Johann Müller, known as Regiomontanus, "A thousand years after the virgin birth and after five hundred more allowed the globe, the wonderful eighty-eighth begins and brings with it woe enough. If, this year, total catastrophe does not befall, if land and sea do not collapse in total ruin, yet will the whole world suffer upheavals, empires will dwindle and from everywhere will be great lamentation."[4]

Closer to Hobbes's own time, the Protestant reformer Philipp Melanchthon had viewed Luther's defiance of the pope in 1518 as the event leading up to a final cycle of ten times seven years, the length of the Babylonian captivity. According to Melanchthon, 1588 would see the seventh seal opened, the Antichrist overthrown, and the Last Judgment at hand.

In Spain, Italy, France, and elsewhere, the prophecy could be interpreted as auguring well or ill for particular regimes, factions, religious movements, and wars, including that between Spain and England. Dutch almanacs for 1588 predicted "violent tempests . . . terrible floods, hail and snow in midsummer, darkness at midday, bloody rain, monstrous births and strange convulsions of the earth, though after August things would quiet down."[5] An English pamphlet of 1576, reprinted in 1587 despite a ban by the Privy Council, alluded to the prophecy, although it was dangerous to do so; the second of two eclipses of the moon, seen as an especially ominous event, was to occur at the beginning of Elizabeth's own astrological sign, the Virgin, and only twelve days away from her birthday. To hint at or predict, however indirectly, the demise of the sovereign was high treason punishable by death. Two other pamphlets, apparently more acceptable to the queen and her Privy Council, testify to the prophecy's notoriety and its unpopularity at court. One of them was entitled "A preparation against the prognosticated dangers of 1588," while the other was headed "A discoursive problem concerning prophecies, how far they are to be valued or credited . . . devised especially in abatement of the terrible threatenings and menaces peremptorily denounced against the kingdoms and states of the world this present famous year 1588, supposed the Great-wonderful and Fatal Yeare of our Age. . . ."

Long before he wrote his *Autobiography*, Hobbes must also have been familiar with Francis Bacon's essay "Of Prophecies," in which other dire predictions were discussed. Bacon (1561–1626), who briefly employed Hobbes and had him translate into Latin three of his essays, according to Aubrey, recalled hearing "when [he] was a Childe, and Queene Elizabeth was in the Flower of her Yeares," the following "triviall" prophecy:

> When Hempe is sponne;
> England's done.

"Hempe," Bacon explained, represented the "Principiall *Letters*" of the English monarchs *"Henry, Edward, Mary, Philip, and Elizabeth,"* after whose reigns *"England* should come to utter Confusion." Bacon also remembered a prophecy for the year 1588 "which I doe not well understand."

> There shall be seene upon a day,
> Betweene the Baugh, and the May,
> The Blacke Fleet of Norway.
> When that that is come and gone,
> England build houses of Lime and Stone
> For after Warres shall you have None.

"It was generally conceived," Bacon commented, "to be meant of the Spanish Fleet, that came in 88. For that the *King of Spaines* Surname, as they say, is Norway." Bacon regarded "almost all" prophecies as "Impostures, and by idle and craftie Braines, meerely contrived and faigned, after the Event Past."[6]

Perhaps for Hobbes's mother, as for many another subject of Elizabeth's, the rumored appearance of the dreaded Spanish fleet in English waters only confirmed the worst forebodings of the prophecy. Certainly, Hobbes in 1672, with his interest in miracles, signs, and superstitions, must have known of the prophecy connected with the year of his birth, whether or not he also knew, or could guess, what role it had played in his mother's life. The prophecy, based as it was on interpretations of Scripture, could not have appealed much to a nonbeliever, and Hobbes was either a nonbeliever in orthodox religious tenets or an exceedingly skeptical and ambivalent believer. His mother, on the other hand, was married to a clergyman and was in all likelihood a loyal communicant of the Church of England. In writing his *Autobiography* Hobbes may not have wanted attention drawn to the religious beliefs of his mother and to a prognostication he himself knew to be absurd. Even less, we may assume, did he wish to associate, however remotely, his own birth with his mother's conviction that the apocalypse was at hand. The *Autobiography* contains one reference to "Our Saviour, the Man-God," which essentially serves the purpose of dating it, and while the word "God" is used on three occasions, the settings in which it is used are not specifically religious and do not commit Hobbes to any personal belief. Nor does Hobbes mention anywhere that his birthday, April 5, was Good Friday in 1588.

Unhappily, apart from two brief references in John Aubrey's *Brief Lives*, all that we know of Hobbes's mother has already been mentioned. In his account of Hobbes's life, first published in 1813, Aubrey stated that Hobbes's mother was a "Middleton" from Brokenborough, a hamlet close to Malmesbury, and that the Middletons were "a yeomanly family," that is, a family that owned enough land to provide itself, at least in good years, with a comfortable living. Aubrey may have been correct about the family name of Hobbes's mother and the village from which she came, but neither Brokenborough, nor nearby Westport, nor Malmesbury, nor any other Wiltshire town contains any record of a late-sixteenth-century family by the name of Middleton.[7]

On his paternal side, of which more is known, Hobbes was the grandson of a clergyman as well as the son of one. His father's father, John Hobbes, had been at New College, Oxford, 1520–25, and was vicar at Tilshead in 1529. Presumably, he married after Henry VIII declared himself and his country independent of the Church of Rome, and in any case before the birth of Thomas Hobbes senior in 1547. According to Aubrey, Hobbes's father had two older brothers, one of whom, Edmund, never appears in accounts of the family's history, because the first editor of *Brief Lives* assumed that there was no such brother, that Aubrey had confused Hobbes's brother, Edmund, with a nonexistent uncle of the same name. In support of Aubrey is a brass plate at the foot of the altar in Malmesbury Abbey Church with this inscription:

> HERE RESTETH THE BODY OF EDMOND HOBBES
> SOMETYME A BURGES OF THIS TOWNE, WHO DECEA-
> SED THE XXIIth DAYE OF APRIL AÑO DOMINI 1606
> EXPECTINGE THE GENERALL RESVRRECTION

*The market cross in Malmesbury, dating back to about 1490.
Described by Leland, who visited Malmesbury between 1535 and 1543,
as "a right faire costley peace of worke," the cross was intended for
"poor folkes to stande dry when rayne cummith." Hobbes as a boy
must often have taken shelter under the cross.*

Since Hobbes's brother, Edmund, lived until 1667, the Edmond who died when Hobbes was eighteen years old must have been the uncle who, wrote Aubrey, was "more than once alderman of Malmesbury."

Hobbes's other uncle, Francis, who was to play a major role in his nephew's adolescent years, was a well-to-do glover and at various times a Malmesbury burgess and alderman. Apparently, Uncle Francis married late in life, and he died childless in 1638. From him Hobbes inherited a pasture on the outskirts of Malmesbury, known locally as the "Gaston" ground, which produced an annual income of £16, a considerable sum for those days.[8] At some point, Hobbes tells us in his *Autobiography*, he made over "a little farm" to his brother because he "loved him," and in his will, dated 1677, Hobbes mentions that he had hitherto provided for his grandnephew Thomas Hobbes, one of the five grandchildren of his brother, Edmund, by giving him "a peece of land, which may and doth, I think, content him." If the "Gaston" ground is not identical with the "little farm," as it may not be, Hobbes must have owned two properties in or near Malmesbury, although only one tract of land is accounted for in his papers.[9]

Brother Edmund, older than Hobbes by about two years, followed his uncle Francis into the glove-making trade. Aubrey described him as looking somewhat like Thomas, "not so tall, but fell much short of him in his intellect, though he was a good plain understanding countrey-man. He had been bred at schoole with his brother; could have made theme, and verse, and understood a little Greek to his dyeing day." Of his three children, Edmund's only son, Francis, Aubrey reported, "pretty well resembled his uncle Thomas, especially about the eie; and probably had he had good education might have been ingeniose; but he drowned his witt in ale [i.e., was a drunkard]." Mary and Eleanor, the two sisters of Francis (who was the father of Edmund's five grandchildren referred to above), were remembered in Hobbes's will.

Hobbes also had a sister, Anne, of whom we know little more of consequence than we know of his mother. The few facts available include her marriage to a Thomas Lawrence, by whom she had seven children, and her inheriting from her father, according to Aubrey, the house in which Hobbes was born.* Apparently, only one of the seven children, a daughter named after her mother, was still alive when Hobbes died. In a letter of June 5, 1680, Aubrey's brother William suggested to him that Anne Hobbes Gay (she was married to a Richard Gay), who was not remembered in the will, should have inherited at least a token amount. "It is uncertaine whether Anne Gay have any

---

* In April 1659, Aubrey noted, Anne's "daughter or granddaughter possessed it."

brother or sister living," he informed his brother following a visit to Malmesbury, "but it is pitty the poor woman should have something if it be but 5 shillings. If you know the executor speak for her." Unfortunately, Aubrey's response to this solicitation is not recorded.[10]

William Aubrey also wrote his brother several paragraphs about Thomas Hobbes senior, and these paragraphs, which were not wholly true and perhaps not wholly fair, have ever since been accepted by historians and others as an accurate portrait of Hobbes's father by which Hobbes senior may be judged.[11] Basing his account in *Brief Lives* on this information, and adding some knowledge of his own, Aubrey described Hobbes's father as a vicar of Westport (adjoining Malmesbury), which he was not, and "one of the ignorant 'Sir Johns' of queen Elizabeth's time; could only read the prayers of the church and the homilies; and disesteemed learning (his son Edmund told me so), as not knowing the sweetnes of it." Repeating the words of his brother William, Aubrey went on to report, "The old vicar Hobs [*sic*] was a good fellow and had been at cards all Saturday night, and at church in his sleep he cries out 'Trafells is troumps . . . (viz. clubs). Then quoth the clark, 'Then, master, he tha(t) have ace doe rub.' " Hobbes senior, continues Aubrey, was "a colirice (i.e. choleric) man, and a parson (which I thinke succeeded him at Westport) provoked him (a purpose) at the church doore, soe Hobs stroke him and was forcd to fly for it and . . . in obscurity beyound London; died there, was about 80 yeares since." William Aubrey, whose 1680 statement this is, must have meant that the elder Hobbes fled to London, and not that he died there, in 1600. In *Brief Lives* John Aubrey reported that Hobbes's father lived in Thistleworth, where he was a "reader." According to Aubrey, Thomas Hobbes senior died about 1630.[12]

In Elizabeth's time and even afterward, there were a good many "ignorant 'Sir Johns' " in the clergy, and no doubt more than a few gambled, sometimes fell asleep during services, and occasionally brawled. In contemporary accounts we read of ministers who drank, fornicated, and blasphemed, and churchgoers frequently complained of clergy who were absent much of the time on business having no connection with religion. Because of their poverty—the typical parish priest was paid a stipend of between eight and ten pounds a year—some clergymen "kept their cattle in the churchyards. Others neglected their duties in favour of farming. The Rector of Normanton used not to hold the Sunday service 'because he was playing at the tables with the schoolmaster of Hambleton.' "[13]

Historians, nevertheless, have learned not to exaggerate the incompetence and moral laxness of the Elizabethan clergy. "Perhaps the most talked-of parson," one of them has remarked, "was the one who made too many visits to the alehouse and was suspected of worse weaknesses. He comes now and again into the records of the quarter sessions and boroughs, but he was not as common a type as puritan pamphleteers made out."[14] Other evidence suggests that "the wealth, status and education of most of the rural parochial clergy had probably risen during Elizabeth's reign . . . the output of clergy from the universities doubled or perhaps tripled between 1560 and 1600 and continued to rise.[15]

The role of universities in educating clergy is particularly interesting in connection with Hobbes's father. The register of Brasenose College, Oxford, for 1587 contains the following entry: "Hobbs, Thomas (Gloucs.). Priv. matr. pleb. 19 Apr. aged 40; Adm. 29 Apr. 1587."[16] Or, in modern nonabbreviated language: "Thomas Hobbes of Gloucestershire, aged 40, of a working class family ("pleb.," for "plebeius") matriculated privately ("Priv."), that is, without ceremony, April 19. He was admitted to the College April 28, 1587." Prior to his admission, in accordance with Elizabethan regulations, Hobbes's father signed the Brasenose register showing he subscribed to the Act of Supremacy, the Thirty-nine Articles, and the Book of Common Prayer.[17]

While there is no indication in Oxford University records that Hobbes's father remained long enough to graduate—indeed, evidence indicates he was back in Malmesbury by May 1589–his enrollment in Brasenose College casts some doubt on Aubrey's assertion that he was hardly more than an "ignorant 'Sir John.' " Nor is there evidence to support the contention of the Malmesbury historian Bernulf Hodge that Hobbes's father was a "choleric drunkard . . . (who) struck a man and killed him in a drunken brawl."[18] In the version of another Malmesbury author, Hobbes senior was "virtually illiterate . . . (and) was finally obliged to leave the town after killing a parishioner in a brawl."[19] Such assertions, although widely believed in Malmesbury, are not supported by Aubrey or any other source, and no one in Malmesbury appears to know how or when people of the town came to believe that Hobbes's father had committed a murder. Hodge also asserts that Thomas Hobbes, our subject, "was a keen Mason and much given to planting acacia trees."[20] At the other extreme, Peter Laslett has referred to "Sir Thomas Hobbes the curate of St. Mary's . . . and father of Thomas Hobbes, the great philosopher. (Sir, as Shakespeare used it, could mean a clergyman as well as a knight.)"[21]

The earliest known reference to Hobbes senior in Malmesbury, dated May 27, 1589, describes him as a "clerk in holy orders" (the word "curate" has a line drawn through it) and gives his age as thirty-two years. Appearing as a witness in a case against a man named Brooke, Hobbes's father testified that Brooke had said what he was reported to have said about part of a sermon preached shortly after Christmas 1588 by a Mr. Wisedome. The text for Wisedome's sermon, delivered during the course of the archdeacon's visitation at Malmesbury, was, according to the deposition, "yee my brethrene are the salt of the earth and the light of the world." Brooke had affirmed, in the presence of Hobbes senior and others, that applying the quoted statement to the ministry "was naughtie and filthie doctrine." Apparently, Brooke had also stated that at least some ministers "were not chosen of God nor of the holy ghost."[22] The deposition does not record the opinion of the witness Hobbes and does not tell the outcome of the case against Brooke.

One year later, in 1590, the churchwardens of Brokenborough, a chapel of Westport, complained to the archdeacon of Wiltshire that their curate was "a common alehouse goer."[23] Since the curate is not identified by name, we cannot be certain that the complaint refers to Hobbes's father although it is consistent with Aubrey's report that Hobbes senior was "a good fellow." Again, we do not know the outcome. We hear nothing more of Hobbes's father for twelve years, and then, in November 1602, "Magister Hobbes clericus curate de Brokenborow" was complained of for not delivering the quarterly sermon and for failing to catechize the youth. In December the charge was repeated.[24]

We are not told what rebuke or punishment, if any, was accorded Hobbes senior, but by 1602 the elder Hobbes was having a variety of difficulties with his Brokenborough parishioners. One of them, touching on his relationship to the vicar of Westport, had its origins in Henry VIII's dissolution of the Malmesbury Benedictine monastery. When the patronage of the two Malmesbury livings (i.e., ministries) of St. Paul's parish and St. Mary's parish, Westport, passed from the abbot to the king in 1548, land was set aside in Westport for the support of a "Stipendiary" priest, or curate, who would assist the vicar of Westport in attending to the spiritual needs of parishoners in Brokenborough and other outlying areas. On a number of occasions parishes served by a vicar-appointed curate had complained of neglect, but without effect; as one note written on the margin of a report put it, "The vicar's man doe yt well ynough."[25]

In 1602 the "vicar's man" was Hobbes's father, and he clearly was not doing "yt well ynough" in the opinion of his parishioners. In a case brought against Hobbes senior and the Westport vicar, Henry Longe (who had held that position for twelve years), by some Brokenborough churchgoers, Hobbes, who resided in Westport, was charged with refusing to live in Brokenborough in accordance with long-standing practice and tradition. The custom of residing in Brokenborough had begun even before the dissolution of the monastery when, "by reason of the rising of the waters betweene Brokenbury and Malmesbury the functions of the Church as weddinges Christeninges burials and such like could not in due tyme be executed and donne at Malmsbury as they ought and weare accustomed whereupon it was condiscended and agreed togeather with the Bishopp of Saranum then be inge and the Abbott as also with the enhabitants of Brockenbury that the saide Chappelle should be hallowed and that there shoulde be a Curate there resident maintayned partely by the Abbot & partely by the inhabitants of Brockenbury [crossed out] there to doe & performe such ecclesiastical rights as there weare & should be from tyme to tyme in succeding ages to be donne."

To this end, continued the deposition, the Brokenborough inhabitants had agreed to pay the resident curate the sum of twenty-three shillings, four pence, over and above what he was paid by the abbot or, later, vicar of Westport. Furthermore, they had set aside "a Chamber which was and is allowed for to lodge the Curate in . . . the predecessors of the saide Hobbes . . . have lodged there and . . . have bin resident upon the same continually . . . but of late yeares . . . (some) inhabitants . . . have detayned the same moneys from the saide Hobbes and doe forbeare to make payment thereof . . . because the saide Hobbes is not there resident and doth not there inhabit. . . ." Apparently, the vicar's wife sided with the aggrieved Brokenborough parishioners, because she was heard to "intreate the parishioners of Brockenbury to beare with her husband a while for that they had not a Curate to serve theire Chappelle aforesaide and tould them that so longe as they wanted a Curate or minister her saide husbande woulde not have the said sume of (twenty-three shillings, four pence) yerely."[26]

The problems posed by the controversy between Hobbes senior and his Brokenborough parishioners did not admit of an easy solution. As a historian of the period has observed, if somewhat harshly, the alternative to filling village clerical posts with "bakers, butlers, cooks, good archers, falconers, and horsekeepers" was "to return to one of the abuses that had given the Reformation its initial impulse by seeking license to hold several livings together, and sending some bucolic and bibulous hedge priest as curate to the parishes the vicar could not get around."[27]

Apparently, Hobbes's father continued to reside in Westport, because in another, more serious court proceeding he is referred to as "curate of Brokenborow . . . but dwelleth in Westport." Indeed, this case, in which Hobbes senior was the defendant in a libel suit brought against him by another clergyman, anticipated the later action against the elder Hobbes that originated in the exchange of blows mentioned by Aubrey. But Aubrey was not entirely accurate in his account, and others have gone further astray in their reports of the incident.

In this first case of *Jeane* v. *Hobbes*, the hearing of which began on October 12, 1603, Hobbes was accused of calling Richard Jeane, rector of Foxley, "a knave and an arrand knave and a drunken knave and one that would have killed his brother minister Mr. Androwes."* Witnesses also testified that Hobbes senior had "saide further that the saide Jeane was drunke almost every Saturnsday before Mr. Andrewes and he fell out." One of those present when the elder Hobbes had spoken these words swore he heard Hobbes "confesse that he had spoken the saide wordes . . . and hath saide further that he would justefie it in the open Courte."[28]

Apparently Hobbes senior was unable to "justifie" his verbal abuse of Jeane at subsequent hearings on October 25, November 8 and 22, and December 6, though on November 22 he supplied the additional information that Jeane would come to Malmesbury "and there make merry and drink and then he would walk up and down with his hat cast over his face." In December or January 1604 the Salisbury Consistory Court found for Jeane, ordering Hobbes senior to do public penance in Foxley church on February 5, during the time of morning prayer. Hobbes, however, failed to appear on that occasion, and three days later, on February 8, Jeane was back before the court displaying "formal letters of penitence by the said Hobbs" and alleging under oath "that being personally present at morning prayer on the said fifth day in February in the church of Foxleye . . . from the beginning to the end of morning prayer . . . he sufficiently expected the same Thomas would come to do the penance ordered. . . ." Instead, "the said Hobbs utterly did not come . . . but carried himself contumaciously. . . ." The consequence, not unexpected, was that the court revoked the order requiring Hobbes's appearance and listened sympathetically to Jeane's prayer "to have him declared contumacious" and, as punishment, excommunicated. At the close of the hearing, which Hobbes senior also had not attended, the court "pronounced the said Hobbs contumacious and . . . excommunicate accordingly."

Whatever his reasons for not appearing in Foxley church or at the hearing of February 8, Hobbes senior did not quietly or contritely accept the Salisbury Consistory Court's verdict. On February 22, 1604, witnesses appeared once again before the court in connection with Hobbes's "violent assault on Richard Jeane of Foxley." According to

---

* Richard Andrews was rector of Little Somerford, which was about four miles from Foxley. Foxley and Westport parishes adjoined each other.

Malmesbury town clock and bell tower. It was in this church-yard that Hobbes's father, the curate, assaulted Richard Jeane. Photo: Jeremy Fletcher, Wiltshire.

one Robert Graunger of Westport, husbandman,* aged about sixty, "upon a Saturnsday [Saturday again!] either a fortnight or a seve-night last past in the present month . . . [Graunger] standing at a butcher's shop in Malmesbury and neere the churchyearde of Malmesbury . . . sawe Thomas Hobbes standing not farre off . . . and not long after came Mr. Richard Jeane parson of Foxley . . . [who] went into the church yard . . . and as he was going into the saide churchyearde the saide Thomas Hobbes followed the saide Mr. Jeane and begann to revyle at him asking him how chaunce he had excom-municated him whereat the saide Mr. Jeane replyed . . . that he did not excommunicate him and then the saide Thomas Hobbes followed the saide Mr. Jeane revyling him and calling him knave and coming neare unto him strooke him the saide Mr. Jeane with his fiste under the eare or about the head and stroake off his hatt and made him lett fall his cloake from his backe all which the said Mr. Jeane suffered untill the saide Hobbes hanged about him and would not desist from striking the saide Mr. Jeane and then he (Jeane) in his owne defence strooke the said Thomas Hobbes and shaking him off from him threw him to the grounde."[29] Hobbes senior, as may be guessed, was not present when the Salisbury Consistory Court once more heard testi-mony against him, presumably for the last time. By February 22 he had left Malmesbury for the environs of London (Thistleworth, if Aubrey is correct), apparently never to be seen there again.

The Malmesbury from which Hobbes senior fled, and from which his son departed for Oxford in 1603, was (and still is) one of the most pleasant towns in England.[30] Although Malmesbury apparently did not exist in Roman times, as did nearby Bath and Cirencester, the earliest records suggest that the town's famous monastery dated to 675, when Leutherius, the fourth bishop of the West Saxons, provided the land for the site. Even then, religious controversies, not totally unlike those that plagued England in Hobbes's time, were important. The Venerable Bede, referring to the year 705, wrote that Aldhelm, who serves Malmesbury as a kind of patron saint, "when he was still a priest and abbot of the monastery . . . wrote by order of the synod of his people a remarkable treatise against the British error of not celebrating Easter at the proper time and of doing many other things contrary to ecclesiastical purity and peace, and by this book brought over many of the Britons who were subject . . . to the orthodox cele-bration of Easter."[31] Aldhelm wrote, in addition to theological works,

---

* Most husbandmen, whose social ranking was just below that of yeomen, "were work-ers of land they did not own but rented." Laslett, World, 45.

books in both prose and verse, hymns, letters, and, not least, a monograph in praise of virginity.

Hobbes in his *Autobiography* mentioned, "Hither, too [that is, to Malmesbury], was brought by Aldhelm the Latin Muse, here the Latin language had its first school." One wonders what he made of the many miracles attributed to Aldhelm, and whether they had any relationship to his own lifelong interest in miracles. For example, Aldhelm was said to have built a church in Dorset that, although never completely roofed, stayed totally dry within, even in the heaviest rain. He was also said to have thrown his chasuble behind him, thinking someone was there to catch it; he was alone, but the chasuble was suspended in midair, held up by a ray of light coming in through a window. Hobbes's skepticism probably asserted itself in connection with still another miracle, one involving the pope of the time, Sergius, who was widely believed to have fathered a child born in the house of his chamberlain. Aldhelm, conveniently in Rome, questioned the nine-day-old baby about his paternity. The infant, speaking clearly, declared that Sergius "was holy and undefiled and ever had been." To no one's surprise Aldhelm returned to Malmesbury with a papal bull confirming the rights of the abbey, over which he ruled as abbot for thirty-three years.[32]

Little is known of Malmesbury for almost two hundred years following the death of Aldhelm in 709, but in 880, toward the end of the Saxon period, King Alfred made the town a borough, and it has been a borough ever since. Indeed, in 1980, as the oldest borough in England, it celebrated the eleven hundredth anniversary of Alfred's grant of a charter. By the time Hobbes was born, Malmesbury had already been a borough for more than seven hundred years, but Hobbes did not consider that fact among the "many things worth mentioning" in his *Autobiography*, though he did write that the town "sent two burgesses to the Council of the realm and still today retains that ancient privilege."

Malmesbury's next hero, after Aldhelm, was Alfred's grandson Athelstan (895–940), to whom Hobbes gave twice as much space. "Here, too," Hobbes noted, "are buried the bones of great Athelstane, and his image in stone lies upon his tomb. It was he that gave the people, as reward of their valour, the neighboring fields, which they had drenched with the blood of the Danes." Athelstan, the last if not also the greatest of the eminent Saxon kings of England, was a distinguished warrior who, in addition to spilling Danish blood, defeated the Northumbrians, conquered Scotland as far as Aberdeen, attacked the Orkneys, and routed an army of Scots and Welsh. Athelstan also was a great churchman and statesman, a collector of books and art works, a builder of cathedrals who provided the land on which St. Paul's in London is built, and the creator of a rudimentary civil service. Yet Hobbes, the "twin" of fear who hated war and any kind of violence, mentioned nothing of Athelstan's peacetime accomplishments. Having paid tribute to Aldhelm's unique scholarship, he perhaps wanted to emphasize a different talent in whose exercise Athelstan excelled beyond any other ruler of his time. But the possibility, to which we shall later return, should not be overlooked that Hobbes, like many other timid souls, greatly if secretly admired the courage and bravery of others, and identified to some extent with those stalwart heroes of English history who sought danger rather than endeavored to avoid it. His *Autobiography* refers admiringly to Drake and Cavendish, both of them great navigators of hitherto unknown portions of the globe, and Drake a conqueror of the Armada (which Hobbes did not mention). Of perhaps greater significance is Hobbes's frequent recourse in all of his writings to adversary language and aggressive images, and his clear preference for idioms and metaphors based on military experience.

Indeed, Hobbes's intellectual differences with contemporaries are invariably couched in language taken from the battlefield. Referring to a death-threatening illness, Hobbes declared in his *Autobiography*, "But I stood my ground and *she* fled." His book *Leviathan* "now fights for all kings." The later *De Corpore*, he wrote, "turned out to be a cause of perpetual war against me. . . . Both nests of theologians were my foes." Algebra is "This deadly enemy of geometry," and "my adversary [John Wallis, Savilian Professor of Mathematics at Oxford, of whom more later] had at last withdrawn from the field." When he expounded the nature of "Proportion," Hobbes's "victory was acknowledged by all. In other fields my opponents were doing their best to hide their grievous wounds. . . . I pressed home the assault. . . . Wallis enters the fray. . . . And now the whole host of Wallisians, confident of victory, was led out of their camp. But when I saw them deploying on a treacherous ground . . . I resolved on fight, turned, and in one moment scattered, slaughtered, routed countless foes." Toward the end of his *Autobiography*, Hobbes observed to Du Verdus, his French friend and confidant to whom it was addressed, "You have heard of my wars. What more would you like to be told?" Du Verdus, like a modern reader of the *Autobiography* and other works, might well have asked whether Hobbes saw himself as an Athelstan of scholars who had drenched the intellectual soil of Europe with the blood of theologians, mathematicians, and philosophers, but as far as we know, Hobbes never gave explicit expression to this view. Still, the question is an important one, and we shall return to it in a later chapter.

Hobbes made no reference to the third of the great Malmesburians, William of Malmesbury (ca. 1095–1143), the outstanding historian of his time. Half Norman and half Saxon, William was a book collector as well as a theologian, and for a time served as the librarian of the abbey. Of his numerous books, one of which was a life of Aldhelm, the most important was a history of England to the year 1142, which is still consulted by those particularly interested in Saxon history. He also was an authority on the First Crusade, and William, like Aldhelm, was fond of bawdy gossip, accounts of which frequently found their way into his writings.

Perhaps Hobbes was less impressed by William than by Athelstan and Aldhelm. Like Hobbes at Oxford, William had little interest in logic, and he reminds us of the Hobbes who translated Thucydides into English when he writes that history interested him because it "excites its readers by example to frame their lives to the pursuit of good or to aversion of evil."[33] Hobbes in his introductory "To the Readers" with which he began his translation noted that "the principal and proper work of history [was] to instruct and enable men, by the knowledge of actions past, to bear themselves prudently in the present and providently towards the future. . . ."* But any similarities between William of Malmesbury and Hobbes of Malmesbury are more than outweighed by William's religiosity and his rejection of any secular influences in the church. Hobbes also may not have been impressed by William's tribute to his parents, to his father especially, through whom he "became familiar with books"—"Indeed," William remarked, "I was so instructed by my father that had I turned aside to other pursuits, I should have considered it as jeapardy to my soul and discredit to my character."[34] In all of his writings, Hobbes's sole reference to his father is the following line in his *Autobiography:* "From my father, who was minister, I received baptism, and the name he gave me was his own."

The four and one-half centuries between William's death and Hobbes's birth were relatively uneventful ones for Malmesbury, though not for its great abbey. Taking no part in the War of the Roses, Malmesbury devoted itself to the woolen trade, and by the fourteenth century the town had become an important center for the weaving of cloth. With eight mills on the river and looms everywhere, even in the abbey itself after the dissolution in the sixteenth century, Malmesbury was producing 3,000 cloths annually of a quality highly regarded everywhere.

For the abbey, of course, the story was very different. Though it

* Hobbes's translation of Thucydides is discussed below, pp. 78–91.

possessed considerable wealth—its income in 1539 was more than £830, a large sum for those days—it had been allowed to fall into disrepair for some time before the dissolution, and its reputation, as a result of recurrent reports that some monks were frequently drunk or living openly with women, had also suffered. Hence there were no protests, much less opposition, in December 1539 when, as one Malmesbury historian "imagines" the appointed day, "the convent bells ceased to chime their accustomed routine; the gates which had stood hospitably open for so many centuries were closed; the keys were handed over to the King's representative, Sir Edward Baynton; the Abbot with his little pension of 200 marks rode off to the house that had been reserved for him in Bristol; the monks doffed their black habits and scattered to new homes accepting their pittances of from £6 to £10 a year with the best grace they could; and the famous Abbey of Malmesbury with its 900 years history ceased to exist."[35]

The abbey was not unoccupied long. Visiting the town less than three years later, John Leland, the archaeologist, reported, "The hole loggings of thabbay be now longging to one Stumpe, an exceding riche clothiar that boute them of the king. . . . At this present tyme every corner of the vaste houses of office that belongid to thabbay be fulle of lumbes to weve clooth yn, and this Stumpe entendith to make a stret or 2. for clothier in the bak vacant ground of the abbay that is wityn the toune waulles."[36] In converting the abbey to the manufacture of cloth, William Stumpe, who was also a member of Parliament, created one of the first factories in England, and for a time the venture was successful. But by the time Stumpe died in November 1553, the trade in cloth had begun to decline. The earlier prosperity had resulted in the setting aside of more cultivated land for sheep grazing, thereby increasing the number of unemployed agricultural workers. Food prices had also increased sharply. Weavers, threatened by the beginning factory system, apparently enjoyed widespread support, for in 1555–56 an act was passed taking account of the weavers' complaint "that rich and wealthy clothiers do in many ways oppress them, some by setting up and keeping in their houses divers looms." The act prohibited more than one loom in any rural house, or more than two in any town house. The cloth trade, nevertheless, did not regain its former prosperity.

Thus, the Malmesbury in which Hobbes was born on April 5, 1588, had seen better days. While we lack population figures and related information, we known from a 1548 census that the number of communicants resident in Malmesbury was 860. Assuming that most although not all Malmesburians qualified to do so had taken communion that year—until 1690 attendance at church services and participation in communion were compulsory—the population that year must have been something over or under 1,000.[37] But fluctuations in the number of inhabitants—as a result of widespread economic distress, wars, and epidemics, including plague—were very marked in those years, and the latter half of the sixteenth century probably witnessed a population decline. Judging by rough maps and diagrams of Malmesbury at various times in its history, there were never more than 150–200 houses or cottages in and around the town until the late nineteenth century.

Some of these houses, according to the Malmesbury historian Hodge, were inhabited by ancestors of William Penn, George Washington, and Abraham Lincoln. The Penn family, Hodge wrote in 1968, originated in Minety, approximately five miles from Malmesbury; one of the Penns, who died about 1590, was Malmesbury's law clerk. The Washingtons of Garsdon Manor, two miles from Malmesbury, included Sir Lawrence Washington, member of Parliament in 1661, the son of "the Sulgrave Washingtons, from whence came the famous George." Lincoln's mother, Nancy Hanks, "was a Malmesbury woman. . . . The Hanks are one of the oldest families in Malmesbury and have been here from Saxon days. . . . In fact the name means 'The Weaver' in Saxon."[38]

The typical Malmesbury house in the late sixteenth century was built of local limestone and tiled, and usually contained one room and a buttery or pantry on the ground floor and one or two bedrooms upstairs. In one of these houses in Westport, Aubrey wrote, "the farthest howse on the left hand as you goe to Tedbury, leaving the church on your right," Hobbes was born. Aubrey did not describe the furnishings of the house, and no trace of the house or its furnishings remains, but perhaps its contents were not unlike those of another stone cottage which were inventoried in 1663. This cottage in Writtle, consisting of "a hall and a parlour downstairs and a bedroom above," had been owned by a widow, one Mary May, and when she died in April 1663, she left the following possessions, as listed and valued in a contemporary account:

> In ye hall—One cubard, one Table, Tressells, and forme, one Setle & an old chair, 15s.
> In ye parlour—One old Bedstead, one featherbed, two Boulstars, two pillowes, three Blanckets, & one flock bed, 3 li. 10s.
> In ye chamber—Two Chairs, one old bedstead, Curtans, one Covering & a Blackit, 10s. 6d; two Cobeireons (andirons), one pair of tongs, one fire shovel, one Spitt, & one broken Warming pan, 8s. 6d; one Wainscott Chair, two Stooles, two

Wheeles, thre old pillowes, one table, and flaskitt, two Chists,
& Severall other Small implements, 1 li. 6s. 8d. Wearing
apparell & redy Money 1 li. 9s. 6d.
Some Totall—8 li. os. 2d.[39]

By the standards of the time, the widow May was not poor, and her
cottage may have been better furnished than the Hobbes house in
Westport. Unfortunately, we do not know how much Hobbes's father,
the curate of Brokenborough, was paid by the vicar of Westport; we
know only, from a document already cited, that the aggrieved Brokenborough parishioners would have paid their curate an additional
twenty-three shillings, four pence, had he resided in their village.
According to Aubrey, the livings of Westport and Charlton were "both
worth £60 or £80 per annum," but, as we have seen, the senior Hobbes
was not the vicar of Westport or Charlton. Perhaps his stipend as one
of the lesser clergy was not far from the estimate quoted earlier for a
"typical parish priest" of between eight and ten pounds a year. If so,
he deprived himself and his family of more than a tenth of his potential income by refusing to live in Brokenborough.

Of his childhood Hobbes wrote in his *Autobiography* only, "I was
four years learning to speak, and four more learning to read, count,
and shape my letters indifferently well." Aubrey added to this that
Hobbes "at four yeares old . . . went to schoole in Westport church,
till eight; by that time he could read well, and number four figures.
Afterwards he went to schoole to Malmesbury, to Mr. Evans, the minister of the towne. . . ." Because his hair was black, Aubrey further
reported, Hobbes's "schoolfellows were wont to call him 'Crowe.' "
Edmund Hobbes, the brother, and a Mr. Wayte who had attended
school with Hobbes, told Aubrey that when Hobbes "was a boy he
was playsome enough, but withall he had even then a contemplative
melancholinesse."

By "playsome" they may have meant that Hobbes, like other boys
of the town, engaged in mock fights and wrestling matches, fished
and swam in the Avon, rolled hoops, practiced archery, and ran foot
races; as will be seen later, Hobbes in middle and old age exercised
regularly, and his habit of exerting himself physically may well have
begun early in life. At Oxford, Hobbes enjoyed trapping birds, and
earlier in Malmesbury he probably often joined his friends in "'birds-
nesting," the aim of which was to collect as many different birds'
eggs from as many different nests as possible. Pinholes were then made
in the eggs, the contents blown out, and the eggs threaded on a string.
Boys with a complete collection of eggs were much admired.

The game of conkers was another favorite local sport. "Conkers," or horse chestnuts, were pierced by a hole through which a string was passed, knotted at one end. The game was played by two boys, each of whom was allowed several strikes with his conker at his opponent's conker. The boy whose conker was damaged or destroyed in this manner was the loser.[40]

At Malmesbury fairs, of which there were a number during the year, individual and group games of all sorts, Punch-and-Judy shows, jesters, dances, songfests, and other diversions were popular. The woolsack race, a team affair usually involving four runners, consisted of carrying a woolsack weighing about sixty-five pounds a total distance of one thousand yards or more. Since part of the course was uphill, winning was far from easy. Hobbes may have been too young to participate, but he must have attended the fairs and watched more than one woolsack race during his years in Malmesbury. If Aubrey is correct, Hobbes delighted in the music played and sung at fairs. Aubrey twice mentioned that Hobbes "when young . . . loved musique," and in one reference he has Hobbes playing the lute, in another the "base-violl."

Still, one can infer from the reference to "contemplative melancholinesse" quoted earlier that Hobbes was a serious youth more interested in books than in games and sports. In his *Autobiography* Hobbes himself stated that for six years, until he was fourteen and went to Oxford, he applied himself to Greek and Latin. During all or most of those years Hobbes was a favorite student of Robert Latimer, then a young university graduate and bachelor of nineteen or twenty, according to Aubrey, and therefore Hobbes's senior by no more than ten years.* Latimer, who "wore a dudgeon [i.e., a wooden-handled dagger], with a knife and bodkin [i.e., stiletto]," "delighted" in Hobbes's company "and used to instruct him, and two or three ingeniose youths more, in the evening till nine a clock." Apparently, Latimer was an inspired teacher and Hobbes an apt student: before he left for Oxford, Hobbes translated Euripides' *Medea* from Greek into Latin and presented his work to Latimer. Unfortunately, this translation, which must have been Hobbes's first important written effort, could not be found when Aubrey searched for it among Latimer's papers many years later, allegedly because "the good huswives had sacrificed (it)," that is, burned it in their cooking oven.

Did the idea of translating Euripides' *Medea* from Greek into Latin originate with Latimer or with Hobbes? We cannot answer that ques-

---

* There is a problem about this. Aubrey implied elsewhere that Latimer was seventy when he died in 1634. If so, Latimer must have been at least thirty when Hobbes was his student.

tion, but in stating that Hobbes "presented his work to Latimer" on the eve, apparently, of his departure for Oxford, Aubrey seems to imply that the translation was Hobbes's parting gift to his tutor, and thus perhaps something of a surprise. But whether or not Hobbes's version of *Medea* was the result of a class assignment—so far as we are aware, the modern requirement of a final paper or essay of some sort was unknown in those days—Hobbes's undertaking the translation of *Medea* rather than of a play by, say, Aeschylus or Sophocles is not without interest. For in Euripides, Hobbes even as a boy of fifteen may have discerned, as he did in Thucydides more than twenty years later, a kindred spirit, and in *Medea*, an episode of which he was to mention at least four times in his writings, Hobbes may have recognized a family tragedy that, its murders and filicides apart, bore some relevance to his own history.

Euripides (ca. 485–407 B.C.), the author of approximately eighty-eight plays (of which only nineteen survive), was regarded in his own time as a realist; Sophocles is supposed to have remarked that whereas he, Sophocles, depicted men as they ought to be, or as one ought to show them to be, Euripides depicted men as they actually were.[41] Living through the horrors of the Peloponnesian War, as did Thucydides, Euripides viewed human life as tragic and pitiful, and war, whether it ended in victory or defeat, as the worst evil of man's fate. A disbeliever in religion, Euripides could not endorse the conventional Greek view that the gods were motivated by the same jealousies and lusts that stirred mankind. "If gods do evil," he admonished his contemporaries, "then they are not gods," and he was too much a skeptic to accept uncritically the existence of immortality, heaven, and hell. "Of certainties," the distinguished classicist Edith Hamilton has observed of Euripides, "he had few," and she quotes his lines

> For who knows if the thing that we call death
> Is life, and our life dying—who can know?
> Save only that all we beneath the sun
> Are sick and suffering, and those gone before
> Not sick, not touched with evil.[42]

The mature Hobbes could well have written these words during the Civil War, and that Hobbes, too, could have been accused, as Euripides was accused by Aristophanes in *The Frogs*, of having taught his countrymen "to think, see, understand, suspect, question, everything."[43]

In *Medea*, as in other plays of Euripides, a woman is the chief character. The legend upon which the play is based has Medea, a sorceress partly descended from the god Helius, meeting Jason when he comes, with the Argonauts, to the extreme eastern end of the Black Sea seeking the Golden Fleece. Falling in love with him, Medea helps him escape her father, King Aeetes, the guardian of the Fleece, by murdering her brother and throwing parts of his body into the water, thereby guaranteeing Jason's and her own escape, since the pursuing ships of her father stop to collect the scattered pieces of her dead brother. Established in Iolcus, Jason's hereditary kingdom, Medea, now Jason's wife and mother of his two children, takes vengeance against Jason's uncle Pelias, who has cheated Jason of certain rights. She manages to persuade Pelias's daughters that their father will regain his youth if they kill him, cut him up, and boil him for a time with herbs and incantations. The death of Pelias, far from having the desired effect of restoring Jason's rights, forces Jason and Medea into a second exile, together with their two children.

Corinth, their new home, is the setting of Euripides' play. Jason, allegedly motivated by the desire to advance his fortunes, dissolves his marriage with Medea in order to take a new wife, the daughter of Creon, king of Corinth. Believing that she has been put aside because Jason has tired of her, Medea resolves to destroy Creon and his daughter by presenting them with robes that, if worn, exude a substance that clings to flesh and burns it. Medea, whose rage at Jason and hunger for revenge are still not satisfied when she receives news of the deaths of Creon and his daughter, and who believes that her children will not be safe in Corinth, murders the two boys. The play ends with Medea's departure for Athens, where she has been promised the protection of King Aegeus.

Whatever the meanings and merits of *Medea* to Hobbes, no other dramatic or literary work is referred to as often in his writings. The futile effort of Pelias's daughters to rejuvenate their father is related, with slight modifications of wording, in *De Corpore Politico; or, The Elements of Law, Moral and Politic,* copies of which Hobbes circulated in 1640, though it was not formally published until 1650; in *De Cive* (1642); and in *Leviathan* (1651). The thrice-repeated tale of Pelias's fate serves Hobbes as an example, by analogy, of the dangers attendant upon civil unrest, whether in behalf of reform of government or of other change. As he uses the legend in *Leviathan,* "they that go about by disobedience, to do no more than reform the commonwealth, shall find they do thereby destroy it; like the foolish daughters of Pelias, in the fable; which desiring to renew the youth of their decrepit father, did by the counsel of Medea, cut him in pieces, and boil him, together with strange herbs, but made not of him a new man."[44] In *De Corpore Politico,* the context of the story is the "eloquence and want of discretion [that] concur to the stirring of rebellion." Pelias's daughters,

Hobbes continues, "desiring to restore their old decripit father to the vigour of his youth, by the counsel of Medea, chopped him in pieces, and set him a boiling with I know not what herbs in a cauldron, but could not revive him again. So when eloquence and want of judgment go together, want of judgment, like the daughters of Pelias, consenteth, through eloquence, which is as the witchcraft of Medea, to cut the commonwealth in pieces, upon pretence or hope of reformation. . . ."[45]

In *Of Liberty and Necessity* (1654), Hobbes's discussion of free will in reply to Bishop Bramhall, Medea herself is cited in proof of Hobbes's contention that "the *last* dictate of the understanding does *necessitate* the *action*, though not as the whole cause, yet as the last cause, as the last feather necessitates the breaking of a horse's back, when there are so many laid on before, as there needed but the addition of one to make the weight sufficient." To Bramhall's quoting the statement *"Video meliora, proboque, / Deteriora sequor"* ("I see and approve of better things, but I follow the worse which I condemn"), Hobbes's rejoinder was that the "saying, as pretty as it is, is not true; for though Medea saw many reasons to forbear killing her children, yet the last dictate of her judgment was, that the present revenge on her husband outweighed them all, and thereupon the wicked action *necessarily* followed."[46]

Clearly, *Medea* made an impression on Hobbes, but the significance of the play for the boy in Malmesbury, Latimer's apt student, could not have been identical with the uses to which it was put by the Hobbes of *De Cive* and *Leviathan*. In the light of what we know, admittedly too little, of the family history, particularly the history of Hobbes's "collirice" father, we may wonder about the private meanings or resonances of Euripides' tragedy for the elder Hobbes's second son, who could not have been more than fourteen or fifteen years old when he presented his translation to the schoolmaster Latimer. Did he see in Jason's treatment of Medea and their children some elements of his father's treatment of the family, and did he observe in Medea's maniacal rage something of the temper that, in 1604, had led his father to assault Richard Jeane? Was Hobbes himself, and his siblings as well, the occasional target of that anger, thereby leading him to identify to some extent with the victims of Medea's fury? Or did Medea, who had sacrificed much for the husband who ultimately betrayed her, and whose lust for revenge was insatiable, arouse complicated emotions in the youthful Hobbes similar to those ambivalent feelings he may have been experiencing in connection with his mother, left behind in 1603 or 1604 with three adolescent children to support? In Medea, Hobbes perhaps also saw certain images of himself, for he, too, as we shall see, could give expression to aggressive anger and even rage, albeit not in the forms preferred by the jilted, venomous sorceress. Unfortunately, the paucity of evidence does not permit us to do more than speculate about these matters, but we can easily imagine that Hobbes, young as he was, may have recognized elements of his own condition and that of others in such lines as these:

> But now there's hatred everywhere, Love is diseased.

and

> What's strange in that? Have you only just discovered
> That everyone loves himself more than his neighbor?
> Some have good reason, others get something out of it
> [with reference to Jason's desertion].

and

> A person of sense ought never to have his children
> Brought up to be more clever than the average.
> For, apart from cleverness bringing them no profit,
> It will make them objects of envy and ill-will.
> If you put new ideas before the eyes of fools
> They'll think you foolish and worthless into the bargain;
> And if you are thought superior to those who have
> Some reputation for learning, you will become hated
> [Medea's retort to Cleon's calling her "a clever woman"].

Quite apart from possible family resemblances, these lines and many others in *Medea* may well have evoked in Hobbes, if not in Latimer, a sympathetic response.

As a dedicated teacher (according to Aubrey), Latimer presumably could not have agreed that a "reputation for learning" leads one to "become hated," however much he may have endorsed other sentiments in *Medea*. A "good Graecian, and the first that came into our parts hereabout since the Reformation," as Aubrey describes him, Latimer briefly was Aubrey's own teacher in 1634, shortly before his death. He had "an easie way of teaching," Aubrey remembered, "and every time we asked leave to go forth we had a Latin word from him, which at our return we were to tell him again. Zeal to learning extraordinary: but memory not tenacious." Aubrey owed more to Latimer, however, than a Latin vocabulary, for it was through Latimer that Aubrey met Hobbes. "This summer 1634," Aubrey recalled in 1671 when he penned some notes pertaining to his own life, "(I remember it was venison season, July or Aug.) Mr. Thos. Hobbes came into his native country to visit his friends, and amongst others he came to see his old Schoolmaster, Mr. Latimer at Leigh Delamere [of which Latimer had become rector], when I was then a little youth at school in the church. . . . Here was the first place and time I ever had the honour to see this worthy man, who was then pleased to take notice of me, and the next day came and visited my relations. He was a proper man, briske, and in very good equipage: his haire was then quite black. He stayed at Malmsbury and in the neighborhood a weeke or better. . . ."[47]

Aubrey could not have known at the time, and Hobbes himself may not have known, that this was Hobbes's last visit to Malmesbury. Though he lived for another forty-five years, he never again returned to the town where he was born and spent the first fifteen years of his life.

T W O

OXFORD

HILE WE CANNOT KNOW how often Hobbes returned to Malmesbury between 1603, when he left for Oxford, and 1634, the year of his last visit, we probably are close to the truth in believing that his Malmesbury sojourns were not frequent. Apart from the relatively few references to Malmesbury in his *Autobiography*, and his being identified on the title pages of books as "Thomas Hobbes of Malmesbury,"* Hobbes's only other known effort to associate himself with his birthplace was in 1665 when he entertained the possibility of establishing a free school in the town. In a conversation with Aubrey, Hobbes told his young friend that "he was willing to doe some good to the towne where he was borne; that his majestie loved him well, and if I could find out something in our countery that was in his (majesty's) guift, he did beleeve he could beg it of his majestie, and seeing he was bred a scholar, he thought it most proper to endowe a free-schoole there; which is wanting *now*. . . . After enquiry I found out a piece of land in Bradon-forest . . . that was in his majesties guift, which he designed to have obtained of his majestie for a salary for a school-master. . . ." But nothing came of the plan, according to Aubrey, because "the queen's priests smelling-out the designe and being his enemies, hindred this publique and charitable intention."

We have no reason to doubt Aubrey's account, but several observations are relevant. The endowment for the free school in Malmesbury was to come from Charles II, not from Hobbes, and had it been forthcoming would have cost Hobbes nothing. Had Hobbes been determined to establish the school, he could have provided funds for

---

*Birth, death, and marriage records of the time establish that a large number of individuals were named Hobbes and that the given name Thomas was as common as John or William. In all probability, Hobbes or his early publisher added "of Malmesbury" as a way of identifying which Thomas Hobbes of the many bearing that name had translated Thucydides and written the books that followed.

it from the pension he was receiving from the king, which, though paid irregularly, amounted to £100 a year. Failing that, Hobbes could have made provision for the school in his will, which disposed of money and property worth, in Aubrey's words, "neer 1000*li*. [pounds], which (considering his charity) was more than I expected." When Hobbes, who by nature was stubborn and persistent, had set upon a course of action, he was not easily deflected from it, and since he never sought another way by which he could endow a free school in Malmesbury, and never manifested any other interest in the town's affairs after 1634, we have some cause to believe that his desire to "doe some good to the towne where he was borne" was no more than a passing whim, designed in part to please Aubrey, who was a devoted Wiltshireman.

Evidence already presented suggests that Hobbes's childhood in Malmesbury probably was an unhappy one, which he had no wish to remember, much less celebrate. The earnings of his father, the curate of Brokenborough, could not have been such as to permit the family much comfort or security, and they ceased altogether when Hobbes senior lost his position following the altercation with the rector of Foxley. His final excommunication and subsequent departure from Malmesbury, in particular, must have been a painful and humiliating experience for his family, perhaps especially for the son who was named after him.

Whatever Hobbes's feelings about Malmesbury, he apparently retained no friends from his early years there; at any rate, none are mentioned by him or by Aubrey. He may have had a special regard for Robert Latimer, as Aubrey implies, but though he owed a good deal to the old Westport schoolmaster who prepared him for Oxford, Latimer is not among the twenty persons referred to by name or by title in Hobbes's *Autobiography*. Each of Hobbes's books is dedicated to a patron or friend—or in one instance, *Leviathan*, a friend's brother whom Hobbes never met—but no book is dedicated to anyone associated with Malmesbury. Nor are the recollections, in this context, of Edmund Hobbes and "Mr. Wayte" of Hobbes as a boy possessing "even then a contemplative melancholinesse" without significance.

In Latimer's school, and no doubt in other respects as well, the Malmesbury years must have had their positive side, but there can be little question that they provided Hobbes with much to be melancholy about. Since a melancholy and pessimistic view of life pervades all of Hobbes's writings, we must raise the possibility that his assumptions about human nature and behavior, buttressed as they are by powerful arguments and penetrating observations, have their psychological origins in the Malmesbury years. But this is not the only hypothetical connection between Hobbes's political theory and

Malmesbury. His father, the curate, was an occasionally violent man who became embroiled in religious controversies, and Hobbes all of his life abhorred violence and repeatedly warned against the evils of religious strife and the rule of clerics. Indeed, Hobbes's ambivalence toward religion itself, and the reputation he enjoyed, deserved or not, as an atheist, may owe much to his father's failings as a clergyman. When we note, finally, that Malmesbury in the seventeenth century was one of those English towns in which the idea of limited or constitutional monarchy was beginning to be discussed (Malmesbury was on the parliamentary side during the Civil War)—an idea thoroughly repudiated by Hobbes—we are tempted to conclude that Hobbes's whole political theory, in terms of its psychological motivation or inspiration, can be seen as a repudiation of Malmesbury and much that it represented.

Hobbes's departure for Oxford in 1603, in other words, may have been experienced by him less as a fond leave-taking of Malmesbury than as an escape from a parochial and troubled personal environment. His years in Malmesbury may also have led Hobbes to entertain fantasies about university life that were far removed from the realities of undergraduate education at Oxford University in the early seventeenth century. Surely he must have known that the curriculum had its roots in Scholasticism, Christian philosophy, and the writings of the ancients, and yet his references in later years to his Oxford studies complain bitterly of the stale and turgid pedantry of the "Schools" at Oxford, a pedantry Hobbes continued to disparage long after it had given way to approaches more in keeping with the new age of science and discovery.

We cannot be certain that these complaints were contemporaneous with his pursuit of an Oxford bachelor of arts degree. Since no letters or other documents survive from Hobbes's Oxford period, we must take his later word for it, which Aubrey indirectly corroborates, that Hobbes even as a student abhorred the "barbarous Latin of the Schoolmen, the 'charms compounded of metaphysics, miracles and traditions,' the science 'strangled by a snare of words.' "[1] For Aristotle, the supreme source of wisdom at Oxford in those days, Hobbes had an almost obsessional dislike, insisting to Aubrey, among others, that Aristotle "was the worst teacher that ever was, the worst polititian and ethick—a countrey-fellow that could live in the world (would be) as good: but his rhetorique and discourse of animals was rare." In *Leviathan* Hobbes argued that the universities, in teaching philosophy as a "handmaid to the Romane Religion," promoted "not properly Philosophy, (the nature whereof dependeth not on Authors,) but Aristotelity." But if "scarce anything" could be said for what "now is called *Aristotles Metaphysiques*," perhaps even less valuable were other areas of "Aristotelity," for there was nothing "more repugnant to Government, than much of that hee hath said in his *Politiques;* nor more ignorantly, than a great part of his *Ethiques*."[2]

Aristotle, however, was not the sole evil influence. In *Leviathan* and *Behemoth* (1679), Hobbes saw religion in the universities, whether Catholic or Calvinist, as a prime source of sedition, inasmuch as both Papists and Puritans maintained "that it was lawful for a subject, in cause of religion, to forsake his prince, and take up arms against him."[3] With instruction and the discipline of students entrusted to incompetent tutors not much older than their pupils, Hobbes further maintained in *Behemoth*, it was no wonder Oxford undergraduates "were debauched to drunkenness, wantonness, gaming, and other vices."[*][4]

The students in Hobbes's day may have led dissolute lives—although we should note that the criticism is a familiar one of almost every generation—but in levying these charges more than forty years (and where they appear in *Behemoth*, more than sixty years) after his graduation, Hobbes was disregarding his own personal history as well as distorting that of Oxford. Subsequent to leaving Oxford in 1608, Hobbes himself, as will be seen in the following chapter, was no more than a beardless young man of twenty when he began to tutor William Cavendish, later second earl of Devonshire, also beardless and only two years younger than his instructor. The second earl, to be sure, was a "waster," as Aubrey put it, who was "debauched" by high living, but no one in or out of his family, least of all Hobbes, ever attributed the earl's weakness of character to his tutor's comparative youthfulness, inexperience, or incompetence. Some years later, when another of Hobbes's students came to an unhappy end,[†] Hobbes, again, was not held responsible either by himself or by others. The typical Oxford tutor when Hobbes was an undergraduate was not a Hobbes, of course, but perhaps the typical student at that time, to judge by other accounts, was not as sunk in sin and sedition as Hobbes in his later writings implied.

We have no memories of Hobbes himself as an undergraduate other than those he provided in his *Autobiography* and the few anecdotes and reminiscences collected by Aubrey.[‡] For whatever reason,

---

[*] In support of Hobbes, Robertson affirms that "the greatest license prevailed among the students": "In 1606 the evil was at a height. . . . The year 1607 was noted for its excesses. . . ." *Hobbes*, 7.

[†] See below, pp. 96–98.

[‡] In another context, Aubrey recalled Hobbes's saying he had been drunk about one hundred times in his life. Was the first of these occasions, one wonders, at Oxford?

the *Autobiography*, which was written in 1672, did not reiterate the charges against Oxford that Hobbes had made earlier in *Leviathan* and *Behemoth*. The Oxford of the *Autobiography* suffered not from an excess of debauchery, but from an excess of dullness; indeed, to judge by Hobbes's account, Oxford in the years 1603–8 must have been one of the dullest places in England. Finding his courses boring, his tutors uninspiring, and his classmates much inferior to himself, Hobbes apparently devoted as much time to independent study and reading away from the university as to formal classroom instruction. One of these extracurricular excursions may have introduced Hobbes to a lifelong interest in the mysteries of optics, an interest that later resulted in several publications. As Aubrey reported, "At Oxford Mr. T. H. used, in the summer time especially, to rise very early in the morning, and would tye the leaden-counters . . . with pacthreds [i.e., string or twine], which he did besmere with birdlime, and bayte them with parings of cheese, and the jack-dawes [i.e., a bird related to the crow] would spye them a vast distance up in the aire . . . and strike at the bayte, and so be harled [i.e., snarled] in the string, which the wayte of the counter would make cling about ther wings." Hobbes "happened to tell" him this story, Aubrey added, "discoursing of the Optiques, to instance such sharpness of sight in so little an eie."

At other times Hobbes "tooke great delight there to goe to the booke-binders' shops, and lye gaping on mappes." Hobbes himself is more expansive in recalling, "I fed my mind too on maps celestial and maps terrestrial. . . . I observed, too, where Drake and Cavendish had cast a girdle around Neptune's waist and the different regions they had visited. I picked out the tiny settlements of mankind and the Monsters depicted on unexplored lands."*

Hobbes's explanation of his interest in maps and explorations is that geography was one of the "more inviting themes" to which he turned when he found his courses dull or incomprehensible. Accepting this, we still may wonder whether this early interest in islands and continents, stars and planets, far removed from Oxford, does not reflect a continuing "contemplative melancholinesse" and tendencies toward depression. Persons with a depressive outlook are often restless and bored in everyday life; attributing their mood to external circumstances but unable to escape from it anywhere, they may resort to frequent travel in a quest, not always conscious, for relief; or, if travel is not possible, they may indulge in fantasies about remote

---

*Sir Francis Drake (1540?–1596) was famous for a variety of exploits, including, in addition to the victory over the Armada, the circumnavigation of the globe in 1577–80. Thomas Cavendish (1555?–1592) was the third circumnavigator of the globe in 1586–88.

places of excitement or contentment. Whatever Hobbes's fantasies while "gaping on mappes," in observing that "geographers have their own way of filling up gaps," he may have been alluding as much to the empty spaces of his own personal geography as to vacant areas of the globe.

We may also infer that he was an indifferent student, though he admits only to being "put in the lowest class for Logic" upon arrival at Oxford, where he was "slow to learn." Aubrey's addendum confirms our suspicion that Hobbes "'did not much care for logick, yet he learnd it," and characteristically "thought himselfe a good disputant" just as, in later years, he was to think himself a brilliant and original mathematician despite overwhelming evidence to the contrary. Perhaps his performance in "Logic" and difficulties with "Physics," where, he tells us in his *Autobiography*, the instructor taught much that was "too high" for Hobbes to grasp, were the reasons he spent five years instead of the customary four earning his bachelor's degree.

Of these Oxford years between 1603 and 1608, we know little more for certain than the few facts already mentioned. Admitted to Magdalen Hall, which had separated from Magdalen College in 1602, Hobbes must have known that past members of the hall included such distinguished Oxford alumni as William Tyndale (1512), translator of the Bible; John Donne (1584), poet and dean of St. Paul's; and John Selden (1600), the future jurist and historian of English law who was to become an acquaintance some years later.* In Hobbes's own time, Magdalen Hall was exceptionally popular with Oxford undergraduates, averaging twenty-three matriculations (admitted students) annually, more than those of any other hall.[5] James Hussee and John Wilkinson, the two principals who presided over the hall while Hobbes was a student, were extremely able men, the latter especially. Wilkinson, who succeeded Hussee in 1605, greatly expanded the hall, increased the number of its scholarships, and led it to a position of eminence that for a time eclipsed even the reputation of Magdalen College.[6] Wilkinson appears to have been a favorite of the students, but he may not have been much in favor with Hobbes. A convinced Puritan, Wilkinson made the hall a center of Puritan influ-

---

* Future members of the hall (subsequently Hertford College) were no less outstanding. Among them were Sir Matthew Hale (1626), the chief justice; Jonathan Swift (1692), the satirist and dean of Dublin; Charles James Fox (1764), Whig statesman; and the author Evelyn Waugh (1921). Interestingly, Hobbes's own name does not appear in all lists of distinguished hall alumni. Sir John Betjeman, for example, does not mention Hobbes in his *An Oxford University Chest* (Oxford: Oxford University Press Paperbacks, 1979; first published 1938), 140–41.

ence at Oxford, and Hobbes, as will be demonstrated later, was no friend of Puritanism.

Arriving at Magdalen Hall not long after his fifteenth birthday—a not uncommon matriculation age at that time, though entering boys of sixteen, seventeen, and eighteen were more usual—Hobbes, like other students, had to take oaths accepting the Thirty-nine Articles, the Book of Common Prayer, and the Act of Supremacy.[7] The Thirty-nine Articles, promulgated in 1563, established the Church of England as "a Church traditional (or Catholic) in structure, with its hierarchy of bishops and courts under the supreme governor, but in doctrine a compromise which leaned heavily towards full Protestantism. Its ritual owed much to the past, a fact which made it more readily accepted by the mass of the people though distasteful to those more eager Protestants whose desire to purify the Church earned them the name of Puritans."[8] The Book of Common Prayer, the official prayer book of the Church of England, was written in English instead of Latin and was designed to "abolish all ritual for which there was not scriptural warrent . . . and make the services as unlike the pre-Reformation services as possible."[9] The Elizabethan Act of Supremacy declared, among other things, "that the Quenes Highnes is thonelye supreme Governour of this Realme . . . aswell in all Spirituall or Ecclesiasticall Thinges or Causes as Temporall, and that no forreine Prince Person Prelate State or Potentate hathe or oughte to have any Jurisdiction Power Superioritee Preheminence or Aucthoritee Ecclesiastically or Spirituall within this Realme. . . ."[10]

Fees were scaled in accordance with social class, the sons of the nobility paying matriculation fees of thirteen shillings, four pence, while ordinary students, known as "Pleb. fil.," a category to which Hobbes and most students belonged, paid four pence. But some poor scholars paid as little as two pence, and a few paid only half of that amount. Hobbes's fees and presumably his other expenses as well, according to Aubrey, were paid by Uncle Francis, the well-to-do glover in Malmesbury. The amount of financial aid provided by Uncle Francis, and the extent of Hobbes's gratitude to his father's older and more successful brother, must remain forever a matter of conjecture. Hobbes makes no reference to Uncle Francis anywhere in his writings.

Hobbes was probably one of the numerous students who were "not on the foundation," or, in other words, one of those paying their own expenses. Students "on the foundation" were supported by the endowments of their college, whereas those "not on the foundation," usually known as commoners, had to pay their fees and provide for their lodging, food, and clothing. While we cannot be certain how much Hobbes's Oxford education cost, some idea of the expense can be gained from the allowances and stipends of other students. Wealthier students might spend about thirty pounds annually on food, lodging, clothing, fees, and travel. Senior fellows or advanced students "on the foundation" at one college were allowed eight pounds per year; bachelors of arts five pounds, ten shillings; and scholars, that is, younger students, four pounds, ten shillings each. Among the commoners, who began to be more numerous and important toward the end of the sixteenth century, there were other gradations as well, approximating class distinctions. For example, the "Higher Nobility," unlike the "Inferior Nobility" and the "Commons," were permitted to wear fur-lined hoods and enjoy certain privileges. But even the "Higher Nobility" were subject to the same regulations as those "on the foundation," including the requirement of individual supervision by a tutor.[11]

The staples of university education in early-seventeenth-century England were grammar, theology, rhetoric, logic, and moral philosophy. Students arrived at Oxford and Cambridge fluent in Latin, the knowledge of which was essential for university study and most scholarly work; a few, like Hobbes, also knew some Greek and were to learn more of that language during their undergraduate years. At Oxford there were a few courses in mathematics, astronomy, geography, and "Physics"—geometry, including Euclid, was taught at Brasenose College, and French and Italian may also have been taught— but they were elementary in nature, and most students in the arts curriculum, including Hobbes, graduated knowing little or nothing about these subjects.* In logic, philosophy, and other courses, the supreme source of wisdom was Aristotle and his interpreters; indeed, as late as 1636, "the Laudian statues of Oxford required that determining bachelors of arts argue their propositions in logic, rhetoric, politics, and moral philosophy according to the teachings of Aristotle, 'whose authority is paramount.' "[12] Where Aristotle had been silent, the students turned to Plato, Ptolemy, Cicero, Strabo, and other luminaries of the Greek and Roman world. With Pliny as the authority on geography and Copernicus ignored altogether, it was no wonder that Hobbes, whatever his travel fantasies, spent time in bookstores reading about the vogages of Drake and Cavendish.

But however he occupied his time while classes were being held, Hobbes undoubtedly was in residence at Oxford during the four aca-

---

* The well-known story in Aubrey has Hobbes encountering Euclid for the first time in 1628, when he was forty, whereupon he fell "in love with geometry." Hobbes never forgave Oxford for failing to teach him the higher mathematics, but his belated discovery of geometry—his critics alleged it was too late in terms of his ability to understand basic principles—may not have been entirely the fault of the university.

demic terms of Michaelmas, October to December; Hilary, January to March; Easter, April to May; and Trinity, May to July. His summer vactions probably were spent back in Malmesbury, but the manner in which he passed the months—working for Uncle Francis, perhaps?—is unknown. When he did attend class, absence from which was punished by fines, loss of commons, or extra assignments, he may have taken courses similar in content to those required of Corpus Christi students. On Monday, Wednesday, and Friday at 8 A.M., the professor of arts at Corpus Christi read and expounded Valerius Maximus, Pliny, the advanced works of Cicero, and the writings of other Latin authors; on Tuesday, Thursday, and Saturday, he dealt with Virgil, Ovid, Juvenal, Terence, and Plautus. The afternoons of feast days were devoted to public lectures on Horace and Persius. The professor of Greek, holding forth at 10 A.M. on Monday, Wednesday, and Friday, discussed the grammar of Theodorus, Isocrates, and Philostrates. On Tuesday, Thursday, and Saturday, he examined a large number of philosophers and historians, including Aristophanes, Euripides, Sophocles, Thucydides, Plutarch, and, of course, Aristotle. Holiday lectures were given over to Homer and Plato. The reader in sacred divinity, who was paid more than the two professors, discoursed on the Bible each day at 2 P.M.[13]

When Hobbes confided to Aubrey that he "thought himselfe a good disputant" at Oxford, he meant that he had performed creditably in academic exercises known as disputations or debates. These disputations, much more a test of verbal facility in Latin and of skill in oral argument than a measure of knowledge, usually centered upon questions in logic, rhetoric, or philosophy that lent themselves to the application of Aristotelian principles as adapted by Peter Abelard, Peter Lombard, and other Schoolmen.* A disputation began when a participant designated a respondent made an affirmative response to a question or proposition. He was followed by one or more opponents who presented the negative side and the weaknesses in the respondent's position. These arguments, pro and con, were heard by a moderator or determiner, and in the third and final stage of the disputation, the moderator or determiner "summed up the arguments . . . pointed out fallacies in the reasoning of the participants, called attention to treatments of the question that had been overlooked or insufficiently

---

*In *Behemoth* Lombard fared no better than Aristotle. Lombard (1100–1160 or 1164) and "John Scot of Duns" (Duns Scotus) (1265?–1308?) were called by Hobbes "two of the most egregious blockheads in the world, so obscure and senseless are their writings. [From them] the schoolmen . . . learnt the trick of . . . [confusing] true reason by verbal forks; I mean, distinctions that signify nothing, but serve only to astonish the multitude of ignorant men." Dialogue 1.

emphasized, reconciled differences where possible, bestowed praise and blame where each was due, and handed down the decision or 'determination' of the question."[14]

Disputations served as the final examinations, but the student began to take part in disputations long before that. Following his first year of residence, he was required to attend disputations engaged in by third- and fourth-year students three afternoons each week from one to three o'clock. During his own third and fourth years, the student was expected to participate in four disputations, twice as a respondent upholding the affirmative side and twice as an opponent supporting the negative side. Finally, toward the end of his fourth year, when he had completed his lecture courses and performed satisfactorily in the required number of disputations, the Oxford student could petition to be admitted to the degree of bachelor of arts. If his petition was accepted, he would, in the normal course, take part in at least two more disputations, following which, if all went well, he could refer to himself as a bachelor of arts.

While we do not know which questions Hobbes debated, we do know some of the topics favored at the time. These included "Can love be induced by philtres?" "Is there any certain knowledge of things?" and "Is a comet helpful or harmful?" A medical topic, to which Hobbes was to return sixty years later, was "Whether a man can live more than seven days without food or drink."[15] Hobbes's answer to that question in his student days, assuming he had an opinion, is not recorded, but in 1668 he thought it possible that a woman could survive without eating for more than six months.*

Possibly the food at Magdalen Hall was such that Hobbes was tempted to fast for days at a time. Breakfast at six in the morning— the students customarily rose at five or earlier in the summer—was a light meal that might include a piece of bread and a glass of beer. Dinner, the main meal of the day, usually was at eleven, and supper was served at five. Dinner normally consisted of salt fish, beef, mutton, and small beer, but feast days, which must have been eagerly awaited by students, were, on the whole, well named. One feast day dinner at Brasenose College was celebrated by the fellows with beef, pork, rabbit, cabbage, wine, sugar, apples, and cheese. The supper menu included rabbit, sack, ale, and, again, apples and cheese. Brase-

---

* Her survival without food was not necessarily a miracle. "I myself in a sickness," he observed, "have been without all manner of sustenance for more than six weeks altogether: which is enough to make mee think that six months would not have made it a miracle." Letter to Mr. Beale, October 20, 1668, in *E.W.*, VII, 463–64. But that thought was not intended to be a judgment, Hobbes cautioned, because "examining whether such a thing as this bee a miracle, belongs I think to the Church."

nose fellows also had a special allowance for a tablecloth and nap-
kins. Some of this food must have been provided by the college itself,
which, like the other colleges, did its own baking and brewing.[16] Grace
was said in Latin before and after meals, and at some colleges students took turns reading from the Bible while their classmates ate. If
no chapel or lecture was scheduled, at which attendance was compulsory, students were free to return to their rooms, read in the library
(in those days many books were chained to shelves and could not be
moved elsewhere), or wander about the college grounds. Most academic work was done on mornings when the light was good.

Students generally slept two, three, four, or more to the room.
Each student usually had a straw bed to himself, but sometimes those
under fifteen years of age shared a bed. Rooms were drab and sparsely
furnished; only the wealthier students owned books, furniture, and
wall hangings (the latter serving mainly to keep out some of the chill).
Very few rooms had fireplaces or, if they did, the wood with which to
keep a fire going, and in winter, especially, the typical student was
cold much of the time, and not infrequently wet or at least damp. A
Cambridge report of 1550 described students retiring for the night as
"fain to walk or run up and down half an hour, to get a heat in their
feet when they go to bed." Since sanitary arrangements were primitive and bathing was relatively unknown, students dealt with lice,
fleas, and bedbugs on a regular basis, and from time to time with rats
and other rodents, ticks, and bats. Rabies was not unknown, and in
1603, the year of his matriculation at Oxford, Hobbes was to live
through the first of six major and a much larger number of minor
plagues that were to ravage England in the seventeenth century. Oxford
was not spared, but it suffered less from the first outbreak than from
some of the later ones.[17]

Student life was subject to a multitude of rules and regulations,
not all of which were strictly enforced. Students could be punished
for neglecting studies, frequenting alehouses and other undesirable
places, being irreverent in chapel, returning to college after its gates
were closed (usually 8 or 9 P.M.), being drunk, being rude to elders
(especially to college heads), making noises at inappropriate times,
skipping classes and disputations, wearing fashionable (i.e., stylish)
clothes, being late for meals, swearing, fighting, and taking food from
the kitchen without permission. In addition, students could not keep
birds, animals, or guns or remain off compus overnight or entertain
a guest without prior approval, and fornication and adultery were
strictly forbidden. Departures from the college could take place only
in groups of two or more. Penalties for violations of these rules included
flogging, fines, imprisonment, withdrawal of privileges, suspensions,

and, in extreme cases, expulsion or, as it later was called, "being sent down."

In addition to these regulations, certain colleges specified in detail the dress or costume to be worn by students. At All Souls, for example, fellows were required to wear gowns reaching to their heels, "sewn together in front, the shirts plain, and not gathered around the collor or arms, or ornamented with silk." At other colleges, "white doublets were forbidden, as well as laced gowns, long hair, furs, velvet, satin, ruffs, and gold and silver decorations."[18] New College fellows were provided with an annual wardrobe, of identical cut and color, that could not be sold for four years. In the fifth year, however, a senior student could give to a junior "his fifth-best suit," presumably the outfit he had received as an entering student.[19] At some colleges bachelors of arts in clerical dress were permitted to wear fur-lined hoods, while masters of arts could wear black capes, and doctors red ones. Students found to be not properly dressed were punished by the loss of commons, which amounted to a fine, the duration of the loss depending on the frequency of the offense.

Somehow Hobbes, like most students, survived all this; unhappily, we do not know how well or successfully he managed. Did he find the rules and regulations too restrictive or, since he later remembered Oxford as somewhat dissolute, not restrictive enough? We do not know. Was he liked by his fellow students, and was he involved in any of their escapades? Again we have no information, but perhaps we have a hint in Hobbes's never mentioning the name of any classmate or Oxford friend in any of his writings. Did he attend the performance at Oxford of Shakespeare's *Hamlet* in 1607?* We do not know. How was he affected by the death of Elizabeth on March 24, 1603, not long before his fifteenth birthday? We have no knowledge.

Of one event at Oxford, Hobbes certainly must have known, and he also may have been personally involved, at least in a small way. In late August 1605, when Hobbes had been a student somewhat more than two years, the city and the university celebrated a three-day visit by King James I. The king was reputed to favor Cambrige over Oxford, and the Oxford elders were determined to spare nothing to make his visit as pleasant and memorable as possible. Weeks and even months before the king's arrival on August 27 fresh paint was applied to buildings James and his entourage were to visit or ride

---

* There may have been an earlier performance. The title page of the first quarto *Hamlet*, which was published in 1603, states that the play was acted "in the two universities of Cambridge and Oxford." Thompson, *Universities*, 29. Not until 1635 did Shakespeare's name appear in the Bodleian Library catalogue. Hobbes never mentions Shakespeare.

past, roads and streets were swept and made as smooth as possible, and the royal lodgings at Christ Church College were enlarged. Heads of colleges were advised that all graduates, fellows, and students were to wear caps and gowns appropriate to their houses and stations and that fines of ten shillings and possible imprisonment were to be the fate of anyone "otherwise apparalled" while the King was in residence. Each college was to prepare "Verses to be disposed and set [i.e., displayed] upon St. Marie's, or to other Places convenient," and to be ready to provide "a short Oration . . . to entertain his Majesty, if his Pleasure be" to visit the college. Scholars who could not be admitted to the plays and other scheduled entertainments were warned to "not make any Outcries or indecent Noises, upon pain of present Imprisonment, and other Punishment."[20]

The numerous orations and disputations enacted in the king's presence included a disputation in which the principal of Magdalen Hall, Dr. Hussee, participated. Dr. Hussee argued the negative side of two questions in civil law, one of which was "In making a judgment, is a judge bound to follow legal proofs contrary to the truth privately known to himself."

The king also heard arguments about whether "Saints and Angels know the thoughts of the heart" and whether the "habits of wet-nurses are imbibed by infants with the milk." Other questions debated before His Majesty included "When a plague is raging, are Ministers of the Churches bound to attend to their congregations?" and "Can the imagination produce real effects?" The king, who was strongly opposed to smoking, listened intently when the disputants held forth on the topic "Is frequent breathing of nicotine wholesome for healthy people?" One wonders whether James, an apt spectator and occasional unscheduled disputant, was satisfied with these presentations. When he was pleased, he would say as much or express his feelings in approving gestures; when speeches "were long, and not very excellent, he would say, Away, away, tush, tush, or such like, not very lowde."[21]

We can never know whether Hobbes attended these disputations, but we can be certain that some of the topics, reflecting as they did the logical canons and substantive interests of the Schoolmen, were among those he had in mind when he later criticized the influence in the universities of Aristotle and the "Schools." But was Hobbes as a student critical of these influences, or were the fulminations recorded in *Leviathan* and *Behemoth* of much later origin? Even if the Oxford curriculum was as antiquated in 1603–8 as Hobbes, more than forty years later, insisted it was, we lack evidence showing that as a student "he had already an insight into the weakness of the School-philosophy. When, long afterwards, he is vehemently denouncing Scholasticism, and helping complete its overthrow, he shows little real acquaintance with the object of his scorn. As far as we can now make out, it may be doubted whether, as an undergraduate, he would be introduced at all to the study (in scholastic paraphrase) of the Aristotelian physics and metaphysics, and whether he was not referring back to these early days the impressions of a much later time. . . ."[22]

But the "impressions of a much later time" cannot have been based on Hobbes's observations forty to sixty years after he himself had been a student. By the mid-seventeenth century science and mathematics courses had become prominent in the curriculum, and they were taught mainly, not by Aristotelians, Papists, or beardless youth, but by men as distinguished as John Wallis, Savilian Professor of Geometry; Jonathan Goddard, an inventor of the telescope; Seth Ward, Savilian Professor of Astronomy; the noted chemist and man of science Robert Boyle; and in medicine Thomas Sydenham, William Petty, and William Harvey (for a brief time), the latter to be renowned as the discoverer of the circulation of the blood. Petty was a friend of Hobbes's and Harvey, also a friend, remembered Hobbes in his will.* The great Christopher Wren was successively student, fellow, and Savilian Professor of Astronomy between 1646 and 1660; among the undergraduates in 1652, who may or may not have been less dissolute than the undergraduates Hobbes knew two generations earlier, was John Locke.

Since Hobbes was well informed about many of the changes at Oxford, the charge cannot be substantiated that he "did not realise how much his old university had altered" in the two-score years that had elapsed.[23] Hobbes, on the contrary, was only too aware of some of the new faculty appointments, the holders of which were among his most bitter and determined critics. Oxford luminaries accorded a cool reception to his De Cive of 1642 and Leviathan of 1651, De Cive arguing that Aristotle, Plato, Cicero, Seneca, and Plutarch promoted civil disobedience by teaching that "tyrannicide is lawful"; similar views, De Cive maintained, were promulgated in the universities and churches by well-meaning but ignorant men.[24] Probably no one at Oxford agreed with Hobbes that, as he put it later, political philosophy was no older than De Cive,[25] and surely no more than a few could

---

*Harvey, who died in 1657, aged seventy-nine, left Hobbes ten pounds. Hobbes, who apparently observed, or assisted in, some of Harvey's dissections of the king's deer, may have met Harvey as early as 1621 through Francis Bacon, a patient of Harvey's whom Hobbes served for a time as a kind of amanuensis. The Hobbes-Bacon relationship is dealt with below, pp. 64–68.

have shared his outrage when, in 1654, *De Cive* was placed on the papal *Index Librorum Prohibitorum*.

But these later writings, to which we shall return presently, do not tell us anything of his attitudes as a student or of experiences at Oxford which may have been formative influences; by 1608, when Hobbes left the university, he had spent a fourth of his entire life, and almost all of his adolescence, at Oxford. Surely he could not have come away from those five years untouched, but touched by what? By whom? Since Hobbes and Aubrey do not have much to tell us about those years, perhaps we can surmise that Hobbes was no happier at Oxford, whatever his expectations had been in 1603, than he had been in Malmesbury, and that the Oxford years were, like the earlier ones, years he had little desire to remember or have recorded in detail. Indeed, Hobbes himself provided some indirect support for this view when he observed, toward the end of his life, that his first years in the employ of the Devonshires, during which he served as the tutor and companion of the second earl, were the happiest of his life.

These years, which began with his departure from Oxford in 1608 and ended with the death of the second earl in 1628, in a sense mark the birth of the Thomas Hobbes known to his contemporaries and to us, the Hobbes of temper, charm, arrogance, and wit; the Hobbes who was by turns timid and audacious, insecure and boastful, superstitious and incredulous, atheistic and religious; the Hobbes of *De Cive*, *Leviathan*, and *Behemoth;* and, finally, the Hobbes who, fearful of death, led a life he believed—correctly, as it turned out—would take him to a very old age.

Of these years we know somewhat more than we know of the earlier period, but perhaps no more than Hobbes wanted us to know. What we do know, however, as Hobbes himself would have been the first to tell us, is more than interesting enough.

HARDWICK AND CHATSWORTH

HOBBES'S GREAT GOOD FORTUNE was to graduate from Oxford on February 5, 1608, in time to be recommended as a tutor to one of England's wealthiest and most distinguished families. Early that year William Cavendish, the first baron Hardwick—he was not to become first earl of Devonshire until 1618—was seeking an instructor for his eldest son and future successor, also named William, who, because he was married, could not attend a university; for reasons unknown he turned to the principal of Magdalen Hall. According to Aubrey, young William, then about eighteen, "had a conceit that he should profitt more in his learning if he had a scholar of his owne age to wayte on him then if he had the information of a grave doctor." Principal Wilkinson, again for reasons not known, proposed Hobbes, and not long afterward Hobbes entered the service of the Cavendish family as young William's "page," as Aubrey put it. With the exception of his self-exile in France during England's time of troubles and Civil War, and two other brief periods, Hobbes was to remain in the service of the Cavendishes almost seventy years, or until the end of his life. Had it not been for this attachment, and the security and opportunities it afforded him, Hobbes's life, like the lives of many other fatherless young men, might well have been, to borrow a phrase from his *Leviathan*, "solitary, poor, nasty, brutish, and short."

Though Hobbes could hardly have been aware of it, on that fifth day of February, the founding matriarch of the Devonshires, Elizabeth Hardwick, countess of Shrewsbury, was still alive but barely so, dying eight days after Hobbes's graduation. Born between 1520 and 1525 (the exact date is uncertain), in the time of Henry VIII, Elizabeth, countess of Shrewsbury, known familiarly to history as Bess of Hardwick, was one of the most formidable women of her time. From inauspicious beginnings—her father, who belonged to the minor gentry, died when Bess was still a small child—Bess by 1544 had made the first of a number of marriages that were to propel her, finally, into the ranks of the wealthy nobility. Robert Barlow, her first husband, who was also a cousin, came from a family somewhat higher in the social scale, and he apparently died not long after they were married, he at age fourteen, leaving Bess, who at twenty was six years older, a very young widow. Her second marriage, in 1547 to Sir William Cavendish, made her the wife of an extremely wealthy widower of forty-two who had already been twice married. Sir William, the father of two daughters, had made a good deal of money in connection with the dissolution of the monasteries, and at the time of his marriage he owned properties distributed over five counties. Selling these possessions in accordance with Bess's wishes, Sir William bought new properties in Derbyshire and Nottinghamshire, among which were the house and land of Chatsworth.*

Bess's marriage to Sir William, which lasted until his death in 1557, was the only one that produced children, eight in all, of whom six lived beyond infancy. The eldest son, Henry, who died in 1616, had no legitimate children, though he was referred to by contemporaries as "'the common bull to all Derbyshire and Staffordshire.'"[1] Charles, the third son (after Sir William, who has already been mentioned), also founded a dynasty of distinguished dukedoms and noble families, some of whose members became important scientists and statesmen, and his son William, duke of Newcastle, was a special friend of Hobbes's. Bess's three daughters fared less well in life, one of them, Elizabeth, probably at her mother's behest marrying Charles Stuart, the brother of Mary, Queen of Scots' former husband, Lord Darnley, thereby incurring the enmity of Queen Elizabeth. Bess, for her own purposes or those of her family, was prepared to take risks, and in promoting or arranging a marriage, the offspring of which might have a claim to the throne, she was taking a risk that verged on the foolhardy. Considering the circumstances and what might have been her fate, she was fortunate to spend only the winter of 1574–75 confined to the Tower of London, as her punishment.[2]

With her second marriage, the duration of which was ten years, Bess "emerged out of obscurity and the main aspects of her character became clear. She was capable, managing, acquisitive, a businesswoman, a money maker, a land-amasser, a builder of great houses, an indefatigable collector of the trappings of wealth and power, and inordinately ambitious, both for herself and her children. She was

---

*The existing house was torn down, and a new Chatsworth built, but not the Chatsworth that now occupies the site. Present-day Chatsworth, the result of extensive rebuilding and remodeling by successive dukes of Devonshire, bears little resemblance to the Chatsworth of Elizabethan times.

neither cultured nor religious. She was immensely tough, but it would be a mistake to think of her as either cold or calculating. She was capricious, rash, emotional, fond of intrigue and gossip, easily moved to tears, the best of company when things were going her way and spitting with spite and fury when crossed. . . . Her unrelenting acqui-sition of property and worldly goods especially of property in the countryside of her birth, and if possible connected with her family and relatives, suggests the ambition of a local girl to demonstrate that the dim squire's daughter had made good in a sensational way."[3]

"Making good in a sensational way" may well have been the object of Bess's third and fourth marriages, each to a man of higher social status and greater wealth than those of Sir William Cavendish. Two years after his death in 1557, Bess married a rich landowner, Sir Wil-liam St. Loé, a member of the royal household and a favorite of the queen's. Dying five years later, St. Loé left much of his property to Bess, a widow for the third but not the last time. By now she was a woman of considerable wealth, but her fortune was as nothing com-pared with that of her fourth and last husband, George Talbot, sixth earl of Shrewsbury. The earl, a widower with six children, was at forty some years younger than Bess, and one of the wealthiest men in England. When Bess married him in 1568, he owned, in addition to many houses and thousands of acres of farmland, iron, steel, and lead mines, foundries, ships, glassworks, and coal mines. Not being told by Bess of the marriage of Elizabeth and Charles Stuart, Shrewsbury, to whom Queen Elizabeth had entrusted the custody of Mary, Queen of Scots, was understandably upset, and whether for this reason or because Bess was spending too much of his money on Chatsworth, the marriage came undone. Bess also may have had a hand in two other marriages: that of her daughter, Mary, to the earl's son and successor; and the marriage of her son, Henry, to Grace Talbot, the earl's daughter. Perhaps Bess wished to ensure that her husband, no matter what happened between them, would never be able to sepa-rate himself from the Cavendishes.

No doubt Bess's temper contributed to the difficulties. When she was angry, she could express herself in language most upper-class women of her time were incapable of using—language, in fact, not unlike that of Hobbes when he was addressing Wallis and other crit-ics. To one antagonist, Sir Thomas Stanhope, Bess sent the following message: "Tho you be more wretched, vile and miserable than any creature living, & for your wickedness become more ugly in shape than the vilest toade in the worlde and one to whom none of reputa-tion would vouchsafe to send any message, yet she hath thought good to send this much unto you: that she can be contented you should live, and doth no wayes wish your death, but to this end that all the plagues and miseries that may befall any man may light upon such a caitiff [base coward] as you are."[4]

By 1583 Bess and her sons were spreading rumors that Shrewsbury was having an affair with Mary, and in 1584 the marriage collapsed entirely. Shrewsbury insisted that Chatsworth belonged to him by virtue of the marriage settlement, and Bess, while she never agreed, turned her attentions to Hardwick, which she had inherited from her father. By 1590 she had replaced the original building with what became known as Hardwick Old Hall, and after Shrewsbury's death that year she began construction of a much larger and finer Hardwick a short distance from the Old Hall. Despite her estrangement from Shrewsbury, she was left a widow's share of his estate which, added to the wealth she had already accumulated, made her at seventy one of the richest women in England. More or less abandoning Chatsworth, in which she had only a life interest (Henry, her eldest son, whom she disliked, was to have it after her death), Bess spent the remaining eighteen years of her life enlarging and furnishing Hardwick, which she and her son William, who was to inherit it, regarded as their principal home.

Hence it was to Hardwick, not to Chatsworth, that Hobbes made his way in the late spring or early summer of 1608, when he took up his duties as tutor and "page" to Bess's grandson, young William Cavendish. Upon Henry's death in 1616 William's father, Bess's second son, inherited Chatsworth, but Hardwick continued to be his main residence and therefore the house where Hobbes was employed most of the time. The Devonshires moved back and forth between the two great estates, which were about fifteen miles apart, throughout the seventeenth century, except for relatively brief periods in London, and Hobbes usually moved with them. When he fell ill in October 1679, he was at Chatsworth, and although he was on his deathbed, he insisted upon accompanying the family to Hardwick when it moved there in late November, and it was there, on December 4, that he died.

We have no record of Hobbes's arrival at Hardwick more than seventy years earlier, but we can imagine that he must have been impressed by the house that was regarded then, and still is regarded, as a gem of Elizabethan architecture.* Approaching it from the front,

---

*In his *De Mirabilibus Pecci: Being the Wonders of the Peak etc.*, written about 1627, Hobbes celebrated the virtues of Chatsworth, and no writing of his makes any clear reference to Hardwick. But since Chatsworth adjoins the Peak country of Derbyshire, about which he was writing, and since it was from Chatsworth that he and his companions set out, we may doubt that his praise of Chastworth reflects any preference on Hobbes's part for one Devonshire estate over the other. See below, pp. 68–70.

Hardwick Hall, Bess's crowning achievement, looking much the way it looked in 1603, when Hobbes first saw it. Note Bess's initials "E.S.," for Elizabeth Shrewsbury, at the tops of the towers.

Hobbes would have seen a facade that was less stone or wood than glass; the west front displayed fifty great windows, each of them containing between six and sixteen leaded glass panes (only when he was inside would he have noticed that several of these windows faced chimneys on their interior side, thus giving a false impression of the space within). The sixty-odd rooms, one of which, probably adjoining young William's on the second floor, Hobbes was to occupy, were spread over three levels enclosed by six massive towers. Nearby stood Hardwick Old Hall, occupied by servants and occasional guests until it was allowed to fall into ruins during the eighteenth century; Hobbes may have frequented the path beside its walls because the belief persists that on certain nights he may be seen walking there still.[5] Whether observant or not of Hardwick's unique architectural features, Hobbes surely must have been aware of Bess's special effort to make sure no one ever forgot that Hardwick was hers and hers alone. At the top of each of the towers, Bess had had inscribed the initials "E.S." (for Elizabeth Shrewsbury).

Compared with the little cottage in Malmesbury and the crowded rooms of Magdalen Hall, Hardwick may have seemed to Hobbes a palace in which almost all the things he had ever dreamed of were possible. Of the thirty or more indoor servants, he probably was included among the upper servants, many of whom were the younger sons or daughters of respectable families, usually addressed as "Mister," "Mistress," or "Miss." Unlike the lower servants, who had to sleep somewhere within calling distance (there were no bellpulls for summoning servants in those days), often in hallways, outside bedroom doors, on landings (or even on the floor at the foot of beds), Hobbes had his own quarters, and he probably also ate alone in his room or took his meals with young William. As William's tutor, he had access to Hardwick's library—which Hobbes considerably expanded beyond the *total* of six books Bess owned when she died— and he and William may have been present on ceremonial occasions when dinner was served in the high great chamber on the top floor. Presumably, the stable and grounds were open to him, and he, like the other upper servants, was waited upon, to some extent, by the cooks, waiters, scullions, maids, and laundresses that composed the bulk of the lower servants.

But for Hobbes and everyone else who lived there, Hardwick had the inconveniences typical of even the greatest of English houses at that time. The entrance hall was also the lower servants' meeting place, where they ate, talked, played cards, or otherwise amused themselves when not working, and therefore was almost unbearably noisy much of the time. Situated on a wind-blown elevation, Hardwick was cool and damp in all seasons, and in the winter its fire-places, no matter how well supplied with wood, seemed to have little effect on the cold. Cooked food, which often had to be carried great distances from the kitchen, usually arrived lukewarm (if warm at all), and hot water was not easily available. Sanitary conditions, of course, were primitive, and since containers holding the contents of chamber pots had to be carried down the main stairways (backstairs were still unknown), unpleasant odors penetrated to all corners of the house. And from time to time, both the high and the low at Hardwick were only too conscious that they shared their dwelling place with an impressive variety of other living creatures: fleas, flies, lice, bedbugs, bats, and worst of all, rats.

Hobbes, of course, was to survive all this and to live longer than anyone else connected with Hardwick, including Bess (who, at the most, was eighty-eight when she died). But when he came to Hard-wick for the first time, he was a young man of twenty, and his pupil, William Cavendish, eighteen. Despite William's youth, he was already a husband, albeit reluctantly, having the preceding April married Christian Bruce, twelve years old at the time, the pretty, red-headed only daughter of Edward, Lord Bruce of Kinloss (Scotland), to whom King James was indebted for assistance in his obtaining of the throne five years earlier. Young William's resistance to the marriage was occasioned, as Bess discovered on her deathbed, by his passion for a certain Margaret Chatterton, "one of the ladies of her household," whom he had seduced, or been seduced by, some years earlier. Wil-liam was not without some support in the family. "Alas, poor Wylkyn!" Uncle Charles Cavendish sympathized. "He desired and deserved a woman already grown, and may evil stay twelve weeks, much less twelve months. They were bedded together, to his great punishment, some two hours."[6] But whomever William "desired and deserved," when his father informed him that "Kinloss was well favored by the queen, and if he refused it would make him the worse by £100,000,"[7] William abandoned Chatterton in favor of Christian (whose name derived from her having been born on Christmas Day). The view may be correct that the first earl shattered the boy's happiness and blighted his life by his "determination to use his son's marriage to improve his political prospects,"[8] but we have no evidence that the second earl became "a spendthrift, a brawler and a rake" because he was unhappily married.[9]

William's father, Baron Hardwick until 1618 when in return for a payment to the crown of £10,000, or approximately $1 million dol-lars, he became earl of Devonshire, may have had some of the char-acter and spirit of his mother. In the four years between 1608 and

1612, he spent more than £1,163, a considerable sum for those days, on building improvements at Hardwick, and probably much more was expended in 1619–21 when a wing was added to the east end of the Old Hall.[10] He also was capable of entertaining on a grand scale when required or expected to do so. In August 1619, when the Prince of Wales, later Charles I, came to dinner, the first earl employed some sixteen cooks to prepare the prince's dinner, and in addition he gave presents to the servants of neighbors who arrived with gifts of food (fish and fowl, a calf, half of a stag, cheeses, fruit). The entertainment for the prince required the services of musicians, who were paid by the earl, and he made payments as well to the prince's servants and even to "my Lady to play with the Prince at Cardes" (£5 10s.). Hobbes and young William are not mentioned in any account of this occasion, but it is likely they were present at the dinner in the high great chamber decorated with a frieze, tapestries, portraits of all the Tudor monarchs, a magnificent chimneypiece, and the royal coat of arms.[11]

In 1610, two years after Hobbes had joined the household at Hardwick, he and his pupil embarked on a tour that took them, wrote Hobbes in his *Autobiography*, to "foreign cities . . . of Germany, France, and Italy." Hobbes and young William may have been in France when King Henry IV was assassinated in May by François Ravaillac, an event to which Hobbes referred at least twice in his later writings,[12] but he does not mention it in his brief reference to the tour in his *Autobiography*, and no letters or other documents survive to tell us where, how, and with whom the two novice travelers spent their time. Whatever their experiences, Hobbes and William Cavendish did not make another visit to the Continent; Hobbes's next European sojourn, with the young son of another family, was not until 1629. But the tour of 1610, close in time to the murder of Henry IV, if not overlapping it, may have been decisive in convincing Hobbes of the dangers to society and civil peace of religious fanaticism. Guy Fawkes and his coconspirators in the 1605 Gunpowder Plot[13] and François Ravaillac were all fanatical Catholics, and Hobbes, although he wrote nothing about these conspiracies at the time, may have decided when still a young man that the single most important condition for domestic order and stability was the total and absolute submission of religion to political authority. But he was not to say so for another thirty years.

Hobbes's writings of this early period are his *De Mirabilibus Pecci*, or long poem to the Peak, mentioned earlier; his first known political work, the translation in 1629 of Thucydides; and, probably, the translation into Latin of two or three of Francis Bacon's essays. Neither Bacon nor Hobbes referred anywhere to these translations, but according to Aubrey (who could have obtained this information only from Hobbes, Bacon having died in 1626, the year Aubrey was born),

"The Lord Chancellour Bacon loved to converse with [Hobbes]. He assisted his lordship in translating severall of his Essays into Latin, one, I well remember, is that *Of the Greatnes of Cities:* the rest I have forgott. His lordship was a very contemplative person, and was wont to contemplate in his delicious walkes at Gorambery, and dictate to Mr. Thomas Bushell, or some other of his gentlemen, that attended him with inke and paper ready to sett downe presently his thoughts. His lordship would often say that he better liked Mr. Hobbes's taking his thoughts, then any of the other, because he understood what he wrote, which the others not understanding, my Lord would many times have a hard taske to make sense of what they writt."

The essay mentioned by Aubrey, which he mistitled, was "Of the True Greatnesse of Kingdomes and Estates," regarded by an authority on Bacon as "one of the best translated of all," while the two others Aubrey "forgott" may have been "Of Simulation and Dissimulation" and "Of Innovations."[14] Certainly, the literary characteristics of the three essays remind the reader of Hobbes's prose style, which was sharp, acerbic, and, in the words of a Bacon biographer commenting on one of Bacon's works, "uncompromising . . . grim, witty, conducive rather to mental shock than to laughter, and some of it unforgettable."[15] Indeed, one has no difficulty understanding why Bacon, according to Aubrey, preferred dictating his thoughts to Hobbes. Despite differences of personality and principle, the area of agreement between the two was vast and important, and there also were many smilarities in attitude and outlook. Both attacked Aristotle and Scholasticism, Bacon describing Aristotle's philosophy as a "philosophy only strong for disputations and contentions, but barren of the production of works for the benefit of the life of man."[16] Both were critical of the universities for teaching Aristotelian doctrines, and both held it "to be an error . . . that scholars in universities come too soon and too unripe to logic and rhetoric arts fitter for graduates than children and novices . . . [thus] the wisdom of those arts, which is great and universal, is almost made contemptible, and is degenerate into childish sophistry and ridiculous affection."* Both intensely disliked theological arguments, and both were inclined, as C. D. Broad said of Bacon, to regard "the Church of England as a branch of the Civil Service, and the Archbishop of Canterbury as the British Minister for Divine Affairs."[17] While neither was a scientist or a mathematician and each tended to minimize the contributions of scientists and mathematicians, both claimed, as Bacon put it, to "have taken all knowledge" for their "province," and left writings in many fields of

---

* Bacon, *Of the Advancement of Learning* (London, 1605), bk. 2. Bacon was twelve when he entered Trinity College, Cambridge, in April 1573; he resided there for three years.

learning.[18] Both claimed, somewhat untruthfully, to have read few books, Hobbes stating that "if he had read as much as other men, he should have knowne no more than other men" (Aubrey), Bacon asserting, according to his chaplain-secretary, that "he wasted none of his time or mental reserves on what he could learn from other men's books."[19] While Bacon was an exponent of experimental induction and Hobbes an advocate of abstract deductive logic, they resembled each other "in their attempt to systematize all human knowledge; in their laying hold of science as the key to truth; in their ideal of utility and power as the end of knowledge; in their conception of reality as more or less mechanical and of sense-impressions as subjective; in their dismissal of final causes and separation of the realms of knowledge and faith; and in their extension of naturalistic principles from the physical to the moral and social worlds."[20] Even Hobbes's "discovery" that everything known and sensed derives from types and degrees of motion was to some extent anticipated by Bacon's hypothesis that heat is nothing more than motion: "A motion expansive, restrained and acting in its strife upon the smaller particles of bodies ... Heat itself, in its essence and quiddity is Motion and nothing else."[21]

Bacon and Hobbes shared other, less significant characteristics as well. Though their only known physical similarity was the color of their eyes, which, according to Aubrey, were lively and "of a hazell colour," both believed in the importance of exercise and careful diet (a regimen far more beneficial to Hobbes, who died at ninety-one, than to Bacon, who died at sixty-six).[22] Unlike Hobbes, Bacon was married, unhappily so toward the end of his life and probably long before that, but both much preferred, and chose their close friends from, the company of men, and in their attitudes toward women there is more than a hint of misogyny.* Both, finally, were admirers of Thucydides, and Bacon may have played a role in Hobbes's decision to

---

* In the case of Bacon, much more than a hint. A number of Bacon's contemporaries, perhaps including his mother, and several later historians believed he was homosexual, or at least bisexual. The evidence, however, is circumstantial at best, though even a biographer who disputes the allegation, Catherine Drinker Bowen, has admitted (in *Francis Bacon*, 15) that Bacon "never loved a woman," that the two persons he loved best were his father and his brother. Hobbes, too, may never have loved a woman, but no one has ever hinted that he was homosexual. Aubrey's references to Hobbes's interest in women, to be sure, are somewhat short and cyptic. Putting it in negative rather than positive terms, Aubrey declared, " 'Tis not consistent with an harmonicall soule to be a woman-hater, neither had he [Hobbes] an abhorrescence to good wine but ... .— this only *inter nos*. . . . He was, even is his youth, (generally) temperate, both as to wine and women. . . ." Hobbes probably agreed with Bacon, who wrote in his essay "Of Marriage and Single Life," "He that hath wife and children hath given hostages to fortune; for they are impediments to great enterprises, either of virtue or mischief.

translate into English the great Greek historian's *History of the Pelo-ponnesian War.** Thucydides, of an aristocratic family, was in disgrace when he wrote the *History,* and one wonders whether it was more than coincidence that Bacon, too, was an aristocrat in disgrace when Hobbes was employed by him to translate some of his essays and take down his thoughts. Was Hobbes, perhaps, drawn to those of the upper classes whose careers had succumbed to vox populi?

Bacon, of course, was no Thucydides either in his own eyes or in those of anyone else, but Hobbes may have seen certain parallels between Bacon's impeachment and Thucydides' banishment. In 1621 Bacon as lord chancellor was charged by Parliament with twenty-eight counts of bribery and misconduct and was subsequently found guilty. His punishment, which was severe, included a fine of £40,000, indefinite imprisonment in the Tower of London, and disqualification forever from holding any state office or seat in Parliament. He was also forbidden to come "within the verge" of the court, which in effect meant he was to remain at all times twelve miles or more from London, and a motion to strip him of all titles and honors failed by only two votes. Fortunately for Bacon, the verdict in its entirety was not carried out, but his career in government was at an end.

While there is no doubt that money was given to Bacon (and to his servants, as well) before and during legal proceedings in which he was officially involved, his judgments and decisions do not appear to have been influenced by such payments. Many of his contemporaries, and most later historians, therefore believed that though Bacon was wrong to accept money from litigants in cases, he was not, in the vulgar sense of the word, bribed. In the opinion of some, Bacon would never have been tried and convicted had it not been for the machinations of his enemies and rivals in Parliament and at the court. Hobbes may have held this view and regarded Bacon, as later he was explic-

---

Certainly the best works, and of greatest merit for the public, have proceeded from the unmarried or childless men. . . . Wives are young men's mistresses; companions for middle age; and old men's nurses. . . . But yet he was reputed one of the wise men, that made answer to the question, when a man should marry?—'A young man not yet, an elder man not at all.' "

* In the second book of his *Of the Advancement of Learning,* Bacon maintained, "History which may be called Just and Perfect History is of three kinds . . . for it either representeth a Time, or a Person, or an Action. . . . Of these . . . the third (excelleth) in verity and sincerity. . . . Narrations and Relations of actions, as the War of Peloponnesus . . . cannot but be more purely and exactly true than Histories of Times, because they may choose an argument comprehensible within the notice and instructions of the writer . . . the text of Thucydides and Xenophon [as related to Greek history] . . . to be kept entire without any diminution at all, and only to be supplied [added to] and continued."

itly to regard Thucydides, as a more or less innocent victim of reck-
less and irresponsible demagoguery masquerading as concern for the
public good—for surely Hobbes knew that many of Bacon's judges in
the House of Commons and in the Lords were men motivated much
more by personal ambition, jealousy, and rivalry than by a concern
for morality in high position. Where affairs do not go well, even though
their conduct lacks "neither providence nor courage," Hobbes was to
write in his introduction to his translation of Thucydides, "the way
to calumny is always open" for persons who "judge only upon events,"
and "envy, in the likeness of zeal to the public good, easily findeth
credit for an accusation." In making this observation not long after
Bacon's death, Hobbes may have had the impeached lord chancellor
in mind as much as the exiled commander of Athenian naval forces
at Amphipolis. But even before his contact with Bacon and Thucydides, perhaps as early as his stay at Oxford, Hobbes seems to have
developed a profound dislike and distrust of legislative assemblies,
especially those whose composition reflected democratic principles,
a dislike and distrust that the histories of Bacon and Thucydides could
only have served to confirm.

Hobbes's political views, however, were hardly apparent in his
first literary effort, the full title of which was *De Mirabilibus Pecci:
Being the Wonders of the English Peak in Darby-Shire, Commonly Called
the Devil's Arse of Peak.** Written in Latin verse between 1626 and 1628
although not published until 1636, the *Peak* (as it will be referred to
here) was dedicated to Hobbes's pupil, the second earl of Devonshire,
with whom Hobbes had visited Peak Cavern and the surrounding area.
While the *Peak* has little if any value as poetry and reveals nothing of
Hobbes's maturing thought, the poem is not without interest. The
first of two books Hobbes dedicated to the second earl—for which the
earl rewarded him with a gift of five pounds—the *Peak* was almost as
much a celebration of the Devonshires as it was a commemoration of
the visit to the caves and caverns of Derbyshire. The first seven of its
pages proclaim the glories of Chatsworth itself: "it's Pile, and Lord,
for both are grand," and, in addition, the Derwin River that flows by
it, the gardens and fruit trees, the water that enters the house and is
used by "Cook and Butler,"† the fountains and walls, the fishponds,

---

* Until recently, Hobbes was believed by Leo Strauss and others to be the author of a
collection of essays, *Horae Subsecivae*, published anonymously in 1620, but this attribution has proven to be false. Hobbes, however, apparently annotated a copy of *Horae
Subsecivae* in the Chatsworth library. The controversy surrounding the authorship of
the essays, and Hobbes's annotations, are discussed in Appendix 1.

† Water from the river was diverted into the house, where it was used for cooking,
cleaning, and other purposes. Chatsworth may have been the first English house with
a primitive version of indoor plumbing and running water.

Elizabethan Chatsworth, by Richard Wilson, after Siberechts.
Perhaps this vista was Hobbes's first view of Chatsworth.

and much else. Hobbes also manages to mention favorably "fam'd Shrewsbury's great Countess"

> Who left an Offspring numerous and great
> With which the joyful Nation's still repleat.

Much tribute is paid the second earl and his wife, Christian, and their three children, one of whom, the only daughter, Ann, is described as "a Nymph, whom Jove himself may love." Turning to the two sons, William the future third earl, and Charles, who was to be killed at Gainsborough in 1643, Hobbes concluded his praise of the family:

> With two Sweet Youths, who Angells might be said,
> The commonpledges of the Marriage bed.
> These with their Parents may be wonder'd at
> What else of Miracles thou may'st repeat,
> Fall short of these, and are not night so great.[23]

The journey itself, though it began well, with a view of Chatsworth seen from a distance, was not far along when two men were killed in the collapse of a lead mine passed en route. Hobbes is not without sympathy for the dead man and their families, but his sympathy lacks tears or any trace of emotion:

> A lazy people drawn from e'ry Town,
> To see the mournful spectacle came down.
> Two women weeping in the crowd we spi'd;
> One for the loss of joyes that she had tri'd,
> T'other for want of hopes are now denied.
> Ones flame continual use had near expir'd,
> T'other with itch of novelty was fir'd.
> Both mourn, because that both their joyes have lost,
> But she who last had tasted them, the most.
> Let them still mourn. We in our way go on.

Whether to please his patron, the second earl, or to amuse himself, Hobbes misses no opportunity to compare hills and caves to parts of the human body. The local name for Peak Cavern, long celebrated as one of the seven wonders of Derbyshire, was the "Devil's Arse," but Hobbes is not content with that allusion. The two segments of the hill surrounding the cave are likened to "buttocks amply sticking out," while the "Devil's Arse" is described as being "like a furnace, or as Hell" following the Day of Judgment:

> Swallowing with open Jawes the Damned croud
> After the sentence is pronounce'd aloud.

Within the cave Hobbes and his party employ as their guide "a she Native of the place . . . Handsome enough, and Girle enough she was," who encourages them on with a "cheer." Later that day they come to another cave, Eldon Hole, before which Hobbes's "Muse" is silent because the mouth of Eldon Hole has a "form obscene." "Tell, me, Tell't me alone, tell't in my ear," Hobbes begs his "Muse,"

> Whisper't, that none but thou and I may hear.

Finally, in a footnote we learn that the "mouth of the hole is of a cnunoid form or like the privities of a woman."*

Memories of his tour of the Peak district were to haunt Hobbes's dreams and waking life until well into his old age.† Although he never again visited the caves and caverns described in his poem, so far as we know, similes and images based on them sometimes appeared in his writings and in his conversations as reported by contemporaries. In one such discussion, with the third earl of Devonshire in the last decade or two of his life, Hobbes maintained that "it was lawful to make use of ill Instruments to do ourselves good." Clarifying what he meant by "ill Instruments," Hobbes declared, "If I were cast into a deep Pit, and the Devil should put down his Cloven Foot, I would take hold of it to be drawn out by it."[24] His reference to "the Devil's Mountain," at the beginning of *Behemoth*, perhaps owed something to the cliffs high above Peak Cavern ("Devil's Arse"), and perhaps, too, his last reported statement, when he was dying, had some connection to conscious or unconscious fantasies that originated on the tour more than fifty years earlier. Informed that his disease was incurable, Hobbes a11supposed to have said, "I shall be glad then to find a Hole to creep out of the World at."[25]

References to human anatomy in the *Peak* do not establish that Hobbes and the second earl shared an interest in the more intimate physical aspects of life, but we may doubt that Hobbes would have included these references had the earl, for whom the poem was written, been displeased by them. Some common interest may also be reflected in a notebook entitled "Epigrams in Imitation of Martial," found among Hobbes's papers after his death. The epigrams, in a handwriting that "might easily be that of Hobbes himself in his early

---

*A local story, repeated by Hobbes, was that in the time of Queen Elizabeth, the earl of Leicester paid a "poor Peasant" to descend into the hole on a rope. The "Peasant" was to drop stones, the sounds of which as they fell providing, it was hoped, the earl with information about the depth of the hole. When the "Peasant" was retrieved, he was found to be raving mad, and he died eight days later. In his poem, Hobbes had the earl learning from this experience "how far the Cave went down," namely, "to Hell."

†Somewhat embarrassed in later life by his effort to celebrate the tour in writing, he did not favor the translation into English of *De Mirabilibus Pecci* in 1678. The translation, however, was an immediate success and circulated widely; the only book by Hobbes in the library of Isaac Newton was *De Mirabilibus Pecci*. John Harrison, *The Library of Isaac Newton* (Cambridge: Cambridge University Press, 1978).

days," are for the most part rather earthy, not to say bawdy (in the seventeenth-century style), and since several of the notebook's pages carry the signature of "William Cavendish," we may specualte that the epigrams, like the *Peak*, were a literary effort Hobbes shared to some extent with the second or third earl of Devonshire.[26] Certainly, the second earl, a married man and the father of three children by 1620, might have thought these lines witty:

> Jenkin his love meeting in a wide field
> Persuaded her, her fort to him to yield:
> And least that any might espy their play
> One should looke one, th'other another way.
> But, when into her fortress he was climbed,
> She cried, O Sweete! looke both ways, I am blind.

Another epigram, perhaps more in the style of Hobbes than of Martial, ran,

> What gentlemen? Can you abstain from laughter
> To hear a merry tale of Symon's daughter?
> Who had by his wife a daughter named Sue.
> Not fair nor foul, but of a comely hew.
> The only child they two had them between
> Being about the age then of sixteen.
> Her mother's care watched her so narrowly,
> She could not piss without her privily.
> She, wearly grown of being so at home,
> Got leave one day to ride into the town:
> Where met her Sam, a man of mickle power,
> And rode with her three long leagues in an hour.
> Thenceforth the wench (stayed) at home abiding,
> And now could have her belly full of riding;
> For twenty weeks and more: then waxing full,
> Symon and his wife perceived well the gull.

But not all epigrams celebrated carnal love. One of the shorter ones observed sadly,

> I poor was in my youth but rich now old
> In neither fortune fitting find I could:
> When I could use wealth, fortune kept all back,
> Now nothing I can use, I nothing lack.*

Some of the epigrams had economic and social overtones, as in the following:

---

*I have modernized spelling and punctuation throughout.

Young Matho, say his friends all what they can,
In's humour now will be a gentleman.
A gentleman? you jest. Yes by the Lord!
By his gentry he doth swear at every word,
And takes tobacco like a young knight's page,
And not his word but his honour doth engage.
He would not now, for all his grandsire's wealth,
Be drunk, unless it were to his mistress's health.
He scorns on the base viol for to play
In barber's shop, but on the market day.
His skin and face are much more soft and clear
Than is an egg steeped in vinegar.
He eats, drinks, speaks, he sleeps and all by art,
And (withal) that he scorns to let a:(: :):
These qualities are good and passing rare,
And sure few with him for them may compare.
Yet his sire a butcher was. He was a pox.
The cruelest man that ever slew an ox.
Yet in his gentle son much unlike him,
That though an ass should kick him, he'd not strike him.
We shall our stormy age a muddily gee,
If yet our butchers' sons so gentle be.

In his *Peak*, Hobbes, in the verses praising his pupil and patron, had observed of the second earl,

Magnificent, not lavish, still he spends
His riches freely, and amongst his Friends.

By that time Hobbes was well aware of the earl's extravagance, but he may not have known the extent to which his employer was in debt. The second earl, who succeeded to the title in 1626, the "waster," as Aubrey stigmatized him, "sent him [Hobbes] up and downe to borrow money, and to gett gentlemen to be bound for him, being ashamed to speake him selfe." One consequence was that Hobbes "tooke colds, being wett in his feet (then there were no hackney coaches to stand in the streets)." Hobbes also "rode a hunting and hawking" with his patron and as a result "almost forgott his Latin. . . . He therefore bought [for himself] bookes of an Amsterdam print that he might carry in his pocket (particularly Caesar's Commentarys), which he did read in the Lobbey, or ante-chamber, whilst his lord was making his visits."

Hobbes's own account of his twenty years with the second earl to some extent contradicts Aubrey's, or at least strikes a wholly different note. In his *Autobiography*, Hobbes wrote that the earl "was not so much a master as a friend, and this was by far the sweetest portion of my life. Still now it often gives me happy dreams. Through all those years he gave me leisure and supplied me with books of every sort for my studies. . . . [He was] my sweet and indulgent master. . . ." Hobbes's dedication to *Thucydides*, written closer in time to his service with the earl and dedicated to him, commends his departed patron's devotion to "those that studied the liberal arts liberally," and adds that there was no one "in whose house a man should less need a university than in his." The second earl, moreover, gave himself to "that kind of learning which best deserveth the pains and hours of great persons, history and civil knowledge. . . . For he read, so that the learning he took in by study, by judgment he digested, and converted into wisdom and ability to benefit his country: to which also he applied himself with zeal, but such as took no fire either from faction or ambition."

For reasons not clear, neither Hobbes nor Aubrey mentions Hobbes's involvement, and that of the second earl, with companies concerned in the settlement of Virginia and the Bermudas. Hobbes, in fact, became a member of the Virginia Company on or about June 19, 1622, and he subsequently was also a shareholder in the Somer Islands Company, an independent but largely subsidiary enterprise of the Virginia Company that was responsible for settlement in the Bermudas. Attending "no fewer than thirty-seven meetings in the following two years," meetings at which the second earl usually was also present, Hobbes voted on issues brought before the Virginia Company's stockholders, apparently always on the side taken by his patron and employer.[27] Both the Virginia Company and the Somer Islands Company almost continually were involved in major controversies about finances and management, and Hobbes must have been present in July 1623 when Robert Rich, earl of Warwick, accused the second earl of lying. Though dueling was officially banned, the second earl, who was hot-tempered by nature, challenged Warwick to a duel, in connection with which they both made arrangements to meet, and fight, in Holland. King James, however, heard of these plans, and as a consequence "all the ports were ordered to be watched. Cavendish was caught at Shoreham and detained there in a gentleman's house. Warwick, disguised as a merchant, got away to the Netherlands, but was discovered at Ghent, and the whole affair apparently blew over."[28]

Hobbes, perhaps, had this affair in memory when he wrote, in *Leviathan*, that "private duels are, and always will be honourable, though unlawful, till such time as there shall be honour ordained for them that refuse, and ignominy for them that make the challenge . . . for the most part they be effects of rash speaking, and of the fear of dishonour, in one, or both the combatants; who engaged by rashness, are driven into the lists to avoid disgrace."[29] But he never made ref-

William Cavendish, second earl of Devonshire (1590–1628). By an unknown artist, Hardwick Hall collection. Toward the end of his life Hobbes remembered his years in the service of the second earl as the happiest period of his life.

erence, directly or indirectly, to the disputes that occupied the Virginia and Somer Islands companies during the years he was a member, and only with difficulty can a connection be made between his experiences as a shareholder in the companies and his political views. Hobbes's total silence about these experiences may be due, as a student of the subject has suggested, to his wish not to be associated, in Restoration England, with such leading figures in the companies as "Sandys, Digges and Danvers, whose sympathies lay, in general terms, with Country against Court, Common Law against Chancery, and parliamentary privilege against royal prerogative."* After 1660, as will be seen later, Hobbes was frequently occupied in defending himself against accusations that following his return from France during the winter of 1651–52, he had been "much caressed" by Cromwell and his supporters, or, in other words, against charges that he had been a partisan and even a "lackey" of the "usurper." Anxious about the possible effects of this indictment, Hobbes would surely have had no wish to call attention to his earlier association with the Virginia Company, which may have seemed to him, "in retrospect . . . tainted with anti-royalism."[30]

Less understandable, perhaps, is his failure to draw upon the knowledge he and other members of the Virginia Company had gained of the American Indian. The four references in *Leviathan* to the Indians generally make the point that the "savage people in many places of America, except the government of small families, the concord whereof dependeth on natural lust, have no government at all," whereas Hobbes must have been familiar with Virginia Company reports establishing that "some Indian tribes did conform to his model of a commonwealth."[31] The suggestion has been made that Hobbes's neglect of these reports and their implications was occasioned by "his distaste for anything that might tie his argument to empirical questions of fact" and by his awareness that Indian government, however rudimentary, "must have been embarrassing for his subsidiary theory that all the benefits of civilization sprang directly from the leisure provided by secure government."[32] An alternative explanation is that Hobbes did not regard the Indian chief as analogous to the absolute sovereign or monarch he held to be essential for peace and security, and did not view the benefits of Indian society, in which intermittent tribal warfare often succeeded in making life, if not "solitary," nonetheless "poor, nasty, brutish, and short," as equivalent to those of European civilization. By 1622, moreover, if not earlier, Hobbes prob-

---

* Malcolm, "Hobbes," 301. Three of Sandys's sons served as colonels in the parliamentary army, and Danvers was one of the regicides of 1649.

ably had in mind the main outline, though not all the details, of his political theory; certainly, the fundamentals of this theory were in place when, some years before 1629, when it was published, he embarked on his translation of Thucydides. Convinced, by then, that man needed strong government as much as he needed air to breathe and water to drink, Hobbes was no more inclined to alter his views in order to accommodate the American Indian experience than he was to modify them in an effort to placate Sandys, Digges, Danvers, and other pro-Parliament sympathizers in the Virginia Company. In all likelihood, Hobbes's opinions on most important subjects were little influenced by meetings or proceedings of the Virginia Company.

Between these meetings, as has been mentioned, the second earl, regularly attended by Hobbes, "applied himself with zeal" to good living. A favorite of King James, the earl was a leader of fashion fond of giving lavish parties and entertainments, which made his house appear "rather like a prince's court than a subject's."[33] Though an extremely wealthy man, "he lived beyond his means" to such an extent that he required, and received from the House of Lords, a bill enabling him "to sell some of his entailed estates, an unusual measure in those days." However, the earl did not live long enough to benefit from the measure, dying at the age of thirty-eight on June 20, 1628. His death, it was said, was due to "excessive indulgence in good living."[34]

Christian, left a widow with three children, was immediately involved in some thirty lawsuits concerned mainly with the payment of her late husband's debts. Since the sale of the entailed estates did not produce a sum equal to these debts, she was forced to take certain measures to economize, but we cannot be certain the subsequent dismissal of the deceased second earl's tutor, "secretary," and friend was among them. Hobbes, in any case, was to return to her service in 1631, but meanwhile there was another young man to be instructed, another tour of the Continent, and the appearance of his first published work, the translation of Thucydides.

F O U R

THUCYDIDES

B EFORE Thucydides," Aubrey reported about Hobbes, "he spent two yeares in reading romances and playes, which he haz often repented and sayd that these two yeares were lost of him—wherin perhaps he was mistaken too. For it might furnish him with copie of words." Hobbes did not say when he began his translation of Thucydides, but on March 18, 1628, it was far enough advanced for him to have it listed in the *Register of the Company of Stationers of London.** Three months later, on June 20, the second earl of Devonshire died, and perhaps for that reason publication of the Thucydides translation was delayed. Early in November, Hobbes's draft of the book's "Epistle Dedicatorie" to the deceased second earl was sent to Christian, the earl's widow, for her approval. In his letter to her, the earliest of his letters to survive, Hobbes wrote that while he had followed "the forme which your Ladyship gave me leave to use," he was concerned that he "may faile through ignorance to do what I intend, and it is my duty to acquaint your Ladyship with my doings, in things that conerne my Lord." Requesting Christian to return the proposed dedication "as soon as conveniently may be, because the Presse will shortly be ready for it," Hobbes "beseeched" her "to hold a good opinion of me (especially touching my dutifull respect to you and just estimation of your noble Virtues) without which no benefit bestowed upon me can be comfortable."[1]

What changes, if any, Christian made in the draft that Hobbes sent to her from the Devonshire house in London, where he was residing at the time, is not known. But she could hardly have been dis-

---

* The listing was equivalent to royal permission or license to publish, without which no book could be printed or sold. Forty yerars later, when Charles II refused his assent to the publicatrion of *Behemoth: The History of the Causes of the Civil Wars of England,* Hobbes observed to Aubrey, "The priviledge of stationers is (in my opinion) a very great hinderance to ye advancement of all human learning."

pleased with Hobbes's fulsome praise of her late husband, some of which was quoted earlier. Nor, probably, was she less satisfied with the sentiments expressed in Hobbes's preface to his translation, entitled "To the Readers," and in his introductory "Of the Life and History of Thucydides," both of them stating opinions that, whether or not they were entirely those of Thucydides, were certainly close to, if not identical with, those of King Charles I and his closest advisers. The book as a whole, dated 1629, was in fact an immediate success. Reprinted in 1634 and again in 1648, *Thucydides* in 1676 reappeared in a second edition, and a third edition "Corrected and Amended" was published in 1723, forty-four years after Hobbes's death.*

In his *Autobiography*, Hobbes wrote that Thucydides, his "special favorite" among historians, taught him "how stupid democracy is and by how much one man is wiser than an assembly." He went on, "I made it my business that this author should speak to the English in their own tongue and warn them against the temptation to listen to rhetoric." Hobbes was saying, in other words, that a new translation of Thucydides' great *History*—the book had previously been translated into English in 1550—was particularly relevant to the England of 1629 in that Thucydides had shown "how stupid democracy is" and had warned against listening to "rhetoric," by which term Hobbes meant the impassioned and emotional appeals of demagogues (such as those of Cleon in the *History*). But were the "lessons" of Thucydides those Hobbes emphasized in his *Autobiography* and also in the prefatory pages of his translation? More important, why was it essential to caution, in the early Stuart period, that democracy was "stupid," and who was producing the "rhetoric" that the English, Hobbes hoped, would refuse to hear?

Thucydides, to begin with, was writing not against democracy or against "rhetoric" but about a war and its effects that were, up to that time, without precedent in the history of mankind. The Peloponnesian War, between Athens and Sparta, 431 to 404 B.C., in the course of which there occurred the worst plague ever experienced by Greece, was not a war between ideals or ideologies, whether of democracy or oligarchy, but one between empires. Sixty years earlier

---

* The full title of the first edition, first issue (1629), was *Eight Bookes of the Peloponnesian Warre, Written by Thucydides, the Sonne of Olorus: Interpreted with Faith and Diligence Immediately out of the Greeke by Thomas Hobbes, Secretary to the Late Earle of Devonshire.* I have modernized the printing (i.e., substituted "u" for "v" and so on). According to Aubrey, the poets Ben Jonson and Robert Ayton gave Hobbes, at his request, "their judgment on his style of his translation of Thucydides." Hobbes himself drew the maps of Greece that accompany the text and composed the list of place-names mentioned by Thucydides.

Athens, at the head of a coalition, had fought and won a war against Persian despotism, and perhaps no war in history had ever been fought, in the words of Edith Hamilton, "for purer motives."[2] But the fifty years following the Athenian victory at Salamis had witnessed the rise of Athens to a dominant position in the Mediterranean world, a position that led the Athenians, who were already powerful and wealthy, to demand more power and wealth. Thus, the "real cause" of the Peloponnesian War "was greed, that strange passion for power and possession which no power and no possession satisfy. ... The Athenians and the Spartans fought for one reason only—because they were powerful, and therefore were compelled (the words are Thucydides' own) to seek more power. They fought not because they were different—democratic Athens and oligarchical Sparta—but because they were alike."[3]

Toward the end Athens, bled white by military expenditures, disunited and confused by political turmoil, and deserted by its allies, bungled a naval-military expedition to Sicily that was intended to reverse the tide of the war. The result was defeat, but not merely defeat in battle. Thousands of Athenians were hacked to pieces, or drowned, or died of starvation and exposure. Thousands of others became slaves, most of whom perished from hard labor in the stone quarries of Syracuse. Although the war continued for another nine years, during which Athens occasionally managed a minor victory, the cause was doomed, and in April 404 the Spartan commander Lysander sailed into Piraeus and occupied Athens.

Thucydides himself, as was mentioned earlier, was in disgrace when he wrote his *History;* a general in 424, he and his forces were defeated in a battle off the Thracian coast, as a result of which he was banished to his estate.* But the major themes of the work are not the defeat of Athens by Sparta (much less anger over his own fate) or, as Hobbes implied, the "stupidity" of democracy. Thucydides' main concerns, apart from telling the story of the war, were to establish the decisive role of human nature in the rise and fall of both societies and individuals, to demonstrate the corrupting effects of war upon morality and decency, and to raise the question whether freedom or democracy, and discipline or self-control, can coexist. He was inclined to believe that, given peace and able leadership (of the sort Solon and Pericles had exemplified), coexistence was possible. After Pericles' death, and increasingly as the war progressed, he became convinced

---

*Thucydides may have died between 404, when he apparently was in Athens, and 399, but the exact dates of his birth (possibly about 460) and death are not certain. Because his *History* was unfinished, ending in the middle of a sentence, some biographers and commentators believe he was murdered.

that democratic government, by which he meant government based upon "a reasonable and moderate blending of the few and the many,"[4] could not withstand the strains of war.

Far from believing that democracy was the cause of Athens's downfall, Thucydides attributed to democracy Athens's sensational rise to power in the first half of the fifth century B.C. As John H. Finley, Jr., has noted, "Athens' career as a first-class power dated only from the Persian wars, but in the less than five decades between them and the Peloponnesian war, she had already climbed to a position which menaced and overshadowed the rest of Greece. . . . The force which carried her to these heights was democracy, the effects of which had been seen, internally, in the liberated energy of her citizens and the material progress which was its fruit and, externally, in the loyalty of the lower classes of the empire and even in the friendliness of the same classes everywhere. . . . [Athens] represented all the revolution-izing forces of the era, democracy, imperialism, material progress, a commercial economy, while [Sparta] stood for the oligarchic, agri-cultural, cantonal Greece of the past."[5]

By democracy, Thucydides meant *not* modern representative government, characterized by an elected executive and legislature in office for a given term of years, but a government of all the people ruling in behalf of the most numerous element, the lower classes. Such a government "was, at best, infinitely more precarious, because infi-nitely more exposed to the winds of popular feeling. The reason was in part that, the city-state being small, the assembly could still be looked on as a meeting of all the people . . . and, in part, because the executive college of generals was annually elected. Moreover, at a stated monthly meeting of the assembly, these generals were subject to review and even to impeachment, a process apparently followed in the cases of both Pericles and Thucydides. This practice was the more dangerous because . . . the assembly tended to be dominated by the urban population. The same element was not less important in determining policies, approving peace or war, and even in voting expeditions. . . . Accordingly, when [Thucydides] bases the whole lat-ter part of his *History* on the idea that, fundamental as democarcy was to the growth and power of Athens, it proved incapable after Pericles' death of a temperate policy or consistent leadership, one must recognize that he was demanding this temperance and consis-tency of a form of democratic government which was perhaps least capable of providing them, especially under the conditions of siege and plague which obtained at Athens at various times throughout the war."[6]

Thucydides, according to Hobbes, "least of all liked the democracy," and while he praised Athenian government "when it was mixed of *the few* and *the many*," he much preferred it when "it was democratical in name, but in effect monarchical under Pericles." Being of "regal descent," Hobbes added, Thucydides "it seemeth . . . best approved of the regal government."[7] In reality, however, for Thucydides, if not for Hobbes, the alternative to the irresponsible and self-serving "rhetoric" of a demagogue (such as Cleon, described by Hobbes as "a most violent sycophant . . . thereby also a most acceptable speaker amongst the people") was not "regal government" but a return to the sane and rational leadership of the Periclean Age.

For Hobbes as for Thucydides, Cleon, described by Thucydides as "the most violent man at Athens," possesses no redeeming features. But the classicist John V. A. Fine has recently called attention to Thucydides' "blatant bias against Cleon," which generations of scholars have accepted without question. Fine has suggested that Cleon was intensely disliked by Thucydides, Aristophanes, and others partly because he was a critic of Pericles' "military strategy" and perhaps his prosecutor in the second year of the war, and partly because he was, as the owner of a tannery, not an aristocrat or a farmer. Thucydides, Fine has observed, "was thoroughly convinced that all Athenian leaders in the war after the death of Pericles were woefully inferior to him, and as an aristocrat he had an instinctive contempt for the "vulgarity" of Cleon. . . . The fact that his banishment in 424 . . . may have resulted from a prosecution instituted by Cleon would not have contributed to his liking of the man. . . . It cannot be emphasized too often that Athenian authors, and Greek authors in general, who wrote history or discussed historical persons were almost exclusively oligarchic, aristocratic, or at least, conservative. . . . In the final analysis it is necessary to admit that an accurate characterization of Cleon will never be possible. . . ."[8]

In overlooking Pericles' own commitment to democracy, Hobbes also forgot that one of Thucydides' greatest laments was that Athens during the years of the war, as compared with Syracuse led by Hermocrates, "lacked a second Pericles to lead the people sanely." For Thucydides, the "great dilemma," which he undoubtedly believed other peoples would face in the future, was how democracy and responsible leadership, both of which had been responsible for Athens's greatness, could be preserved "under the stress of war and the hot demands of the populace."[9] Surely, this issue, and the relevance of the Peloponnesian War to the wars that were to follow it, were what he had in mind when he wrote that he would be satisfied with his *History* "if these words of mine are judged useful by those who want to understand clearly the events which happened in the past and which (human nature being what it is) will, at some time or another and in much the same ways, be repeated in the future. My work is not a piece of writing designed to meet the teaste of an immediate public, but was done to last forever."*

In making Thucydides into an antidemocrat, Hobbes, in effect, was making him into a Hobbesian, for by 1629 Hobbes himself was passionately in favor of "regal government" and a strong supporter of the crown against parliamentary challenges. But Hobbes had other reasons to admire Thucydides and to identify with him, and though these led Hobbes to slight or distort the differences between them, we still do well to remember that by 1629 Hobbes had developed, or was in the process of developing, attitudes and opinions not unlike some of those manifested two thousand years earlier by Thucydides.†

These similarities extended even to personality, Hobbes being, like Thucydides in one description, "pessimistic, sceptical, highly intelligent, cold and reserved, at least on the surface, but with strong inner tensions."[10] In Hobbes's writings, as in the *History*, "the gods are chiefly remarkable by their absence. . . . [Thucydides] seems to go out of his way to deny their intervention in human affairs." Hobbes could well have been writing of himself when he noted of Thucydides (together with Anaxagoras and Socrates) that he was thought to be an "atheist" by the "vulgar" because he regarded their religion as "vain and superstitious."[11] Like Thucydides, who wrote almost nothing about Athenian art and literature. Hobbes rarely concerned himself with any aspect of English culture—apart from his essay in Davenant's *Gondibert* (1651), which was dedicated to him, and his personal interest in music—though he lived in one of England's most fertile literary periods. Yet both were aware that words, as Hobbes put it, "are wise men's counters, they do but reckon by them; but they are the money of fools . . . ," and both knew that the meaings of words

---

* This quotation from *Thucydides*, and other quoted statements, unless otherwise identified, are from Rex Warner's translation published as *Thucydides * History of the Peloponnesian War* (Harmondsworth, Eng.: Penguin Books, 1978; first published 1954). The statement quoted above appears on p. 48. Hobbes's own translation, acclaimed as "muscular" (M. I. Finley) and "exact, masculine and emphatic" (Warner), was not wholly accurate, and in any case his early-seventeenth-century English vocabulary and phrasing are not as easily understood as later versions. Where there are revealing differences of meaning between translations, Hobbes's and perhaps other translations will be compared with Warner's.

† On at least one occasion Hobbes alluded to a self-identification with Thucydides. Sending the third earl of Devonshire a letter of paternalistic advice in 1638 (the earl by then was fatherless), Hobbes wrote, "[C]all me fool or Thucydides for my presumption. . . ." See below, p. 118.

change with changing events, such as war. "What used to be described as a thoughtless act of aggression," Thucydides wrote, "was now regarded as the courage one would expect to find in a party member; to think of the future and wait was merely another way of saying one was a coward. . . ." Hobbes's own comment in *Leviathan* seems almost an addition: "for one man calleth *wisdom*, what another calleth *fear*; and one *cruelty*, what another *justice*; one *prodigality*, what another *magnanimity*; and one *gravity*, what another *stupidity*, &c."[12] Thucydides and Hobbes were alike in believing that while they were writing for the timeless future and not the limited present, they were addressing themselves to "wise men" rather than to the "common people"; and both disdained any "desire at all to meddle in the government," as Hobbes put it with regard to Thucydides. Indeed, Hobbes was uncannily forecasting his own noninvolvement in the Civil War, still more than a decade away, when he noted that Thucydides declined to take an active part in politics "that he might not be either of them that committed or of them that suffered the evil."[13]

As was noted earlier, Hobbes's translation of the *History* suffered from certain inaccuracies; this led Benjamin Jowett, the most distinguished Regius Professor of Greek in the history of Oxford University, and himself a translator of Thucydides, to condemn it as "rough" and as having been "praised beyond its merits."[14] A few inaccuracies may owe less to "roughness" and carelessness than to Hobbes's desire, albeit unconscious, to make Thucydides say or not say things that Hobbes, had he written the *History*, would have said or not said. Hobbes was also eager to defend Thucydides against the charge, first made by certain ancient Greek historians and since repeated by some modern critics, that Thucydides occasionally made significant errors and distortions in reporting speeches, such as Pericles' famous Funeral Oration. Thucydides' own account of his method in reporting speeches has been translated by Jowett and Warner as follows:

HISTORY
BOOK I, 22

Jowett	*Warner*
As to the speeches which were made before or during the war, it was hard for me, and for others who reported them to me, to recollect the exact words. I have therefore put into the mouth of each speaker the sentiments proper to the occasion, expressed as I thought he would be likely to	I have found it difficult to remember the precise words used in the speeches which I listened to myself and my various informants have experienced the same difficulty; so my method has been, while keeping as closely as possible to the general sense of the words that were actually used, to make the

express them, while at the same
time I endeavoured, as nearly as I
could, to give the general purport
of what was actually said.*

speakers say what, in my opinion,
was called for by each situation.

In the Jowett and Warner versions, Thucydides admits that, to some
extent, he has had to improvise the speeches in terms of what was
"proper to the occasion" or "called for by each situation." Hobbes,
on the other hand, translates the passage in such a way as to suggest
that Thucydides' rendering of the speeches was more literal:

> What particular persons have spoken when they were about
> to enter the war or when they were in it were hard for me
> to remember exactly, whether they were speeches which I
> have heard myself or have received at the second hand. But
> as any man seemed to me that knew what was nearest to
> the sum of the truth of all that had been uttered to speak
> most agreeably to the matter still in hand, so I have made
> it spoken here.

In his introductory commentary, Hobbes goes even further in the
direction of insisting on the accuracy of the speeches, writing of Thucydides, "The grounds and motives of every action he setteth down
before the action itself, either narratively, or else contriveth them
into the form of deliberative orations. . . ."[15]

When Hobbes composed his translation, crown and Parliament
were engaged in a verbal war about the power to tax, both James and
Charles insisting they could levy taxes without Parliament's consent,
Parliament taking the opposite view. Hobbes, who supported the
crown's position, was perhaps influenced by this conflict in translating a section of the *History* dealing with an Athenian effort to raise
money for the war. For purposes of comparison, the translations of
Jowett, Warner, and Hobbes are given below:

HISTORY
BOOK III, 19

Jowett	*Warner*
The Athenians, being in want of money to carry on the siege, raised among themselves for the first time a property-tax of two hundred talents, and sent out twelve ships to collect tribute among the allies, under the command of Lysicles and four others.	The Athenians still needed more money for the siege, though they had for the first time raised from their own citizens a contribution of 200 talents. They now sent twelve ships to collect money from their allies, with Lysicles and four others in command.

---

*Benjamin Jowett, *Thucydides*, 2d ed. rev. (Oxford: Clarendon Press, 1900).

Hobbes
The Athenians, standing in need of
money for the siege, both contributed themselves, and sent
thither two hundred talents of this
their first contribution, and also
dispatched Lysicles and four others with twelve galleys, to levy
money amongst the confederates.

The Jowett and Warner translations make it clear that the Athenians were taxing themselves for the first time; until the war, no
general tax or levy was paid by Athenians.[16] Hobbes's version, however, makes it appear that the levy of 200 talents was not a novel or
unprecedented undertaking, that the money was only the first of a
number of contributions. Hobbes, in effect, implies that Athenians
were accustomed to paying taxes, especially in time of war, as a matter of course, without protest or fanfare. Here, too, Hobbes perhaps
wanted his translation of Thucydides to convey a message to his fellow English who, in Parliament and elsewhere, were resisting the
imposition of new taxes and increases in old levies to finance not only
wars but also the enormous and rising costs of royal households.

Thucydides' references to actions taken by public assemblies and
tribunals, particularly those seeking scapegoats for the calamities
Athens was experiencing, are frequently translated by Hobbes into
language stronger or more perjorative than that of the Greek original.
Because Hobbes has less use for these assemblies than did Thucydides, who himself was no admirer of popular despotisms, he loses no
opportunity, through his choice of words, to influence his translation's readers against them. But as the following example demonstrates, some of the words belong more to Hobbes than to Thucydides:

HISTORY
BOOK VI, 53

Jowett	*Warner*
They [the Athenians] did investi-	Instead of checking up on the char-
gate the character of the informers,	acters of their informers, they [the
but in their suspicious mood lis-	Athenians] had regarded every-
tened to all manner of statements,	thing they were told as grounds for
and seized and imprisoned some of	suspicion, and on the evidence of
the most respectable citizens on	complete rogues had arrested and
the evidences of wretches; they	imprisoned some of the best citi-
thought it better to sift the matter	zens, thinking it better to get to the
and discover the truth; and they	bottom of things in this way rather
would not allow even a man of	than to let any accused person,

good character, against whom an accusation was brought, to escape without a thorough investigation, merely because the informer was a rogue.

however good his reputation might be, escape interrogation because of the bad character of the informer.

Hobbes

And making no inquiry into the persons of the informers, but through jealousy admitting of all sorts, upon the reports of evil men apprehended very good citizens and cast them into prison, choosing rather to examine the fact and find the truth by torments, than that any man, how good soever in estimation, being once accused should escape unquestioned.

In other words, Thucydides paints a black picture of these interrogations, but Hobbes, in translating the Greek terms as "jealousy" and "torments" (i.e., torture), makes the picture even blacker.

Hobbes himself could not have believed that these "people's tribunals" in any form existed in England when, sometime before 1628, he completed his translation of the *History;* reliance on informers, use of torture to obtain evidence or confessions, and imprisonment without trial were prerogatives of the crown, not of Parliament. Nor were the English at that time moving toward democracy, whether of the Greek city-state variety or of the type that now characterizes modern Britain. In his "warnings" against "rhetoric," Hobbes may have had Sir John Eliot (1592–1632) and John Pym (1584–1643) in mind, but surely no one else, not even James and Charles, could have believed that Eliot and Pym were, like Cleon, "violent sycophants" motivated by "envy" and self-aggrandizement.[17] England's Peloponnesian War— if the Civil War can possibly be called that—was in no man's dream or nightmare of the future, in 1629, and yet England's Thucydides—if

---

* In his "To the Readers" Hobbes noted that the translation "lay long by me" after he had finished it, presumably because "other reasons taking place, my desire to communicate it ceased." How long he withheld publication, he did not say, but apparently the "other reasons" included his becoming aware that "for the greatest part, men came to the reading of history with an affection much like that of the people in Rome: who came to the spectacle of the gladiators with more delight to behold their blood, than their skill in fencing. For they be far more in number, that love to read of great armies, bloody battles, and many thousands slain at once, than that mind the art by which the affairs of both armies and cities be conducted to their ends." *E.W.,* VIII, ix.

Hobbes can be called *that*—was writing as if the war had already begun.*

To do so, Hobbes had to view the conflicts between crown and Parliament as, in effect, unresolvable conflicts between the wisdom of monarchy and the "stupidity" of democracy. To this end, he also had to overlook, or dismiss as irrelevant, significant differences of character between Elizabeth and some of her predecessors, notably her father, Henry VIII, and her successors James and Charles, the first Stuarts. James, for instance, was widely believed, with good reason, to be a coward and, though married and a father, to have strong homosexual inclinations.† These did not preclude voyeuristic interests that led him, on one occasion, to demand from his daughter's husband a complete report on their first night together. He frequently could not, to use a modern expression, hold his liquor, and he was less successful holding his tongue in situations calling for, if not silence, temperate speech. He often had difficulty making up his mind and keeping it made up, with the consequence that he was regarded as indecisive and vacillating. He also was generous, extravagant, and wasteful on a scale that had not been seen in royalty for a century or more. Finally, he was Scots and therefore, from the English point of view, of an inferior race; for to be a Scot in early-seventeenth-century England (or even in some circles of England today) was somewhat comparable to being a southern "red-neck" in early-twentieth-century America.

With these differences between James and his predecessors, and not unrelated to them, had come parliamentary demands for changes in the relations between crown and Parliament. The early Stuart Parliaments insisted on the right to be consulted about taxes and expenditures. They disputed the contention that the king and clergy alone could legislate matters of ecclesiastical concern, and demanded toleration for the Puritans who were becoming influential in the Commons.[18] The extent to which court-appointed ministers were accountable to Parliament was a disputed issue, as were questions concerning the rights of members to speak freely without fear of arrest and imprisonment. Indeed, the whole range of civil liberties of mem-

---

* One would never gather from Hobbes that "from 1570 to 1639 England had its longest period of domestic peace since 1066 and, unlike the nearly comparable period 1330–80, was only engaged in foreign wars for just over a third of the time." Cooper, ed. *Decline of Spain*, 531.

† A contemporary account of James observing a military exercise noted that he "was much more interested in watching the boy cadets than in watching the soldiers." His alleged homosexuality was disapproved less on moral grounds than for its influence in his making appointments and dispensing patronage. Cooper, ed., *Decline of Spain*, 258.

bers and subjects alike was frequently a topic of debate.

Had James spent less lavishly on himself, his family, his servants, and his favorites, Parliament might have been less inclined to challenge his right to levy taxes. But unlike Elizabeth, whose ordinary expenditures (i.e., those unrelated to war) had remained well within her income of about £300,000 annually, James from the beginning spent amounts far greater than his income. From a starting point of £400,000 annually, James's expenditures by 1614 had risen to £522,000, of which £77,000, or almost twice what Elizabeth had spent, represented the court's day-to-day living expenses. By 1612 James was £500,000 in debt, and despite increasing difficulties with parliament over money, the debt increased. By 1624 it had reached a total of £1,000,000.

Nevertheless, James's fourth and last Parliament, which met in February 1624, was the least contentious of his reign. In return for voting three subsidies, the amount of which fell short of James's need, Parliament received the right to advise the king on matters of war and foreign policy, and to be consulted on royal marriages and other business formerly regarded as being within the court's exclusive jurisdiction. For once, both sides were conciliatory, and perhaps such harmony would have continued had Charles, whose first Parliament met in June 1625, been willing to make concessions. Charles, too, needed money, large amounts of it for the war with Spain, but he would not tolerate such innovations as parliament's renewing of customs duties for a year only (rather than, as was usual, for life), or accept the demand that Buckingham, his favorite minister, be cast aside. Instead, he dismissed Parliament after two months, and his second Parliament, which convened in February 1626, sat for less than five months. Rumors were heard that the king intended to rule without Parliament altogether, but if Charles wished to abolish Parliament at that time, he was unable to do so. Unable to raise sufficient funds for the war on his own, he had no alternative to summoning a third Parliament, which gathered in March 1628 (by which date Hobbes had completed his translation of Thucydides). In January 1629 it was dissolved for having manifested, in the king's words, "a disobedient and seditious carriage." There was not to be another Parliament for eleven years.[19]

Hobbes may have seen in the "disobedient and seditious carriage" and its consequences a perfect example of "how stupid democracy is," but one may doubt that Thucydides himself would have regarded the conflicts between crown and Parliament as analogous to the turmoil in Greece following the death of Pericles. Hobbes to the contrary notwithstanding, democracy, in the sense of government by a popularly chosen executive and legislature serving for a fixed term of office, was still more than two centuries away. Moreover, Thucydides would not, in all probability, have seen Eliot and Pym as Cleons reincarnate. Sir John Eliot, of an old Devonshire family, began his parliamentary career as a protégé of Buckingham, Charles's favorite, and a supporter of the war with Spain. Eventually convinced of Buckingham's incompetence and corruption, Eliot became a leader of the move to impeach Buckingham, and by 1626, offended by the king's treatment of Parliament, Eliot was playing a prominent role in the parliamentary opposition to the king. For his outspokenness in connection with Buckingham and his resistance to arbitrary taxation, Eliot was imprisoned three times and, on the occasion of his last confinement to the Tower of London, harshly treated. His death at the age of forty, not long after his final imprisonment, led to the suspicion that he had been murdered. Whatever the truth, the circumstances of his imprisonment and death further embittered the struggle between Charles and Parliament. A gifted orator (gifted in "rhetoric," Hobbes would have said), Eliot was not without faults, but he was motivated by high principles, not demagoguery, and did not deserve the fate that was accorded him.*

John Pym, of a family even more ancient than Eliot's (tracing its ancestry as far back as Henry III), was a lawyer who entered Parliament in 1614. An upholder of the Elizabethan principle that Catholic politics, not religion, was subversive,† Pym in his early parliamentary career was concerned with religious affairs. Like Eliot, he supported the war against Spain, and he, too, was prominent in the Buckingham impeachment. He also took part in the 1628 impeachment of Bishop Roger Manwaring (to which we will return later in connection with Hobbes's departure for France in 1640), and insisted that Parliament should be consulted on matters of religion. During the eleven years, 1629–40, when Parliament did not meet, Pym was

---

*Eliot's death in prison, the "tragic sacrifice of a man so gifted and patriotic, and actuated originally by no antagonistic feeling against the monarchy or the church, is the surest condemnation of the king's policy and administration." *Encyclopaedia Britannica*, 13th ed. IX, 277.

†A principle with which Hobbes did not disagree, whatever his other differences with Pym and his fellow parliamentarians. As G. R. Elton has commented, the excommunication of Elizabeth by Pope Pius V in 1570 was "an unmistakable declaration of war . . . (posing) the fatal dilemma from which neither the Catholics nor the government could thereafter escape. Obedience to Rome now meant acceptance of the excommunication and deposition of Elizabeth, and therefore at least treason *in posse*. It may well be true that the national loyalties of English Catholics were not affected by the bull; at least, except for a few hotheads who got involved in plots, they remained peaceful, and after the outbreak of war with Spain the majority demonstrated that they had chosen England before religion. But the government could not be expected to take this for granted." Elton, ed., *Tudor Constitution*, 411.

relatively inactive, perhaps from a feeling of hopelessness. Had he died at that time, or emigrated to America, in which he had some financial interest, he would probably have remained an obscure and unimportant figure in British history. But in the three years of life that remained to him after the first meeting of the Short Parliament in April 1640, Pym came into prominence as the acknowledged leader of the House of Commons in its struggle with the king, a struggle that culminated in the outbreak of the Civil War in May 1642. During the ensuing months, Pym initiated several efforts to arrange a peaceful settlement, but his efforts were in vain, and on December 8, 1643, not long before his sixtieth birthday, he died. A more eloquent and persuasive orator than Eliot, Pym ranks as one of the two or three greatest leaders of the House of Commons and is remembered, for all his opposition to the crown, as an enlightened conservative who anticipated Edmund Burke in declaring "time must needs bring about some alterations . . . those commonwealths have been most durable and perpetual which have often reformed and recompensed themselves according to their first institution and ordinance."[20]

Hobbes's translation of Thucydides, in short, despite the claims he put forward, had little relevance to the England for which he intended it to serve as a "warning." But the work does tell us a good deal about Hobbes himself. The *History* reveals, to begin with, that Hobbes, long before the Civil War and even before 1629, was intolerant of challenges to established order, however moderate and reasonable such challenges were. Driven, therefore, "to take the side of settled and visable authority,"[21] Hobbes could only be contemptuous of the political aspirations of the merchants, tradesmen, and other entrepreneurs who were beginning, in the Parliaments of James and Charles, to demand a share of power in the governing of Britain. Hobbes at forty, the Hobbes of *Thucydides*, was already the Hobbes of the later *De Cive* and *Leviathan*: pessimistic, skeptical, ironic, and sarcastic, laying stress on the dark side of human nature, ambivalent about religion, wary and self-protective, arrogant but deferential toward superiors, and evidencing no great affection for his fellow man. Indeed, one does not exaggerate too much in suggesting that *Thucydides* presents in outline form the thesis that Hobbes, in his later writings, was to propound in detail.

But between the *History* and the earliest of these writings, Hobbes was briefly to change his employment, spend several years in Europe, and make new and important friends. This expansive phase of his life began with the death of the second earl on June 20, 1628, when Hobbes was forty. The passing of his former pupil and patron inaugurated a period of about two years during which Hobbes's relations with the

Devonshires, for the first but not the last time, were severely strained. The earl's will apparently settled on Hobbes a yearly pension of eighty pounds, which, had it been paid, would have enabled Hobbes to devote himself entirely to his studies. But the earl's debts were greater than had been anticipated, leading most students of Hobbes to conclude that because of these debts Hobbes was denied not only his pension but also his continuing employment as tutor to the third earl, then between ten and eleven years of age. Hobbes, understandably, felt "neglected," as he put it in his *Autobiography*. According to this account, he "tarried" the following eighteen months in Paris, whence he was recalled to the service of the Devonshires. The clear implication is that the financial condition of the Devonshires had improved sufficiently by late 1630 to make possible his reemployment. He did not mention that another tutor had served in his absence and that in Paris he had been accompanied by the young son and heir of another distinguished family to which he had been appointed tutor.

Assuming that Hobbes's replacement in the Devonshire household was paid, his departure from the family's service toward the end of 1628 may have been due to factors other than financial stringencies. Perhaps Christian, the earl's widow, was unhappy with Hobbes's role in her late husband's life; she may have held Hobbes, the earl's tutor, companion, and confidant, at least partly responsible for his dissolute life and resulting burden of debt. She may also have been unwilling to pay Hobbes a pension in addition to his tutor's salary, some part of which probably was in arrears by 1628, and the repayment, with interest, of money Hobbes had lent to the second earl. The Devonshire household accounts of the time, admittedly incomplete, do not indicate that Hobbes received any pension until late in his life, but there is evidence that interest on the loan, if not on the principal itself, was paid in 1637 and 1638. Christian, in short, may have been able to afford a tutor immediately after her husband's death, but not the payment of all the money owed or due Hobbes.

The second earl's indebtedness to Hobbes, however, could not have been very significant in comparison with his other debts, the total of which, when he died, was more than 22,000 pounds. Shortly before his death, and despite having inherited 15,000 pounds from his father, the first earl, in 1625, the second earl, in order to pay his debts and provide for his second son and daughter, had successfully petitioned Parliament for permission to sell portions of his entailed estate, principally land in four English counties. The proceeds of the sale, in accordance with the act of Parliament, were to be used to settle the earl's indebtedness, to increase Christian's annual income to 4,000 pounds, and to create inheritances for the two children who would not succeed to the title. No doubt anticipating what was to come, the earl in his will provided that if the properties sold were not sufficient to pay his debts, the additional amount needed should be taken from the income of his heir, the third earl, during the latter's minority. This provision was to create difficulties between Christian and her eldest son, in the settlement of which, as will be seen, Hobbes was to play a major and wholly uncharacteristic role.

As late as November 1628, or more than five months after the earl's death, Hobbes was still residing in the London mansion of the Devonshires, though no longer employed by them, and he may have remained there during the early months of 1629. Sometime in 1629 he became the tutor of Gervaise Clifton, then about seventeen years of age, the oldest son and heir of Sir Gervaise Clifton of Nottinghamshire, known popularly as Gervaise the Great or Gervaise the Golden. The Cliftons, the first of whom came to England with William the Conqueror, were a distinguished and colorful family long resident in Nottinghamshire, and Sir Gervaise (1587–1666), who was only one year older than his son's tutor, probably met Hobbes through his acquaintance with the first earl of Devonshire.*

Sir Gervaise, who was a member of nine Parliaments in the course of his long life, also was known as Seven Times Clifton by reason of his seven marriages. Father of nine children, Sir Gervaise outlived all but the last of his seven wives, and his seventh wife died within months of his own death in 1666. By that time, he had severed all connections with his oldest son, Hobbes's pupil in 1630 and the only child of his first wife, who, in accordance with family tradition, bore his father's name.

Of this period in Hobbes's life, we know, once again, too little. Hobbes's few surviving letters from 1629–30 and the two surviving letters Gervaise sent his father in 1630 establish that he and Gervaise were abroad a good part of 1630, mainly in France. Most of March was spent in Paris, from which, in early April, they traveled to Lyon by coach. On April 22 and 23 they rode horseback from Lyon to Geneva, where they remained more than two months. By July 10 they were in Orleans, and they apparently stayed there a month or more. A letter from Hobbes to Sir Gervaise, dated November 2 and sent from Hardwick, suggests that by that date Hobbes was back in the employ of the Devonshires.

Hobbes's travel correspondence (if we may give that term to his

---

*Hobbes's Clifton connection so far has undeservedly received little attention from Hobbes scholars. Perhaps for that reason, Clifton is mistakenly rendered as "Clinton" by Laird, *Hobbes*, 7; Peters, *Hobbes*, 20; and Mintz, *Hunting*, 6.

few letters) was rarely longer or more informative than his correspondence on other subjects. In writing to Sir Gervaise, he was, in
general, polite, dutiful, and reassuring as to the health and progress
in study of young Gervaise. In a March 1630 letter from Paris, Hobbes
declared their intention of proceeding to Venice "3 weekes hence, or
sooner," but he added, prophetically, "by what way I knowe not,
because the ordinary high way through the territory of Milan is
encumbered with the warre betweene the French and the Spaniards."[22] In the end, because of the War of the Succession of Mantua,
1629–30, Hobbes and Gervaise were to return to England without
having visited Italy.

In a second letter to Sir Gervaise, dated April 29, 1630, Hobbes
reported that he and young Gervaise had safely arrived in Geneva,
where they were lodged "in the house of one Mr. Provost a minister
of the most estimation of any man in the cittie, a very wise and honest
man and not of the Geneva print, more than is necessary for an inhab-
itant and minister of the place."[23] Then as now, more than 350 years
later, Geneva was "free frō noyse, company, and ill example, free frō
contagion, and warre, and fitte for study and retirednesse, having also
good ayre and walkes w[hich] in other great townes are wantinge."
Intending to remain there until September, Hobbes expressed the hope
of wintering in Italy if there were no "warres"; otherwise they would
spend the winter in France, returning home by the "low countries."
Young Gervaise, he reported to the boy's father, was studying both
spoken and written Italian, and in general spending "his time profit-
ably and to your Content."

Much as Hobbes wished to visit Italy, his characteristic prudence
manifested itself in his refusal to join two Englishmen traveling to
that country. They will proceed, he wrote, "downe the Rhosne a good
way, and then by Land through Provence to Tolon, a journey of seven
or eight days in w[hich] they can ly in no towne that hath not the
plague, and most of the townes in Provence have it in vigor. frō Tolon
they make the rest of their way by water, w[hich] will be 4 dayes at
least, and comminge so into Italy are sure to be receaved into no
towne there till they have bene 40 dayes ayred in the fieldes, on these
termes we might have gone w[ith] them but I refused." Hobbes could
not help adding that the Englishmen, a Mr. Smithy and a Captain
Say or Sale, were foolish to risk the plague "on no greater an errand
than ye curiosity of travellers."[24]

Hobbes's next letter to Sir Gervaise, written two weeks later,
announced the abandonment of his wish to escort Gervaise on a tour
through Italy because "of the warres, and going up and down of troupes
in all partes." Nevertheless, he wrote, Gervaise is learning Italian "so

fast that I doubt not but he will be able to speake the languadge though we be denyed to see the contry"; indeed, Gervaise "studies as much if not more than I desire" and is exercising regularly as well. Hobbes thought it necessary to make plans for the winter, and he sought Sir Gervaise's advice. There were three possibilities: Orleans "or some other towne on the River of Loyre"; the Low Countries, but then they would need passports from "the Archduchesse, or Spaniards"; or Geneva, which, Hobbes wrote, "I like least of the 3 but leave all to your direction and Commandement." Reporting the outbreak of war between France and Savoy, Hobbes observed "this newes is enough to let you see we are not likely to have good passage through Savory. . . ."[25]

In a letter to his father that was probably written at about the same time, Gervaise, who apparently did not believe in punctuation, confirmed Hobbes's report of the disruption of their plans because of war. "Upon the instant of dispatching a packette to you," he began, "wee had the good fortune to receave one from you wherein yr pleasure of delaying our farther proceeding comes as opportune and as answerable to the state of things as if you had bin heere and seene the dangers and inconveniences threatened Monsieur de Bassompiere lyes all most within sight of Geneva, with a great Armie of Swissers hee has hovered hereabout a great whiles and dealt with the Signiorie to declare themselves for the Frenche Theye keepe neuters [neutral] and excuse themselves for the scarcity of people which will spare noe troopes twoards an offensive warre of their owne much lesse to bee Auxiliaryes in a case which belongs not to them I praye God this forreine warre maye decrease and the begginings of our Domesticke feare in England not goe on, I am every daye busie 2 or three houres about the Italian and beggin to have poche parole which poche I hope to turn to Molte ere I goe hence and it makes mee the more earnest lest the Impossibility of passage should continue till the time that you should please to call mee backe and soe the country being denyed to see the getting of the language maye satisfye in some kinde the disappointing of your purpose. Thus praying daylie for your health I begge on my knees your blessing. . . ."[26]

Neither Hobbes nor Gervaise may have received any reply to their

---

*A friend of Sir Gervaise, Walter Waringe, who was traveling with Hobbes and Gervaise, wrote the boy's father on May 9 from Geneva, "[A]ll those passage (to Italy) are now blockt upp with famine the sword and pestilence, the last of these desperately threatens Geneva and admonishes us retreat: for should wee not depart in due time, flight (the only refuge in such feare) would be debard us. upon these considerations your sonne (so advised by Mr. Hobbes) resolves to depart the towne this next morninge. . . ." University of Nottingham, Manuscript Department Catalogue No. C 561.

letters until July 8, when a letter sent from England on May 30 by a
Robert Leeke, who was handling Sir Gervaise's business affairs,
reached Hobbes in Orleans. Answering Leake two days later, Hobbes
after a discussion of financial matters informed him of his plan to
winter in Paris, "the best place to stay . . . for us that have allready
vewed so much of the contry." The war, meanwhile, was generating
little news inasmuch as "they do no wonders on neyther side (although)
the French use to do much at first." Concluding his letter, which was
brief, Hobbes looked forward to their "merry meeting in England,"
which he hoped would be "next spring [1631] at farthest."[27]

But Hobbes and young Gervaise were not to spend the winter in
Paris. By November 2, 1630, Hobbes was back at Hardwick, where he
again was in the employ of the Devonshires. Presumably, a letter of
recommendation to Christian had preceded him because Hobbes wrote
Sir Gervaise, "That I am welcome home, I must attribute to yo[ur]
favorable Letter, by w[hich] my Lady understandes yo[ur] good
acceptance of my service to Mr. Clifton. This favo[r] of yours I esteeme
no small part of your Liberality. . . ."[28] For Hobbes, Hardwick was
clearly "home," and perhaps something like homesickness accounted
for his return to the Devonshire household as soon as the opportunity
to do so presented itself. He continued on good terms with the Cliftons, writing Sir Gervaise on November 23, 1632, that while he preferred to "Kisse your hands" to sending a letter, the letter would have
to suffice because his schedule did not allow for more than one night's
visit to Clifton, which, for a variety of reasons, was not practical.
Hobbes also mentioned that he was "sorry to heare from Mr. Clifton
[Gervaise] that you entend to stay in the contry," suggesting that he
had recently seen Gervaise or was corresponding with him.*[29]

By 1636 Gervaise had obtained, through the influence of his father,
a position at court, but by that time, or very soon afterward, Sir Gervaise was about to sever relations with him. In a letter to "J.B." (possibly Sir John Beaumont, a friend and occasional correspondent) of
March 12, 1637, Sir Gervaise wrote, "I would have you goe to my son
and lett him know from me that till he carry himself more piously to
God, more worthyly and soberly to his wife, more without scandall
and intemperancy in his generall courses, and leave of to wast and
consume his estate as he doth, which I shall pray God to lett me see,

---

*Hobbes continued to correspond with Sir Gervaise when he was in Paris in 1635. The
surviving letters appear to have had no other purpose than to assure Sir Gervaise of
Hobbes's affection, gratitude, and sense of obligation; a representative example, at the
beginning of a letter dated January 30, 1635, ran, "No newes, nor service I can do you,
but the ambition to remayne in your memory hath produced this letter, which is an
acknowledgement of your favour. . . ." Ibid., No. C 564.

the world takes such notice of thes particulars as I have no great joy to see him at my howse, and I may not be an Eli to connive at or sooth his obliquityes least I share in the guilt and punishment, which will too soone fall, if not repented and amended."[30] Two year later, Sir Gervaise excused himself for not attending the earl of Newcastle in the Scottish wars as his wife "lyes att this present gaspinge and my sonne gaping not for what I leave dyinge but what I have livinge my backe beinge turned to make a prey of all my convertible goodes within dores and without."[31]

Sir Gervaise's references to his son's failure to behave "soberly" to his wife and abandon "intemperancy" and "wast" of his estate could be taken to mean that Gervaise, like Hobbes's earlier pupil, the second earl of Devonshire, was a "waster." Several of Gervaise's letters to his father, not dated, established that he was a defendant in one or more suits brought before the Star Chamber and the Assizes; in one of these letters Gervaise informed his father that he had been ordered to answer "in the Starrechamber, within ten days, allsoe I heare there is another order Peremptorie for my remoove to London," and he asked his father for "Counsell . . . as allsoe your mercie which has beggun this Assizes."[32] Gervaise's troubles almost certainly included unpaid debts, but whatever its cause, the breach between father and son was never healed. When Sir Gervaise died in 1666, his estates passed to his second son, Sir Clifford Clifton, rather than to Gervaise, who was still living. Sir Gervaise could not prevent his oldest son from inheriting the baronetcy, but Gervaise, apparently, was left nothing else, and when he died in 1676, the title reverted to William, Sir Clifford's son.*

Sir Gervaise's rejection of his son, accompanied as it was by anger and distrust, was reason enough for Hobbes not to mention his tutelage of young Gervaise in his *Autobiography* or in any other writing. Sir Gervaise was not only his friend and occasional patron but a friend of the Devonshires as well and of others in the circle of the earl of Newcastle, a circle that included, as well be seen shortly, Hobbes himself. Given the social usages and customs of the time, Gervaise,

---

* The Clifton genealogy, as recorded in Thoroton's *Nottinghamshire* and in G. E. Cokayne, ed., *Complete Baronetage*, vol. 1, *1611–1625*, lists Penelope, Sir Gervaise's first wife, as "the Mother of the wretched unfortunate Sir Gervaise his Father's greatest Foil" (108). Since Penelope died in October 1613, when she was twenty-three years old, Gervaise, her only child, must have been at least sixteen when Hobbes became his tutor in 1629. According to the *Complete Baronetage*, p. 19, Sir Gervaise and Penelope were married "in or shortly before 1613," raising the possibility that Penelope died in or not long after childbirth. Sir Clifford, the second son and heir, was the fourth of five children born to Sir Gervaise's second wife, Frances, who died in November 1627, aged thirty-three. Sir Clifford, probably, was not born before 1620.

we can imagine, must by 1638 or 1639 have found most doors closed to him, including, no doubt, those that led to Hobbes's own chambers. Hobbes was never one to favor the underdog, least of all the disinherited son of an aristocratic family.

Less understandable is the Cliftons' silence about Hobbes. The family archives record the correspondence before the Civil War between Sir Gervaise and Hobbes, but there is no reference to Hobbes's serving as tutor to any Clifton.[33] Did the Cliftons eventually hold Hobbes in some way responsible for the profligate and dissolute behavior of Gervaise? Were they reluctant, in later years, to acknowledge an earlier connection with anyone reputed to be, as was Hobbes after publication of *Leviathan*, an atheist and antiroyalist? Perhaps both Hobbes and the Cliftons wished to forget their associations with the "wretched unfortunate" Gervaise; perhaps they also hoped Gervaise himself would be forgotten. Coincidentally or otherwise, no account of Hobbes's European tour of 1630 with Gervaise mentions that the young man became in subsequent years his father's "greatest Foil."

Indeed, until now the only effort to connect Gervaise with Hobbes was that made in 1904 by Sir Leslie Stephen in his study of Hobbes. A letter of April 4, 1628, from the provost of Eton to Sir Thomas Wentworth (the future, ill-fated earl of Strafford), a friend of Sir Gervaise, advised Wentworth, according to Stephen, to "tell him [Sir Gervaise] that when he sent his son hither [to Eton] he honoured, and when he took him away he wounded us. For in this Royal Seminary we are in one thing and only one like the Jesuits, that we all joy when we get a spirit upon whom much may be worked." Stephen added, "We may hope, therefore, that Hobbes had a satisfactory pupil." The Provost, of course, was referring to Clifford, who, about nine years old at the time, was the right age for Eton, whereas Gervaise, then fifteen or sixteen, would have been too old. Stephen must have thought it obvious that the boy who had been withdrawn from Eton was the same one who had become Hobbes's pupil, thereby failing to notice that in April 1628 the second earl was still living, and Hobbes was still in his service. Sir Gervaise's reasons for terminating Clifford's study at Eton are unknown.[34]

Whatever the explanation of the failure to identify the young man whom Hobbes accompanied to France and Switzerland in 1629–30, Hobbes, if not Sir Gervaise, was clearly far from unhappy when he and his pupil once again were back in England. While we cannot be certain about the time and place, the most significant event of that experience probably occurred in Geneva, and Hobbes may well have recognized that it was an event that was to affect the whole course and direction of his future thought. Indeed, the years that follow it mark the beginning of the most creative and productive period of his life. At an age when the lives of most seventeenth-century Englishmen were coming to an end, or were already over, Hobbes's life, which was to continue for almost fifty years, was, in a sense, just beginning.

In Motion and on Motion

THE DECISIVE EVENT of Hobbes's second visit to the Continent, in 1629–30, and one that was profoundly to influence his thought in the years that followed, may have occurred in Geneva. Unable to travel into Italy because of the dangers involved, Hobbes and Gervaise Clifton were forced to remain in Geneva for at least a month, lodging with a certain Minister Prévost.* Prévost's library may therefore have been the "gentleman's library" where, according to Aubrey, Hobbes first "looked on geometry; which happened accidentally." If Aubrey was slightly mistaken in stating that Hobbes was then "40 yeares old"—Aubrey could not recall exactly when or where Hobbes discovered geometry, and he may have been guessing Hobbes's age—Hobbes, who was forty-one or forty-two at the time, may have been in Geneva and not in London when he glanced at an opened copy of Euclid's *Elements*. Reading proposition 47, Hobbes, Aubrey reported, exclaimed, "By G—
—, this is impossible!" (Aubrey originally deleted Hobbes's expression, writing instead, "He would now and then use an emphaticall oath.") "So he reads the demonstration of it, which referred him back to such a proposition; which proposition he read. That referred him back to another, which he also read. Et sic deinceps, that at last he was demonstratively convinced of that trueth. This made him in love with geometry."

Perhaps Hobbes's reputation in his own time would have suffered less had he not read Euclid when he was almost forty. Ever loyal to his old friend, Aubrey quoted the laments of Sir Jonas Moore and others that Hobbes had not studied mathematics earlier; had he done so, the lamentors and Aubrey agreed, he "would have made great advancement in it . . . [and] would not have layn so open to his learned

---

* Prévost may have been Pierre Prévost, "born at Issoudon 1549, died at Geneva 1639." De Beer, "Some Letters," 200.

mathematicall antagonists." Aubrey was referring to John Wallis and his Oxford colleagues, who had no difficulty demonstrating the fallacies in Hobbes's efforts to "prove" a number of unprovable propositions in geometry, thereby making Hobbes appear ridiculous.* Had Hobbes confined himself to mathematics from age forty onward, he would be remembered today, if remembered at all, only for his translation of Thucydides, which, as was noted earlier, is not unanimously regarded as distinguished. Moreover, there is no consensus that Hobbes's intellectual temperament and habits of mind would have lent themselves, at any age, to the study of mathematics. His impatience with detail work and his preference for generalizations, his marked indifference to scientific methodology and experimentation, his confusion of inference and evidence, and his tendency to treat hypotheses as facts suggest that Hobbes was fortunate to fall "in love with geometry" when he was almost twice the age at which many of the great mathematicians of history have made their most important discoveries.

We cannot be certain that Hobbes was approaching middle age when he first encountered Euclid. As was mentioned earlier, Euclid was not wholly unknown at Oxford in the early seventeenth century, whether or not he was known to Hobbes. Hobbes's course of studies may have precluded any exposure to Euclid, or, alternatively, Hobbes as a student may not have been interested in either mathematics or geometry. During the years that followed, however, Hobbes may have had every opportunity to discover Euclid. In the four-volume *Catalogue of the Library at Chatsworth*, published in 1889, books by Euclid, the earliest of which was published in 1482, occupy more than three pages. Assuming that not all of these books were added to the Hardwick-Chatsworth collection after Hobbes's encounter with proposition 47, Hobbes, who functioned for the Devonshires as a part-time librarian, may have been familiar with at least some of Euclid's books, although this is not to say that he necessarily read them.

A possible explanation of Hobbes's "By G——, this is impossible!" in 1629 or 1630 is that Hobbes, if indeed he looked into Euclid while at Oxford or Hardwick, earlier was not much interested in geometry. But by 1630 Hobbes, who had already published his first book related to politics, was becoming convinced that political principles based on "dogmatical" learning or even repeated experience would never be accepted by most men as self-evident or demonstrable truths. History itself, he had observed in *Thucydides*, can at most teach men "to bear themselves prudently in the present and provi-

---

* See below, pp. 195–204.

dently towards the future," but though experience teaches prudence (which is why old men tend to be more prudent than young), it cannot establish the truth. From experience, Hobbes stressed in 1640, "we cannot . . . conclude, that any thing is to be called *just* or *unjust*, *true* or *false*, or any proposition universal whatsoever. . . ."[1]

Suppose, however, politics could base itself not wholly on experience, but on laws, rules, and principles analogous to, and as provable as, those of mathematics. "Mathematical" learning, as opposed to "dogmatical" learning, "is free from controversy and dispute, because it consisteth in comparing figure and motion only; in which things, *truth*, and *the interest of men*, oppose not each other: but in the other way ["dogmatical" learning, of which the study of politics was one variety] there is nothing indisputable, because it compareth men, and meddleth with their right and profit; in which, as oft as reason is against a man, so oft will a man be against reason."[2] Hobbes's confidence in "mathematical" learning as a source of truth "free from controversy and dispute" no doubt owed something to the achievements of Galileo and Descartes, both of them mathematicians whose writings were challenging and transforming traditional views about the nature of man and the universe; indeed, mathematics, especially geometry, and science in general were very much discussed and argued about in the social and intellectual circles of which Hobbes was a member during the 1630s. A wish to establish himself in these circles and to be "numbered," as Hobbes put it in his *Autobiography*, "among the philosophers," unquestionably played a role. But we may hypothesize that one root of Hobbes's interest in mathematics was a need, traceable to the insecurities and uncertainties of his childhood, to establish a scientific politics of authority and stability. Hobbes's personal quest for older and security, and the political as well as intellectual culture of the time, were fused, as it were, in his determination to make a science of his own political principles, to prove, in the later words of his friend Mersenne (of whom more later), that *De Cive* and other works "demonstrated no less than the *Elements* of Euclid!"*

---

*Letter of Marin Mersenne to Samuel Sorbière, April 25, 1646, in *De Cive*. We cannot know whether the comparison of *De Cive* with Euclid's *Elements* originated with Mersenne or with Hobbes. Sorbière, a French physician and intellectual gadfly, was attending to the publication in Holland of *De Cive*. Mersenne, a Minim friar whose interests were as broad as his theology was narrow, met Hobbes in 1634 on the occasion of the latter's third visit to France. A staunch friend and admirer of Hobbes, he nevertheless was not happy about Sorbière's unauthorized publication of his letter commending *De Cive* as "that golden book" of "the incomparable Mr. Hobbes." Presumably, he did not, as a cleric, wish to be understood as endorsing all of Hobbes's views, especially not his relgious opinions. Pierre Gassendi, Hobbes's older and closer clerical friend in France, also contributed a preface extolling *De Cive* but excepting "those matters pertaining to Religion, with regard to which we have different opinions." For more on Mersenne and Gassendi and their relationship to Hobbes, see below pp. 141–44.

Given such demonstrations, Hobbes must have hoped, political truths could perhaps be safeguarded from the destructive rantings of demagogues and fanatics, and ultimately triumph.

His first efforts toward the establishment of politics as a science may have coincided with his "discovery" of Euclid, as reported by Aubrey. In 1630 or soon thereafter, Hobbes became fascinated by the idea that laws or principles of motion, in the body and in the universe alike, lay at the heart of all physical and mental activity. According to Hobbes's own account (in his Latin prose autobiography, *Thomae Hobbesii Malmesburiensis Vita*), his preoccupation with motion and its consequences had its origins in a discussion of "learned men," at which he was present, that focused on the meaning of sensation. To his amazement, none of those present could give a precise meaning to the phenomenon of sensation, much less account for its existence. Determined to resolve these difficulties, Hobbes began to ponder the nature and causes of sensation, eventually arriving at the conclusion that all senses and sensations, such as those involved in the seeing of light or color, the hearing of sounds, and the feeling of heat or cold, derived not from properties inherent in the objects seen, heard, or felt but from motions carried to the brain, which itself was not at rest. As he put it in his *Human Nature* of 1650, portions of which were written in 1640, "As colour is not inherent in the object, but an effect thereof upon us . . . so neither is *sound* in the thing we hear, but in ourselves. . . . Nothing can make any thing which is not in itself: the *clapper* hath no *sound* in it, but *motion*, and maketh motion in the internal parts of the bell; so the *bell* hath motion, and not sound, that imparteth *motion* to the *air;* and the *air* has motion, but not sound; the *air* imparteth motion by the *ear* and *nerve* unto the brain; and the brain hath motion but not sound; from the *brain*, it reboundeth back into the nerves *outward*, and thence it becometh an *apparition without*, which we call sound. . . . So likewise the *heat* we feel from the fire is manifestly in *us*, and is quite *different* from the heat which is in the *fire:* for *our heat* is *pleasure* or *pain*, according as it is *great* or *moderate;* but in the *coal* there is no such thing."[3]

By 1634, when he was in Paris for the third time, Hobbes was persuaded that behavior of all sorts, including thinking, desiring, imagining, and fearing, was caused by types or varieties of motion. Then and later, Hobbes was eager to claim originality for his views; as we saw earlier, Hobbes characteristically was not one to give credit where credit was due, and he was particularly loath to share with anyone his ownership of the theory of motion. The evidence for sole proprietorship, however, is not conclusive. In favor of Hobbes's claim is his authorship of a brief treatise entitled *A Short Tract on First Principles*, first published by Tönnies in 1889. While no one can be

certain when Hobbes wrote the *Short Tract*, scholars are generally
agreed that the probable year of composition was between 1630 and
1638, Tönnies himself believing 1630 to be the correct date. Tönnies
apparently based this belief on the following passage in a 1646 letter
from Hobbes to the earl of Newcastle: "about (16 years since I affirmed
to your Lordship) at Welback, that light is a fancy in the minde, caused
by motion in the braine, which motion again is caused by the motion
of the parts of such bodies as we call lucid" (*E.W.*, VII, 468).*

Whatever its date of compostion, the *Short Tract* does not contain
assertions identical with those "affirmed" by Hobbes at Welbeck, much
less with those set forth at length in *Human Nature*. Nor does it, sub-
stantively viewed, compare in interest with the translation of Thucydides. Whether Hobbes's intention was, as some scholars believe,
to undermine "the scholastic doctrine of 'intelligible species' which
was part of their theory of sense perception,"[4] or to organize his own
views, in somewhat Euclidian fashion, about the extent to which certain aspects of Aristotelian belief could be reconciled with some of
the newer ideas associated with Galileo and others, the *Short Tract*
cannot be regarded as anything more than a transitional work or, in
Laird's classification, as one of Hobbes's "Minor Philosophical Pieces."[5]
The *Short Tract* also reminds us, as we shall be reminded again when,
later, Hobbes turns his attention to mathematics and related sciences, that Hobbes's "passionate concern and most inspired writing"
was about politics, not just when he was a young man, as Tönnies
mistakenly maintained, but always.[6]

Still, the *Short Tract* is not without interest as a partial reflection
of Hobbes's philosophical principles in or not long after 1630. The
three sections of the work feature a large number of definitions presented in propositional form, all of which ultimately interact with
each other in a schema that Hobbes may well have regarded as a
preliminary geometry of motion. The *Short Tract* opens with the
statement "That, whereto nothing is added, and from which nothing
is taken, remains in the same state it was."[7] To the twentieth-century
reader, Hobbes's assertion seems wholly innocuous, but upon it Hobbes
constructed the entire edifice of his theory of motion. For, having
observed that nothing changes unless something is added or taken
away, Hobbes could then proceed to identify the instrumentalities by

---

* Ferdinand Tönnies, ed., *Thomas Hobbes: The Elements of Law, Natural & Politic* (Cambridge: Cambridge University Press, 1928), xii–xiv. The *Short Tract* appears as "Appendix I," 152–67. Hobbes, as was stated earlier, was abroad much of 1630, but the
conversation at Welbeck, Newcastle's estate in Sherwood Forest, could still have taken
place. On the other hand, Hobbes's letter is the only corroboration of Tönnies's belief
that Hobbes was thinking and writing about motion as early as 1630.

which changes, or, in his word, "moves," can be effected.

Among these instrumentalities are "Agents," defined as "that which hath power to move," and "Patients," defined as "that which hath power to be moved." From this it follows, "An Agent produceth nothing in the Patient, but Motion, or some inherent forme." But Hobbes cannot proceed to discuss motion without identifying two additional terms, "Substance" and "Accident," the former defined as "that which hath being not in another, so as it may be of it self, as Aire, or Gold," and the latter as "that which hath being in another, so as, without that other it could not be, as Colour cannot be, but in somewhat coloured."* These principles, in turn, lead Hobbes to his first conclusion: "Every thing is eyther Substance or Accident. For, Every thing that hath a being in Nature, hath it eyther in another, or not in another. . . . No Accident can be without a Substance." Nor can any "Agent" or "Patient," Hobbes continues, be other than "Substance," as was previously asserted, since each, whether it moves the other or is moved by the other, "hath being not in another" but in itself. Nevertheless, though both qualify as "Substance," every "Agent," defined as that which has power to move, "working produceth Motion in the Patient."

In the third and final section of the *Short Tract*, Hobbes concludes that sense and sensation, understanding, appetite, images in the brain (which he calls "Phantasmas"), and other phenomena originate in "Motions of the Animal Spirits," the latter term presumably referring to the physical and mental apparatuses of sense perception and cognition. Hobbes was to see human behavior as somewhat more complex in his later political writings, especially in *Leviathan*, but he was never to depart from the view that "the Act of Appetite is a Motion of the Animal Spirits towards the object that moveth them. The object is the Efficient cause, or Agent, of desire . . . and the Animal Spirits the Patient. . . . Appetite therefore is the Effect of the Agent. . . ."

Even if we assume that the *Short Tract* was written in 1630, Hobbes was not the first to stress the causal significance of motion, although he may have been the earliest to relate sensation and sense perception to motion. By 1630, laws, theories, and concepts of motion were very much in the air. Most thinking men—or, to employ a modern word, intellectuals—probably believed, with Copernicus, that the universe was in motion, and they were probably familiar with Galileo's discovery of the laws governing the velocity and direction of moving bodies. Blood was in motion, according to William Harvey's

---

*By "somewhat" Hobbes means an object or a thing colored, in terms of which, and only in terms of which, we are able to see color.

great work on the circulation of the blood, published in 1628; Hobbes, as was mentioned earlier, was a friend of Harvey. Geoffrey Keynes, Harvey's biographer, has noted that the views expressed in Hobbes's *De Corpore* of 1655, which include his theory of the senses, "are very much in accord with Harvey's as they appear in his notes for the treatise, *De motu locali animalium*, begun in 1627. . . . A passage in one of Hobbes's latest tracts, 'Of the Causes and Effects of Heat and Cold' (*Decameron Physiologicum*, 1678), discussing the source of the heat of man and animals, strongly suggests that he had perhaps been present at some of Harvey's dissections of the King's deer."[8] Keynes has also suggested that Harvey may have served as Hobbes's medical adviser.

Indeed, Hobbes paid tribute to the extraordinary achievements of Kepler (who was joined in greatness by Mersenne and Gassendi) in his *De Corpore* of 1655, not omitting himself and *De Cive* from such distinguished company. Hobbes did not mention in this context another friend, Sir Kenelm Digby (1603–1665), though on several occasions he linked "his name and those of Descartes and Gassendi."[9] Digby, a Roman Catholic who was by turns an author, diplomat, privateer, would-be scientist, and, according to John Evelyn, "errant mountebank," corresponded with Hobbes in 1636–37 but may have known him much earlier. Married in 1625 to Venetia Hanley, said to have been one of the most beautiful women of her time (who died in 1633 as a result, according to rumor, of having been poisoned by a concoction, brewed by her husband, that was designed to preserve her beauty), Digby was a huge, handsome man of great presence to whom men and women of all descriptions, the latter including an elderly Marie de Medici, queen mother of France in 1623, and Queen Henrietta Maria, were immediately attracted. Like Hobbes, Digby was something of a materialist, and he also maintained, as did Hobbes, that any governing authority should receive support from clergy and laity alike, but he was no scientist, believing, for example, that a mixture of vitriol and rainwater he had devised, the so-called "power of sympathy," would cure wounds.[10] This belief, and others of equal dubiousness, however, did not prevent him, as equivalent beliefs prevented Hobbes, from becoming a member of the Royal Society.

But neither in *De Corpore* nor in any other of his writings did Hobbes indicate what influences these thinkers had exerted on his own intellectual development, and as some scholars have demonstrated, the two philosophers with whom he had most in common, Bacon and Descartes, were not mentioned. While Bacon's omission may have been "purely technical," as has been argued by certain students of Hobbes, in the sense that Bacon was concerned with "natural history" rather than with "natural philosophy," Hobbes's interest, one may also suggest that Hobbes did not refer to Bacon or Descartes, because he did not want attention drawn to similarities between their views and his own. Hobbes's envy and suspicion of Descartes, which will be discussed in Chapter 6, are well known, and Bacon's influence on Hobbes has already been dealt with. Throughout his life Hobbes tended to establish, or try to establish, the maximum possible distance between himself and those among the eminent thinkers of his time whom he most resembled and to whom, philosophically, he was closest. Conversely, he was apt to give credit and even fulsome praise to those whose achievements were in fields far removed from his own, such as astronomy and medicine, or to the Mersennes and Gassendis among his acquaintances, lesser personages Hobbes himself must have known to be relatively minor figures and hence beyond suspicion of having exerted any influence.

One is tempted to conclude, in fact, that Hobbes was most comfortable with those to whom he could feel intellectually superior. The "circles" of learned and gifted men in which he participated during the years 1630–40, "circles" that took their names from the great houses in which they met and were accorded hospitality, were not without their persons of distinction, but the luminaries tended to be individuals whose achievements did not overshadow Hobbes's own accomplishments and those to which he aspired. Thus the "circles" at Great Tew and Burford, the country estates of Lucius Cary, the second viscount Falkland, composed, for the most part, of Oxford dons and clergy with a smattering of literary figures, were "circles" in which no one was Hobbes's intellectual equal; nor could anyone imagine, then or later, that Hobbes had learned much from the clerics Gilbert Sheldon, George Morley, John Earle, William Chillingworth (the ablest of the group), and Henry Hammond, or from the poets Edmund Waller, Sidney Godolphin (a particular friend of Hobbes), and Abraham Cowley, or from Falkland himself.[11] The most distinguished of the company, men such as Edward Hyde, the future earl of Clarendon and lord chancellor under Charles II, and John Selden, the eminent jurist and legal historian, may have been Hobbes's near equals in intelligence and learning, but, again, there is no evidence they influenced Hobbes's thinking in any major respect.

Clarendon, who later wrote a three-volume history of the Civil War, and in 1676 a book-length critique of *Leviathan* (discussed below, pp. 188–95) was to later claim that few men had known Hobbes longer than he "in a fair and friendly conversation and sociableness." The extent of Selden's acquaintance with Hobbes is difficult to determine. Aubrey recounted the following story, probably apocryphal: "When

(Selden) was near death, the minister was comeing to him to assoile him: Mr. Hobbes happened then to be there; say'd he, 'What, will you that have wrote like a man, now dye like a woman?' So the minister was not let in." Selden's opinions, as recorded in his *Table-Talk: Being the Discourses of John Selden, Esq.*, first published in 1689, bear some resemblance to those of Hobbes, particularly his views of a religion and witchcraft. For example: "We cannot tell what is Judgment of God; 'tis presumption to take upon us to know. . . . Commonly we say a Judgment falls upon a Man for something in him we cannot abide. An example we have in King *James* concerning the death of *Henry* the Fourth of *France;* one said he was killed for his Wenching, another said he was killed for turning his Religion. No, says King *James* (who could not abide fighting), he was killed for permitting Duels in his Kingdom." Almost identical with Hobbes's is Selden's view of "witches," as the following comparison demonstrates:

Selden	*Hobbes*
The Law against Witches does not prove there be any; but it punishes the Malice of those People, that use such means to take away Men's Lives. If one should profess that by turning his Hat thrice, and crying Buz, he could take away a Man's Life though in truth he could do no such thing, yet this were a just Law made by the State, that what-soever should turn his Hat thrice, cry Buz, with an intention to take away a Man's Life, shall be put to death.†	. . . as for Witches, I think not that their witchcraft is any real power; but yet that they are justly pun-ished for the false beliefs they have that they can do such mischiefe, joyned with their purpose to do it if they can; their trade being nearer to a new Religion than to a Craft or Science.*

The other, far more influential "circle" of which Hobbes, at various times, was a member was centered at Welbeck, the estate of another William Cavendish, earl and, from 1665, duke of Newcastle (and a grandson, like the second earl of Devonshire, of Bess of Hardwick). The Welbeck "circle" included several leading literary figures, among whom Ben Jonson, John Dryden, and William Davenant were most prominent.‡ More significant for Hobbes was the inclusion of

---

* *Leviathan*, in *E.W.*, III, 9.

† S. W. Singer, ed., *The Table-Talk of John Selden*, 2d ed. (London: John Russell Smith, 856), 164–65.

‡ Davenant's *Gondibert* (1651) was dedicated to Hobbes, prompting Hobbes to adjoin to its publication a long essay of analysis and appreciative exegesis. For an extended discussion of this venture of Hobbes into literary criticism see Reik, *Golden Lands*, 133–64.

Newcastle's brother, Charles Cavendish, mathematician and patron of science and scientists both in England and abroad. Probably through Cavendish, Hobbes became acquainted with a number of persons engaged in research of a scientific nature or related to scientific inquiry. The mathematicians John Pell and Walter Warner, in company with Cavendish's chaplain and secretary Robert Payne, may have been responsible for Hobbes's interest in optics and the mysteries of refraction; Warner is known to have written several papers on optics and to have been highly regarded by Cavendish, Hobbes, and others.[12] But perhaps Cavendish's most important service to Hobbes was to bring him into contact with leading scholars and scientists on the Continent. Cavendish, a friend of Descartes, may have introduced Hobbes to Mersenne and Gassendi, and to the French mathematician and optics experimenter Claude Mydorge, all of whom Hobbes met in the course of his third European tour, of 1634 to 1636 or 1637.[13]

Both Cavendish brothers may have facilitated Hobbes's interest in the work of Galileo, and one or the other, with the assistance of Mersenne, may have been instrumental in arranging a meeting between Galileo and Hobbes in 1635 or 1636. Two years earlier, in London, Hobbes had been commissioned by Newcastle to procure for him a copy of Galileo's great *Dialogo dei due massimi sistemi del mondo,* published in Florence in January 1632. Hobbes had expected to find the book easily, but after an unsuccessful search he was forced to write Newcastle, "[I]t is not possible to get it for mony—There were but few brought over at first, and they that buy such bookes, are not such men as to part w[ith] them againe. I heare say it is called in, in Italy, as a booke that will do more hurt to their Religion than all the bookes have done of Luther and Calvin, such opposition they thinke in betweene their Religion and naturall reason. I doubt not but the Translation of it will here be publiquely embraced. . . ."[14]

Hobbes never wrote any account of his later meeting with Galileo in Arcetri, near Florence.* Did the two discuss their respective theories of motion, or exchange views regarding the nature of ethics and moral philosophy, or reflect together about the cruel and stupid ways of men as mirrored in the exile of Thucydides, the trial of Bacon, and the recent ordeal of Galileo himself before the inquisitors of the

---

*Hobbes's *Vitae Auctarium* lists Pisa as the meeting site, but as Tönnies first noted, basing himself on Hobbes's letters at the time, the two must have met at "Il Giojello," Galileo's Arcetri villa. In June 1633, after some months in the custody of the Inquisition, during which he was repeatedly interrogated and threatened with torture, Galileo formally recanted his views, above all, his endorsement of the Copernican theory. Condemned nevertheless as "vehemently suspected of heresy," he was ordered held at the pleasure of the examining tribunal and as penance commanded to recite the seven penitential psalms once each week for three years. By December 1633 he had been allowed to return to Arcetri, where he spent the remaining eight years of his life.

Holy Office?* Was Galileo, seventy-one or seventy-two years old at the time, favorably impressed by his younger English visitor (Hobbes was forty-seven or forty-eight), who could not have been known to him except through intermediaries, Hobbes having published only his translation of Thucydides? Did Hobbes, then and afterward, ponder the implications of Galileo's appearances before the Inquisition and resolve to avoid situations that could lead him to suffer similar or worse consequences? On July 29, 1636, Hobbes wrote to Newcastle, who had complained of his enemies at court, "I am sorry your Lordship finds not so good dealing in the world as you deserve. But my Lord, he that will venture to sea must resolve to endure all weather, but for my part I love to keepe a'land. And it may be your Lordship now will do so to. . . ."[15] One wonders whether such characteristically prudent advice was reinforced by Hobbes's recent visit to Arcetri.

Whatever the roles of Newcastle and his brother, Charles Cavendish, in directly or indirectly making possible Hobbes's meeting with Galileo, they were influential patrons of Hobbes until the end of their lives, but Newcastle was a good deal more. While we do not know when Hobbes and Newcastle, four years apart in age, first met, Newcastle, first cousin to the second earl of Devonshire, must have been an occasional visitor to Hardwick and Chatsworth, and after the death of the second earl in 1628, a frequent one. Newcastle was forced to assume certain family responsibilities, including the lord-lieutenancy of Derbyshire, previously held by the first and second earls, which the earl's son and successor, a boy of ten or eleven, could not undertake for some years. By 1630 Hobbes and Newcastle were corresponding regularly, and the surviving letters often refer to meetings and discussions at Welbeck, such as the letters, already quoted, in which Hobbes reminded Newcastle of his "affirmation" in approximately 1630 "that light is a fancy in the mind, caused by motion in the brain."[16] Other letters of Hobbes declare his affection and respect for Newcastle or thank him for gifts of money and, in one instance, "silver spurres," though there came a time during the Civil War when Newcastle, impoverished by his support of Charles I, had to borrow "about ninety" pounds from Hobbes.[17] Two of Hobbes's books, *Elements of Law* (1640)

---

*The only known account of Hobbes's meeting with Galileo, discovered by Tönnies in an obscure mathematics history of 1800, claims that they discussed *"Sittenlehre,"* which could be translated as "ethics" or, according to Brandt, "psychology as a whole." The author of the treatise, A. G. Kästner, wrote, in translation, "Joh. Albert de Soria, former teacher at the University of Pisa, assures us that according to word of mouth, Galileo gave Hobbes (while strolling near the Grand-ducal Pleasure Palace) the first idea that the doctrines of ethics *[Sittenlehre]* can be brought to a mathematical certainty by applying the principles of geometry." Quoted in Brandt, *Hobbes's Conception of Nature*, 393.

and *Of Liberty and Necessity* (1646), the latter written at the suggestion of Newcastle, were dedicated to Newcastle, and in October 1636 Hobbes was willing to relinquish his post with the Devonshires in order to devote full time to his studies at Welbeck. Writing Newcastle from Byfleet,[18] where he and the third earl were delayed by illness on their return from the Continent, Hobbes confided to Newcastle, "For though my Lady and my Lord [Christian, the second earl's widow and her son, the third earl] do both accept so wel of my service as I could almost engage my self to serve them as a domestique all my life, yet the extreame pleasure I take in study overcomes in me all other appetites. I am not willing to leave my Lord, so as not to do him any service that he thinkes may not so well be done by another; but I must not deny my selfe the content to study in the way I have begun, and that I cannot conceave I shall do any where so well as at Welbecke, and therefore I meane if your Lordship forbid me not, to come thither as soone as I can, and stay as long as I can without inconvenience to your Lordship."[19] Hobbes's interest in moving to Welbeck no doubt reflected ambitions that, if not inspired by his European tour, were at the very least enlarged by it, especially the reception accorded Hobbes by leading thinkers, during the course of which he began, as he put it in his *Autobiography*, to be "numbered among the philosophers." As such, he would not have wanted to remain, in his words, "a domestique," and the prospect of joining the Newcastle household as a kind of resident intellectual must have seemed to him almost irresistible. But on October 26, ten days later, Hobbes was still at Byfleet, where, his illness apparently "decreasinge," he expressed hope in another letter to Newcastle of joining him at Welbeck "within little more then a moneth." The main reason for the delay, he explained, was his fear that the "sicknesse," undoubtedly the plague, might bring "danger . . . to your family, by receiving such as must lodge by the waye in common juries."[20] Two months later, Hobbes, in another letter from Byfleet, repeated once more his intention of coming to Welbeck. Thought not free of "sicknesse," he would long since have been with Newcastle, he wrote him on December 25, "if two thinges had bene, that is, fayre weather, or tolerable wayes, and free accesse to London." He added, "But as soone as I have beene but a weeke in London which I hope will be about three weekes hence I meane to goe" to Welbeck.*

---

*The "sicknesse" may have been pneumonia, or at least a severe "flu," Hobbes having been ill, apparently, more than two months. "I have a cold," Hobbes's letter continued, "that makes me keepe my chamber, and a chamber—in this thronge of company that stay Christmas here—that makes me keepe my cold." *Manuscripts of . . . the Duke of Portland*, 130.

In the end, however, Hobbes remained with the Devonshires; Chatsworth accounts books record salary payments to him of 50 pounds per year in 1637 and 1638, and 65 pounds in 1639. During those years Hobbes was also receiving annual interest payments of 12 pounds on money owed him, amounting to 200 pounds. These payments may have related to money lent by Hobbes to the second earl or to his widow, Christian, in the form of loans or deferred wages. Since Hobbes was relatively well paid by the Devonshires, the prospect of financial gain probably had played no role in his contemplated move to Welbeck. In Dorset in 1635 a "bailiff or servant of the best sort capable of directing the work of others" earned an annual wage of 80 shillings (4 pounds) if his apparel was provided, or 100 shillings (5 pounds) if he had to supply his own apparel.[21] While we have no records of annual salaries paid to tutors and secretaries, the wages recorded above suggest that Hobbes was exceptionally well treated by the Devonshires.

We can only speculate about the reasons behind the decision, whether Hobbes's or Newcastle's, that led Hobbes to remain in the service of the Devonshires. Perhaps the treatment accorded Newcastle by the court of Charles I in 1636 and 1637 inclined Hobbes to reconsider. For some years prior to 1636, Newcastle had been very eager to procure a high court position, and that year the position he wanted most was that of sole gentleman of the bedchamber to the Prince of Wales, or, in effect, governor of the future Charles II. But as 1636, and then 1637, passed with no announcement from the court—he finally was appointed Charles's governor in March 1638—Newcastle became convinced the coveted position was not to be his. Hobbes, always one to calculate carefully his main chance, may have decided early in 1637 that his fantasies of becoming an influential figure in Prince Charles's entourage by becoming an influential figure at Welbeck were not to be realized, and perhaps other factors also suggested to him that his own fortunes would be better served by his remaining where he was. The advantages of the Devonshire connection, Hobbes may have decided finally, were far richer and more secure than any that Newcastle could offer, and Christian and her son may have made the connection more attractive by replacing some of Hobbes's "domestique" duties with less menial, more respectable chores. By 1637 the third earl was twenty years of age, contemplating marriage, and beginning to turn his attention to the creation of a remarkable library, books being one of his enduring passions. Hobbes, who some years earlier had begun to think of, and occasionally sign, himself a "Secretary" to the late second earl, surely must have found the opportunities afforded him as Devonshire librarian extremely appealing.

But a conflict over his inheritance between the third earl and his mother, into which Hobbes reluctantly was drawn, may have made Hobbes wish, more than once, that he were serving as librarian at Welbeck. A document of April 12, 1639, dictated by Hobbes and signed at the bottom of each page by him and the third earl, signifying their approval of the text, gives a revealing insight not only into Hobbes's relationship to the Devonshires at that time but also into the complex interrelationships of persons and property in a titled family of early-seventeenth-century England. In the document, entitled "A Narrative of Proceedings both Publique & Private concerning ye Inheritance of ye Right Hon[orable] William Earle of Devonshire, from ye time of ye decease of his Grandfather, to this present," Hobbes reported the earl's suspicions that his mother, Christian, in addition to reducing his inheritance by using some portion of it to pay his father's debts, had spent other sums on the purchase of certain properties for herself. One such acquisition, land holdings in Derbyshire producing an annual income of almost 2,000 pounds, the earl originally "did believe, or hope, were purchased for him with such monies as otherwise would have accrued unto him ... because he was allways told by such as were likeliest to know ye truth thereof, that it was impossible for any sonne to have a better mother, which he thought was not sayd without reference to that purchase, at least he thought ye same was irrevocably assured him & his heyres after her decease." When Christian asked her son, who had come of age in 1638, to sign a statement granting her a "discharge of all things done by her in his Estate during his minority," the earl consulted Hobbes. Though Hobbes "understood not ye reason of such procedding," he "did nevertheless persuade ye said Earle not to take any exceptions thereat, but to endeavour to please his Mother as before."

Christian could not have been pleased when, as seems certain, she learned of these discussions between her son and his tutor. The earl, determined to obtain an accounting, but not knowing how to proceed, turned to Hobbes for advice. After threatening to leave home, the earl was able to persuade Hobbes "not to acquaint his Mother therewithall without his leave; which he yealded unto, ye said Earle first promising he would doe nothing afterwards, but what should become a good and dutifull sonne to doe." Hobbes then advised the earl to obtain from the auditor "which was now lately dismissed of his imployment," presumably by Christian, an accounting of all receipts and payments made during his minority, and an inventory of his estate. In Hobbes's analysis for the earl of the resulting audit, he advanced the view that Parliament, in coming to the aid of the second earl, had not intended to charge all properties of his son and widow for payment of his debt, but "onely ye lands allowed to be sold, and ye personall estate of [the second earl], together with such things as in equity wer lyable to ye said debts before ye revenue of ye Heyre," estimated at "about £50000."

Hobbes then dealt with one of the most disputed issues between the third earl and his mother (and perhaps his brother, Charles Cavendish, as well), namely, the issue whether the Devonshire house in London and its silver, jewelry, and furnishings, were "lyable to the said debts" or, instead, part of the third earl's inheritance. Had Hobbes held that the London property was "lyable," he would have enabled Christian, at least insofar as her eldest son agreed, to dispose of the house and contents and to use the money to pay debts and, if there was any surplus, to acquire other properties for herself and the two remaining children. But Hobbes, in an opinion that must have infuriated Christian, informed the third earl that "seeing in ye Act of Parliament it is put down as a motive to cause ye said Earle to pay his father's debts, that the said debt was partly contracted by ye purchase of Devonshire house, of Bishops-fee (a manor in Leicester), of Plate, Jewells & Household-stuffe, he thought it against equity & the expectation of ye Parliament that ye same, or any part thereof should be devised from him either for ever, or for any time at all." If the land holdings allotted to be sold were not sufficient to pay the debt, Hobbes continued, properties in the counties of Gloucester and Derby (no doubt including those that had been acquired by Christian) should be sold "before ye revenue of ye heyre." In the event that funds remained after all debts and legacies had been paid, "the same should be wholly to ye benefitt of [the third earl]."

Apparently, Hobbes himself was in favor of the existing system of inheritance, known as entail, in accordance with which the eldest son was the principal heir, to the disadvantage of his siblings. For "if it were reasonable to bequeath away those goods & lands by which ye debt was contracted," Hobbes argued, "from him that was to pay ye debt, there would be no use of Entayles, nor need of a Parliament to cutt them off. For ye father might buy what quantity of land he pleased, for which he might enter into debt; & giving ye said land to whom he pleased, might enjoyne his sonne and heyre to pay ye said debts; which would be (if ye father pleased) equivalent to ye disinheriting of his sonne." Perhaps Hobbes even believed that Parliament had intended, in 1628, partially to disinherit the third earl, because "it was point worthy ye considering that by this Act ye undoubted property he had in his estate, was without pretence of benefit to ye Publique, without Crime, & against his will taken from him."

Having taken the side of the third earl against his mother, his siblings, and the Parliament of 1628, Hobbes thought it wise, in con-

*William Cavendish, third earl of Devonshire (1617–1684). By
Van Dyck. As is noted in the text, this portrait of the third earl is not
without some resemblance to the engraved face of the "Mortal God"
on the title page of* Leviathan.

cluding the documents, to express some goodwill toward Christian and to make clear he had not personally benefited from the foregoing "Proceedings." The third earl "living at this present in ye house of his said Mother," the document ended, "The said Thomas Hobbes hath councelled him, & doth still councell him to continue so; & not to commence any suite against her. And for this information ye said Thomas Hobbes neyther hath receaved, nor demanded, nor expecteth any reward, but onely ye testimony of having performed ye parte of a faithfull Tutor, & to be justified against aspersions to ye contrary." We do not know what these aspersions were or by whom they were made.[22]

The "Proceedings," whatever their effect on the relations between Hobbes and Christian, must have drawn Hobbes and the third earl more closely together. But though he remained with the third earl most of the remainder of his life (the earl's death in 1684 came only five years after his own), Hobbe's friendship with Newcastle continued to be close. The relationship between the two may at first strike us as a curious one. Newcastle, a handsome man whose ambition and vanity drew encouragement from Hobbes and others of his "circle," was as pretentious about his literary accomplishments as he was proud of his stable, reputedly one of the best in all of Europe. Without question Newcastle was a fine horseman, and in manners and deportment almost as fine a gentleman, but he fancied himself a poet and playwright as well, which he was not. When the Civil War began, he raised a small army at his own expense, and imagining himself to be skilled in military arts, managed to have himself made commander of the king's forces in the north. The appointment proved disastrous to both Charles and Newcastle: the king lost the north and with it, as events ultimately demonstrated, the war; and Newcastle, defeated and disgraced, fled abroad to Hamburg, to Paris, and, finally, to Antwerp, where he occupied the house that had belonged to the painter Rubens. According to Margaret, duchess of Newcastle, his second wife, his losses as a result of the war, the confiscation of his properties by Cromwell, his expenses in exile, and his loans to the royal court and cause, most of them never repaid, amounted to more than 940,000 pounds.

A talented seducer of women, especially of the female servants of his own household, Newcastle made a provident first marriage to an heiress whose money and titles enhanced his own. His second marriage, in 1645, not long after the death of his first wife, was another matter. Margaret Lucas (ca. 1625–1673), the future duchess of Newcastle, was a lady-in-waiting to Queen Henrietta Maria, and also, like her husband, an aspiring poet, playwright, and biographer (of her husband) whose writing compulsions verged on mania. Eccentric in dress and manner, capable of unexplained bizarre behavior on occasions that called for the utmost propriety, Margaret was viewed, much of the time, as a comic, even ridiculous figure despite a vast literary enterprise that filled some thirteen thick volumes.*

A typical story has a French nobleman describing to Charles II "the extraordinary apparition he had seen as he stepped from his sedan chair" upon arriving at a court masquerade. " 'I bet,' said the King, 'it is the Duchess of Newcastle.' " It was not the duchess, but the story is illustrative of Margaret's standing.[23] Perhaps the fairest short summary of Margaret's life and reputation was that of Virginia Woolf in 1925. The duchess of Newcastle, she observed three hundred years after Margaret's birth, was "garish in her dress, eccentric in her habits, chaste in her conduct, coarse in her speech [and] she succeeded during her lifetime in drawing upon herself the ridicule of the great and the applause of the learned."[24]

One of those applauding "learned" was Hobbes. Margaret's writings, he wrote, in a contribution to a volume of eulogies, had given him "more and truer ideas of virtue and honour than any book of morality he had ever read." Comparing her plays with those of others, he concluded in 1661, "[I]f some comique writers have been able to present vices upon the stage more ridiculously and immodestly, by which they take their rabble, I reckon that amongst your praises. For that which most pleases lewd spectators is nothing but subtle cheating or filch, which a high and noble mind endued with virtue from its infancy can never come to the knowledge of."[25] Margaret, in turn, expressed approval of Hobbes and his principles, though she hinted several times that some of the more important principles had originated with her husband in discussions with Hobbes.

Undoubtedly, Newcastle's influence on Hobbes's intellectual development was negligible, but he may have had some effect on certain other interests. When Hobbes was "past ninety," he wrote a short love poem, some lines of which were reminiscent of Newcastle's "The Gossip's Hand." which may have been composed as early as 1626. In "The Gossip's Hand," Newcastle declared,

---

*Margaret's quirky behavior and prodigious literary output may have owed something to her remaining, much against her will, childless (Newcastle was the father of several children by his first marriage). As Antonia Fraser has suggested, her failure to conceive led her "to write with considerable acerbity about her fertile sisters," noting of one such "sister" who was pregnant after only four weeks of marriage that she already was "rasping wind out of her stomache . . . making Sickly faces . . . and bearing out her Body, drawing her Neck downward, and standing in a weak and faint posture as great bellied Wives do." Margaret, in short, was jealous. Fraser, *Weaker Vessel*, 63.

> With love's hopes long my phansy thou hast fed;
> Now, since my wife is safely brought to bed,
> Thou art my Gossip, honour me to stand . . .
> Think not, though I grow old, I am no other
> But a dull handycraft Mechanique Lover:
> What though my youth's declin'd; I am afraid
> You'll think me a Patriarch with my handmaid.*

Hobbes's poem contained the lines

> Thinke not the man a fool tho he be old
> Who loves in body fair a fairer mind.†

Hobbes's influence on the duchess and her works is unknown, but
there can be no doubt of his influence on Newcastle. Newcastle's draft
of instructions that he drew up for Prince Charles's guidance contained advice and admonitions similar to those Hobbes had tendered
the second and third earls of Devonshire. Thus the prince was urged
to study history, but not too much, and to be devout, but, again, not
too much, because "a good man might make a bad king."[26] He was
to be moderate in his speech, courteous and civil, and even in the
bedchamber he was to avoid too great a familiarity, lest he lose respect.
To women, especially women of high degree, he always was to be
polite and considerate.‡

Sometime after 1650 Newcastle presented Prince Charles with a
lengthy political document or handbook of his own composition, but
one that was unmistakably Hobbesian in substance though not in
style. In its fifteen chapters, ranging in topic from "The Militia" and
"The Church" to "For Forayne States" and "For France and Spayne,"
Newcastle advised the prince how to conduct himself when he was
"Inthronde" in every area of statecraft, not excluding "ceremoneye
and Order" and "Your Majesty's Divertisements" (Newcastle recommending hunting, hawking, coursing, riding and racing horses, tilt-
ing, dancing, and "the Maske"—"Etaliens makes the Seanes beste").
In "For the Church," one of the longest chapters, Newcastle instructed
Charles that a monarch is "Governmente In Cheef off the whole Bodye

---

* Quoted in Trease, *Portrait*, 56–57.

† For the poem in full, see page 131.

‡ In a letter of August 22, 1638, to the third earl of Devonshire, who was twenty-one at
the time and visiting in Paris, Hobbes cautioned the earl "to avoid all offensive speech
not only openly reviling but also that Satyrical way of niggling that some use. The
effect of it is a cooling of the Affection of your servants, & the provoking of the hatred
of your Equals. . . . I think it no ill counsell that you profess no Love to any Woman
which you hope not to Marry or otherwise to enjoy. For an Action without Design is
that which all the World calls Vanity." Oxford University, Rawlinson Manuscripts, no.
232, fol. 80. The entire letter is reproduced in Reik, *Golden Lands*, 197–98.

Willm: Cavendishe 1st
of Newcastle married
1st. Eliz.th Daughter
Willm: Basset of Blore
2.d Margaret Lucas
Daughter to Tho.s Lucas
COLCHESTER

William Cavendish, first earl (later duke) of Newcastle (1593–1676). By Van Dyck. This portrait of Hobbes's friend was painted in the 1630s.

Poletick, In all Itt Partes, & Capaseties by one Person only." There should thus be no rival figure claiming sovereignty over any body of subjects on religious grounds. Lest there be any doubt whom or what he had in mind, Newcastle reminded Charles of the "sturrs the Pope hath made in Englande & the Presbeterians much worse. . . . For Indeed, Popery, & Presbytery, though they looke divers wayes, with their heads, yett theye are tied together like Samsons Foxes by theye Tayles Carienge the same fierbrandes off Covetusnes & Ambition, to putt all Into a Combusion whersoever theye coume, thatt will nott Submitt to them. . . ." Hobbes would have put it better but less color-fully, and certainly no more forcefuly.[27]

In the *Life* of her husband, Margaret recorded some eighty-five statements and observations of Newcastle, many of which could be, perhaps even should be, attributed to Hobbes. For example, "I have heard My Lord say," Margaret wrote, "That ther should be more praying, and less preaching: for much preeching breeds faction; but much praying causes devotion." And "That all books of controversies should be writ in Latin, that none but the learned may read them, and that there should be no disputations but in schools, lest it breed factions amongst the vulgar. . . ." Newcastle had also declared, "That power, for the most part, does more than wisdom: for fools with power, seem wise; whereas wise men, without power, seem fools; and this is the reason that the world takes power for wisdom; and the want of power for foolishness." He further "had observed, that seldom any person did laugh, but it was at the follies or misfortunes of other men; by which we may judge of their good natures."[28] Perhaps such senti-ments were original with Newcastle, but they are identical or similar to those appearing in Hobbes's writings.

In his *Elements of Law* (1640), for example, Hobbes noted as one cause of laughter that "men laugh at the infirmities of others, by com-parison of which their own abilities are set off and illustrated . . . laughter proceedeth from the sudden imagination of our own odds and eminence; for what is else the recommending ourselves to our own good opinion, by comparison with another man's infirmities or absurdities?" He added, "I may therefore conclude, that the passion of laughter is nothing else by but a sudden glory arising from sudden conception of some eminency in ourselves, by comparison with the infirmities of others, or with our own formerly. . . ."[29] In *Leviathan* (1651) Hobbes repeated, "*Sudden Glory* is the passion which maketh thos *Grimaces* called *Laughter;* and is caused either by some sudden act of their own, that pleaseth them; or by the apprehencion of some deformed thing in another, by comparison whereof they suddenly applaud themselves."[30]

In one branch of knowledge and experience, however, Hobbes was almost beneath Newcastle's notice, though that did not prevent him, probaby in response to a Newcastle request, from writing a short essay on the subject. A celebrated horseman and author of two authoritative works on horsemanship, Newcastle may have asked Hobbes for his "Considerations touching the facility or Difficulty of the Motions of a Horse on streight lines, & Circular," the title Hobbes gave to his essay. Hobbes, of course, was interested in motion, but he was no student of the horse, and notwithstanding Newcastle's gift of "silver spurres," he was "never any," as he wrote Newcastle on one occasion, "ranke [i.e., accomplished] rider."[31] His undated essay, which included such statements as "The most naturall & easy posture of the body of a Horse, at rest, is in a streight line: for in that posture every Horse, standing still, and at liberty, naturally putts himself," could not have told Newcastle anything he did not already know, but his response to it is unrecorded. Whatever his reaction to what one commentator has termed Hobbes's "irrelevant superfluity of reasoning"—and it probably was an appreciative or at least polite one since the friendship continued unaffected—Hobbes, one must agree, "hardly appears to advantage." Perhaps, however, the judgment is too harsh that "the sage on the high horse resembles the tailor in 'Gulliver's Travels,' who measured his man with the help of a sextant and other mathematical instruments."[32]

If Hobbes, on one occasion, could be compared to the tailor in *Gulliver's Travels*, Newcastle on a great many occasions could be seen as an English Don Quixote. Early in 1639, commanding a small force of men he himself had equipped, Newcastle rode to Scotland to help put down the thousands of Scots, the so-called Covenanters, who had refused to approve the king's new prayer book. Embroiled in matters of protocol from the beginning, Newcastle refused to allow his troop, which he had named after the Prince of Wales (he still was counseling Charles), to be preceded in any engagement by another contingent. But in the end there were no battles apart from those between Newcastle and the other commanders, also noblemen, who were in charge of troops equally insistent upon precedence. So far as is known, Newcastle neither fired nor heard a shot during his first campaign in the north; even the duel to which he challenged a rival commander came to nothing. By June he was back in London, attending the prince and writing plays, but neither activity was to continue for long. A member of both the Short and the Long Parliaments of 1640 (the latter was not to end until 1660), Newcastle became involved in plots to free the doomed Thomas Wentworth, earl of Strafford, from the Tower of London, the consequences of which were his near impeachment by the House of Lords in May 1641, and, two months later, his dismissal as sole Gentleman of the bedchamber to the prince. Early that fall he was back in Welbeck, where, according to faithful Margaret, he "settled himself with his lady, children and family, to his great satisfaction."[33]

By that time Hobbes had been in France for almost a year. He and Newcastle were not to meet again until 1645, by which date the Civil War had taken a deadly toll of their friends. Falkland, Sidney Godolphin, and Charles Cavendish (second son of the second earl of Devonshire) had been killed on the battlefield; Chillingworth had died a prisoner of war. Whatever the outcome of the war and the future of England, Hobbes and Newcastle in 1645 must have known that their lives would not be the same again. But neither could have known or guessed, then, that the combined years of their self-exile abroad would total more than a quarter of a century. Though the Civil War ended several years earlier, Hobbes did not return to England until 1651, and Newcastle not until 1660.

THE FIRST TO FLEE

H OBBES'S DEPARTURE FOR Paris in 1640, probably a week or two after the Long Parliament first met in November, was preceded by a series of crises. The outbreak of renewed fighting in Scotland (the so-called Second Bishop's War) and the Scots' invasion of England, the increasingly embittered conflict between Archbishop Laud and the Puritans, the refusal of John Hampden to pay ship money,* John Pym's inflammatory speech in the House of Commons that culminated in the impeachment of Strafford, the king's principal advisor, for high treason, and other dire events persuaded Hobbes that Charles I no longer was the undisputed sovereign ruler of his kingdom. Hobbes, by reason of his convictions even more than by way of his connections, was a staunch royalist, and to a man who regarded the collapse of government as the single worst calamity that could befall humankind, England seemed to be moving toward that anarchic state in which life, as he was to put it in *Leviathan*, would become "solitary, poor, nasty, brutish, and short."[1] Such life, of course, was not for him, and the desire to escape was clearly much stronger than any ties that bound him to family and friends, or to the Devonshire household of

---

* Ship money, a levy on coastal towns the proceeds of which paid for the arming of ships, was applied in 1636 to the inland counties where most well-to-do taxpayers lived. Hampden, a country gentleman and a member of Parliament, refused to pay the tax on the grounds that only Parliament could establish a new tax. While he lost his case before the judges, the seven-to-five decision was a close one, the majority stating unequivocally that the decision was not to be construed as an endorsement of extraparliamentary taxation in general. In *Behemoth* (written in 1668 but not published in an authorized edition until 1682), Hobbes was contemptuous of Hampden and his suit, observing incredulously that the "oppression" complained of by Parliament had been expressed "by one of their members that had been taxed but 20s. (Mark the oppression; a Parliament-man of 500£ a year, land-taxed at 20s!). . . ." *E.W.*, VI, 209. He did not mention that Hampden, whose opposition to ship money and other "oppressions" led him to volunteer his services on the parliamentary side in the Civil War, had been mortally wounded at Chalgrave Field in 1643.

which he had been a member, except for one brief period, more than thirty years. So far as we know, no friend of Hobbes was apprehensive enough, or frightened enough in 1640 to join him in flight. Indeed, Hobbes, by some process of twisted thought or timorous logic, was sufficiently proud of his decision to boast afterward that he had been "the first of all that fled." He apparently believed that his escape to France demonstrated his loyalty and devotion to the royal cause. The idea never occurred to him that those most loyal and devoted to Charles I had been those who argued and fought—and in some cases died—for the king, on English soil. But Hobbes was not the only one to seek safety abroad as early as 1640.

He had done so, he later wrote, because of a "little treatise" on sovereignty he had composed in English during the Short Parliament which "had not his Majesty dissolved the Parliament, it had brought him into danger of his life." Claiming to have been "the first that had ventured to write in the King's defence," Hobbes had observed, when the Long Parliament met in November, that those elected "proceeded so fiercely in the very beginning, against those that had written or preached in the defence of [the king's] power, which they also intended to take away, and in gracing those whom the King had disgraced for sedition, that Mr. Hobbes, doubting how they would use him, went over into France . . . and there continued eleven years, to his damage some thousands of pounds deep."* Aubrey, repeating this account, added, "[Bishop] Manwaring (of St. David's) preach'd *his doctrine* [of absolute sovereignty]; for which, among others, he was sent prisoner to the Tower. Then thought Mr. Hobbes, 'tis time now for me to shift for my selfe, and so withdrew into France. . . "

The historical record does not support either Hobbes or Aubrey. The "little treatise," henceforth to be referred to as *The Elements of Law* (1640), was "not printed" at that time, and though "many gentlemen had copies, which occasioned much talk of the author," no scholar of the period believes that Hobbes was in any real danger.[2] While the number of copies and the names of recipients is not known—six manuscript copies have been identified—parliamentary and other documents of the time do not reveal that *The Elements of Law* was known about, let alone widely discussed. Hobbes's belief that he was in as much danger as Strafford, who was subsequently executed, or even Manwaring, an extreme royalist who was imprisoned briefly by the Long Parliament, tells us more about Hobbes's fearful fantasies, or

---

* Ibid. In his *Autobiography* Hobbes revealed he had £500 when he arrived in France, adding "[F]rom my native land also came to me a pension of £80 a year." The pension, presumably, was awarded him by the third earl of Devonshire.

as Peters suggests, about his "exaggerated sense of his own importance," than about the realities of 1640. At worst, he might have been imprisoned in the Tower, like many another in the decade that began with the Long Parliament and ended with the beheading of Charles I, but such a fate was unlikely. Unlike Bishop Manwaring, who defended royal absolutism weekly in his sermons, Hobbes was a private person whose views were known only to a small number of persons.* Moreover, his opinions, whether or not subversive of Parliament, could not easily be obtained by those who were suspicious or merely curious. As late as 1641, we need to remind ourselves again, by which time he was safely in France, Hobbes had published *only* his translation of Thucydides.

Nevertheless, fear of the Tower, whether real or imaginary, may have been a reason why Hobbes deserted to France. Another, more powerful reason, perhaps, was that Hobbes, anticipating the Civil War, may have believed that when the conflict came, his friends would expect him to become personally involved. Hobbes, to be sure, was not trained in military arts, as far as we know; but as a secretary, scribe, or record keeper, he would have been useful to commanders in the field, since every war, not excluding those of ancient Egypt and Greece, has needed soldiers or civilians who do only paperwork. He may have had reason to think that Newcastle would ask him to join his staff and perform services similar to those he had rendered the second and third earls of Devonshire. Four years older than Newcastle, Hobbes could not have claimed he was too old to serve; his friend William Harvey, ten years older than Hobbes, was part of the King's entourage at the Battle of Edgehill in October 1642, where, according to Aubrey, he sought shelter under a hedge with the Prince of Wales and the duke of York, then boys of twelve and ten years of age, "and tooke out of his pockett a booke and read; but he had not read very long before a bullet of a great gun grazed on the ground neare him, which made him remove his station." Harvey, who was sixty-four at the time, apparently remained with the king until July 1646.

Hobbes, who lacked physical courage, would have found Harvey's Edgehill experience intolerable, and he would have been

---

* Roger Manwaring's troubles had begun in 1628 when he was impeached by the House of Lords for insisting on the king's right to levy taxes without parliamentary consent. Almost immediately thereafter he was pardoned by Charles and, in effect, rewarded by being appointed to a higher and more munificent "living." In trouble once more in 1640, he was "imprisoned and persecuted by Long Parliament," according to the *Concise Dictionary of National Biography*, but he survived, eventually to die in 1653, at age sixty-three. Laird, however, states (*Hobbes*, 10) that in 1640 "the House *desisted*, on the King's appeal, from an attempt to censure him."

extremely unhappy to find himself in or near any battlefield. Whatever other reasons he may have had for fleeing to France, he knew
that in Paris he would be safe from the bullets of either side and able
to resume his discissions with the philosophers and scientists. His
intuition may also have told him that the royal cause would ultimately be lost, and perhaps with it his Devonshire connection, and
that he would do better to measure the consequences of that loss in
Paris rather than in London or, if the thought ever came to him, in
Malmesbury, which was on the parliamentary side.

When he arrived in France in November or December 1640, he
brought with him, as has been mentioned, a manuscript copy of *The
Elements of Law*, which, though not published until 1650, was his first
major work on politics.[3] His first *published* book about politics, therefore, was *Elementorum Philosophiae Sectio Tertia: De Cive*, which
appeared, in Latin, in 1642. As we noted earlier, Hobbes regarded *De
Cive*, "privately" printed in a small edition, as the foundation of political science, and though the English translation was not published
until 1651, the book was known to, and highly regarded by, eminent
men of the time, including, in addition to Mersenne and Gassendi,
Grotius and even, in a guarded fashion, Descartes, who was not otherwise an admirer of Hobbes.[4] But Hobbes had hardly less regard for
his earlier *Elements*, observing to Newcastle, to whom the book was
dedicated, with characteristic immodesty that "it would be an
incomparable benefit to commonwealth, if every man held the opinions concerning law and policy here delivered." Whether or not Hobbes
was accurate in his appraisal, he clearly regarded both books, then
and later, as supplying the basis of his own political philosophy, and
in this view he undoubtedly was correct. For the similarities are great,
and the differences relatively minor, between his first two important
works and his later writings, including the book by which he is better
known than any other, his great and enduring *Leviathan*. Hobbes, in
other words, at the age of fifty-four, had brought to maturity the
political theory that had begun to take form at Oxford, to find expression in *Thucydides*, and to receive further development in letters and
discussions involving leading thinkers in at least three countries.
Though epic political events still lay ahead and though he was to
write and publish more books and monographs, he was not to make
any significant changes in this theory other than those dictated by
political expediency and concern for his own well-being. *Leviathan*,
as will be seen, was to be his longest and most comprehensive work
on politics, but in no sense was it a revison, much less a refutation,
of *The Elements* or *De Cive*.[5]

In all three books much attention was paid to religion, but one measure of the increasing significance of religious controversy in 1640–51 is the amount of space Hobbes devoted to the issue. In *The Elements*, perhaps a fifth of the book was given over to religion. Two years later, in *De Cive*, religion occupied fully a third of the pages. When *Leviathan* was published in 1651, the triumph of Cromwell and the ascendancy of Parliament had settled, temporarily, certain doctrinal controversies, but Hobbes still was very much occupied with religious matters: more than half of *Leviathan* was about religion. Religion did not cease to interest Hobbes in his declining years, but by then he was mainly concerned to defend himself against charges of atheism. While scholars are not agreed among themselves about the merit of these charges (a matter to be explored later), almost all hold the view that Hobbes's writings on religion, however far apart in time, manifest a remarkable congruity of opinion.

Discussing the nature of God in *The Elements*, Hobbes emphasized that we can know only that God is; we cannot know what he is or have any "conception or image of the Diety." Arguing that all effects have causes and that causes are themselves the effects of prior causes, Hobbes held that the first and original cause was "an eternal" or "first power of all powers, and first cause of all causes. And this is it which all men call by the name of God: implying eternity, incomprehensibility, and omnipotency." Though we imagine, he continued, that God is capable of "seeing, hearing, speaking, knowing, loving, and the like," we have merely attributed to him qualities or abilities that we enjoy. None of these attributes enables us to understand the nature of God; they only express "our incapacity (to understand), or our reverence."[6]

Though such opinions were hedged with frequent assertions that there is a God, Hobbes in all of his books disputed the conventional Christian view that God is knowable and that his principles are or can be known to each one of us through "reasoning" or the "spirit" within us. Moreover, we cannot know, except on faith, that the Scriptures are the word of God, since there is no knowledge or evidence, natural or supernatural, that can establish such a connection. The identification of God's principles and the interpretation of Scripture, Hobbes always maintained, must be the function of the church and, above it, the supreme authority to which the church was responsible, namely, the secular sovereign power. In such matters no man should trust his own opinion or even that of numerous others, he wrote, in a statement reminiscent of his introduction to *Thucydides*, "For commonly truth is on the side of the few, rather than the multitude."[7]

If we cannot know what God is but only that he exists, neither can we know "by natural means only" the nature of "spirits" or angels. We "who are Christians" can only acknowledge "that there be angels good and evil; and that they are spirits, and that the soul of man is a spirit; and that these spirits are immortal. But, to know it, that is to say, to have natural evidence of the same: it is impossible." Some men, he went on, as if he had not raised enough questions about traditional views, regard spirits as "incorporeal, and some corporeal'" but to himself "it seemeth, that the Scriptures favoureth them more, who hold angels and spirits for corporeal, then them that hold the contrary."[8]

The certainties and uncertainties of religion clarified (and some of the former disposed of), Hobbes could then turn his attention to the requirements of good and sound government. While much had been written on the subject in the two thousand years since Aristotle, he observed, no one could claim to know more than the ancient Greek philosopher, and yet every man thought he knew as much as any other man without "study" or any recourse other than "natural wit." They could consider themselves authorities, Hobbes commented drily, because "in their writings and discourses they take for principles those opinions which are already vulgarly received, whether true or false, being for the most part false." Opposed to these men, whom Hobbes called *"dogmatici,"* and their false principles were the *"mathematici,"* men who were familiar with "magnitudes, numbers, times, and motions, and their proportions one to another," in short, men like Hobbes himself. From their studies have come the arts and sciences of navigation, geography, astronomy, and geometry, all of them the result of the "most scrupulous ratiocination" proceeding "from most low and humble principles, evident to the meanest capacity; going on slowly." Unfortunately, those who had written about moral philosophy, law, and government had come from the ranks of the *dogmatici* and had succeeded only in multiplying doubt, controversy, and confusion.[9]

Basic truths, neglected or denied by the *dogmatici*, were that the diversity of passions, among which were ambition and vanity, and the tendency of the strong to dominate the weak, make men insecure and fearful of death. Hence the natural state of mankind was that of "offensiveness" of one man to another, and when "there is added a right of every man to every thing, whereby one man invadeth with right, and another with right resisteth; and men live thereby in perpetual diffidence, and study how to preoccupate each other; the estate of man in this natural liberty is the estate of war." No wonder, then, that in countries where "natural liberty" exists (such as America, which Hobbes thought of as mainly occupied by savages), "We find the people few and short lived, and without the ornaments and comforts of life. . . ." If the "estate of war" is to be avoided, Hobbes stressed in

The Elements and in his later books, "natural liberty" must be given up in favor of a compact or social contract establishing a political authority that citizens are obligated to obey.[10]

The compact or social contract could not be broken, Hobbes made clear, and the political authority, once established, could not be overthrown by those who had created it. Unlike other theorists before and after him, notably John Locke, Hobbes went so far as to argue that a covenant resulting from fear was no less binding than one based on freely given consent. If a man, he wrote, using a homely example, "for fear of death, have promised to give a thief an hundred pounds the next day, and not discover him," the promise or covenant "is not therefore void, because extorted by fear. For there appeareth no reason, why that which we do upon fear, should be less firm than that which we do for covetousness. For both the one and the other maketh the action voluntary. And if no covenant should be good, that proceedeth from fear of death, no conditions of peace between enemies, nor any laws could be of force which are all consented to from fear . . . the covenant of things lawful is obligatory, even towards a thief."[11]

In a passage written more than ten years before Hobbes made his peace with Cromwell and urged, in *Leviathan*, his fellow citizens to do the same, Hobbes argued that conquered subjects were as obligated to obey their conquerors as they previously had been to obey the ruler who was conquered. A man is released from any duty or obligation to a government, he insisted, when that government yields to conquest, for "when it cometh to pass, that the power of the commonwealth is overthrown, and any particular man thereby, lying under the sword of the enemy yieldeth himself captive, he is thereby bound to serve him that taketh him, and consequently discharged of his obligation to the former. For no man can serve two masters."[12]

For developing this argument at some length in *Leviathan*, Hobbes was accused by John Wallis and others of having sought "to flatter *Oliver* . . . or purpose to make way for his return," as Hobbes put it in a defense of himself not published until after his death, *Considerations upon the Reputation, Loyalty, Manners, & Religion of Thomas Hobbes of Malmesbury* (London, 1680). Even Clarendon, who, unlike Wallis, was not engaged in a feud with Hobbes, suggested that Hobbes's motive in propounding such doctrines had been a desire to return to England, where he would be like a "Man that commanded thirty Legions, (for Cromwel had bin oblig'd to have supported him, who defended his Usurpation)."[13] While there can be no question that Hobbes had always favored submission to any ruler, however he came to power, who would protect his subjects' life and liberty, he may have had Cromwell prominently in mind when he elaborated and extended his view of the matter in 1651. In addition, he was not entirely convincing when he argued, in his self-defense, that he could hardly have wished to flatter Cromwell in 1651 since Cromwell "was not made Protector till three or four years after." In fact, Cromwell became lord protector in 1653, but in 1651, if not a year or two earlier, few could have doubted that eventual outcome, in view of his prominence.

Hobbes's stress on the preservation of life as the chief end for which men establish government and submit to its decrees is the major theme in all of his political writings, and it also plays an important role in his discussions of the family, which he views, in effect, as possessing political attributes. Hobbes, of course, was not the first political theorist to regard relations between parents and children as analogous to relations between rulers and subjects, but he may have been drawing on his own, personal history and experience in placing special emphasis on the powers and responsibilities of women. Taking issue, in *The Elements*, with earlier writers who had assigned dominion over children to both parents or to the father alone, Hobbes argued that neither "generation" as such nor the physical strength of the father justifies giving him "propriety in the child" that is exclusionary of the mother, for it is not "generation" that bestows dominion but the "preservation" of the child, which, in a state of nature, is within the power of the mother. So long as the mother chooses to care for her child, Hobbes was saying, she is the child's parent or ruler, but if she abandons the child or exposes it to death, "whatsoever man or woman shall find the child so exposed, shall have the same right which the mother had before; and for the same reason, namely for the power not of generating, but preserving." While Hobbes is not unaware that husbands and fathers are those to whom women usually "yieldeth the government," he almost goes out of his way to note exceptions arranged by covenant, such as those between men and their concubines assigning custody of children.* But even in marriage "sometimes the government may belong to the wife only, sometimes also the dominion over the children shall be in her only; as in the case of a sovereign queen, there is no reason that her marriage should take from her the dominion over her children."[14]

Such statements hardly establish that Hobbes was an early advocate of women's rights, but, qualified and incomplete as they are, they do suggest that his view of family relations was somewhat at variance with his generally pronounced antipathy toward equality.

---

*Another example was "in the copulation of the Amazons with their neighbours, the fathers by covenant had the male children only, the mothers retaining the females." *The Elements*, 104.

In reminding his readers that, as he phrased it in *De Cive*, "the birth follows the belly," and in drawing attention to those rare circumstances in which men "yieldeth the government" to women, Hobbes could not have been influenced by the political or social thought of his time, which was silent on the subject of women and their rights. Even less likely is the possibility that Hobbes, like John Stuart Mill two centuries later, was reflecting the opinions of any particular woman, let alone of women as remarkable as Mary Wollstonecraft and Harriet Taylor. Though there is the merest hint in Aubrey, as was already noted, that Hobbes, who never married, was a misogynist, we have no reason to believe that Hobbes eschewed women acquaintances or that he was wholly without heterosexual interests.

According to Bishop Kennet, Hobbes was the father of an illegitimate daughter by an unidentified woman. Kennet's statement (referred to by Laird, Peters, and others) is indirectly supported by Hobbes's will. In that document, dated September 25, 1677, Hobbes bequeathed "to Elizabeth Alaby the Daughter of Thomas Alaby two hundred poundes and because she is an Orphan and committed by me to the Tuition of my Executor my will is that she should be maintained decently by my Executor till she be sixteene yeares of age and that then the said two hundred poundes be delivered unto her hands being intended for her furtherance in marriage but let her dispose of it as she please. . . ." If Elizabeth Alaby was in fact Hobbes's daughter rather than his granddaughter, he must have been at least seventy-four years of age when she was born, an achievement for Hobbes not out of keeping with a poem he wrote shortly after he dictated his will. As recorded by Aubrey, the poem, which has similarities with one written by Newcastle (see above) ran,

> Tho' I am now past ninety, and too old
> T' expect preferment in the court of Cupid,
> And many winters have mee ev'n so cold
> I am become almost all over stupid,
> Yet I can love and have a mistresse too,
> As fair as can be and as wise as fair;
> And yet not proud, nor anything will doe
> To make me of her favour to despair.
> To tell you who she is were very bold;
> But if i' th' character your selfe you find
> Think not the man a fool tho he be old
> Who loves in body fair a fairer mind.

Nothing is known either of Alaby or of the "wise as fair" mistress who inspired the poem.

But since we know nothing of these relationships and of their

significance in Hobbes's life, we are forced to conclude that his entire
experience of family life, apart from the years spent in the service of
the Devonshires, during the early part of which Bess must have been
a ghostly presence, was confined to the first fifteen years of his life in
Malmesbury. Perhaps, then, Hobbes's view of women and their roles
in the family owed much to that occasion during those years when
the curate, possibly long before his disappearance, was forced by his
character and circumstances to yield the government to Hobbes's
mother.

Whatever the origins of his opinions, Hobbes in *The Elements* and
later books was not primarily concerned with family relations. In all
of his political works, his paramount interest was in establishing
absolute sovereignty, preferably through the institution of absolute
monarcy, as the only alternative to chronic civil disorder, and in
defending sovereign power against any and all challenges based on
appeals to religion, natural law or natural rights, the social contract,
or any other body of principles that was inimical to, or that could be
interpreted by *dogmatici* and "orators" as inimical to, sovereign power.
If such challenges tending toward "rebellious actions" were to be
avoided, he asserted toward the end of *The Elements*, the "rooting
out" of certain opinions was necessary, among which were the following: "that a man can do nothing lawfully against his private conscience; that they who have the sovereignty, are subject to the civil
laws; that there is any authority of subjects, whose negative may hinder
the affirmative of the sovereign power; that any subject hath a propriety distinct from the dominion of the commonwealth; that there
is a body of the people without him or them that have the sovereign
power; and that any lawful sovereign may be resisted under the name
of a tyrant. . . ."[15]

Hobbes was never to abandon this view that certain opinions were
by their very nature seditious, or the appended belief that their "rooting out" required a complete change of climate in the universities. As
he put it, in the penultimate chapter of *The Elements*, "because opinions which are gotten by education, and in length of time are made
habitual, cannot be taken away by force, and upon the sudden: they
must therefore be taken away also, by time and education. And seeing
the said opinions have proceeded from private and public teaching,
and those teachers have received them . . . in the Universities, from
the doctrine of Aristotle and others . . . there is no doubt, if the true
doctrine concerning the law of nature, and the properties of a body
politic, and the nature of law in general, were perspecuously set down,
and taught in the Universities, but that young men, who come thither
void of prejudice, and whose minds are yet as white paper, capable

of any instruction, would more easily receive the same, and afterwards teach it to the people, both in books and otherwise. . . ."[16] To
the end of his life, Hobbes was to hold the universities in large part
responsible for the turmoil that culminated in the Civil War and its
immediate aftermath.

These doctrines and principles of *The Elements*, however, were
not formally published until 1650, by which time, as has already been
mentioned, Hobbes's reputation was based on *De Cive*. First published at Paris in 1642 in a small edition, and signed only with the
initials "T.H.," *De Cive*, in Latin, immediately attracted favorable
attention in France, where it served Hobbes as a kind of introduction
to influential circles of learning. One of these early admirers who was
important in facilitating this introduction was the French physician,
translator, traveler, and official historiographer royal to Louis XIV,
Samuel Sorbière (1610?–1670). Born near Uzès, in the south of France,
to a Protestant family, Sorbière while still a young man abandoned
both medical practice and Protestantism in favor of, respectively, the
cultivation and promotion of intellectual celebrities and their works,
and a militant Catholicism—which, however, did not preclude "much
addiction," as a biographer put it, "to his Pleasures."[17] Ingratiating
himself with two popes, Alexander VII and Clement IX, and several
prominent cardinals, among whom was Richelieu's successor, Maza-
rin (who awarded him a pension), Sorbière devoted much of his adult
life to writing polemics against Protestants and Protestantism, and
to translations. The works of Camden, More's *Utopia*, and other writings were rendered into French by Sorbière prior to his meeting
Hobbes, probably in 1645, to whom he may have been introduced by
Mersenne or Gassendi. In addition to being the first to translate *De
Cive* into French, Sorbière was responsible for the 1652 publication in
French of *The Elements*, and he considered for a time undertaking a
translation of *Leviathan*. Because of his background and familiarity
with Hobbes's thought and style of expression, Sorbière would have
been ideally qualified to produce a French *Leviathan*, but for unknown
reasons, and despite his view of Hobbes as the greatest of all political
philosophers, Sorbière did not translate Hobbes's greatest book.
Hobbes, meanwhile, remained on good terms with Sorbière for many
years after returning to England in 1651, and in 1661 he dedicated to
him his *Dialogus Physicus*, a critique of Boyle and the Royal Society
(and a republication of his discredited "demonstration" that the circle could be squared).

Undoubtedly, Sorbière's greatest service to Hobbes was as a kind
of literary agent, in which capacity he arranged the 1647 publication,
in Amsterdam, of three separate Latin editions of *De Cive*, followed

by two French editions in 1649.* Unhappily for Hobbes, Sorbière's promotional talents occasionally subverted his judicious instincts, with the result that some copies of the first 1647 edition featured an engraved portrait of Hobbes beneath which was the caption "Tutor to . . . the Prince of Wales," and the third edition printed the letters in praise of *De Cive* written by Mersenne and Gassendi, previously referred to, which were not intended for publication. Apparently, Hobbes's portrait and the inscription attached to it were deleted from all but a few copies of the first edition, but not before Hobbes, in a letter to Sorbière of March 22, 1647, had protested, "[T]he times are such, that I would willingly have paid a high price for [the portrait] either not to have been affixed, or at least for that inscription 'Principal Tutor to His Most Serene Highness the Prince of Wales' to have been removed, erased or torn out." Instructing Sorbière that Prince Charles's enemies would use the alleged association with himself and his doctrines as "pretexts for hurling the Royal Line into disfavor with the masses," Hobbes went on to admonish Sorbière that "whatever evil may arise thence . . . will, with my worst disgrace, be imputed to my foolishnes and vain ambition." Furthermore, he continued, "by this title my return to my country, if ever a desire of returning seizes me, has been precluded, and I do not see why, if England should be at peace, I should not wish to return, if it should be permitted in any way; for I am not the Teacher of the Prince of Wales, nor at all a part of the household . . . but such as any one of those who teach for a month. . . ." Sufficiently concerned to urge that the portrait or inscription, preferably both, be removed from copies already printed and at booksellers in London and Paris, Hobbes ended his letter with a message calculated to propel Sorbière into action: "Mersenne and all our very great friends say that is of importance both to me and the Prince of Wales that the inscription or better the whole portrait be removed. If there should be need of a moderate sum of money to do it, I shall pay it willingly."[18]

Hobbes's concern in 1647 that neither he nor *De Cive* be associated with the Prince of Wales appears, in retrospect, almost as exaggerated as his anxiety in 1640 about remaining in England. The thoroughly secular principles of *De Cive*, to be sure, were not popular

---

* The 1647 and 1649 editions of *De Cive* may have been published in Amsterdam because Sorbière was unable to obtain royal consent for a Paris edition. *De Cive*, however, was published in Paris in 1651 and 1660, in French translation, despite a Vatican decree at Rome of June 16, 1654, placing the book on the *Index Librorum Prohibitorum*. *De Cive*, in Latin, was again published at Amsterdam in 1657, 1669, and 1696, in addition to the English translation published in London in 1651 under the title *Philosophical Rudiments concerning Government and Society*.

in certain circles attached to the court of the exiled prince, notably in those dominated by Queen Henrietta Maria and her fellow Catholics, and allegations, now beginning to be heard, that Hobbes was an atheist, were capable of arousing to anger or worse many non-Catholics at the court and elsewhere. But Hobbes had friends as well in high places, including, in addition to the earl of Newcastle (through whom Hobbes may have procured his appointment to the prince as tutor in mathematics, "not Politics," as he insisted to Sorbière in a letter of October 4, 1646); Henry Bennet (1618–1685) first earl of Arlington and himself a secret Catholic; Sir Kenelm Digby, also a Catholic and chancellor to the queen (see above, p. 106); Sir William Petty, economist, statistician, and anatomist (who read Vesalius with Hobbes); the third earl of Devonshire, self-exiled in France from 1642 to 1645; the earl's cousin, the scientist Sir Charles Cavendish; and, at various times, such literary acquaintances as Abraham Cowley, William Davenant, and Edmund Waller. Clearly, Hobbes was not an isolated figure in exiled royalist circles in the years 1640–51, and though he undoubtedly had his enemies in Paris and Saint-Germain (where he resided much of the time), he was never as endangered by them as he sometimes suggested.

Hobbes, moreover, did not retrieve *De Cive* from his Dutch publisher in 1647, much less refuse his assent to the ten separate editions, in three languages, that appeared between 1647 and 1669. Despite the quoted letter to Sorbière, his concern about the damage he and his book could inflict upon the royal cause could not have been very great, and he may have had other, more cogent reasons to proceed with *De Cive*'s publication minus the portrait and inscription. Indeed, he hinted at such reasons when he shared with Sorbière his anxiety that his putative "title" might preclude his return to England "if England should be at peace." These remarkable sentences seem to indicate that as early as March 1647, the Civil War being virtually over, with Charles I a prisoner of Cromwell and his Roundheads, Hobbes, despite his royalist views and avowed loyalty to the king, was contemplating the end of his exile in France. Regarding the war as lost and well aware of Charles's inability to compromise even with the throne at stake, Hobbes may have considered his remaining longer in France a futile undertaking. No doubt he also was nudged in a homeward direction by the sucessful effort of his employer, the third earl of Devonshire, to reclaim his estates, which, had he remained abroad, might have been confiscated. But above all, Hobbes guessed that *De Cive*, however offensive some might find it, would not preclude his return to England provided nothing in the book connected him officially and formally with the royal family. Whatever his reasoning, our assumption that Hobbes was in 1647, in effect planning to be among "the first of all that returned" is compatible with his insistence to Sorbière and his Dutch publisher that neither his name nor any title conferred upon him be associated with the Prince of Wales. Hobbes's intention, in short, was much less to protect the prince than to protect himself.

But he did no return home for more than four years. Perhaps illness was a contributing factor in the delay; he was seriously ill in August 1647, and as late as November was still not fully recovered. About the middle of August, Hobbes wrote Sorbière on November 27, 1647, "I fell into a very serious and continual fever, so that not only sick in body but also damaged in mind, I could not even recognize friends who were visiting me, standing at my bedside. This fever kept me in bed for six weeks, afterwards departing [but then] breaking out into abcesses which confined me to bed for another four weeks, finally when the abcesses healed, an illness of the hips afflicted me, accompanied by the greatest pain. Now, however, the illness treats me more mildly and allows me occasionally to turn my attention to the affairs of friends." Hobbes's symptoms suggest he may have been suffering from septicemia, or blood poisoning, perhaps the result, not uncommon in those days, of an infected tonsil or septic sore throat. Typhoid fever, however, cannot be ruled out entirely.[19]

Even before his illness he may well have begun to doubt that "England should be at peace" for some time to come. The agitations across the Channel of John Lilburne and his Leveler followers (which must have impressed Hobbes as far more dangerous and seditious than any actions previously urged by Pym and Hampden), repeated mutinies in the New Model army, and, finally and no doubt decisively for Hobbes, the renewed outbreak of war culminating, in 1648, in yet another Scots invasion of England, may have convinced Hobbes that the uncertainties of France, where a civil war known as the Fronde began in the winter of 1648–49, were much to be preferred to those of his homeland.

In postulating that Hobbes's reaction to the initial title page of De Cive was motivated by self-interest or, more precisely, by a desire to safeguard his return to England, we are saying only that Hobbes in 1647, as well as before and afterward, was being true to his own principles, among which the preservation of life was paramount. In De Cive, as in The Elements and other books, Hobbes emphasized repeatedly that "the first foundation of natural right" is that "every man as much as in him lies endeavour to protect his life and members" and "use all means, and do all the actions, without which he cannot preserve himself."[20] Moreover, no other man's judgment as to means and actions can be rated equal to one's own, much less superior, for it is "contrary to right reason" that another man can be a better judge of the peril to oneself. Even in his defense of compacts obtained through fear, when he again resorted to the homely example of the robber promised a hundred pounds in return for sparing his life, Hobbes excepted contracts inimical to self-preservation. No one is obliged by any agreement, he insisted, "not to resist him who shall offer to kill, wound, or any other way hurt his body," even if resistance results in the "evil" of war, because "certain death is a greater evil than fighting." The right of self-preservation also nullifies contracts requiring a man "to accuse himself, or any other, by whose damage he is like to procure himself a bitter [sic] life." In addition, members of a family are not obligated by any compact to testify against each other "for in vain is that testimony which is presumed to be corrupted from nature."[21]

Surprisingly, Hobbes did not rule out testimony obtained by torture, notwithstanding his aversion to any proceeding that inflicted pain or death. Noting that "in a public trial [a man] may by torture be forced to make answer," Hobbes would go only so far as to justify any response, no matter how honest or dishonest. As he put it, "whether the party tortured . . . answer . . . true or false, or whether he answer not at all, whatsoever he doth, he doth it by right."[22] By "right" Hobbes meant right of self-preservation, or in the stated context, the right to attempt to avoid torture and the threat of death by giving any answer, or no answer. Unlike others of his time, and in defiance of certain ethical and moral codes, Hobbes did not insist on veracity, or the requirements of honor and integrity, in all circumstances. Though he did not make his disapproval explicit, he clearly did not believe that any dogma, religious or secular, justified the sacrifice of life individually or collectively; as he implied in referring to the death in battle of his friend Sidney Godolphin, no cause was worth a war, and no war was worth even a single death.

Security of life, for Hobbes, was not possible in a state of nature, that is, in a state without government, because such a state (as he was to repeat later in Leviathan) "is nothing else but a mere war of all against all." Since, without government, all men had equal right to all things, and one man was as good as another with even a weaker man finding "how easy a matter it is" to kill someone stronger, the state of nature was a state of fear. The natural condition of man, in other words, is not characterized by brotherly love, and "all great and lasting societies" originated "not in the mutual good will men had towards each other, but in the mutual fear they had of each other." The motive force that drew men together to establish a civil society, Hobbes insisted, was not affection, or trust, or respect, but distrust and suspicion of each other, "heed," and "a certain foresight of future evil"—or, in short, chronic anxiety about what could or would happen at any time.[23]

Those who disagree, he added, need only consider the lengths to which men go to lessen their fears even in "well-governed states, where there are laws and punishments." For instance, "particular men travel not without their sword by their sides . . . neither sleep they without shutting not only their doors . . . but also their trunks and coffers. . . . Can men give a clearer testimony of the distrust they have of each other, and all of all?" Indeed, Hobbes attached such importance to his argument, and perhaps was so impressed by his examples, that he repeated himself, adding some additional illustrations, a few pages further along in De Cive: "They who go to sleep, shut their doors; they who travel, carry their swords with them. . . . Kingdoms guard their coasts and frontiers with forts and castles; cities are compact with walls. . . ."*

But man's fears and apprehensions in civil society were as nothing compared with those of the "perpetual war" of the state of nature. In such a state even the victorious were so unsafe "it were to be accounted a miracle, if any, even the most strong, should (live) many years and (reach) old age." Where the state of nature rules, as in America "in this present age" and other countries in the past, nations are "few, fierce, short-lived, poor, nasty, and deprived of all that pleasure and beauty of life, which peace and society are wont to bring them." Hobbes was to condense and polish this statement in his much-quoted sentence in chapter 13 of Leviathan, reducing the evils of the natural state to five in number ("solitary, poor, nasty, brutish, and short"), but in De Cive he was not yet willing to overlook any and all calamities that beset man removed from established government, calamities that included, besides those mentioned above, "dominion of passions, war, fear, poverty, slovenliness, solitude, barbarism, ignorance, cruelty," murder, and theft.[24]

The alternative to the state of nature was strong, effective government, preferably in the form of absolute monarchy. In De Cive and other books, Hobbes stressed that the sovereign authority was to have the sole power to make war and peace, to decide disputes between

---

* The same argument appeared once more in Leviathan: ". . . consider . . . when taking a journey, he arms himself, and seeks to go well accompanied; when going to sleep, he locks his doors; when even in his house he locks his chests; and this when he knows there be laws and public officers, armed . . . [consider] what opinion he has of his fellow-subjects, when he rides armed; of his fellow-citizens when he locks his doors; and of his children, and servants, when he locks his chests. Does he not there as much accuse mankind by his actions, as I do by my words?" E.W., III, 114.

contentious religious and secular factions, to allocate and dispose of subjects' wealth and property, and to frame and interpret civil and ecclesiastic laws. Perhaps his most significant point was that the sovereign power, although in a crucial sense created by a social contract, was not a party to the contract and therefore not obligated in any way to honor its provisions. The sovereign, in effect, was above the contract, as he was above any particular interpretation of divine, natural, or civil law other than his own. In a century marked, in England, by two revolutions based to some extent on claims that the sovereign was bound by and responsible to a social contract, Hobbes's views could be regarded not only as unique but as reactionary. On the other side, his total indifference to any theory of sovereignty based on divine right could only offend royal fundamentalists. His essential message, that any government was better than no government, was at once too conservative for social-contract theorists and too radical for those who insisted the monarch held his appointment from God. Given Hobbes's extreme royalist views, the latter might have held their fire had Hobbes raised fewer questions in their minds, not about his belief in divine right, but about his belief in divinity itself. In that direction, however, Hobbes would go only so far.

Of lesser significance in *De Cive* and his other books, but of possible importance in understanding Hobbes, are his frequent fulminations, first encountered in *Thucydides*, against "orators" and those who preached and taught; generally, he is inclined to link "eloquence," especially in public assemblies and debates, with "want of judgement," unscrupulous ambition and demagoguery, or "democracy." Thus, "democracy" in *The Elements* "is no more than an aristocracy of orators, interrupted sometimes with the temporary monarch of one orator."[25] In *De Cive* "the tongue of man is a trumpet of war and sedition. . . . Pericles . . . sometimes by his elegant speeches thundered and lightened, and confounded whole Greece itself."[26] "Another reason why a great assembly is not so fit for consultation is, because every one who delivers his opinion holds it necessary to make a long-continued speech; and to gain the more esteem from his auditors, he polishes and adorns it with the best and smoothest language. Now the nature of eloquence is to make *good* and *evil, profitable* and *unprofitable, honest* and *dishonest*, appear to be more or less than indeed they are; and to make that seem *just* which is *unjust*. . . ." Again we hear that most "vulgar received opinions . . . are erroneous" and that "eloquence . . . as all the masters of rhetoric teach us" has as its end "not truth (except by chance), but victory . . . not to inform, but to allure." Finally, in *De Cive*, we are told that the notion one can know good and evil from "private knowledge" obtained through "natural reason" originated in "sick-brained men, who having gotten good store of holy words by frequent reading of the Scriptures, made such a connextion of them usually in their preaching, that their sermons, signifying just nothing, yet to unlearned men seemed most divine. For he whose nonsense appears to be a divine speech, must necessarily seem to be inspired from above."[27]

Hobbes may have derived these views from observations and reflections dating back to his Oxford student days, when regular church or chapel attendance was required of undergraduates. But as an adult he was not known to attend religious services frequently—he once confided to Aubrey that sermons could teach him nothing he did not already know—and we have no record of his presence at sessions of Parliament or other "great assemblies."* We can hardly question, however, that as a child Hobbes must often have been present when his father, the curate of Brokenborough, read the weekly "lesson" and delivered a sermon. Since we know that the elder Hobbes was in difficulties with his parishioners much of the time and that he was a "choleric" and occasionally violent man, we may speculate that Hobbes must have had many occasions to ponder the contrasts and contradictions between his father's "good store of holy words" and the use he made of them in everyday life. We have no information about the elder Hobbes's virtues as a preacher, but surely the possibility exists that he was skilled in making all manner of words "appear to be more or less" than they were, at least in connection with his own behavior, and that Hobbes may have entertained the thought more than once that the curate's sermons, homilies, and other pronouncements from the pulpit were an "eloquence . . . signifying just nothing." In other words, Hobbes's lifelong distrust of "orators," preachers, and teachers may have had its roots in his father's very considerable shortcomings and deficiences as a cleric.

This distrust was even more manifest in *Leviathan*, but almost ten years separated the first appearances of *De Cive* and Hobbes's *magnum opus*. The generally favorable reception accorded *De Cive* may have persuaded Hobbes not only to write a third original political work but to write it in his native language. *De Cive*, as has been noted, did not appear in English until 1651, and in publishing the English *Leviathan* almost twenty years prior to the Latin version, parts of which may have been written first (see below, 160–62), Hobbes knew

---

* Hobbes may well have been in attendance upon the second earl of Devonshire when the earl, as MP for Derbyshire, took his seat in the House of Lords. Whatever his personal experience of parliamentary "democracy" under James I and Charles I, it could not have extended beyond 1629, when Parliament was adjourned, not to meet again until 1640.

he would reach a much larger and somewhat different audience. Though he had frequently aired reservations about making political tracts available to the mass public—he clearly was of the opinion that the less ordinary people read, the better—he had no doubt of the suitability of his books, all of which urged submission, obedience, and unquestioning loyalty to the sovereign power.*

Hobbes's decision to embark upon *Leviathan* may also have received encouragement from his three closest French friends, Mersenne, Gassendi, and François Bonneau, seigneur du Verdus, who usually signed himself, and is known in the Hobbes literature as, Du Verdus. Marin Mersenne (1588–1648), to whom Hobbes devoted more grateful and affectionate attention than to anyone else in his *Autobiography*, was a friar at the Minim Convent de l'Annonciade in Paris, where his cell functioned as a kind of salon for such intellectual luminaries as Descartes, Peiresc, Roberval, Fermat, the Pascals, and Hobbes himself. Mersenne's own thought and writings, which were "characterized by wide scholarship and the narrowest theological orthodoxy,"[28] were much less important than his ability to recognize brilliance in others and his willingness to act, not always successfully, as their intermediary or go-between. To Hobbes he was particularly useful, introducing him to savants of almost all philosophical schools, acquainting him with the latest scientific discoveries, and offering him constructive criticisms of his ideas both written and unwritten. In his *Autobiography* Hobbes described Mersenne's role as follows: "If anyone discovered an important porism of a new principle it was to Mersenne he brought it; and in his own clear style, stripped of all figures of rhetoric, sententiousness, show, or subterfuge, he discussed with the learned the problems they brought him so that they could either weigh his answers on the spot or carry them home with them for further thought. Out of many discoveries he published the best, marking every one with its author's name. Mersenne was the Pole round which resolved every star in the world of science."

Born to a peasant family in northwestern France in the same year as Hobbes, Mersenne as a youth attended the famous Jesuit college of La Flèche, where he met and became a lifelong friend of Descartes.

---

*In his *Autobiography*, Hobbes mentions that from 1642 to 1646 he "was busy day and night" preparing to write *De Corpore*, eventually published in 1655, but that he abandoned the project when Prince Charles came to Paris in 1646. He then taught the prince mathematics for approximately six months and was seriously ill for another six months, afterward managing to finish *Leviathan*. He also was able to complete, though he does not refer to it in the *Autobiography*, a monograph entitled *A Minute or First Draught of the Optiques*, which he sent to Newcastle in 1646. The implied date for his beginning *Leviathan* is sometime between 1646 and 1648.

From 1611, when he was ordained a Minim friar, he devoted himself
to philosophy, but by the time he first met Hobbes, in 1635 or 1636,
his interests had begun to shift to mathematics and science. Though
as a friar his intellectual freedom was necessarily limited, Mersenne
was an admirer and even popularizer of Galileo as well as a vigorous
defender of Descartes against Catholic charges that his *Meditations*
and other writings were tainted by heresy. The conclusion of Galileo's trial in June 1633, however, seems to have inspired in him a
greater caution (which it also inspired in Descartes), and his scientific
and philosophical writings thereafter tend to be somewhat equivocal.
For example, a book of 1634 supported the church's role in interpret-
ing Scripture, provided a summary of Galileo's views and the first
two days of his trial, and disagreed with Galileo's claim that he had
supplied "necessary demonstrations" of his theories. According to
Mersenne, the question of the earth's motion was as yet undecided;
the truth of the matter could be established only by new data.[29]

Mersenne, whom Hobbes seems to have known longer than anyone else in France, probably introduced him to Pierre Gassendi (1592–
1655). Though he did not mention Gassendi in his *Autobiography*,
Hobbes, according to Aubrey, regarded him as "the sweetest-natured
man in the world": "they loved each other entirely." A native of Provence, Gassendi was educated in Digne and the University of Aix, where
he studied philosophy and theology. After taking holy orders in 1617,
he was appointed to the chair of philosophy at Aix, where, for a time,
he was an exponent of Aristotelian philosophy. Coming under the
influence of Galileo and Kepler, he grew disenchanted with Aristotle
and in 1624 published the first of several books critical of Aristotelian
philosophy. He seems not to have reached Paris until Hobbes arrived
there in 1640, by which time he had traveled in Flanders and Holland
and served as provost of the cathedral church of Digne. In 1642, at the
request of Mersenne, Gassendi published his objections to certain
fundamental propositions of Descartes, objections that must have
pleased Hobbes to exactly the same extent they displeased Descartes.
Six years later, illness forced him to retire to Toulon, where he spent
more than two years, but he was back in Paris in 1653 and died there
in October 1655, from what appears to have been tuberculosis.

Gassendi, however close he was to Hobbes, could not have influenced him much, and if he performed services similar to those of Mersenne, they are unknown. Though Gibbon termed him "le meilleur
philosophy des littérateurs, et le meilleur littérateur des philo-
sophes,"[30] his books, with the exception of biographies of Copernicus
and Peiresc, were, like those of Mersenne, less important than his role
as a critic and popularizer of the work of others. His clumsy empiri-

Pierre Gassendi (1592–1655). According to Aubrey, Hobbes and Gassendi "loved each other entirely."

cism and crude Epicureanism did not attract Hobbes, and thus when Hobbes placed Gassendi in the first rank of philosophers, we can assume that he did so more out of friendship than out of a genuine belief that Gassendi was the intellectual equal of the great thinkers of his time.

Hobbes may have met François Bonneau (1620–1675), known as Du Verdus, through Mersenne, directly or indirectly; possibly, the two first became acquainted at the home of still another member of Mersenne's "circle," the "rich 'virtuoso'" Montmor, "whose house became a chief meeting-place of the learned after Mersenne's death in 1648."*[31] The friendship between Hobbes and Du Verdus, however it began, was apparently closer and more intimate for many years than any other of Hobbes's friendships, though in intellectual terms it was distinctly one-sided.

Du Verdus, who until now has unaccountably been viewed by Hobbes scholars as a shadowy figure,[32] was the scion of a wealthy family from Bordeaux that had long been represented in the local parlement. Born in 1620, Du Verdus went to Paris in 1639, when he was nineteen years old, presumably to study mathematics. In the years immediately following he wrote an impressive exposé of the "méthode des tangents," which was long attributed to Roberval, and perhaps as a result became friendly with Mersenne. Early in 1644, by which time he must have met Hobbes, Du Verdus accompanied the French ambassador to Rome, where he became acquainted with Evangelista Torricelli (1608–1647), the brilliant pupil of Galileo who in 1643 invented the barometer; Du Verdus thereby became familiar with vacuum experiments even before Mersenne did. While he was in Italy, his former tutor somehow managed to place in jeopardy his inheritance, forcing his return home toward the end of 1645. Thereafter he was involved in interminable lawsuits, which may have been a reason why Hobbes, who in 1646 was considering taking up residence in the Du Verdus household, decided to remain in Paris.

Du Verdus apparently spent the tumultuous years of the Fronde

---

*According to Stephen (*Hobbes*, 40), Mersenne died in September 1648, "after great suffering under the hands of blundering surgeons." Perhaps Hobbes was present: "He was wont to say," reported Aubrey, "that he had rather have the advice, or take physique from an experienced old woman, that had been at many people's bed-sides, then from the learnedst but inexperienced physitian." Between Mersenne's death and that of Charles II in 1685, little had changed: "The poor King's body was purged and bled and cauterized and clystered and blistered. Red-hot irons were put to his shaven skull and his naked feet. His urine became scalding throught the lavish use of cantharides. Cupping-glasses and all the many weird resources of medicine at the time were applied. They all had one thing in common: they were extremely painful to the patient." Fraser, *Royal Charles*, 446.

in Bordeaux, but by 1653 he was back in Paris, where on September 29 he was granted permission to publish his translation into French of Bacon's *The Advancement of Learning (La Sagesse mystérieuse des anciens)*. But no copy of this book has ever been found, presumably because he was unable to find a printer.[33] In the following years Du Verdus wrote Hobbes a large number of letters, which are preserved at Chatsworth, about events in France and which, according to Robertson, were "(more and more suggestive of monomania) concerning the persecution to which he was subjected by his family, in league with the ecclesiastical authorities at Bordeaux."[34] Finally, in 1660, his own translation of the first two parts of *De Cive*—he omitted the part dealing with religion—was published in Paris. In dedicating the book to Louis XIV, Du Verdus, an unswerving supporter of absolute monarchy, pleaded with the king to make *De Cive* required reading in the schools; the only two "demonstrative sciences," he informed Louis, were Euclid's *Elements* and Hobbes's *Elements (De Cive)*.[35] Though Du Verdus had earlier considered also translating *Leviathan* and had in January 1657 sent Hobbes a preliminary version in French of chapter 4, he did not further pursue the project. In view of certain reactions to his *De Cive* translation, perhaps it was just as well.[36]

Du Verdus's last years were unhappy ones. Depressed by events in his own life and apparently out of favor with the French court as well as the Catholic hierarchy—in connection with which his befriending Hobbes could not have helped him—he turned somewhat misanthropic with, as a French account put it, "a taint of mysticism."[37] When he died at Bordeaux on August 20, 1675, aged fifty-nine, he left a will with the curious sentence "Dieu m'avait donné des amis; il me les ôtés; ils m'ont laissé; je les laisse et n'en fais point mention" ("God gave me friends; he took them away; they abandoned me; I leave them and make no further mention of them").[38] Presumably, he was referring to "friends" other than Hobbes; Hobbes's *Autobiography* of 1672 was addressed to Du Verdus, who was writing Hobbes as late as March 7, 1674. But we cannot be certain. Though Hobbes usually was a faithful and prompt correspondent, no letters from Hobbes to Du Verdus have survived. Did Du Verdus destroy them, or were they lost during the subsequent centuries? At three hundred years' distance, no student of the subject can venture more than a guess.

No guesswork is called for, however, in assessing the relationship between Hobbes and René Descartes (1595–1650), the most famous mathematician and philosopher of his time. Familiar with Descartes's work, principally his *Discourse on Method* (1637), while still in England, Hobbes shortly after arriving in France was asked by

Mersenne to comment anonymously on Descartes's *Meditations*, which had not yet been published. Mersenne had been requested by his friend and former fellow student to circulate the manuscript for criticism; in sending it to Hobbes, Mersenne undoubtedly entertained hopes that an exchange of views between the two would mature into friendship or at least mutual respect. But despite his efforts and those of Sir Charles Cavendish and Sir Kenelm Digby, Hobbes and Descartes were wary of each other almost from the start. Whether they were individually and privately aware, as scholars have been ever since, that their agreement was more fundamental than their disagreement, neither ever gave any evidence that he had anything important to learn from the other.[39] Indeed, the area of agreement may have been the main source of difficulty; any similarity of thought may have raised questions, in their minds if not in the minds of all others, about priority and originality of ideas. As was mentioned earlier, Hobbes probably was most comfortable in the company of those whose intellects he regarded as inferior to his own. We have no reason to suspect that Descartes, who quarreled with many of the leading mathematicians and who was remarkably sparing even in his praise of Galileo, was very different. In character and personality there were also resemblances: Descartes "was not disposed to be a martyr" for his beliefs, and neither was Hobbes;[40] both prided themselves on having read few books (which may not have been true); neither had any visual sense (no work of art or miracle of scenery is ever mentioned in their writings); neither married or is known to have had a long relationship with a woman (or, enjoying such a relationship, let others know of it); and both, in their private habits, were somewhat egocentric and idiosyncratic (Hobbes with his rubdowns and "prick songs" [see below, pp. 224–26], and Descartes spending much time in bed).

Of these latter similarities, however, they were totally unaware, and had they been conscious of them, they would undoubtedly have insisted that any personal resemblances were far outweighed by doctrinal differences. These differences, as expressed in Hobbes's "Objections" to Descartes's *Meditations*, had at their core Descartes's dualism and, in particular, his claim that he had established the existence of the soul. Taking exception to Descartes's "Cogito ergo sum," in the third meditation, Hobbes argued that while the act of thinking supposes an "I" that thinks, as Descartes had postulated, the act of thinking cannot be understood apart from that which thinks, and, Hobbes continued, contrary to Descartes's assertion, thinking cannot be attributed to such noncorporeal things as "the mind, the spirit, the understanding, the reason." If such attribution made sense, one could "say: I am exercising thought, *hence* I am thought; *or* I am using my intellect, *hence* I am intellect. *For in the same way I might say,* I am walking; *hence* I am the walking. . . . *Yet all Philosophers distinguish a subject from its faculties and activities, i.e., from its properties and essences; for the entity itself is one thing, its essence another. Hence it is possible for a thing that thinks to be the subject of the mind, reason, or understanding, and hence to be something corporeal; and the opposite of this has been assumed, not proved."*[41]

As a materialist who insisted on the tangible and corporeal nature of things, and who believed that through faith and reason man can know only that God is, not what he is, Hobbes could hardly accept, much less endorse, a dualism which maintained that God, the soul, and spiritual essences were as real as visible and measurable objects in the physical world. Hobbes took particularly strong exception to Descartes's assumption that he had "proved" that God exists, and he apparently always suspected that Descartes's religiosity was more opportunistic than sincere. "When I think of a man," Hobbes commented in his "Objection V," "I recognize an idea or image, with the figure and colour as its constituents; and concerning this I can raise the question whether or not it is the likeness of a man. . . . [But] with the most holy name of God; we have no image, no idea corresponding to it. . . . But just as one born blind who had frequently been brought close to a fire and has felt himself growing warm, recognizes that there is something which made him warm, and, if, he hears it called fire, concludes that fire exists, though he has no acquaintance with its shape or colour, and has no idea of fire nor image . . . so a man, recognizing that there must be some cause of his images and ideas, and another previous cause of this cause and so on continuously, is finally carried on to a conclusion, or to the supposition of some eternal cause . . . and calls it God."*[42]

Descartes, as may be imagined, was not impressed by these arguments, and his replies to Hobbes's "Objections" became shorter and sharper. To Hobbes's "Objection VII"—stating, in part, "If there is no idea of God . . . as seems to be the case, the whole of this argument collapses"—Descartes replied little more than "If there is an idea of God (as it is manifest there is), the whole of this objection collapses."[43] Accusing Hobbes of "bad reasoning" throughout the "Objections," Descartes was even more incensed when he received, from Mersenne, also in 1641, Hobbes's criticisms of his *Dioptric* (1637), subsequently published in Mersenne's *Optique* (1644). Suspecting that the author of these criticisms was the same Englishman who had

---

* Hobbes's reasoning and phrasing is very close to that of the *The Elements,* more than ten years earlier. See above, pp. 127–28.

written *De Cive*, which he apparently read shortly after its first appearance in 1642,* Descartes accused Hobbes of plagiarism in connection with Hobbes's view of subjective sense phenomena (which Hobbes claimed, in the letter to Newcastle quoted earlier, he had advanced as early as 1630) and refused to have anything more to do with him. Though they apparently met in 1648 and, according to Charles Cavendish, "had some discourse" and areas of agreement (which he did not identify), they disagreed "extreamelie" on the nature of hardness.[44] Hobbes, on his part, had somewhat more respect for Descartes than Descartes had for him, but his final judgment appears to have been, in Aubrey's words, that had Descartes "kept himself to Geometrie he had been the best geometer in the world but that his head did not lye for philosophy. . . . (Hobbes) could not pardon him for his writing in defence of transubstantiation, which he knew was absolutely against his opinion and donne meerly to putt a compliment [on] the Jesuites." Adding a critical note of his own, Aubrey reported hearing "Mr. Oates [presumably Titus Oates (1649–1705), the infamous fabricator of the "Popish Plot"] say that the Jesuites doe much glorie that (Descartes) had his education under them. 'Tis not unlikely that the Jesuites putt him under that treatise."

Slightly more than three years separated Hobbes's meeting with Descartes from his return to England, and for a variety of reasons they could not have been happy ones. Mersenne's death in September 1648, Gassendi's departure for the south of France at about the same time, and Du Verdus's protracted absence from Paris on family business deprived Hobbes of his most loyal admirers and closest companions in France, and in a sense marked the beginning of a long period of intellectual isolation and perhaps personal loneliness that was not to end when Hobbes was once more on home ground.[45] No longer

---

* Descartes wrote of *De Cive*, "I think the author, [whose name he could not have known at that time] a much greater Master of Morality than of Metaphysicks, or natural Philosophy, tho' I can by no means approve of his Principles or Maxims, which are very bad and very dangerous, because they suppose all Men to be wicked, or give them occasion to be. His whole design is to write in favour of Monarchy, which might be done to more Advantage than he has done, upon Maxims more virtuous and solid. He has wrote likewise greatly to the disadvantage of the Church and *Roman* Catholic Religion, so that if he is not particularly supported by some powerful interest, I do not see how he can escape having his Book censured." Quoted in "The Author's Life" (by John Campbell), in *The Moral and Political Works of Thomas Hobbes of Malmesbury* (London, 1750), xiv. Hobbes may have been alluding to this opinion, or he may have had other reasons to believe, as he confided to Sorbière in 1646, that "if M. Descartes should find out that publication of my book is under way (this book or any other) I know for certain he will block it, if he can, this is one thing I know, please believe me." Letter of May 16, 1646, in G. C. Robertson, "Some Newly Discovered Letters of Hobbes," *Mind*, 15 (1890), 442.

welcome at the English court in exile, because of *De Cive*, and for the same reason disliked and regarded with suspicion by the French court and the Catholic church, Hobbes began to fear, as he expressed it in his *Autobiography*, that he would suffer the same fate as the regicides Ascham and Dorislaus, that is, assassination by royalists. Once again, no doubt, he was exaggerating his personal peril, but his sense that he was in danger, whether well-founded or not, could only have added to his unhappiness.

He also was seriously ill at least twice between 1647 and 1651. Though Aubrey reports that Hobbes "grew healthier" after he reached forty years of age and developed at that time "a fresh, ruddy, complexion," two major illnesses in four years and other health problems tend to suggest either than Hobbes as a young man was afflicted by frequent sickness or that the faithful Aubrey, as sometimes happened, had his facts wrong. Hobbes, of course, did survive to celebrate his ninety-first birthday, but he also suffered from illnesses related to aging and to the times in which he lived.

One of these illnesses may have induced or contributed to the "shaking Palsey in his handes" (Aubrey) that began in Paris before 1650 and grew worse in the following years. From the time he was sixty, or beginning about 1648, Hobbes himself told Sorbière, he suffered from pain in his side and unsteadiness in gait. Shortly before or after 1650 Hobbes may have begun to manifest symptoms not unlike those of paralysis agitans, or Parkinson's disease. Usually a progressive disorder of middle or late life, paralysis agitans is characterized by "stooped posture . . . stiffness and slowness of movement . . . rigidity of facial expression, and the rhythmic tremor of the limbs which subsides on active willed movement or complete relaxation." The mind is not usually affected, but emotional factors play an important role, the disease being aggravated by anxiety, tension, and unhappiness in general.[46] Unfortunately, we have too few facts about Hobbes's health to make any diagnoses of his illnesses.

While we do not know when Hobbes began to employ household servants and others to take dictation of both his books and his letters, we learn from Aubrey that he could not write legibly after 1665 or 1666 and that for several years before he died he was "so Paralyticall that he wase scarce able to write his name."

In August 1651 Hobbes again was seriously ill, and on this occasion he was seen by the French physician, scholar, and bibliophile Guy Patin (1601–1672), who reported, in a letter of September 22, "I found him in a very bad state: constricted breathing, pain, vomiting—such suffering that he must have had thoughts of killing himself. He is a stoic philosopher, melancholic, and in addition to that English.

I made him a little better with food and baths, but he refused to be bled, though in great need of it, under the pretext he was sixty-four years old. The following day, I being a little more in his good graces, he permitted me to bleed him, which brought him much relief. He alleged to me afterward, as an excuse, that he did not think anyone his age could have so much bad blood. After that, we became comrades and great friends. I let him drink a little beer he wanted, and after a purgative, he felt much better. He thanked me very much and said he wished to send me something beautiful when he returned to England. May he soon return there gay and joyous, and without more thoughts of repaying me."[47] Whether Hobbes, who was in England a few months later, remembered his wish, is not known.*

Patin's letter provides the last detailed glimpse we have of Hobbes in France.[48] The final months of his fourth and by far his longest visit to the Continent marked the end of his travels anywhere but in England, and they also brought to a conclusion the years when he had been most creative, most respected, and—the hypothesis is reasonable—most loved.

---

*The illness treated by Patin may have lingered on. According to the biographical sketch of Hobbes in the 1750 English edition of his works, his return to England was "partly on Account of an Indisposition in his Stomach, from which by the Use of proper Medicines he perfectly recovered." *Moral and Political Works*, xvii.

"LEVIATHAN"

WHEN HOBBES DISEMBARKED AT Dover in November or December 1651, full of apprehensions about the future, he was returning to an England very different from the country he had left.* Of all the vast changes that had taken place during the preceding eleven years, the most far-reaching was the transformation of the government from a monarchy to a commonwealth (in disregard of the claim of Hobbes's former mathematics pupil to be Charles II). The third earl of Devonshire remained in charge of his estates, but he was prohibited from taking up his seat in the House of Lords, and rarely visited London. Many of Hobbes's friends were dead or remained abroad, and the "circles" of Great Tew and Welbeck were gone forever; never again was Hobbes to know or be part of a gathering of minds similar to those that had been brought together before the Civil War by Falkland and Newcastle. The English counterparts of Mersenne, Gassendi, and Du Verdus simply did not exist.

Hobbes, too, was a different man. Practically unknown to his countrymen in 1640, he now was a controversial figure whose views of politics and religion were familiar to royalty and commoners alike. In 1650 his earlier *Elements of Law* had been published in two parts, *Humane Nature* and *De Corpore Politico*, and the first English translation of *De Cive* was issued before his arrival. *Leviathan*, which had been published while he was still in France and which was to generate more argument than any other book, was beginning to stir discussion. (Two further printings of *Thucydides*, in 1634 and 1648, had also made an appearance.) While Hobbes was not yet as famous or as

---

*"I returned to my native land," he wrote in his *Autobiography*, "not well assured of safety, but because there was nowhere else I could be safer. It was cold, the snow was deep, I was old, the wind was biting and fierce, my horse restive, and the road full of pot-holes."

notorious as he was to become, he was already, so to speak, a remarked man, and above all, in late 1651, there was the question how his writings and he himself would be treated by Cromwell and his government. Aware of his cautionary nature and reluctance to take physical risks, we can imagine that Hobbes must have made certain inquiries and received certain assurances before packing for London, but he also knew very well that some covenants, contrary to his teachings, were made only to be broken.

Because he was uncertain of his treatment by Cromwell, Hobbes may not have wanted to reestablish immediately a close relationship with the royalist Devonshires, or perhaps, for similar reasons, the third earl did not wish to be closely identified with his controversial and possibly dangerous former tutor. Whatever the case, Hobbes made his residence in London and remained there for some years. The future fourth earl and first duke of Devonshire, then a lad of eleven, was dividing his time between Hardwick and the smaller family estate at Latimers, in Buckinghamshire (his father did not wish to be seen too often at regal, costly Chatsworth), with frequent visits to his grandmother Christian's house in Roehampton.[1] The boy's education had not been neglected while Hobbes was in France, but records do not indicate whether his tutor during some of those years was the minister and playwright Dr. Henry Killigrew, who in 1658 accompanied him to France and Italy when he, like his father and grandfather before him, made the grand tour. So far as we know, Hobbes had little if any direct contact with this latest scion of the Devonshires, which was fortunate for Hobbes, if not for the future first duke. As an adolescent, the young man resembled his "waster" grandfather rather more than his less colorful father, and he resembled him to excess. By the time he was thirty years old, in 1670, he was an accomplished rake who had compiled a record of brawls, duels, debts, mistresses, and illegitimate children that was unmatched in the entire history of both Cavendish branches. Long before then, Hobbes must have thought, if he thought about the future duke at all, that he was well out of it.

While in France, however, he had not been totally removed from involvement in matters affecting the fourth generation of the Devonshires. In October 1646, when the third earl was seeking a tutor for his six-year-old son, Hobbes wrote Sorbière that he was prepared to suggest a "M. du Prat" on the recommendation of Gassendi and others, and that if du Prat desired "a situation suiting his merit," he would try as much as he could, "for the sake of both, (to help him) move from Lyons to London."[2] Du Prat, however, apparently was not appointed to the position, and two years later the third earl again turned to Hobbes for advice concerning the education of his heir and the proper allowance to bestow upon the eight-year-old boy. Writing the earl from Saint-Germain in 1648, Hobbes observed, "It is a great allowance, 50*li* (pounds) ayere for a young university scholler, unlesse he hath better learning then is usually taught in the University. That which is requisite, for my young Lord is the Latine tongue and the mathematiques, I mean whilst he is yonge; for other knowledge, as the knowledge of the passions and manners of men, of the nature of Government, and the reading of history or poets otherwise than to exercise his Latine tongue, he is and will be a great while too yonge. If the young man propounded by Mr. Payne can teach him Latine well, and the beginnings of Mathematics, and be such as will imprint in him piety without superstitious admiration of preachers, he may deserve his allowance. In these partes I find none yet that can do this."[3]

Hobbes may have had other thoughts about education that he never communicated to the third earl or to anyone except Aubrey. Aubrey, who was interested in theories of pedagogy and who in 1669 wrote an essay entitled *An Idea of Education of Young Gentlemen . . .* , was persuaded by a friend, a "Mr. J. Ward," that "the only time of Learning is from nine to sixteen, afterwards Cupid beginns to Tyrannize." Perhaps Hobbes strongly agreed, for he told Aubrey that the "Duke Of Buckingham [George Villiers (1628–1687), second duke of Buckingham] had at Paris when he was about twenty yeares old, desired Him to Reade Geometrie to him: his Grace had great naturall parts, and quicknesse of wit; Mr. Hobbes read, and his Grace did not apprehend, which Mr. Hobbes wondered at: at last, Mr. Hobbes observed that his Grace was at mastrupation (his hand in his Codpiece)." In concluding his account of this vignette, Aubrey observed, "This is a very improper age; for that reason for learning."[4] Aubrey seems also to have believed that French boys of *any* age were uneducable; "like the shearing of Hogges," he noted in his essay, "they make a great crie and little wool; thir mindes do chiefly run on the propagation of their race."[5] On this point, Hobbes, who was far more familiar with the ways of the French, would probably not have agreed.

But whether he agreed or not, he had more urgent business on his mind than the sexual proclivities of young Frenchmen or even those of the almost-adolescent future duke of Devonshire. *Leviathan*, which may have preceded him to London by six months,* had been accompanied by stories and rumors, not all of them false, of the most

---

* According to Stephen (*Hobbes*, 40) and Robertson (*Hobbes*, 69), *Leviathan* was published "about the middle of 1651." Hobbes's dedication of the book to Francis Godolphin, the brother of his dead friend Sidney, was dated "Paris. April 15. 1651."

damaging kind. Many had heard of the treatment accorded Hobbes in late October when he had presented a handwritten copy of *Leviathan*, beautifully bound in vellum, to his former pupil, the future Charles II; Charles, who had returned to Paris following his defeat at Worcester, had accepted the book, but not long afterward Hobbes found he was persona non grata at the exiled royal court.* There were also reports, believed and perhaps facilitated by Clarendon and others, that much of *Leviathan*, the final "Review and Conclusion," especially, had been written to gain the favor of Cromwell; Clarendon even cast doubts on Hobbes's motives in dedicating *Leviathan* to Francis Godolphin. Claiming to have been the first to inform Hobbes of the legacy of 200 pounds that had been left him by Sidney Godolphin, Clarendon had suggested, according to his own account, that if Hobbes "found some way secretly (to the end there might be no public notice of it in regard of the Parliament) to demand it of his Brother *Francis Godolphin,* (who in truth had tole me of it) he would pay it. This information was the ground of the Dedication of this Book to him, whom Mr. Hobbes had never seen." *(Brief View and Survey of . . . Leviathan,* 7.) But if Hobbes was not paid the 200 pounds, ostensibly in the form of a "gift" expressing Francis Godolphin's gratitude, until the "Dedication" was published in 1651, his reference to the legacy in his *Autobiography* makes little sense, for he wrote there, "To these (500 pounds in his possession when he fled to Paris) another £200 were added together with a great and lasting blow. Godolphin, thou art dead! . . . From my native land also came to me a pension of £80 a year." The clear implication is that he received the legacy not long after Sidney Godolphin's death in 1643. Whatever the facts of the matter, Clarendon's main thrust was that Hobbes had promulgated certain doctrines in *Leviathan* because, Hobbes had admitted to him, *"The truth is, I have a mind to go home."* Such reports gained credence when royalist agents observed, or thought they observed, as one of them put it, that "Hobbes is caressed at London for his traitorous and rebellious tenets."[6] Perhaps some were even persuaded that the most malicious rumor of all was true, namely, that Cromwell's esteem for *Leviathan* was such that he had asked Hobbes to serve as his secretary.[7] Those who trusted the rumor would have had no difficulty also believing that the face of *Leviathan*, shown on the pictorial title

---

* The king's copy of *Leviathan* eventually made its way to the British Library, where, with special permission, it may be seen today. The royal copy is identical to the first printed versions except for minor changes, mostly typographical, and the title page, which is drawn by hand rather than printed from an engraving (see below, pp. 158–60). The penman employed by Hobbes to transcribe *Leviathan* expressly for the king is unknown.

page as a human figure wearing a crown (Hobbes's "Mortal God"), was the face of Cromwell himself.[8]

If Cromwell read *Leviathan*, or had any particular feeling for or against Hobbes, he did not share this information with anyone. The reception accorded *Leviathan* when it was first published, however, does not suggest that the book was better received by the men of the Protectorate than by those who had advised the exiled Charles II in Paris not to see Hobbes again. Although there were three separate printings of *Leviathan*, all carrying the date 1651, careful research has established that only the first was published in London in 1651. So far as is known, despite the demand for copies and what appears to have been a flourishing black market for the book, *Leviathan* in English was not published again in London until the eighteenth century; the only other London editions prior to that time were two in Latin, which appeared in 1676 and 1678, respectively.* The first separate edition in Latin (1670), a Dutch edition (1667), and a Latin edition of Hobbes's works that included *Leviathan* (1668), were published in Amsterdam.[9] The "caressing" of Hobbes by the Roundheads that was alleged to have taken place, in short, either was greatly exaggerated by his enemies or did not extend to permitting the publication of a second English edition of *Leviathan*.

The first three issues of Hobbes's greatest book, each dated 1651, are most readily distinguished from each other by ornaments at the foot of the printed title pages. The first issue, and true first edition, has a "head" as its ornament and is therefore known as the "head" edition or issue; Andrew Crooke, the printer "at the Green Dragon in St. Paul's Church-yard," subsequently was to print other books by Hobbes until his death in 1674, following which his son William continued the practice. The second edition or issue, with a "bear" at the foot of its printed title page, is referred to as the "bear" edition, and while it also lists "Ckooke" as the printer, it was probably published in Holland "not long after 1651."[10] The third edition or issue, called the "ornaments" edition because of the ornaments at the foot of the printed title page, again has Crooke as the printer but may also have been printed in Holland sometime after 1668, perhaps even as late as 1680. Nothing is known of the size of the three printings, but the first could not have been large, in view of the demand for books that led to the second and third editions or issues.

---

* On September 3, 1668, Pepys wrote in his diary, "To my bookseller's for Hobbes's 'Leviathan,' which is now mightily called for; and what was heretofore sold for 8s. [shillings] I now give 24s. for at the second hand, and is sold for 30s., it being a book the bishops will not let be printed again." Quoted in Robertson, *Hobbes*, 196.

The three editions can be further distinguished from each other by differences in the engraved pictorial title page. Though the same plate may have been used for all three editions, the reproduction in the "head" edition is darker and sharper than those in the other two editions. That of the "bear" edition is usually somewhat fainter and worn, and in the "ornaments" edition the reproduction "has been retouched, a comparison revealing differences in, for instance, Leviathan's crown and sword-hilt, his hands and face, and in the shading of the landscape in the background."[11]

There are also textual differences between the three editions. In the first, or "head," edition, the list of errata that follows the table of contents corresponds exactly to errors or misprints in the text, none of which have been corrected. In the second, or "bear," edition, the list of errata is identical to that of the "head" edition, but some errata, such as spelling mistakes, have been corrected. The list of errata in the third, or "ornaments," edition includes a misprint, and more of the errata in the first and second editions have been corrected. In addition, the type and paper used in the printing of the "ornaments" edition differ from those of the other two editions.

Clearly, the "head" edition is *the* first edition of *Leviathan*, but apparently copies were not uniform. The five or more different watermarks that have been found on engraved title pages of this edition—some engraved title pages have no watermarks whatever—and minor printing differences perhaps indicate there are at least six different issues of the "head" edition, even without taking into account the existence of several so-called large-paper copies, the pages of which are more than one and one-half inches longer and wider than those of other copies.*[12] These variations do not admit of any simple explanation, but one possible reason for them is that Crooke, overburdened with work, or unwilling to accept total responsibility for the publication of *Leviathan*, found other printers with whom he could share both the work and the responsibility.†

Still another mystery of the first edition is the identity of the

---

* In 1984 Jeremy Norman, a San Francisco antiquarian book dealer, offered for sale a large-paper *Leviathan* first edition priced at $15,000!

† Though Andrew and William Crooke printed more works of Hobbes than any other London printer, Hobbes's books between 1650 and 1660 were issued by a variety of printers. A detailed study of the books and pamphlets published by them could reveal whether any was involved in printing the first "head" edition of *Leviathan*, or other editions.

Title page of the first edition, first issue, of Leviathan (1651).

Non est potestas Super Terram quæ Comparetur ei Iob. 41. 24.

LEVIATHAN
Or
THE MATTER, FORME
and POWER of A COMMON-
WEALTH ECCLESIASTICALL
and CIVIL

By THOMAS HOBBES
of MALMESBVRY.

London
Printed for Andrew Crooke
1651

artist who engraved the title page depicting Leviathan, one of the masterpieces of English engraved title pages. In 1898 a catalogue of the works of Wenceslaus Hollar (1607–1677), the Prague-born artist and engraver who emigrated to England and was an acquaintance of Hobbes, credited him with the engraving, but in 1934 a definitive catalogue of English engraved title pages recorded the engraver as unknown. In the interval, those who doubted that the engraving was Hollar's work had argued effectively that the engraving was too crude, the details too inexact, to have been done by Hollar. The buildings shown, especially a fortress-type structure in the small left-hand panel and the small church directly across from it, one close student of the engraving insisted, did not reflect Hollar's knowledge of architecture, and the inscription beginning "Non est potestas" at the top of the engraved page could not be recognized as one of Hollar's lettering styles. Other comparisons demonstrated "a slackness of attention, failure of intelligence . . . and indifference to possibilities of perspective, all of which seem equally un-Hollar like."[13] On the other hand, the drawing of the pictorial title page (in the copy presented in Paris to Charles) was suggestive of Hollar: "The peculiarly 'soft' quality of the drawing, especially noticeable in the representation of Leviathan's face, is almost a Hollar trade-mark in itself, for instance, and his slight clumsiness with the human figure might be thought to be reflected in Leviathan's somewhat nerveless wrists. A stronger indication, however, is to be found in the treatment of Leviathan's eyes: this can be matched elsewhere in Hollar's work."[14]

The "inescapable" conclusion, therefore—or at least "inescapable" until nullifying evidence is provided—is that "Hollar is the artist of the drawn title-page presented to Charles II, and the engraved title-page was made in England from a Hollar drawing sent over by Hobbes along with his manuscript . . . the engraving's slightly reduced degree of effectiveness in expressing the sense of the book also might be thought to suggest a craftsman not in touch with either the original artist or the author."[15] For the presentation copy, which Hobbes must have taken great pains to acquire, he may well have turned to Hollar for the drawing, knowing him to have been "Charles's old tutor in drawing, whose style could be expected to suit the royal taste."[16] Since Hollar spent the Civil War years in Holland, Sorbière, who was often there arranging publication of Hobbes's works and attending to other business, may have made the arrangements, but the likelihood is greater that Hobbes dealt directly with Hollar in either Paris or Amsterdam. For the engraving and even more for the drawing, "doubling the functions of today's (book) blurb and dust-jacket design," are succinct summaries of Hobbes's thought and *Leviathan's* principal themes, themes that Hollar, who probably had not read the lengthy and as yet unpublished manuscript, could have known about only from contact with Hobbes himself.[17]

Close collaboration between Hobbes and Hollar is reflected in the extraordinary images and organization of the pictorial title page, and while not all the symbolic meanings are clear, Hollar's ability to understand and appreciate Hobbes's intention in *Leviathan* is manifest throughout. On the lower left side, Hollar drew five small panels depicting the emergence of civil society from the state of nature and the "war of all against all" (the battlefield of the bottom panel) through the termination of fighting (the stacked weaponry and silent cannon of the next two panels), to the crown, symbolizing sovereignty (the fourth panel), and the fortified castle or fortress, representing the seat of power (the topmost small panel). On the lower right side, the panels of which deal with religious equivalents of the themes shown on the other side, the artist portrayed (reading upward) a church council deciding a doctrinal dispute, a collection of two- and three-pronged theological weapons perhaps symbolizing both the division between Catholics and Protestants and the schism within the English church between Puritans, Presbyterians, and Anglicans,* what appears to be a cloud emitting lightning bolts (God's wrath raining down on the warring factions?), a miter, or bishop's hat, symbolizing religious authority, and a church, the seat of religious power. Commanding these ten panels and the landscape above them of city and countryside is, of course, Leviathan, Hobbes's "Mortal God," who holds in his right hand the sword of state, and in his left hand the pastoral staff of religion. Leviathan's body is made up of innumerable heads and upper backs of tiny figures, all of them facing Leviathan rather than the viewer, the meaning of which, for Hobbes, was that Leviathan, or the "State, (in latine CIVITAS) which is but an Artificiall Man," moves and is moved by "Naturall Man."[18] But in presiding, God-like, over the world, and in impressing us as greater and mightier than the sum of these figures, Leviathan may be seen as much more than an "Artificiall Man," and this, too, was Hobbes's intention.

Less easy to evaluate, perhaps, is the claim, already mentioned, that the face of Leviathan was drawn in such a way as to resemble Charles I or Cromwell (see above, note 8). The difficulty of believing that Hobbes would in 1651 have wanted his book adorned by a por-

---

* Robertson *(Hobbes,* 69) sees the subject matter of this panel as "the weapons of logical fence (three-pronged fork of syllogism and other forks, with the dilemmatic horns," and, directly across from it, "armour." Each of the nine prongs carries a label that reads, from left to right, "Syl-," "logis-," "me," "Spiritual," "Direct," "Indirect," "Temporal," "Real," "Intentional"; the horns connecting the prongs are labeled "Dilemma."

trait of the dead Charles I as a "Mortal God" is more than equaled by the greater difficulty of thinking that Hobbes, eager for the favor of the future Charles II, would have presented the king with a likeness of his enemy Cromwell. In an effort to resolve the matter, the rather ingenious suggestion has been made that the engraved title pages of the "head" and "bear" editions display a face "suggestive of the features of Oliver Cromwell," while the face on the drawn title page, "if one reduces the luxuriance of facial hair, is in fact strongly suggestive . . . of Charles II himself . . . we need only turn to Hollar's own acknowledged engraving of Charles, dating from 1650, in which appear the same pouched eyes as in the drawing . . . and the same rather heavy strong nose, in an otherwise somewhat suety face, marked by thick eyebrows. . . . In both versions of the title-page the only real difference between the face depicted (which had to be generalized a little for iconic purposes) and that of [Charles II] lies in the addition of a beard too small to conceal the features being portrayed, and a fuller moustache." In other words: Hobbes may have wanted "both potential leaders of Great Britain . . . to see their own image in that of Leviathan."[19] The assertion is not out of keeping with Hobbes's acute and overriding interest in his own welfare, but whether the likenesses of the pictorial title page are indeed those of Charles II and Cromwell, the readers will have to judge for themselves.

A final mystery of *Leviathan* is the relationship between the English edition that first appeared in 1651, and the Latin version, first published in 1668. The assumption, which seemed only commonsense, that the English *Leviathan* had clearly preceded the Latin edition was challenged in 1932 by claims that many passages of the Latin version, though hardly the entire book, had been written some years prior to 1651.[20] Related arguments in favor of an earlier Latin text were that the Latin edition as finally published was shorter than the English *Leviathan* suggesting but not proving that the English version might have been expanded from an earlier Latin draft; that the superior quality of the English version, with its clarity of thought and polished style of expression, as compared with the duller, cruder, and often incorrect and difficult Latin edition, makes it appear that the Latin *Leviathan* published later could not have been translated from or significantly based on the English version, for which it may originally have served as a very rough and inexact first draft; and that certain references to the Civil War in the Latin edition are in the present tense, that is, as if written before the war had ended rather than long afterward. For example, where the English text reads "it were very absurd for men to clamour as they doe, for the Liberty they so manifestly enjoy," the Latin phrasing is "absurdissime conquererentur

Libertatemque flagitarent hodie rebelles nostri qui ea manifestissime fruentes rebellaverunt" ("it were very absurd for our rebels of today to complain and to call for liberty, they who rebelled when they so manifestly enjoyed it").[21] Again, where the English version is "And I doubt not, but many men, have been contented to see the late troubles in England," the Latin edition reads "Ne que dubito quin nostrorum multi bellum, quod nunc geritor in Anglia libenter videant" ("And I doubt not that many of our own look with favor on the war that is presently being waged in England").[22] Clearly, these contrasting sentences from the English and Latin *Leviathans* were not written in the same time frame; the tone and substance of the Latin statements, which are hostile to the parliamentary side in the Civil War and which would therefore have been inappropriate in the *Leviathan* of 1651, leave no doubt they predated their equivalents in the English text. In 1668 and thereafter, however, Cromwell's revolution having long since given way to Charles II, the Latin assertions, though somewhat dust laden and irrelevant, did not require judicious editing.

Thorough study of the differences between the two *Leviathans* may ultimately establish, as some Hobbes scholars are already prepared to argue, that "a large proportion of the Latin *Leviathan* was written before the English [version], around 1648–1649," and "corresponds to a state of Hobbes's thought intermediate between the doctrine of *De Cive* and that of the English *Leviathan*."[23] Unfortunately, the Latin *Leviathan* has not yet been translated into English; though detailed comparisons have been made between the two *Leviathans*, the comparisons are based on a translation of the English *Leviathan* into French, the copious footnotes of which consist mainly of sentences and phrases from the Latin *Leviathan* also translated into French.* Because the Latin *Leviathan* is not accessible in English and only partially translated into French, there has been very little agreement about its contents and the extent to which it differs from its English counterpart. According to Macdonald and Hargreaves, the bibliographers of Hobbes, "The Latin version of *Leviathan* differs considerably from the English: it is the Latin version in which Hobbes really expressed his opinions. . . . In his Latin version he was less con-

---

* Tricaud, trans., *Hobbes: Léviathan*. For editing this French translation and annotating it from the Latin *Leviathan*, François Tricaud of the Faculty of Letters and Human Sciences of Lyon, deserves the gratitude of Hobbes scholars everywhere, whatever their language. We do not detract from his accomplishment in suggesting that any student of Hobbes who wishes to become familiar with the Latin *Leviathan* may choose to learn French for that purpose, thanks to M. Tricaud, but he also has the option, if he chooses to learn Latin, of reading the entire Latin *Leviathan* in the original and the Latin *De Cive*, which may or may not have been changed significantly when Hobbes translated it into the English *Philosophical Rudiments*.

cerned with personalities."[24] The French translation previously referred to, on the other hand, stresses conceptual differences in Hobbes's view of sovereignty and in the meanings he assigns to *Civitas*, in addition to arguing the priority of the Latin edition. Laird's view is that Hobbes "clearly regarded the Latin edition as the definitive one . . . designed for the learned. But *the* book is the English book."[25] Robertson, more expansive, observed of the "altered" Latin *Leviathan* that "the exposition was considerably shortened and occasionally toned down in the political and ecclesiastical sections. A few of the more hazardous expressions on points of theology were abandoned in deference to the outcry they had excited; though, when they turned upon the interpretation of actual passages in Scriptures, he was not afraid still to maintain his most peculiar opinions. He gave, as the reason for his Latin rendering now of a book originally written in such different circumstances, that he wished its principles, of lasting importance as they were, to be rescued from suppression at the hands of those who most had profited by their bold statement."[26] Still others claimed that in the Latin edition Hobbes expressed a greater preference for monarchy.[27] The only broad agreement among those who have contrasted the two editions, an agreement that no one could possibly dispute, is that the final "Review and Conclusion" of the English edition does not appear in the Latin and that the three appendixes of the Latin version—"On the Nicene Creed," "On Heresy," and "On Certain Objections against *Leviathan*"—do not appear in the English."*

Moreover, there is no dispute about the source of the name Hobbes chose for his great work. The Latin inscription on the pictorial title page, "Non est potestas super terram quae comparetur ei," or "Upon earth there is not his like," was from the Book of Job, chapter 41, in which God, asserting his omnipotence and omniscience before the contrite Job, invokes the mythical monsters of the land and sea, Behemoth who prevailed on land (and who was to give Hobbes the title for his book on the Civil War), and Leviathan, the mighty ruler

---

*Robertson may have been correct about the "toned down" character of the Latin version, but there can be no certainty about this claim or any other assertion relating to the Latin *Leviathan* until it is translated in full into English. Here and there, perhaps, the "toning" may have been in the opposite direction: in part 1, chapter 4, for example, where the English states "The first author of *speech* was God himself, that instructed Adam . . . ," the Latin text is *"Sermonis* author primus fuit Adam . . . ("The first author of *speech* was Adam . . ."). And, in English, ". . . for I do not find any thing in the Scripture (to the effect) that Adam was taught the names . . . ," but in Latin "Non enim invenio in Scripturis Sacris (to the effect) imposuisse Adamum . . . nomina . . ." ("I find nothing in Sacred Scripture (to the effect) that Adam . . . gave the names . . .") These examples, of course, unless they can be multiplied innumerable times, hardly refute Robertson.

of the oceans. "Canst thou draw out Leviathan with a fishhook?" God asks rhetorically.

> Or press down his tongue with a cord?
> Canst thou put a rope into his nose?
> Or pierce his jaw through with a hook?
> Will he make many supplications unto thee?
> Or will he speak soft words unto thee?
> Will he make a covenant with thee,
> That thou shouldest take him for a servant for ever?

Hobbes, who always insisted the sovereign was not bound by any covenant whereas his subjects were, may have been particularly taken with the last two lines, and with

> His heart is as firm as a stone;
> Yea, firm as the nether millstone.
> When he raiseth himself up, the mighty are afraid;
> By reason of consternation they are beside themselves.
> If one lay at him with the sword, it cannot avail;
> Nor the spear, the dart, nor the pointed shaft.
> . . . .
> He beholdeth every thing that is high:
> He is king over all the sons of pride.*

For Hobbes, who manifested little interest in the literal aspects of the Book of Job, the "sons of pride" were those of any faith or creed who challenged the authority of Leviathan, the "Mortal God." But the name he selected for his title, from one of the most moving and influential books of the Old Testament, reminds us that much of *Levithan* is concerned with religion, not politics. According to one precise calculation, "371 out of 714 pages in *Leviathan* deal with religious matters,"[28] and Hobbes himself recognized, in his "Epistle Dedicatory," that his opinions about religion were likely to prove the most controversial of all. "That which perhaps may most offend," he wrote, "are certain Texts of Holy Scripture, alledged by me to other purpose than ordinarily they use to be by others. But I have done it with due submission, and also (in order to my Subject) necessarily; for they are the Outworks of the Enemy, from whence they impugne the Civill

---

* In the Book of Job, as elsewhere in the Old and New Testaments and in many great works of literature, multiple meanings are possible. In Jewish mythology Leviathan was sometimes portrayed as originally a male and a female, until the female was killed and her body preserved as future food for the righteous. Other legends, describing Leviathan as female and Behemoth as male, predict that the two monsters will one day fight a war to the finish. This legend, in part, seems to lend itself to Hobbes's usage.

Power."* Had Hobbes confined himself to interpretations of Scripture, he would have offended less, but, then, he would not have been Thomas Hobbes. Because he was Thomas Hobbes and had scores to settle dating back to Malmesbury and Oxford, he could not refrain, in part 4 of *Leviathan*, from referring to the pope as the "King of the Fairies," and to the papacy as "no other, than the *Ghost* of the deceased *Romane Empire*, sitting crowned upon the grave thereof."[29] Nor could he resist, being Hobbes, comparing "Fairies" and "Ecclesiastiques" in a manner certain to offend English clergy and nonclergy alike who had supported the parliamentary side in the Civil War:"When the *Fairies* are displeased with any body, they are said to send their Elves, to pinch them. The *Ecclesiastiques*, when they are displeased with any Civill State, make also their Elves, that is, Superstitious, Enchanted Subjects, to pinch their Princes, by preaching Sedition; or one Prince enchanted with promises, to pinch another."[30] No wonder the "Fairies," "Ecclesiastiques," and "Elves" everywhere were only too eager to pinch Hobbes or, worse, apply pincers to him and his books!

Apparently, they were too enraged to notice that Hobbes also had insulted them by reserving his discussion of religion for the latter half of *Leviathan*, thus making both certain and clear that, in his view, "Of Man" (part 1) and "Of Commonwealth" (part 2) came before "Of a Christian Commonwealth" (part 3) and "Of the Kingdome of Darknesse" (part 4). For him, as for other doctrinaire secularists since his time, religion, to the extent it is recognized and tolerated at all, follows rather than precedes man and the state; in effect, religion is dependent upon the civil authority and not merely subservient to it. Indeed, Hobbes implies in *Leviathan* that man and society can exist without religion altogether, and at times he almost goes so far as to suggest that religion creates more difficulties than it resolves. For Hobbes, in short, religion is more a problem than a solution, whereas Leviathan, or the state, is capable of solving all problems including that of religion.

The "Mortal God" or "Artificiall Man," moreover, is created by the "Art of man," not by God, though the act of creation by which all component parts of Leviathan are brought together and set in motion resembles "that *Fiat*, or the *Let us make man*, pronounced by God in the Creation."[31] The "Mortal God," then, is man-made, and by "man" Hobbes means mankind or, better, men, each of whom in essentials

---

* In the Latin *Leviathan*, the sentence beginning "But I have done it . . ." was replaced by ". . . but I also took great care not to write anything that goes against the official teaching of our church (it is, in fact, permitted not to agree with individual opinions)." Tricaud, trans., *Hobbes: Léviathan*, 1–2, where the whole of the "Epistle Dedicatory" is translated from the Latin into French.

is very much like the others. As Rousseau was to argue later, and Freud was to demonstrate much later, Hobbes maintained that if we follow the prescription *"Nosce teipsum"* ("Read thy self," in his translation), we are bound to discover that "the thoughts, and Passions of one man [are similar] to the thoughts, and Passions of another, whosoever looketh into himself, and considereth what he doth, when he does *think, opine, reason, hope, feare,* &c, and upon what grounds; he shall thereby read and know, what are the thoughts, and Passions of all other men, upon the like occasions."[32] Hobbes was careful to distinguish desire, fear, hope and other "Passions" from "objects of the Passions, which are the things *desired, feared, hoped,* &c: for these the constitution individuall, and particular education do so vary. . . ."[33] Again anticipating Freud, Hobbes shrewdly observed that the objects of passion are easily kept from our knowledge, and therefore "the characters of mans heart, blotted and confounded as they are, with dissembling, lying, counterfeiting, and erroneous doctrines, are legible onely to him that searcheth hearts."[34] Freud would hardly have disagreed with this very early, unsophisticated version of his theory of repression, or with Hobbes's insistence "He that is to govern a whole Nation, must read in himself, not this, or that particular man; but Man-kind: which [is] hard to do, harder than to learn any Language, or Science. . . ."[35]

But such a "reading," while difficult, was not impossible provided one began with the source of all thought and perception, namely, the phenomenon of sense. The years since 1630, when he had first raised the topic with Newcastle (see above, pp. 104–5) had not altered Hobbes's conviction that "there is no conception in a mans mind, which hath not at first, totally, or by parts, been begotten upon the organs of Sense. The rest are derived from that originall."[36] Once again Hobbes took issue with the traditional view, based on Aristotle and the doctrine of the Schools, that what was seen, heard, or understood was an emanation from the objects seen, heard, or understood, in short, the belief that there existed species, audible species, and intelligible species. On the contrary, Hobbes repeated, "Sense in all cases, is nothing els but originall fancy, caused (as I have said) by the pressure, that is, by the motion, of externall things upon our Eyes, Eares, and other organs. . . ."[37]

Imagination ("decaying sense"), memory, and even dreams ("the reverse of our waking Imaginations") derived from sense and the sense organs. Doubting that visions were anything more than dreams or fancies traceable to past sense perceptions, Hobbes noted that even when awake those who were "timorous, and supperstitious, possessed with fearfull tales, and alone in the dark" could believe they had seen "spirits and dead mens Ghosts walking in Church-yards," whereas the reality was that they had imagined such things, or been fooled by the "knavery" of persons pretending to be ghosts. While he was careful not to deny that God can make apparitions, he doubted that he did so often, and quickly made the point that apparitions, superstitions, "Fayries," ghosts, "Prognostiques from Dreams," "false Prophecies, and many other things" were mainly devices enabling "crafty ambitious persons [to] abuse the simple people."[38] Here, as in past writings, Hobbes was not willing to dispense with God and the supernatural entirely, but God in all of Hobbes's scenarios is rarely more than a character offstage and invisible (in all ways) to the audience, or, to vary the image, a ghost-like presence in one of the small panels on the pictorial title page.

In writing about the "Trayne of Thoughts" or "Mentall Discourse," Hobbes seems almost modern in his conception of what he termed thought "Unguided, without Designe." Where there is no "Passionate Thought" to direct or focus thought processes—or, as we might put it in today's language, no conscious effort to channel thought in one direction—"thoughts are said to wander, and seem impertinent one to another, as in a Dream. Such are Commonly the tho[u]ghts of men, that are not onely without company, but also without care of any thing . . . without harmony." Yet there may be coherence in such thoughts, once we understand how the first thought relates to the second, and the second to a third, and so on. Hobbes is talking about free association or the stream of consciousness, thought without planned sequence or thematic organization, and he contrasts it with thought "regulated by some desire, and designe," and moving toward a given end. The two types of thought, however, cannot give us any "Idea, or conception of any thing we call Infinite. No man can have in his mind an Image of infinite magnitude; nor conceive infinite swiftness, infinite time, or infinite force, or infinite power." We are very soon back to God in the small panel: "And therefore the Name of God is used, not to make us conceive him; (for he is Incomprehensible; and his greatnesse, and power are unconceivable;) but that we may honour him." Honor him in the breach, some theologians, sharply sarcastic, might have added, and perhaps some actually did make such a comment.[39]

Thoughts become verbal through speech, and, again, there are two varieties: the first, which Hobbes calls "Markes" or "Notes," enable us to remember the "Consequences of our Thoughts" ("Marke" them for recall); the second, "Signes" or words, are used by many to represent what they think, desire, fear, "or have any other passion for." Both "Markes" and "Signes" make use of "Names" and the "Connexion" between "Names," but the effectiveness of the use depends on "the right ordering of names in our affirmations, [for] a man that seeketh precise *truth*, had need to remember what every name he uses stands for; and to place it accordingly; or else he will find himselfe entangled in words, as a bird in lime-twiggs; the more he struggles, the more belimed."* Definitions, especially, are important, for "in the right Definition of Names, lyes the first use of Speech, which is the Acquisition of Science. And in wrong, or no Definitions, lyes the first abuse; from which proceed all false and senseless Tenets. . ." Without "Letters" no man could become either very wise or very foolish, but with "Letters" there was no guarantee of truth: "For words are wise mens counters, they do but reckon by them: but they are the mony of fooles, that value them by the authority of an *Aristotle*, a *Cicero*, or a *Thomas*, or any other Doctor whatsoever, if but a man."†[40]

Having demonstrated the importance of correct or precise language, Hobbes could then proceed to specify the elements, which were also anchored in sense, setting this language, and man himself, in motion, and those elements were nothing more than "Appetites" and "Aversions." "Appetites," or desires, originate in "Endeavour" or the "small beginnings of Motion, within the body of Man, before they appear in walking, speaking, striking, and other visible actions." While some "Appetites," though not many, "are born with men; as Appetite of food, Appetite of excretion," and some others, the larger number "proceed from Experience, and triall of their effects upon themselves, or other men." Most "Appetites," in other words, are a positive response to the effects of external motions upon the senses, whereas most "Aversions" are a negative response to the effects of still other motions upon the senses. The "appearance" of "Appetites" is accompanied by "Delight," "Pleasure," "sense of good," "Love," and other sensations that seem to be "a corroboration of Vitall motion, and a help thereunto;" "Aversions," on the other hand, are accompanied by "Hatred, "Displeasure," "Payne," "Offence," "Griefe," and other negative feelings. "Deliberation" enables men and beasts to calculate what motions ("Endeavours") will satisfy "Appetites" or "Aversions," and in asserting that will itself was *"the last Appetite in Deliberating,"* Hobbes, as

---

* Pt. 1, chap. 4; *E.W.*, III, 23. This is one of many instances in *Leviathan* when Hobbes invoked an image or example we can trace back to his Malmesbury or Oxford years (cf. Aubrey's account of his snaring birds at Oxford as one way of passing time [see above, p. 46]). Such instances suggest that the residues and inner meanings of these earlier exieriences were never entirely lost or recalled only in the form of anecdotes.

† By "a Thomas," Hobbes presumably meant Saint Thomas Aquinas, but since his own first name was Thomas, he may have been insinuating, half jokingly but also half seriously, that his own "authority" was no better than that of the others.

he must have known, was inviting the strongest possible censure from those who believed that men, unlike animals, could employ free will and knowledge of God's commandments to rise above both "Appetites" and "Aversions."[41] But Hobbes was writing not for the "Schooles," whose "Definition of *Will* that it is a *Rationall Appetite,* is not good," but for those who shared his belief or who could be persuaded to share his belief that human behavior was reducible to simple cause-and-effect principles not unlike those of other sciences. He was also, in a philosophical sense, preparing the way for those who were later to stress the importance of the pleasure-pain and stimulus-response mechanisms in behavior as well as for those, later still, who were to establish the foundations of behavior conditioning.

Hobbes also anticipated the future in defining power as one's present ability "to obtain some future apparent Good," a definition that has yet to be improved on by political scientists of the present day. For him, as for most students of power since, the varieties of power are almost as numerous as man's "Appetites" and "Aversions," and with power, as with them, there are degrees or differences of "more or lesse." The varieties included natural (qualities of body or mind), and civil power ("The Greatest of humane Powers . . . compounded of the Powers of most men, united by consent, in one person . . . ."), and power based on "Riches" ("because it procureth friends, and servants"), "Reputation" (because it gaineth love"), eloquence, "Nobility" (but "not in all places"), weapons, the "Sciences" (though "small power; because not eminent"), and other special attributes or qualities, each of which is valued and possessed differently by different men. But all men are alike in one respect, Hobbes insisted, and that is in their wish to possess the objects of their desire not just today, or tomorrow, but forever. The ubiquity of such a wish, he observed, in one of the most provocative and quoted sentences in all of *Leviathan,* was such "that in the first place, I put for a generall inclination of all mankind, a perpetuall and restlesse desire of Power after power, that ceaseth onely in Death."[42]

By "generall inclination" Hobbes did not mean, as is sometimes maintained, that man harbors an innate "power drive" or seeks power merely for its own sake. The cause of the "generall inclination," he explained, "is not always that a man hopes for a more intensive delight, than he has already attained to; or that he cannot be content with a moderate power: but because he cannot assure the power and means to live well, which he hath present, without the acquisition of more." But he was saying something beyond this when he cited as an example that "Kings, whose power is greatest, turn their endeavours to the assuring it at home by Lawes, or abroad by Wars: and when that is done, there succeedeth a new desire; in some, of Fame from new Conquest; in others, of ease and sensuall pleasure; in others, of admiration, or being flattered for excellence in some art, or other ability of mind." Power, and more power, is sought, Hobbes was emphasizing, with an end in view, and therefore it cannot be understood without reference to an "Appetite" or "Aversion" that power of some type enables one to satisfy.[43]

The "Appetites," "Aversions," and powers of one individual collide with those of another, and for Hobbes this collision and its consequences supply the fundamental reason for civil society. Though men are relatively equal in body and mind, this equality leads not to harmonious relations but to warfare, because each man, entertaining an "equality of hope" in the attainment of his ends, becomes an enemy of every other man who pursues similar ends; for this reason, "men have not pleasure," as he expressed it, "(but on the contrary a good deale of griefe) in keeping company." While the ends may be varied, the particular ends that cause the most trouble are those that relate to the desire for increased wealth, the desire to be secure in one's person and property, and the desire to be deferred to and to enjoy respect. The result, Hobbes asserted, and for the second time in *Leviathan* he made a broad statement with profound implications, demonstrated that "in the nature of man, we find three principall causes of quarrell. First, Competition; Secondly, Diffidence; Thirdly, Glory."[44]

The first of these "causes," he continued, "maketh men invade for Gain; the second, for Safety; and the third, for Reputation. The first use Violence, to make themselves Masters of other mens persons, wives, children, and cattell; the second to defend them; the third, for trifles, as a word, a smile, a different opinion, and any other signe of under-value, either direct in their Persons, or by reflexion in their Kindred, their Friends, their Nation, their Profession, or their Name." Unless there is "a common Power to keep them all in awe, they are in the condition which is called Warre; and such a warre, as is of every man, against every man."[45]

By "Warre" Hobbes meant not just the actual state of warfare but also the continual prospect of war that leads men constantly to feel acutely insecure because they have only their own strength for protection. In such circumstances, Hobbes wrote, in still another of his sweeping declarations, which subsequently became the most famous of all, "there is no place for Industry; because the fruit thereof is uncertain; and consequently no Culture of the Earth; no Navigation, nor use of the commodities that may be imported by Sea; no commodious Building; no Instruments of moving, and removing such things as require much force; no Knowledge of the face of the Earth;

no account of Time; no Arts; no Letters; no Society; and which is worst of all, continuall feare, and danger of violent death; And the life of man, solitary, poore, nasty, brutish, and short."*[46]

So described, the state of nature is the antithesis of civilized existence, and much of the remainder of *Leviathan,*, excepting the chapters devoted to religion, which are not wholly irrelevant, is given over to a discussion of the conditions, in the broadest sense, that make civilized life possible. The first and most essential of these conditions, Hobbes insisted, as he had insisted before in his earlier books, is that "every man should say to every man, *I Authorize and give up my Right of Governing my selfe, to this Man, or to this Assembly of men, on this condition, that thou give up thy Right to him, and Authorise all his Actions in like manner*. This done, the Multitude so united in one Person, is called a COMMONWEALTH, in latine CIVITAS. This is the Generation of that great LEVIATHAN, or rather (to speak more reverently) of that *Mortall God*, to which wee owe under the *Immortall God*, our peace and defence."[47]

As may be expected, Hobbes's view of this covenant creating Leviathan had not changed during the preceding years. The sovereign was not bound by the covenant, and no man could violate it on the grounds that it was antithetical to his covenant with God, for there was no such thing; "this pretence of Covenant with God," Hobbes affirmed, using some of his strongest language, "is so evident a lye, even in the pretenders own consciences, that it is not onely an act of an unjust, but also of a vile, and unmanly disposition." Nor could anyone acting as the sovereign, who was capable of "Iniquity" but not of "Injustice" or "Injury," be put to death. The sovereign had the power to censor speech and publications, to determine the kinds and amounts of property a man could possess, to decide all questions of law, to reward or punish subjects according to their merits as citizens, to make war or peace, to appoint all lesser officials, and, finally, since men value decorations and symbols of respect, to bestow "titles of Honour" and determine "what Order or Place, and dignity, each man shall hold." Since sovereignty was indivisible, none of the powers mentioned could be divided; indeed, Hobbes added, if this opin-

---

* Hobbes's references to navigation and geography, when he could have written simply "no Science," reminds us, once again, of his Oxford student days almost fifty years earlier, during some of which he "tooke great delight to goe to the book-binders' shops, and lye gaping on mappes." (See Aubrey and Hobbes's *Autobiography*, and above, pp. 46–47.) His specifying navigation and geography as pursuits impossible in the state of nature suggests that these particular areas of knowledge possessed some special significance for him.

ion had been adhered to in recent years, the people of England would never have "been divided, and fallen into this Civill Warre."[48]

Hobbes's sovereign, clearly, was a "Free-Man," defined by him as "he, that in those things, which by his strength and wit he is able to do, is not hindred to doe what he has a will to." But were there any other "Free-Men" in the Commonwealth? Hobbes's answer to this question, which he had given previously in other books, was that a man was free to disobey the sovereign if commanded to kill, wound, or maim himself or to permit others to take such actions against him; moreover, he could not be required to go without food, air, or medicine. He also could freely refuse to testify against himself, and, somewhat surprisingly, he could sue "for his right" against the sovereign if the conflict with the sovereign was based "on a precedent Law," not on the sovereign power as such. A "Free-Man"—and here, Hobbes almost certainly had his own example in mind—could refuse to serve in the army, "without injustice," even if such refusal resulted in his being put to death. If the objector finds someone to take his place, Hobbes urged, in a tone that is more supplicatory than analytic or coolly objective, he cannot be accused of desertion. Moreover, allowance should be made "for naturall timorousnesse, not onely to women, (of whom no such dangerous duty is expected,) but also to men of feminine courage." Nevertheless, when the survival of the commonwealth requires the help of all those able to bear arms, everyone is obliged to serve.[49]

But the sovereign also has certain obligations, among which the foremost, indeed, the one that defines his title, is the obligation to protect and preserve his subjects. His subjects are bound to him only "as long, and no longer, than the power lasteth, by which he is able to protect them. For the right men have by Nature to protect themselves, when none else can protect them, can by no Covenant be relinquished." Hence, if the sovereign is "subdued by war," in which event he no longer can protect his subjects, he no longer is sovereign and his subjects "become obliged to the victor." If he abdicates, or leaves no heir, the obligation of his subjects also comes to an end. Here, again, Hobbes is making the point, familiar to readers of his earlier books but entirely overlooked by Clarendon and other critics, that a Charles I or a Cromwell or any monarch is sovereign only so long as he is able to rule effectively, that is, preserve the peace and security of his subjects. For Hobbes, long before Cromwell, and even, one suspects, long before Charles I and James I, there never was any other test or measure of sovereignty than the capacity to protect subjects from dangers within and without corresponding to those of the state of nature. A sovereign, Hobbes was saying, is he or she or it that is sovereign not just according to law, custom, or tradition but according to *fact*.[50]

While Hobbes was more concerned, in *Leviathan* and other books, with the political powers of the sovereign than with his economic role, he did not neglect the topic or, as was usually the case, avoid arousing controversy in his discussion of it. Clarendon, in still another misunderstanding of Hobbes's principles, accused him of displaying in *Leviathan* an "extreme malignity to the Nobility, by whose bread he hath ben alwaies sustain'd, who must not expect any part, at least any precedence in his Institution . . . in a conjuncture when the Levellers were at highest, and the reduction of all degrees to one and the same was resolv'd upon, and begun, and exercis'd towards the whole Nobility with all the instances of contemt and scorn, he chose to publish his judgements. . . ."[51] Somewhat related to this view of Hobbes is the modern opinion that, in the words of Strauss, "however much Hobbes personally esteemed the aristocracy . . . his political philosophy is directed against the aristocratic rules of life in the name of bourgeois rules of life. His morality is the morality of the bourgeois world. Even his sharp criticism of the bourgeoisie has, at bottom, no other aim than to remind the bourgeoisie of the elementary condition for its existence. This existence is not industry and thrift, not the specific exertions of the bourgeoisie, but the security of body and soul, which the bourgeoisie cannot of itself guarantee."[52]

More recently, Macpherson, building on Strauss's thesis and carrying it a good deal further, has argued that Hobbes's political theory was developed for the "possessive market society," or, roughly, the emergent early capitalist society, in which labor was a commodity along with energy and skill and in which all three, as possessions, could be sold for a price much the way other commodities were sold. In such a society, "market relations so shape or permeate all social relations that it may properly be called a market society, not merely a market economy."[53] In Macpherson's view, Hobbes is essentially a bourgeois political theorist whose concepts of the "sovereign's duties" and "of taxation" and whose other economic ideas were, like his attitude toward taxes, "bourgeois through and through." Macpherson is aware, of course, that Hobbes expressed dislike for bourgeois morality and had little use for the merchant class (most of which had probably supported Parliament in its struggles with the crown), but he explains these inconsistencies by pointing to Hobbes's alleged unawareness "that these models, which he offered as models of man as such and society as such, were valid only as models of bourgeois man and society."[54]

Whatever the source and nature of Hobbes's "models," they do not give substance to Clarendon's charge that Hobbes had an acute dislike for the nobility, or even support Strauss's claim that his political philosophy was "directed against the aristocratic rules of life." Hobbes's assertion in *Leviathan*, cited by Clarendon as evidence, is that "Good Counsell comes not by Lot, nor by Inheritance; and therefore there is no more reason to expect good Advice from the rich, or noble, in matter of State, than in delineating the dimensions of a fortresse. . . ." Clarendon did not quote the remainder of the sentence or the one following, the themes of which sharply affect the meaning he imputed to Hobbes, for Hobbes continued, "unlesse we shall think there needs no method in the study of the Politiques, (as there does in the study of Geometry,) but onely to be lookers on; which is not so. For the Politiques is the harder study of the two."[55] Hobbes's point, made long since by Bacon and others, was that wealth and breeding as such do not necessarily make for "Good Counsell" or governance; both require study, and not ordinary study but study "harder" than that required to learn geometry. Hobbes did not write anywhere in *Leviathan* that wealthy and noble citizens should give way as counselors to the middle class and ordinary ranks of people, educated or otherwise. To insinuate or imply, as Clarendon did, that Hobbes somehow deliberately coordinated the publication of *Leviathan* with the agitations of the Levelers, whom he intensely disliked, as if to give them support, suggests that the defeats and disappointments of Clarendon's last years may have been more serious in unsettling his judgment than historians and his biographers have so far believed.[56]

The bourgeois character and possessive individualism that have been attributed to Hobbes also are difficult to reconcile with his stated views. Hobbes believes in private property though he insists that such property is dependent on, and in some sense at the disposal of, the sovereign, but nowhere does he recommend the getting and keeping of wealth as the most desired end in life, or urge the benefits to the individual and society of what later came to be called the Protestant ethic, or stress the virtues of trade and commerce above those of other occupations, or discuss work or labor as if they were nothing more than commodities to be freely bought and sold in the marketplace. In his economics, as in his politics, the supreme emphasis is on the preservation of life and all that conserves life: preservation of the sovereign because protection of life is his most vital function; preservation of the commonwealth because secure life is possible only in a civil society; preservation of the supremacy of the state and subordination of the church because the reverse leads to war and the destruction of life. Hence taxes "layd on the People by the Sovereign" are justified as "the Wages, due to them that hold the publique Sword, to defend private men in the exercise of severall Trades, and Callings." While rich and poor theoretically owe the same taxes, "the rich, who have the service of the poor, may be debtors not onely for their own persons, but for many more" (as no doubt were the earls of Devonshire, who employed armies of servants and paid taxes accordingly). Let the taxes be based not on the wealth possessed (today's term would be "assets") but on the wealth consumed or spent; and Hobbes implied there should be no limits placed on consumption, because the commonwealth is not "defrauded, by the luxurious waste of private men." Those unable to provide for themselves because of physical weakness or accident should be provided for by the commonwealth, not by private charity; those "as have strong bodies . . . are to be forced to work," with agricultural, manufacturing, fishing, and other enterprises being encouraged to provide jobs. The surplus population is to be transported to countries with a small population, where it is to live in peace with the natives, not exterminate them; and when that overseas recourse is not longer available, "then the last remedy of all is Warre; which provideth for every man, by Victory, or Death." Hobbes may have been the first to posit a connection between overpopulation and "the last remedy of all."[57]

Surely, no orthodox bourgeois thinker then or now would have justified, as Hobbes did, committing a crime against property and resorting to violence, but for him there was no contradiction between such a crime, when committed for certain reasons, and one's obligation to obey laws of the sovereign. Again, as always with Hobbes, the supreme value is not wealth or possessions but life itself. "When a man is destitute of food, or other thing necessary for his life, and cannot preserve himself any other way, but by some fact against the law; as if in a great famine he take the food by force, or stealth, which he cannot obtain for money or charity . . . he is totally excused."* In short, the justification for theft is identical to the justification for law, for sovereignty, and for the commonwealth—namely, preservation of life. One supreme paradox of Hobbes's fame and reputation is that no other major philosopher, not even Adam Smith, who was a professor of moral philosophy as well as an economist, ever went so far in upholding the sanctity of life; and yet no other philosopher, with the

---

* Pt. 2, chap. 27; E.W., III, 288. As a lad in Malmesbury, Hobbes may have been familiar at first hand with hunger and destitution as a consequence of the prolonged slump in the woolen trade and a long period of rising food prices. In 1614, in order to avoid starvation, Malmesbury weavers had been forced to steal.

exception of Karl Marx, has ever been thought of as more of a materialist.

About midway in *Leviathan*, at the very conclusion of "Of Commonwealth" (part 2), Hobbes confessed, "I am at the point of believing this my labour, as uselesse, as the Commonwealth of *Plato;* For he also is of opinion that it is impossible for the disorders of State, and change of Governments by Civill Warre, ever to be taken away, till Soveraigns be Philosophers." But he added, "I recover some hope, that one time or another, this writing of mine, may fall into the hands of a Soveraign, who will consider it himselfe . . . without the help of any interested, or envious Interpreter. . . ."[58] Perhaps, had he ended his great work there, it would have found its way into some enlightened circles of power, serving as a kind of "Guide to the Perplexed" monarch or ruler. But as was already noted, the remainder of *Leviathan* was largely devoted to a critical and occasionally acerbic examination of religious beliefs and practices, both Catholic and Protestant, and in this Hobbes went far beyond his ostensible purpose, which was to establish the ascendancy of civil over religious authority. Since the final chapters are almost wholly given over to an excoriation of traditional religious dogmas, especially those of the Catholic church, we may wonder whether they were written in France at approximately the time Hobbes began to fear for his life at the hands of the ultraroyalists and higher French clergy who, according to Clarendon, were attempting "to apprehend him."[*] If so, Hobbes may have wished to strike at those who were driving him from France with the only weapons he possessed: the language of scorn, wit, and ridicule. For the language of this final section of *Leviathan*, as in the references to the papacy quoted earlier, appears to have been chosen not merely to jar or bruise but to draw blood, and by expressing himself in such language, Hobbes must have known, or at least guessed, that *Leviathan* was less likely to "fall into the hands of a Soveraign" than into those of an ecclesiastic or secular censor.

While he did not explicitly identify the Catholic church as a "Confederacy" of those who believe that nothing is "impossible . . .

---

[*] ". . . he was compell'd secretly to fly out of Paris," Clarendon wrote, "the Justice having endeavour'd to apprehend him" (*Brief Survey*, 8–9). Robertson (*Hobbes*, 72) attributes Hobbes's near arrest to the "French clerical authorities, made aware of the contents of 'Leviathan,' and exasperated by such an open and unsparing assault . . . on the Papal system." But he quotes (p. 73) Clarendon as writing to Nicholas, somewhat inconsistently, "I had indeed some hand in the discountenancing of my old friend, Mr H. . . . What the Catholics wished, I know not, but sure they contributed nothing to that justice."

to be done [and] to bee beleeved," he clearly had it in mind when he wrote that "two men conspiring, one to seem lame, the other to cure him with a charme, will deceive many: but many conspiring, one to seem lame, another so to cure him, and all the rest to bear witnesse; will deceive many more."[59] Perhaps the "many conspiring" include "the secular Clergy, besides Monks and Friars, which in many places, bear so great a proportion to the common people, as if need were, there might be raised out of them alone, an Army, sufficient for any warre the Church militant should imploy them in. . . ."[60] But the "many conspiring," Hobbes made clear, were nothing compared with the multitude of those deceived. Deceived, for example, by the sacrament of the Lord's Supper;* by the "Exorcismes" that attend "Marriage, . . . Extreme Unction, . . . Visitation of the Sick, . . . Consecrating Churches, and Church-yards, and the like"; and by practices that originate not in Scripture but in pagan superstition and idolatry, such as the painting or carving of images, the canonization of saints, the carrying of images in processions, the burning of candles or torches before images, and the naming of the pope *pontifex maximus*. For the heathen *aqua lustralis*, Hobbes continued, the Church of Rome has substituted *holy water;* for *bacchanalia, wakes;* for *saturnalia,* "Carnevalls";* and for their "Procession of *Priapus,*" "our fetching in, erection, and dancing about *May-poles.*" There are many more examples of "these old empty Bottles of Gentilisme, which the Doctors of the Romane Church, either by Negligence, or Ambition, have filled up again with the new Wine of Christianity. . . ."[61] The pope, Hobbes seemed to imply, was not just sitting on the grave of the Holy Roman Empire; he was attempting to bring the corpse back to life, and with it the position of religious ascendancy he had occupied in England a little more than a century before.

When he addressed the pope as "King of the Fairies," Hobbes must have known that he would not be welcome again in a Catholic country, but at the age of sixty-three, somewhat tired and not fully recovered from his illnesses in France, he probably had little or no thought of further travels abroad. But he may not have anticipated

---

* Regarding the ritual of the sacrament Hobbes remarked, "The Egyptian Conjurers, that are said to have turned their Rods to Serpents, and the Water into Bloud, are thought but to have deluded the senses of the Spectators by a false shew of things, yet are esteemed Enchanters: But what should wee have thought of them, if there had appeared in their Rods nothing like a Serpent, and in the Water enchanted, nothing like Bloud, nor like any thing else but Water, but that they had faced down the King, that they were Serpents that looked like Rods, and that it was Bloud that seemed Water? That had been both Enchantment, and Lying. And yet in this daily act of the Priest, they doe the very same." Pt. 4, chap. 44; *E.W.*, III, 611.

the extent to which *Leviathan* and other writings would provoke and turn against him some of his own countrymen, including, in addition to those at court before and after 1660, the community of scientists gathered in the Royal Society as well as influential professors of his old university. He was not without friends, but almost none were prepared to come to his defense in writing or even to assist him in efforts to get his books published. Perhaps, then, more than once in the decades following his return to England in 1651, Hobbes remembered, with nostalgia, the years in Paris and Saint-Germain when his adversaries had been insignificant in comparison with his friends. Perhaps he even wished, at particularly low points in his later life, that there was a way to return to the salon of Montmor, Mersenne's successor, and resume his discussions, or at least pay a lengthy and leisurely visit to the château of Du Verdus near Bordeaux. But such ventures were not possible. He was to be reminded, however, of certain other experiences in France, not among the most pleasant or rewarding he had known, which he had thought were well and long behind him, experiences that revived old controversies and inspired new ones.

EIGHT

DISQUISITIONS AND DISPUTATIONS

I N MAKING HIS SUBMISSION to the council of state in the winter of 1651–52, thereby signifying his willingness to accept the authority of Parliament and, not far off, the rule of Cromwell, Hobbes was acknowledging in accordance with his own principles that he owed allegiance to the present government that held de facto power, not to an absentee monarch whose claim to sovereignty was de jure at best. But in declaring himself a loyal subject of the Commonwealth, he also was certifying, in effect, that for him, if not for many friends and acquaintances who remained abroad, the Civil War was over. Perhaps he believed, as well, that many if not most of these friends and acquaintances would regard his submission as honorable and, under the circumstances, inevitable, even though they did not wholly approve of it. No doubt a large number, notably Newcastle and Arlington, did so, but others took a different view, and two of those who disapproved, each of whom wrote a critique of *Leviathan*, may have been motivated as much by envy and resentment as by ideological differences. For not everyone was as successful as Hobbes in making amends, first to Cromwell and later, in 1660, to Charles II.

John Bramhall (1594–1663), bishop of Derry, the first of these critics, was a devout Anglican and staunch royalist who earlier had served in Ireland as chaplain to Wentworth, later the earl of Strafford. Excluded by the Uxbridge convention from the general pardon, as were Archbishop Laud and others, Bramhall fled abroad in 1644. Excluded, once more, as was Clarendon, from the Act of Indemnity of 1652, a purpose of which was to reconcile royalists to the new regime, Bramhall, often ill and impoverished, was forced to remain abroad until the Restoration in 1660. Even then, apparently, he was not convinced that England's trials and his own sorrows were over, observing, in "A Sermon upon His Majesty's Restoration," that while "we sit in the beauty of peace, every man under his own vine and his own fig-tree," no one can "know how soon our ringing of bells may be changed to roaring of Cannons."[1]

Clarendon (1608–1674), whose service to the royal cause was responsible for his suffering exile twice, the second time at the express command of Charles II in 1667, believed, not without reason, that he had sacrificed more for the king, and offended him less, than Hobbes had; his resentment of Hobbes's more favored status, manifest in the "Epistle Dedicatory" and elsewhere in his *Brief View and Survey of Leviathan* (1676), may have been a factor in his writing, while in exile, the most important critique of *Leviathan* published in the seventeenth century. Until his second exile, Clarendon as lord chancellor had been one of the most powerful men in England following the Restoration. He gradually fell into disfavor, however, as a result of his economic policies, the unsuccessful Second Dutch War, for which he was unfairly blamed, and his hardly concealed disapprovel of the profligate and disorderly court of Charles II, not to mention the succession of royal mistresses and their bastard offspring. The king's curt "Bid the Chancellor begone!" sent Clarendon into an unhappy, seven-year exile in France that was to end, despite his pathetic pleas to return home, with his death at Rouen in 1674, aged sixty-six. His two exiles, the first of which was from 1648 to 1660, came to a total of nineteen years.

Hobbes apparently first met Bramhall in Paris, perhaps at the residence of Newcastle, in 1645 or 1646. Bramhall, who believed firmly in the divine right of kings and whose Church of England orthodoxy inclined him to be almost equally antagonistic to Catholics, Presbyterians, and atheists, was probably not much interested in Hobbes's views on any topic, but the two somehow became involved in a discussion of free will.[2] Newcastle, who was present, asked them to put their opinions in writing, and both agreed to do so, Hobbes insisting as a condition that his paper, which was in the form of a long letter or report to Newcastle, not be published. Unfortunately for this stipulation, a Frenchman present who was not fluent in English prevailed upon Hobbes to permit a translation of his views into French, a translation subsequently undertaken by one John Davys of Kidwelly, Wales, an admirer of Hobbes, of whom little more is known. Davys must have made a copy of Hobbes's paper for himself, because eight years later, in 1654, by which time Hobbes was well known, Davys published the paper, in the form of a long letter from Hobbes to Newcastle, with a brief, unsigned introduction of his own, without Hobbes's permission or any notification to Bramhall, who was still in France. Unfamiliar with this history, Bramhall believed he had been doubly deceived by Hobbes—he complained that even the date at the end of Hobbes's letter, "Aug. 20, 1652," was a deception, since the discussion had taken place six years earlier—and his ire was fueled by the title, which, favoring Hobbes, read in full, "Of Libertie and Necessitie: A Treatise wherein all Controversie concerning *Predestination, Election, Free-will, Grace, Merits, Reprobation,* &c. is fully decided and cleared, in answer to a Treatise written by the Bishop of London-derry, on the same subject."

Bramhall's angry rejoinder appeared one year later, in 1655, and to it Hobbes replied, in 1656, with a book-length restatement of his position. The controversy, however, was not over: in 1658 Bramhall published still another effort to rebut Hobbes, and to this he attached "an Appendix concerning The Catching of the *Leviathan,* Or the great Whale." In 1668 Hobbes was to have the last word, Bramwell having died in 1663, but his final remarks on the subject were not published until 1682, three years after his own death.

Barred from returning to England or Ireland, and therefore unable to delay, much less prevent, publication of *Of Libertie and Necessitie,* Bramhall must have believed that Hobbes had taken advantage of his involuntary absence to publish only one side, and in Bramhall's view the weaker side, of their argument about free will. He also was unable to understand why Hobbes had permitted Davys to preface the book with the "lewd epistle" Davys had styled "To the Sober and Discreet Reader."[3] As a Christian, Bramhall might grudgingly have accepted Davys's designation of Hobbes as "this great author," and his referring to the book as "a jewl" of unparalleled "preciousness," but as a High Churchman he was understandably outraged by Davys's declaration that Hobbes "in so few sheets hath performed more than all the voluminous works of the *priests and ministers . . .* and to do this, being a person whom not only the averseness of his nature to engage himself in matters of controversy of this kind, but his severer study of the *mathematics,* might justly exempt from any such skir-mishes; we may not stick to infer, that the *black-coats,* generally taken, are a sort of ignorant *tinkers,* who in matters of their own profession, such as is the *mending* and *soldering* of men's *consciences,* have made more *holes* than they found. . . ." As if this were not insult enough, Davys concluded that *Of Libertie and Necessitie* "contains more evi-dence and conviction in the matters it treats of, than all the volumes, nay libraries, which the *priests, jesuits,* and *ministers* have, to our great charge, distraction, and loss of precious time, furnished us with."[4]

In his subsequent rejoinder to these charges, which was prefaced by his own epistle "To the Reader," Bramhall heaped contempt on "the nameless author" who had taken it upon himself to "hang out an ivybush" in front of Hobbes's "rare piece of subliminated stoicism," inviting "passengers to purchase it." No novice himself in the use of invective, Bramhall invited the anonymous Davys to "lick up the spittle of Dionysius by himself, as his servile flatterers did, and protest that it is more sweet than nectar; we envy him not; much good may it do him." Holding that the "Church of England is as much above his distraction, as he is beneath this question," Bramhall cited Davys as yet another proof "into what miserable times we are fallen, when blind men will be the only judges of colours."[5]

Defending himself against Bramhall's accusations of bad faith, particularly the allegation that the book had been published "either through forgetfulness or change of judgment" on Hobbes's part, Hobbes insisted that *Of Libertie and Necessitie* had been published "without my knowledge, and (as he [Davys] knew) against my will; for which he since hath asked me pardon." But he was hardly apologetic in stating his doubts that Bramhall had intended their discussion to remain private, inasmuch as "the Bishop ... saith he writ it to the end 'that by the ventilation of the question, truth might be cleared from mistakes,'" which end would not have been served by nonpublication. Furthermore, Bramhall might have perceived that the substitution of 1652 for 1646 was an error Hobbes could not have known about, since he knew nothing of the book's being printed, and in any case an error of no advantage whatever to Hobbes.[6]

Until now, no scholar has questioned the validity of Hobbes's account, perhaps because insufficient note has been taken of the two editions of *Of Libertie and Necessitie*, both of which appeared in 1654. The first of these editions, according to the standard Hobbes bibliography, carries the end date 1652, whereas in the second the date has been corrected to 1646; except for the change of date, the two editions are identical. Clearly, the controversy between Bramhall and Hobbes about publication, portions of which have been quoted, relates to the first edition, with the date in error. The correction of the date in the second edition suggests that Davys or Hobbes (or someone who had recognized the error) must have contacted the printer in the interval between editions, at which time other changes, such as the inclusion of Bramhall's remarks, might have been made, thereby forestalling the publication of his own book a year later. In any event, whether or not Hobbes knew of the first edition, he almost certainly must have known of the second in 1654, and hence we cannot assume that he was totally innocent of the charges brought against him by Bramhall.[7]

But innocent or not, he clearly did not regret the publication of his side of the argument with Bramhall. *De Cive* and *Leviathan* were

behind him, and as the survivor of more momentous controversies
with divine-right royalists, Papists, and Protestant clergy of various
persuasions, Hobbes in 1654 was not inclined to defer to Bramhall in
any respect, least of all in respect to his theology, which joined Church
of England doctrines to the logic and language of the Schoolmen. In
Hobbes's view, Bramhall's belief in free will, or the idea that man is
free to choose good or evil, obedience or disobedience to divine law—
the belief, in short, that man can *choose* to do or not to do—was contrary to scientific principles of behavior, and above all to the principle that established the centrality of motion. In all of his earlier
writings, and now against Bramhall, Hobbes argued that man is a
creature of "Appetites" and "Aversions," both of which result from
external motions impinging upon internal ones. What Bramhall and
others imagine to be will, Hobbes insisted, is merely "deliberation,"
which itself is the last "Appetite" in a sequence of "Appetites" and
"Aversions" generated by the interactions of external and internal
motions. For Hobbes, in effect, desires, wishes, hopes, fears, wants,
and most other human behavioral phenomena were themselves
"Appetites" or "Aversions"—or, from another point of view, will itself
and not the results of will.[8]

Fourteen years later, in 1668, Hobbes was engaged in another
controversy with Bramhall, which, like the earlier one, deserves more
scrutiny than scholars have given it thus far. In *An Answer to a Book
Published by Dr. Bramhall*, written in 1668 but not printed until 1682,
Hobbes claimed in his "To the Reader" that he would have dealt with
Bramhall's *The Catching of the Leviathan* (1658), in which he was
accused of atheism, much sooner had he known of the book. But he
had not "heard of it till about three months since; so little talk there
was of his Lordship's writings."[9] In other words, Hobbes was asking
his readers to believe that he had known nothing of Bramhall's critique of his *Leviathan* for almost ten years after its first publication,
although Bramhall, who became archbishop of Armagh and primate
of Ireland in 1660, was well known to him as one of his major adversaries. His disclaimer is also difficult to reconcile with his stated
awareness in 1656, only two years before publication of *The Catching
of the Leviathan*, that Bramhall was contemplating writing such a
book. For in his "To the Reader" at the beginning of *The Questions
concerning Liberty, Necessity, and Chance*, which was first published
in 1656, Hobbes referred to Bramhall's designation of *Leviathan* as
"Monstrum horrendum, informe, ingens, cui lumen ademptum." "Words
not far fetched," Hobbes continued, "nor more applicable to my *Leviathan*, than to any other writing that should offend him. ... And
whereas he saith there are two of our own Church (as he hears say)
that are answering it; and that 'he himself,' if I desire it, 'will dem-

onstrate that my principles are pernicious both to piety and policy, and destructive to all relations,' &c.: my answer is, that I desire not that he or they should so misspend their time; but if they will needs do it, I can give them a fit title for their book, *Behemoth against Leviathan.*"[10] Bramhall, of course, did not adopt that title, but Hobbes's suggestion, which was not a frivolous one, tends to indicate not only that he knew that Bramhall might write a book critical of *Leviathan* but also that he attached some probability to the venture.

Assuming, however, that he was unaware of *The Catching of the Leviathan* when it appeared two years later, and remained unaware of it for a decade, why did he choose in 1668, when Bramhall himself had been dead five years, to issue a reply to Bramhall's charges of atheism? If the book had in fact occasioned "so little talk" when it first appeared, it undoubtedly was even less discussed, if available at all, ten years later, and the question therefore arises of Hobbes's motivation in calling attention to a forgotten or almost-forgotten book he regarded as ignorant, malicious, and unjust. We might have expected, instead, that he would have been the first to welcome *The Catching of the Leviathan* into oblivion, and the last to remind himself or anyone else of its existence.

While we cannot be certain of the answers to these questions, we have some reason to believe they reflect the far-reaching changes that occurred both in England and in Hobbes's personal situation between the early confrontations with Bramhall and his 1668 *An Answer.* Relatively secure under the Protectorate, despite his royalist views, Hobbes had been reasonably free to express his opinions and had done so on numerous occasions; between 1650 and 1660 he published or republished seven of his major works, in a total of fifteen editions.*

---

* Books Published or Republished in London, 1650–60:

SHORT TITLE	NUMBER AND YEAR OF EDITIONS	
Leviathan	One	1651
Humane Nature	Five	1650, 1651 (two), 1652 (two)
De Cive (*Philosophicall Rudiments*)	One	1651
De Corpore	Two	1655, 1656
De Homine	One	1658
Of Libertie and Necessitie	Four	1654 (two), 1655, 1656
The Art of Rhetorique	One	1651

Source: Macdonald and Hargreaves, *Hobbes: A Bibliography.*

In the nineteen years between 1660 and his death in 1679, the only books he was permitted to publish were, with one exception, those mainly in Latin, which dealt with mathematics or physics, a second edition of *Thucydides* and a translation of Homer, and two further editions of *De Mirabilibus Pecci*, one of them an English translation. The only book of his published during that period which touched on other matters was *Mr. Hobbes Considered*, of 1662, in which he defended himself against Wallis's accusations of disloyalty to the king and subservience to Cromwell. Although four separate editions of *Behemoth*, Hobbes's book on the Civil War, were published by an unknown printer in 1679, none of them were licensed for publication or issued with Hobbes's approval; *Behemoth*, as was mentioned earlier, was not officially published until 1682, three years after Hobbes's death.

The lack of freedom to publish, however, was not the most important of Hobbes's problems after 1660. The return to the throne of Charles II, who, fortunately for Hobbes, was amicably disposed toward him, was accompanied by the restoration of the Church of England to a position of power over all other sects and branches of religion, both Catholic and Protestant, and with that ascendancy came renewed agitation for persecution of atheists, heretics, Papists, and all others who had offended the episcopal establishment during the preceding twenty years. The old assertion of James I "No Bishop, no King!" was renewed in the widely held conviction that "no man could be a true royalist who was not a true Churchman,"[11] a conviction that Hobbes could only challenge and not share. Hobbes, whose characteristic timidity became more pronounced as he grew older, must have watched these developments with growing anxiety, and when the term "Hobbism," referring to a philosophy compounded of atheism, immorality, and sedition in roughly equal measures, came into disreputable use, the anxiety must have approached panic. Not long afterward, the great plague and the fire of 1666, viewed by the devout as punishments from God, inspired an urgent interest in writings and conduct that might have grievously offended the Almighty, among which Hobbes's books enjoyed a certain but not exclusive pride of place.

In September and October 1666 a House of Commons committee, in connection with a "Bill Against Atheism and Profaneness" before it, was empowered "to receive information touching such books as tend to atheism, blasphemy and profaneness, or against the essence and attributes of God, and in particular . . . the book of Mr Hobbes called the 'Leviathan,' and to report the matter with their opinion to the House."[12] While the bill was approved by the committee on January 31, 1667, and referred to the House of Lords, nothing more was heard of it. But for a time Hobbes apparently believed he was in real danger of being executed as a heretic. According to Aubrey, Hobbes, fearing "that his papers might be search't by . . . order," told Aubrey that "he had burn't part of them," and another account, from Bishop Kennet, quotes the Devonshires as reporting of Hobbes at this time that "terror upon his spirits made them sink very much: he would be confessing to those about him that he meant no harm, and was no obstinate man, and was ready to make any proper satisfaction."*

A successful effort to refute Bramhall's charges of atheism, Hobbes must have decided, would go far toward providing "proper satisfaction." Bramhall, after all, had been a High Churchman from 1660 to his death in 1663—and knowing Hobbes as we do, we can easily imagine him saying to himself, wryly, that *this* time there would be no rejoinder from the Lord Bishop of Armagh. With his alleged atheism as the issue, Hobbes did not feel required to deal with Bramhall's criticisms of *Leviathan*'s politics; "the words *atheism, impiety,* and the like," he observed in his "To the Reader," are "words of the greatest defamation possible," whereas the errors of his "civil doctrines . . . if there be any, will not tend very much to my disgrace."[13] (His attempt to refute Bramhall also gave him the opportunity to write, as an appendix to *An Answer,* a monograph he entitled *An Historical Narration concerning Heresy and the Punishment Thereof.* In *Heresy,* which was not published until 1680, Hobbes argued that since the High Commission Court, which had had jurisdiction over heresy cases, was abolished before the Civil War and not reconstituted, neither he nor his books could be formally charged with heresy. In concluding his monograph, which was not one of his better efforts, he recommended to his prospective persecutors the counsel of Saint Paul "even in case of obstinate holding of an error" that "servants of the Lord" should strive to "be gentle unto all men, apt to teach, patient, in meekness instructing those that oppose themselves."[14] In the eighty years of his life that had preceded *Heresy,* Hobbes had been timorous and perhaps even contrite, but never before so abject.

The hypothesis, in other words, is that Hobbes probably was aware of *The Catching of the Leviathan* long before 1668 but that he saw no need to confront Bramhall until he began to fear for his personal safety. Had Hobbes chosen also to reply to Bramhall's rejection of his "civil doctrines," *An Answer* would hold more interest for the modern reader,

---

* Kennet, *Sermon Preached,* 15. "There was a report," wrote Aubrey, known to Hobbes "(and surely true) that in parliament, not long after the king was setled, some of the bishops made a motion to have the good old gentleman burn't for a heretique."

whose concern with atheism and with religion in general is considerably less than that of his seventeenth-century English ancestors. Bramhall's critique of *Leviathan*'s politics, moreover, is more profound and cogent—in a word, more worldly—than his canonical strictures, and one wishes, as one does in reading Clarendon's later *Brief View*, that Hobbes had been able or willing to respond. Perhaps the acuity of these two assessments owes a good deal to their having been written at a time when Bramhall and Clarendon, both suffering involuntary exile, were free enough of their customary duties and obligations, as well as resentful enough of Hobbes's enjoying (as they believed) the successive favors of Cromwell and Charles II, to give his greatest book their most careful attention.

The general tone of Bramwell's analysis of *Leviathan*, and something of his Anglican zeal, is reflected in the title of his book, the full version of which was *The Catching of the Leviathan, or the Great Whale, Demonstrating out of Mr. Hobbs his own Works, That no man who is thoroughly an Hobbist, can be a good Christian, or a Good Commonwealths man, or reconcile himself to himself. Because his Principles are not only destructive to all Religion but to all Societies; extinguishing the Relation between Prince and Subject, Parent and Child, Master and Servant, Husband and Wife; and abound with palpable contradictions.* Signing himself "John Bramhall, D.D. and Bishop of Derry," he added, for further instruction of his readers, "Proverbs: xii, 19. 'The lip of truth shall be established for ever but a lying tongue is but for a moment.' "[15]

The "lip of truth," according to Bramhall, was that the making of government was a more complex business than "the making of gunpowder," and therefore could not be reduced to certain formulae or self-evident rules. Taking issues with one of Hobbes's most cherished and long-standing convictions—namely, the belief that the art of government could and should be based on scientific principles analogous to those of mathematics—Bramhall insisted that the formulation of public policy was much more like a game of tennis, using Hobbes's own image in *Leviathan* of what government was not, than like any science. "State policy," he argued, "which is wholly involved in matter and circumstances of time and place and persons, is not at all like Arithmetic and Geometry, which are altogether abstracted from matter, but much more like Tennis play. . . . There is no room for Liberty in Arithmetic and Geometry."[16]

Here Bramhall was indirectly reminding Hobbes and his readers, as Clarendon later was also to do in his *Brief View and Survey*, that men of affairs, among whom Hobbes could not be included, were inclined to view government as more complex and involved than theoreticians and observers on the outside were apt to imagine. Bramhall, with his long experience in Ireland of church administration, not to mention his successful management of his own considerable properties, could make such a point with authority. In doing so, he came close to articulating the fundamental disagreement about the nature of politics that has always existed between political realists and practical politicians, on the one hand, and political theorists and idealists, often dubbed "closet philosophers" or "ivory tower dwellers," on the other. Hobbes, to be sure, thought of himself as a realist, but to Bramhall and Clarendon, the realism of Hobbes was akin to the "realism" of dreams and nightmares.*

As an Anglican who believed in free will, Bramhall also could not accept Hobbes's view that the natural state of man was the state of war. Men are not worse than "bears or wolves, or . . . the most savage wild beasts," Bramhall argued, and they do not habitually prey on their own kind any more than animals within a given species prey on each other.[17] The rise of civilization testifies to the fact that war is the occasional rather than the constant condition of mankind, and war when it does occur is not a wholly ruthless, cut-throat affair but is fought in accordance with its own rules and laws. Indeed, the Hobbesian state of nature in its entirety is a chimera: "There was never any such degenerate rabble of men in the world that were without all religion, all government, all laws natural and civil; no, not among the most barbarous Americans, who (except for some criminal habits) have more principles of natural piety and honesty than are readily to be found in his writings."[18] Surely, Bramhall once more insisted, Hobbes in writing about sovereignty, religion, and natural law cannot be describing the real world—"Did this man writ waking or dreaming?" he asked, rhetorically—but perhaps his principles were designed for the unsettled and primitive world of America. Certainly, the possibility deserved a test, and Bramhall, who was not lacking in humor, proposed that Hobbes should seek "a fit place in America, among the savages, to try if perhaps they might be persuaded that the names of good and evil, just and unjust doe signify nothing but at

---

*One wonders whether Bramhall and Clarendon were explicitly aware of the irony that Hobbes, whom they regarded as politically naive and woefully ignorant of governmental realities, was far more successful in accommodating himself to the political realities of his time, as a result of which his own exile abroad was wholly voluntary and much shorter than theirs. Although both men, Clarendon especially, envied Hobbes the favorable treatment he had been accorded by Cromwell and Charles II, and believed that he had deliberately courted Cromwell, neither apparently ever surmised that Hobbes, whatever interpretation might be attached to his writings, was quite adept at "Tennis play."

the pleasure of the sovereign Prince."[19] Indeed, he was all "for an accommodation: that Mr. T. H. should have the sole privilege of setting up his form of government in America, as being calculated and fitted for that Meridian. . . . And if it prosper there, then have the liberty to transplant it hither; who knoweth (if there could but be some means devised to make them understand his language), whether the Americans might not chuse him for their Sovereign? But the fear is that if he should put his principles into practice as magisterially as he doth dictate them, his supposed subjects might chance to tear their Mortal God to pieces with their teeth and entomb his sovereignty in their bowells."[20]

While many of Bramhall's more serious criticisms of *Leviathan* were repeated by Clarendon, the latter made no effort to emulate his wit or, despite the word "Brief" in the title, match his brevity; the 34 pages of *The Catching of the Leviathan* were, in total, little more than a tenth of the 322 pages that constituted the first edition of Clarendon's *Brief View and Survey*.* But perhaps the most extraordinary difference between the two books was Clarendon's inclusion of an "Epistle Dedicatory" to Charles II in which he drew attention, at Hobbes's expense, to his own character and service to the king. These introductory pages, in fact, are so much a plea for Charles's forgiveness and permission to return home, to the point of implying that Hobbes and not the author was the more deserving of exile, that the reader may be tempted to speculate that one of Clarendon's principal intentions in writing his book was to regain the king's favor irrespective of the cost to his own integrity and Hobbes's reputation. But whatever his intentions, his *Brief View and Survey* appeared too late to have any effect either on Charles or on Hobbes. Nineteen months after the "Epistle Dedicatory" was written, and, by coincidence, almost exactly nineteen months before his rebuttal of Hobbes was published, Clarendon was dead.†

The "Epistle Dedicatory" begins with a denunciation of Hobbes's

---

* Clarendon apparently had read one or more of the exchanges between Hobbes and Bramhall about free will, and he may have been familiar with the latter's *The Catching of the Leviathan* though he did not refer to it in his *Brief View*. Declaring that Hobbes would not "entangle" him in the free-will controversy, Clarendon ventured that Hobbes "hath enough exercis'd himself . . . with a more equal Adversary, who I think hath bin much too hard for him at his own weapon, Reason, the Learned Bishop of *Derry*, who was afterwards Arch-Bishop of *Armagh*, and by which he hath put him into a greater choler then a Philosopher ought to subject himself to, the terrible strokes whereof I am not willing to undergo . . ." (p. 80).

† The "Epistle Dedicatory" was dated "Moulins, May 10, 1673," though the book was not published until July 1, 1676, probably because a license to publish could not be

"false and evil" doctrine that a "banished Subject," far from being obligated to support the sovereign who banished him, is entitled to be "a lawful Enemy of the Common-wealth that banish'd him."[21] Assuring the king that despite the "insupportable burden of Your Majesties displeasure, and . . . the infamous brand of Banishment," he was one of his most loyal subjects, Clarendon declared, for emphasis, "I thank God . . . I have not thought my self one minute absolv'd in the least degree from the obligation of the strictest duty to your Person, and of the highest gratitude that the most oblig'd Servant can stand bound in. . . ." Having finished a work requested of him by Charles's "Blessed Father" (he was referring to his *History of the Rebellion*, first published 1702–04, "which I hope will be to the Honor of His Majesties memory, and your own magnanimous Sufferings"), he now was ready "to answer Mr. *Hobbes's Leviathan*, and confute the doctrine therein contain'd, so pernicious to the Soveraign Power of Kings, and destructive to the affection and allegiance of Subjects; notwithstanding which, by the protection the Author hath from the Act of Indemnity, and I know not what other connivance, it is manifest enough, that many odious Opinions, the seed whereof was first sowed in that Book, have bin since propagated, to the extreme scandal of the Government in Church and State."

Harsh words, but Clarendon was not through with Hobbes, whom he acknowledged to be, in his "Introduction," one of "the most ancient acquaintance I have in the World, and of whom I have alwaies had a great esteem." While Charles would have no difficulty detecting and "detesting" the "wickedness" of many principles asserted in *Leviathan*, were he to read the book (which Clarendon implied he had not), Clarendon could not be certain that others would recognize the "iniquity" of such principles, disguised as they were by "the frequent reciting of loose and disjointed Sentences, and bold Inferences . . . novelty and pleasantness of the Expressions, the reputation of the Gentleman for parts and Learning, with his confidence in Conversation, and especially the humor and inclination of the Time to all kind of Paradoxes . . . and the love of his person and company. . . ." Hobbes, moreover, "consulted too few Authors, and made use of too few Books; the benefit of which," Clarendon reminded the king, "my present condition has also depriv'd me of; altho the want which I complain most

---

obtained. According to the "Introduction," the writing of the first draft was completed during the month of April 1670. Clarendon, whose chronic ill health worsened in exile, died December 9, 1674. In June 1671 and August 1674, he formally requested the king's permission to return to England, but on neither occasion was his petition acknowledged, much less granted.

of, is of Friends to examine and controul. . . ." Still, he concluded the "Epistle Dedicatory," his "poor Discourse may be of some use and service to your Majesty; that all the World may know, how much you abhor all those extravagant and absurd Privileges, which no Christian Prince ever enjoied or affected." The "Privileges" referred to were those Hobbes had associated with absolute sovereignty, but since Clarendon had privately lamented other "Privileges" claimed by Charles, above all the king's careless, impatient, and self-indulgent manner of conducting government business, his exaggerated flattery of Charles can only be seen as a measure of his despair and desperate longing to return to his family and home. Once again, however, his wishes were not gratified, though he expressed the hope "that your Majesty will at some time call to your remembrance my long and incorrupted Fidelity to your Person," and signed himself "one of the oldest Servants that is now living, to your Father and your Self."

Repeating, in his "Introduction," what he had already written about Hobbes's qualities in his "Epistle Dedicatory," that he was "a Man of excellent parts" and so forth, all of which enhanced the acceptability of *Leviathan*, Clarendon, as has already been mentioned, insisted that a principal motivation of Hobbes had been to win the favor of Cromwell. Indeed, *Leviathan* had not been refuted when it was published, because of the futility in disputing "with a Man that commanded thirty Legions, (for Cromwel had been oblig'd to have supported him, who defended his Usurpations;) so afterwards Men thought it would be too much ill nature to call Men in question for what they had said in ill times, and for saying which they had a plenary Indulgence and Absolution." In his invoking of the image of "thirty Legions," did Clarendon seek to remind Charles and his readers of the thirty pieces of silver paid to Judas for betraying Christ? Was he making an analogy between Judas's behavior and Hobbes "betrayal" of the king and embrace of Cromwell? While we cannot be certain Clarendon was consciously and deliberately linking Judas and Hobbes, an affirmative answer to these questions is plausible in view of Clarendon's firm conviction that *Leviathan* had been made destructive of all established government and religion because Hobbes in 1650–51 had had "a mind to go home."

In his chapter-by-chapter analysis of *Leviathan*, which to this day is the lengthiest evaluation ever attempted, Clarendon discovered few pages totally unobjectionable. Hobbes, to begin with, was wrong to believe he could divine what all men thought, hoped, or feared by "looking into himself." The truth, rather, was "that much the major part of mankind do not think at all, are not endued with reason enough too opine, or think of what they did last, or what they are to do next."[22]

Men differ in their thoughts and passions to such an extent that, to take one example, "If Mr. *Hobbes*, and some other man were both condemn'd to death, (which is the most formidable thing Mr. *Hobbes* can conceive) the other could no more by looking into himself know Mr. *Hobbes's* present thoughts, and the extent of his fear, then he could, by looking in his face, know what he hath in his Pocket. . . . How comes it to pass, that one . . . undergo's death with no other concernment then as if he were going any other Journy, and the other with such confusion and trembling, that he is even without life before he dies; if it were true that all Men fear a-like upon the like occasion."[23] We may wonder, for the second time, whether Clarendon, in making a general point, wished also to insinuate a negative characterization of Hobbes, namely, that he feared death more than most men did, or should.

Hobbes was wrong, as well, in his "Expressions," which were "incongruous," and in his "Definitions," which were "not so exact as might have been expected from so great an Artist." We do not better understand the nature of laughter, Clarendon argued, when we are informed it is "suddain glory," or the meaning of "Contemt" on being told "it is nothing else but an immobility or contumacy of the heart, in resisting the action of certain things. . . ."[24] As for Hobbes's chapters devoted to the "Schole-men . . . who are in his debt for much mirth which he hath made out of them," Clarendon would leave their examination to the "Schole-men" themselves: "I for my part being very indifferent between them, as believing that the Schole-men have contributed very little more to the advancement of any noble or substantial part of Learning, than Mr. Hobbes hath don to the reformation or improvement of Philosophy and Policy."[25]

Clarendon's most extended criticisms of *Leviathan's* politics, like those of Bramhall, focused on Hobbes's conceptions of human nature, natural law, and sovereign power. When God made man in his image, Clarendon affirmed, "he endued him with Reason, and all the other noble Faculties . . . and therefore to uncreate him to such a baseness and villany in his nature, as to make Man such a Rascal, and more a Beast in his frame and constitution then those he is appointed to govern, is a power that God never gave to the Devil; nor hath any body affirm'd it, till Mr. *Hobbes* took it upon him."[26] Nor did God leave his "master" creation, "Man, in a condition of War of every man against every man, in such a condition of confusion . . . without any notions of, or instinct towards justice, honor, or good nature. . . . Nor had Mr. *Hobbes* any other reason to degrade him to this degree of Bestiality, but that he may be fit to wear those Chains and Fetters which he hath provided for him."[27] The theme that Hobbes's principles, if applied or acted upon by any ruler, would justify tyranny and enslavement is frequently struck by Clarendon, and he is chronically suspicious of Hobbes's motives in advancing such principles; as he warns a little further on, "we have great reason to watch him narrowly, when his Legislative fit is uppon him, least he cast such a net over us, that we be deprived of both the use of our liberty, and our reason to oppose him."[28]

Hobbes's arguments in support of his principles, Clarendon maintained, were as false as the propositions that accompanied them. The reason men locked their chests and doors, for instance, was not the "jealousie and malignity" of human nature, but their adherence to "that common practice of circumspection and providence, which custom and discretion hath introduced into human life. For men shut their Chests in which their mony is, as well that their servants or children may not know what they have, as that it may be preserved from Thieves; and they lock their doors that their Houses may not be common [i.e., open to everyone]; and ride arm'd, and in company, because they know there are ill men, who may be inclined to do injuries if they find an opportunity. . . . If it be known that there is one Thief in a City, all men have reason to shut their doors and lock their chests: and if there be two or three Drunkards in a Town, all men have reason to go arm'd in the streets, to controul the violence or indignity they might receive from them."[29] Besides, Clarendon added, many men, doubting that anyone wants to do them harm, no longer carry swords or wear doublets. In short, the state of nature was not a state of war, and natural law did not presume a war of all against all.

Clarendon was hardly less a royalist than Hobbes—"I shall heartily concur with Mr. *Hobbes* in the preference of Monarchy," he declared at one point (p. 59)—but as a constitutionalist he could not endorse the concept of absolute power residing wholly in the sovereign, nor could he view sovereign authority as primarily based on force. The "extent of power and authority" that Hobbes assigned to the "Soveraign command and Government" of his "Commonwealth as never was in nature" or the world, Clarendon protested, was such "as the Great *Turk* hath not yet appear'd to affect."[30] By this assertion Clarendon did not mean that sovereign power, both for its own security and the peace of society, was wise to take into account, and sometimes defer to, wise counsel and popular opinion. As he put it, in an attempt to correct Hobbes, "There is no doubt there are in all Governments many things don by, and with the consent of the People; nay all Government so much depends upon the consent of the People, that without their consent and submission it must be dissolved, since where no body will obey, there can be no command, nor can one man compel a million to do what they have no mind to do. . . . " But this did not imply that "any Government was originally instituted by an assembly of men equally free, and that they ever elected the Person who should have the Soveraign power over them. . . ."[31]

Had Hobbes truly been informed about the English constitution and monarchy, "of which he knows no more then every other man of *Malmesbury*," Clarendon wrote contemptuously, he would have realized that the sovereignty of the king was derived not from any compact but "from a descent of six hundred years," and that the king "was alone called Soveraign, had the title of Majesty from every one of his Subjects, and was unquestionably taken by them for their King."[32] As for Hobbes's assumption that the "late troubles" or rebellion owed a good deal to the theory of "mixed monarchy," an assumption that Hobbes was to develop further in his later *Behemoth* (where he suggested that Clarendon himself had subscribed to the theory!), the view *"that the power was divided between the King, and the Lords, and the House of Commons* . . . was an opinion never heard of in *England* until the Rebellion was begun, and against which all the Laws of *England* were most cleer. . . ."[33] The causes of the "late execrable Rebellion," Clarendon insisted, were not defects in the law or in the authority of the king, but "the power ill [i.e., evil] men rebelliously possessed themselves of, by which they suppressed the strength of the Laws, and wrested the power out of the hands of the King." While no one, Hobbes included, can doubt that such men "were guilty in the highest degree," some of those who declared as much, notably "Dr. Manwaring, and Dr. Sibthorpe," who did so before Hobbes, lacked "the good fortune to escape punishment as he [Hobbes] hath don."[34] Once again, Clarendon's enmity toward Hobbes is apparent.

Enmity usually gave way to vilification when Clarendon could prove to his own satisfaction, if not to that of all others, that Hobbes's opinions in *Leviathan* were directly and entirely connected with Cromwell, and on one occasion he accused Hobbes of taking "very officious care that Cromwell should not fall from his greatness" and that England "should remain still captive under the Tyranny of his vile Posterity." In contradiction of the prevailing legal fiction, to which Clarendon wholeheartedly subscribed, that the king never dies (popularly, "The king is dead, long live the king!") and that the succession is by blood descent, Hobbes had held that a reigning monarch could choose his successor or heir "by his expresse Words, and Testament," the purpose of such selection being the avoidance of any return to "Confusion, and to the condition of a War." that would result from succession by a weak or incompetent ruler.[35] Outraged by this assertion, Clarendon expressed his certainty that "in the Year One thousand six hundred fifty one," when *Leviathan* was printed, Hobbes could not have had any other end in view but inducing "Cromwell to break all the Laws of his Country, and to perpetuate their slavery under his Progeny." Indeed, Hobbes's doctrine of succession was so repugnant to all established kingdoms that Clarendon wondered that Hobbes's "own natural fear of danger, which made him fly out of *France*, as soon as his *Leviathan* was publish'd and brought into that Kingdom," had not "terrified him from invading the right of all Hereditary Monarchies in the World."*

Clarendon could not even discover some merits in Hobbes's *Thucydides*, first published almost fifty years earlier, though one might think he would have found much to praise in Hobbes's warnings against democracy and demagoguery. Objecting to Hobbes's charge that civil wars and insurrections everywhere had been "contriv'd or fomented by men who had spent much time in the reading of Greek and Latin Authors," a favorite Hobbesian theme, Clarendon countered that "*Jack Straw* and *Wat Tyler*, whose Insurrection . . . was as dangerous as hath happened in any Age or Climate, had never read *Aristotle* or *Cicero*; and I believe, had Mr. *Hobbes* bin of this opinion when he taught *Thucydides* to speak English, which Book contains more of the Science of Mutiny and Sedition, and teaches more of that Oratory that contributes thereunto, then all that *Aristotle* and *Cicero* have published in all their Writings, he would not have communicated such materials to his Country-men."[36] But much worse, in this respect, was *Leviathan*, which, if believed, "would undermine Monarchy more in two months" than Aristotle and Cicero had done in all the years since their death and would cause men to wish "that the Author of it had never bin born in the English Climate, nor bin taught to read and write."[37]

In the final pages of his *Brief View and Survey*, Clarendon once again linked Hobbes to Cromwell, adding, for good measure, that he had never read a book containing "so much Sedition, Treason, and Impiety." But it was no good asking Hobbes to recant, "because he would be too ready to do it upon his declared *Salvo*" of survival and self-preservation at all costs. Hobbes, instead, would be effectively punished "by knowing that his Book is condemned by the Soveraign Authority, to be publickly burn'd, which by his own judgment will refrain him from publishing his pernicious Doctrine."[38] "I should be

---

* Brief View, 60–61. The only known instance of Hobbes being questioned about his views, in what may have been originally a face-to-face discussion, was with reference to his conception of "hereditary right." The document recording this discussion is printed as Appendix 2.

very glad," he concluded his review of *Leviathan*, striking a note reminiscent of Bramhall, "that Mr. *Hobbes* might have a place in Parliament, and sit in Counsel, and be present in Courts of Justice, and
other Tribunals; whereby it is probable he would find, that his solitary cogitation, how deep soever, and his too peremptory adhering to
some Philosophical Notions, and even Rules of Geometry, had misled
him in that investigation of Policy." The hoped-for result might be
that Hobbes "would rather retire to his quiet corner in the *Peak*" than
continue in the company of those responsible for the conduct of public affairs.[39]

Claredon's seemingly casual reference to "Rules of Geometry" is
one of many comments or asides taking note, usually in a sarcastic
fashion, of Hobbes's intense interest in mathematics and its possible
application to politics. Early in his *Brief View and Survey*, he shrewdly
observed that Hobbes had been greatly disturbed by allegations of
"gross errors, and grosser oversights in those parts of Science in which
Mr. *Hobbes* would be thought to excel," compared with which his
own criticisms would be regarded by Hobbes as less important.[40] Such
allegations "made by Learned Men of both the Universities," he later
commented, "are like to put him more out of countenance then any
thing I can urge against him," Hobbes valuing himself "more upon
being thought a good Philosopher, and a good Geometrician, than a
modest Man, or a good Christian." Far from unhappy about his inferior critical position, Clarendon was gleeful that the "Learned Men,"
in defending their universities against Hobbes's accusations that they
neglected mathematics in favor of Aristotle and the antiquated doctrines of the Schools, had made of Hobbes something of a fool. By
now, Clarendon suggested, Hobbes himself must be aware of his "many
Errors, and of not being enough conversant in [geometry]; insomuch
as the Learned and Reverend Dr. *Ward*, the present Lord Bishop of
Salisbury, and Dr. *Wallis*, the Worthy Professor of Geometry in *Oxford*,
have both produced a Person to him, whom he thought in the beginning of his *Leviathan* impossible to find . . . *who is so stupid, as both
to mistake in Geometry, and also to persist in it, when another detects
his error to him.*"[41]

The "so stupid" individual, of course, was Hobbes, who, for a
considerable number of years before and after Clarendon wrote these
lines at Moulins, was involved in what might be called, in a paraphrase of one of his own famous formulations, a war of one against
all. The more numerous side eventually included, in addition to Seth
Ward (1617–1689), the Dutch mathematician and astronomer Christian Huygens (1629–1695), and many, though by no means all, of the
founding members of the Royal Society. As in other such wars, the

lesser and weaker side lost, and as a result Hobbes's reputation as a scientist was sharply diminished both in England and abroad. While we can be reasonably certain that his defeat was not solely responsible for his exclusion from the Royal Society and consequent difficulty in being taken seriously as a scientist, his papers and letters leave no doubt he was very hurt by the society's refusal to admit him to its ranks.

The chronicle of Hobbes's lost war, which in duration could almost be regarded as a kind of intellectual Thirty Years' War, began with Hobbes's censure, in *Leviathan*, of the universities, and the publication of his views about religion.[42] Ward and Wallis, both Savilian professors at Oxford and clergymen, strongly objected to these opinions and undertook to refute them. Ward, who had four years earlier contributed a friendly preface to Hobbes's *Humane Nature* (1650) signed with the initials "F.B." (for Francis Bowman, an Oxford bookseller), initiated hostilities, in 1654, with a defense of the universities and the extraordinary charge that Hobbes was guilty of plagiarism on at least two counts. In his *Vindiciae Academiarum*, a book mainly directed at John Webster's *Academiarum Examen* but with some attention given to Hobbes, Ward claimed that Descartes, Gassendi, and Digby had anticipated Hobbes in developing the theory that the senses derived from motion, and he alleged further that Hobbes's optical discoveries were based on the research of Walter Warner, a scientist who had done experimental work with lenses and magnifying glasses. He also challenged Hobbes, no doubt certain in advance of the outcome, to publish his latest geometric findings. Hobbes, who believed he had solved the problem of squaring the circle, a conundrum that had eluded the best mathematical minds from the beginning of time, eagerly took the bait, thereby presenting his critics, in *De Corpore* (1655), where his "solution" appeared, with a fish they could hardly resist landing. Hobbes, who eventually produced twelve different circle-squaring "solutions," had not in fact solved the problem, though the more Wallis and others proved he had not, the more Hobbes insisted that he had.

Thus, when Wallis demolished Hobbes's proud achievement, in his *Elenchus Geometriae Hobbianae* (1655) Hobbes simply created another version of his circle squaring, which he published in the English edition of *De Corpore* (1656). Meanwhile Ward, who apparently wrote in partnership with Wallis, each taking turns, as it were, reeling in their fish, published another critique of Hobbes, this one directed at his philosophy, in *Thomae Hobbii Philosophiam Exercitatio Epistolica* (1656). Hobbes, nothing daunted, responded to both Wallis and Ward by writing, as an appendix to the English *De Corpore, Six Lessons to the Professors of Mathematicks of the Institution of Sir Henry*

Savile in the University of Oxford (1656). Far from convinced that his circle-squaring efforts had been wrong to the point of absurdity, Hobbes in his *Six Lessons* took the offensive against Ward and Wallis, an offensive that, despite their counter-attacks, was not to terminate until shortly before his death in 1679.

Almost all of the *Six Lessons* was devoted to establishing that Ward and Wallis together knew less geometry than Hobbes; to their assertions that he, not Joseph Scaliger, was the worst geometrician who had ever lived, Hobbes replied that "my geometry is to yours as 1 to 0."* Taunted by Wallis, who had asked whether Hobbes was angry, or blushed, or could endure to hear Wallis, Hobbes retorted, "I have some reason to be angry; for what man can be so patient as not to be moved with so many injuries? And I have some reason to blush, considering the option men will have beyond sea, (when they shall see this in Latin) of the geometry taught at Oxford. But to read the worst you can say against me, I can endure, as easily at least, as to read any thing you have written. . . ."[43] Geometry, Hobbes admitted, may now be taught at Oxford, but it had little place in the university when he was a student, and while he did not deny *"then* that there were in Oxford many good geometricians," he did "deny *now*, that either of you is of the number."[44]

Defending himself against accusations of atheism and disrespect to religion, Hobbes asked, rhetorically, "Do you think I can be an atheist and not know it? Or knowing it, durst have offered my atheism to the press? Or do you think him an atheist, or a contemner of the Holy Scripture, that sayeth nothing of the Deity but what he proveth by the Scripture?" As for his argument that the "rules of God's worship" should be based on laws or statutes, to which Ward and Wallis had made strong objection, "from whom," Hobbes queried them, "would you have them taken? From yourselves? Why so,

---

* *E. W.*, VII, 291. Scaliger (1540–1609), chiefly remembered as a classicist but described in the *Encyclopaedia Britannica* (13th ed., XXIV, 284) as "the greatest scholar of modern times," was much admired by Hobbes, who defended his mathematical reputation at length in *Six Lessons*. Aubrey suggested that one could say of Hobbes, as someone had said of Scaliger, "that when he erres, he erres so ingeniosely, that one had rather erre with him then hitt the mark with Clavius," and there were other similarities. For Hobbes, like Scaliger, with whom he may have had some identification, "made numerous enemies . . . he despies and hates all who differ from him. . . . Nor was he always right. . . . His emendations, if frequently happy, were sometimes absurd . . . he relied sometimes upon groundless, sometimes even absurd hypotheses, frequently upon an imperfect induction of facts. Sometimes he misunderstood. . . . And he was no mathematician. But his enemies were not merely those whose errors he had exposed and whose hostility he had excited by the violence of his language. The results of his system of historical criticism had been adverse to the Catholic controversialists. . . ." *Encyclopaedia Britannica*, 13th ed., XXIV, 285.

more than from me? from the bishops? Right, if the supreme power of the commonwealth will have it so. . . . From a consistory of pres- byters, by themselves, or joined with lay-elders, whom they may sway as they please? Good, if the supreme governor of the commonwealth will have it so; if not, why from them, rather than from me, or from any man else?" He charged his accusers with breaking "the greatest of God's commandments, which is charity," in calling him an atheist, and accused them, in turn, of being "only ignorant and imprudent Christians." How, Hobbes asked them, "could you think me an athe- ist, unless it were because finding your doubts of the Deity more fre- quent than other men do, you are thereby the apter to fall upon that kind of reproach? Wherein you are the like women of poor and evil education when they scold; amongst whom the readiest disgraceful word is whore: why not thief, or any other ill name, but because, when they remember themselves, they think that reproach the like- liest to be true?"[45] Perhaps he was not far from implying that Ward and Wallis were whores as well as atheists, for he had earlier noted that neither wrote anything "but what is dictated to each of you by a doctor of divinity."[46]

Hobbes's *Six Lessons* elicited more insults from Wallis. In a work entitled *Due Correction for Mr. Hobbes; or, Schoole Discipline For Not Saying His Lessons Right* (1656), Wallis made the further charge that Hobbes had stolen a number of his mathematical formulations from Descartes, Mersenne, Fermat, Roberval, and others, a charge to which Hobbes responded, in 1657, with his *Etirmai; or, Markes of the Absurd Geometry, Rural Language, Scottish Church-Politicks, and Barbarisms of John Wallis, Professor of Geometry and Doctor of Divinity*. In *Markes* Hobbes, in addition to disputing Wallis's geometry and religious views, ridiculed his employing such words as "lurry," which Hobbes declared he did not understand and had heard spoken only once, and resorting to such rustic expressions as "just the same to a cow's thumb."[47] In taking exception to Wallis's language, Hobbes was retaliating, in effect, for the fun made of his name by Ward and Wallis in their references to "fairies which you call in English hob-goblins" and to their "jest for using at every word *mi Hobbi*."* Wallis, completely unchastened, replied with *Hobbiani Puncti Dispunctio; or, The Undoing of Mr Hobs's Points* (1657), in which he informed Hobbes, "My Elenchus, you say, made you angry. Very likely! I'le take your word for that, without

---

E.W., VII, 355. Hobbes's critics often reminded him, teasingly, of the plebeian origins of his name, citing such words and phrases as "Hob," meaning a clumsy, awkward rustic or, in American parlance, a hick; hob-nail; to play hob with; hobble; and hobby- horse.

swearing. And you perceive (you say) your lessons have in some measure moved me. They have so: But not to those passions which I suppose, you could have wished; not much either to Grief, or Anger; but
to mirth sometimes, I confesse they have."[48]

For almost three years there were no further exchanges between
Wallis and Hobbes, but in 1660–61 their warfare began again with
two publications by Hobbes, one of which, his *Examinatio et Emendatio Mathematicae Hodiernae* (1660), was a reassertion of his own
principles and a detailed criticism of Wallis's, and the other was still
another Hobbesian "solution" to a hoary problem, a duplication of
the cube. The latter, entitled *Dialogus Physicus* (1661), also inaugurated a dispute with Robert Boyle, whose experiments with the air
pump Hobbes found unconvincing. Hobbes, who had doubts about
the existence of the vacuum, took issue with Boyle's discoveries and
with the Royal Society's whole bent toward experimentation; perhaps he surmised, by that time, that unless he was able to gain some
credence with both Wallis and Boyle, he would not be admitted to
the society, which, after meeting informally for some years, was issued
a royal charter in 1662. Boyle, in any case, replied politely but firmly
in 1662 to the *Dialogus Physicus*, and he apparently believed that his
corrections of Hobbes settled the matter. But Hobbes, as Boyle might
have known from the continuing warfare between Hobbes and Wallis, was not one easily to admit defeat. When Hobbes proceeded, in
his *Problemata Physica* (1662), to argue the case against the vacuum
and to advance other dubious propositions about the nature of the
physical universe, Boyle was not willing to respond, but when Hobbes
indicated, in 1674, that he stood by his earlier "solutions," Boyle once
more resorted to print. "Upon the coming abroad of Mr. Hobbes's
Problemata Physica," he wrote in the preface to his *Animadversions
upon Mr. Hobbes's Problemata de Vacuo*, "I found, by obvious passages in the third Chapter, or Dialogue, as well as by the title . . . that
I was particularly concerned in it. . . . [But] the natural Indisposition
I have to Polemical Discourses, easily perswaded me to let alone a
Controversie, that did not appear needful: And I had still persisted in
my silence, if Mr. Hobbes had not as 'twere summoned me to break
it by publishing again his *Explications* [*Principia et Problemata Ali-
quot* (1674)] which in my *Examen* of his Dialogue *De Natura Aeris* I
had shewn to be erroneous."[49]

Meanwhile, Hobbes and Wallis, neither of whom was in the least
averse to "Polemical Discourses," remained locked in hostile embrace.
From 1666 to 1678 Hobbes published six additional works sharply
critical of Wallis, and he also submitted papers and wrote letters to
the Royal Society, many of them hostile to Wallis, which were not

circulated to more than a few members. The quality of the substance
and language of the Hobbes-Wallis exchanges had long since deteri-
orated, with Wallis referring to one of Hobbes's books as a "shitten
piece," and Hobbes assailing Wallis's "Geometry and Philosophy" as
"in sum . . . all Errour and Railing, that is *stinking wind*, such as a
Jade [i.e., horse] lets flie when he is too hard girt upon a full belly."[50]
When Wallis, anticipating Clarendon, accused Hobbes of having
written *Leviathan* "in defence of Oliver's Title," Hobbes heatedly denied
the charge and, in return, attacked Wallis for having deciphered during the Civil War "the Letters of the King and His Party, and thereby
delivered his Majesties secrets to the Enemy, and His best Friends to
the Scaffold, and boasted of it in your Book of Arithmetick (written
in Latin) to all the World."[51] Wallis's claim that he had done so "to
the King's advantage," Hobbes asserted, only proved that he had been
a traitor to both sides.

Clearly, these charges and countercharges had nothing to do with
geometry or other purely scientific issues, but they were used to discredit Hobbes, who, unlike Wallis, could not fire broadsides from the
safety of a highly respected chair of mathematics at Oxford. Hobbes
was dealing with Wallis and Ward from a position of weakness, and
his natural stubbornness in defending a vulnerable position, a stubbornness that had its uses in connection with his political and religious views, was an extreme disadvantage to him in dealing with
matters the truth or falsity of which could be more objectively determined. His unyielding efforts, in geometry, to prove the unprovable,
his conviction that the experimental method in science was inferior
to the deductive approach, and his aggressive arrogance in stating
his opinions, whatever the subject, had combined to deprive him, by
1661, of some of the hard-won reputation, and a substantial measure
of the personal satisfaction, he had brought with him from Paris ten
years earlier. Certain circles of admirers, notably those who had succeeded Mersenne in France and including, somewhat improbably,
Cosimo III de' Medici (to whom Hobbes dedicated one of his mathematical works in 1669), remained persuaded of Hobbes's importance
as a scientist, and he was not without allies in the Royal Society itself,
but he no longer was regarded by every savant as "among the philosophers" who mattered. Ironically, perhaps, his loss of status may have
helped protect him, after the Restoration, from those returning royalists and Anglican bishops who were eager to wreak vengeance on
suspected regicides and their supporters. Had Hobbes, who was seventy-two years old in 1660, been perceived as more influential than
eccentric, he might have had a difficult time of it.

His exclusion from the Royal Society, however, an action that
hurt him and embittered his declining years, cannot be entirely

explained in terms of doubts about his scientific stature. Hobbes, to be sure, knew less about the physical world than Boyle did, as he knew less about mathematics than Wallis did, In addition to believing that there were no empty spaces in the world and that as a consequence there was "no vacuum," despite the evidence accumulated by Pascal, Torricelli, and Boyle,* Hobbes disputed the existence of gravity and held some curious notions about the nature of tides, lightning, frost, and ice. The reason stones and other bodies fall to earth after being thrown upward, Hobbes suggested in his *Seven Philosophical Problems*, is "that the globe of the earth hath some special motion, by which it more easily casteth off the air than it doth other bodies . . . when the air is thrown off from the earth, somewhat must come into the place of it, in case the world be full: and it must be those things which are hardliest cast off, that is, those things which we say are heavy."[52] In explaining tides, Hobbes proposed that the earth's motion forces the sea currents "east and west" to the shores of America and India; as to the former, the barrier to the current is a "bar . . . [constituting] the south part of America, which leaves no passage for the water but the narrow strait of Magellan. The tide rises therefore upon the coast of America. . . ."[53] Lightning, which he defined as "the fancy made by the recoiling of the air against the eye," sometimes brings death by killing "men with cold," not with burning or heat.[54] Strong winds, Hobbes also maintained, are the cause of frost and ice; indeed, ice "is nothing else but the smallest imaginable parts of air and water mixed."[55]

While these beliefs reveal that Hobbes was not among the most enlightened scientists of the late seventeenth century, they do not establish that he "was no scientist" or that his writings in that area read "like a travesty of Swift."[56] The great German astronomer Johannes Kepler (1571–1630) was a mystic, and Isaac Newton (1642–1727), perhaps the greatest scientist who ever lived, believed in astrology and practiced alchemy. Moreover, scientific achievement, however defined, was not a requirement for membership in the Royal Society. The society's charter book 1662, the official founding date, is signed by Wallis and Boyle, who were instrumental in guiding the

---

* In his *Problemata Physica* of 1662, published in English the same year as *Seven Philosophical Problems and Two Propositions of Geometry*, which he dedicated to Charles II, Hobbes insisted "that no experiment made with the engine at Gresham College [i.e., the Royal Society], is sufficient to prove that ther is, or that ther may be vacuum." *E.W.*, VII, 22–23. He was even more convinced of the vacuum's nonexistence in his *Decameron Physiologicum*, which appeared in 1678, when he was ninety years old. "If sucking would make a vacuum," he asked rhetorically, using a homely example, "what would become of those women that are nurses? Should they not be in a very few days exhausted, were it not that either the air which is in the child's mouth penetrateth the milk as it descends, and passeth through it, or the breast it contracted?" Ibid., 90.

society from its earliest meetings in Oxford, and a number of other distinguished scientists and philosophers including the diarist and arboriculturist John Evelyn;* Hobbes's friend the physician William Petty; Dr. John Wilkins, the influential warden of Wadham College, Oxford, and subsequently bishop of Chester; and Christopher Wren. But the more then one hundred charter fellows also included John Aubrey, the third earl of Devonshire, Sir Kenelm Digby, and Sorbière, who, apparently by coincidence, was passing through London when the royal charter was presented and was invited, perhaps by Wallis, whom he admired, to take the oath of membership and sign the charter book. Surely in this company, if not in that mentioned earlier, Hobbes would not have been either unfit or unwelcome.

The more probable reason Hobbes was refused admission to the Royal Society was not his mathematics, or his politics, or his obstinacy in both areas, but his religion or, rather, the common perception that he did not believe in God. In the seventeenth century the leading scientists of England, including almost all the founders of the Royal Society, were deeply religious men, some of whom were, like Wallis, Ward, and Wilkins, clergymen as well as philosophers and mathematicians. Robert Boyle, one of those scientists who were not founders, was particularly devout, devoting a good deal of his money and energy to supporting missionary activities and subsidizing translations of the Bible into American Indian, Turkish, Malayan, Gaelic, Welsh, and other languages. Partly as a result of these influences, the Royal Society, far from encouraging thought or speculation about religion, much less any discussion of the compatibility of science and religion (not that such discussion was taking place anywhere in that age), declared at the outset that religion was not a proper subject for research and investigation. As one of its statutes put it, the purpose of the Royal Society was "to improve the knowledge of naturall things, and all useful Arts, Manufactures, Mechanick practices, Engynes and Inventions by Experiments—(not meddling with Divinity, Metaphysics, Moralls, Politicks, Grammar, Rhetorick, or Logick)."[57] Hobbes, of course, had "meddled" with all of these forbidden subjects, especially the first, in *Leviathan*, in connection with which his "meddling" was viewed, by Wallis in a 1659 letter to Huygens, as "furiously attacking and destroying . . . especially ministers and the Clergy and all religion, as though the Christian world had not sound knowledge."[58]

---

*On December 14, 1655, Evelyn wrote in his diary, "I visited Mr. Hobbes, the famous philosopher of Malmesbury, with whom I had been long acquainted in France. . . . Now were the Jews admitted." So far as is known, Hobbes never referred to this reversal by Cromwell of an exclusionary policy dating back to the time of Edward I in 1291.

Since Hobbes had implied, according to Wallis, then "men could not understand religion if they did not understand Mathematics," those opposed to his views could undo the damage by showing that *he* did not understand mathematics. Hence Wallis, Ward, and eventually Boyle, as well, agreed "it seemed necessary some mathematician should show him . . . how little he understands the Mathematics from which he takes his courage; nor should we be deterred from doing this by his arrogance which we know will cast up poisonous filth against us."[59] Three years later, in 1662, Boyle expressed a similar opinion, probably urged on him by Wallis, in observing of Hobbes, "[It] was also suggested to me that the dangerous Opinions about some important, if not fundamental, Articles of religion I had met with in his *Leviathan*, and some other of his writings, have made too great Impressions upon divers persons . . . these Errors being chiefly recommended by the Opinion they had of Mr. Hobbes's demonstrative way of Philosophy; it might possibly prove some service . . . to show that in Physicks themselves his opinions and even his Ratiocinations have no such great advantage over those of some Orthodox Christian Naturalists."[60] In short, the most effective way of nullifying *Leviathan* and undermining Hobbes's influence, Wallis and Boyle agreed, was not a refutation of *Leviathan* chapter by chapter but a successful effort to discredit Hobbes as a mathematician and scientist.

In accordance with this strategy, which was, as has been noted, not without effect, Wallis, Boyle and some others insisted that Hobbes be denied membership in the Royal Society, for to have admitted him would have been to restore at least some part of his creditability. Their strategy, apparently, applied as well to anything written by Hobbes; all books and papers he submitted to the society were either totally ignored or given bad reviews in its official journal, the *Philosophical Transactions*. On at least one occasion, a subject discussed by Hobbes in a letter was presented to a society meeting by one of its members, with no mention of Hobbes either at the meeting or in the report that followed in the society's *Journal Book*.[61] Clearly, as far as Wallis, Boyle, and the scientific circles they dominated were concerned, Hobbes was a nonperson.*

---

*Wallis's animus toward Hobbes, which was much more virulent than that displayed by Ward or Boyle, may have been fed by a recognition, conscious or otherwise, of certain unwanted resemblances. Wallis's father, like Hobbes's, a minister who named his son after himself, died when young John was six years old (he was almost fifty when his son was born). A supporter of the parliamentary side in the Civil War—Hobbes's charge that Wallis had deciphered secret letters and papers of the royalists was accurate—Wallis nevertheless opposed the death sentence of Charles I, despite which he became, in June 1649, Savilian Professor of Geometry at Oxford. Twelve years

Hobbes, angry and bitter about this treatment until the end of his life, may never have fully understood the role his religious views played in his exclusion from the Royal Society. Though he repeatedly defended himself against charges he was an atheist, he apparently believed that his major differences with the scientific community represented by Wallis and Boyle were philosophical ones involving the nature of scientific research and discovery. In some of his remarks on the subject, he seems even to have confused the meanings of experimentation and invention, and to have believed that neither was the necessary foundation of "natural philosophy." Not everyone who experiments or invents, he wrote in 1662, is a philosopher or is qualified "to reason upon their work . . . (and) to discern the differences of things." For the truth is, "Every man that hath spare money, can get furnaces, and buy coals. Every man that hath spare money, can be at the charge of making great moulds, and hiring workmen to grind their glasses; and so may have the best and greatest telescopes. They can get engines made, and apply them to the stars . . . but they are never the more philosophers for all this. It is laudable, I confess, to bestow money upon curious or useful delights; but that is none of the praises of a philosopher. . . . So also of all other arts; not every one that brings from beyond seas a new gin, or other jaunty [i.e., pleasing] device, is therefore a philosopher. For if you reckon that way, not only apothecaries and gardeners, but many other sorts of workmen, will put in for, and get the prize. Then, when I see the gentlemen of Gresham College apply themselves to the doctrine of motion, (as Mr. Hobbes had done, and will be ready to help them in it, if they please, and so long as they use him civilly,) I will look to know some causes of natural events from them, and their register, and not before: for nature does nothing but by motion."[62]

But neither then nor in the remaining seventeen years of Hobbes's life was the Royal Society willing to "use him civilly." Sometime after his death, however, the society made its amends, in a certain fashion, by hanging two portraits of Hobbes, its most prominent non-member, on its walls. No doubt Hobbes himself would have been pleased to know this, and perhaps he would have been even more gratified to discover that as of February 1981 the society owned and displayed two portraits of Robert Boyle, but only one portrait of John Wallis, and none at all of Seth Ward.

---

later he was appointed one of the king's chaplains in ordinary, Charles II either not knowing or not caring about Wallis's services to his enemies during the Civil War. Dying in 1703 at the age of eighty-seven, he lived almost as long as Hobbes. Wallis, in short, like Hobbes, was adept at "Tennis play."

THE BEAR IN WINTER

ROM 1651 TO 1660 Hobbes much preferred the intellectual stim-
ulation and social congeniality of London to life in the country, and as a result he spent little time at Hardwick or
Chatsworth. Far from suffering under the rule of Parliament
and Cromwell, Hobbes prospered, and he knew that this fact
of his existence had been duly reported in Paris, where his enemies
at the exiled court, a small but not wholly insignificant number following publication of *De Cive*, had swelled considerably with *Leviathan* and his abrupt return home. Denied access to the king's person
on the eve of his departure for London, Hobbes may well have wondered, before Charles's triumphal return in May 1660, whether, as a
reputed atheist, traitor to the royal cause, and lackey to the dead
"usurper," he again would be forced to flee for his life.

Perhaps for this reason he spent the winter of 1659–60 in Derbyshire, according to Aubrey, rather than in London, where royalist circles were busy preparing the way for the restoration of the monarchy.
While we do not know that Hobbes shared these anxieties with his
patron and employer, the third earl of Devonshire, he probably would
have found the earl sympathetic had he done so, for the earl, too, was
not without certain apprehensions. In keeping with his position, the
third earl, whose brother Charles was killed at Gainsborough in 1643,
had accompanied other royalists to France during the Civil War,
leaving his mother, the formidable Christian, in charge of the estates.
In 1645, however, the estates were threatened with sequestration,
whereupon Christian, with the assistance of some influential friends,
was able to arrange a settlement: the return of her son from France
and his making peace with the king's enemies, in exchange for the
right of the Devonshires to retain possession of the family properties.
By the end of 1645, the earl, who apparently won few if any arguments with his mother, was back at Hardwick, and he remained there,
or resided at one of the other houses, most of the time until his death

in 1684. His return to England and his estates fifteen years before the Restoration, and while the Civil War was still being fought, may have generated in him, as in Hobbes, a certain uneasiness about the future. Such feeling had some foundation. As an early Devonshire biographer put it, delicately, "After the Restoration, which was in 1660, we do not find that the Earl often went to court, or that the King shewed him any particular marks of favor for the signal services he had done the Royal Family; on which occasion, a modern writer justly observes, 'That one of his disposition was not fitted to shine in great employments, during the reign of Charles II.' However, it ought to be noted, to his honour, that the King's ingratitude made no impression on him . . . he withdrew into the country, where he shewed, by his great charity and hospitality, what an happiness it is for the world, *when such men are blest with ample* fortunes."[1] The earl's mother, who had courted disaster during the Protectorate by her efforts in behalf of the Stuarts, was more welcome at court than her son, and she continued to dominate him and his household until her death in January 1675, aged eighty.

Hobbes, perhaps would have shared the third earl's country exile had not Aubrey, and perhaps others, urged him to come to London for the king's arrival there on May 29, 1660. Aubrey must have known, or at least had good reason to believe, that Charles II was not averse to seeing his former instructor in mathematics, because Hobbes was easily and quickly persuaded. "It happened," Aubrey reported, "about two or three dayes after his majestie's happy returne, that, as he was passing in his coach through the Strand, Mr. Hobbes was standing at Little Salisbury-house gate (where his lord [the third earl] then lived). The king espied him, putt of his hatt very kindly to him, and asked how he did." Hobbes must have been very relieved to find himself once again in the king's good graces, and even more pleased when, a week or so later, "he had orall conference with his majesty at Mr. S. Cowper's, where, as he sate for his picture, he was diverted by Mr. Hobbes's pleasant discourse.[2] Here his majestie's favours were redintegrated to him, and order was given that he should have free accesse to his majesty, who was always much delighted in his witt and small repartees."

The difference between the king's treatment of Hobbes in 1651 and the reception accorded him in 1660 probably owed a good deal to the vast improvement in Charles's situation and prospects during those nine years. In 1651 the king, an exile in a staunchly Catholic country whose advisers were, for the most part, deeply religious men (not to mention his ultra-Catholic mother, Henrietta Maria, who intensely disliked Hobbes), necessarily had to take account of Hobbes's grow-

John Aubrey (1626–1697), Hobbes's much younger friend and lifelong admirer. This portrait depicts Aubrey in 1666, when he was forty years old.

ing reputation as an atheist. Whatever he may have felt privately, Charles could not risk continuing his relationship with Hobbes, who had by late 1651 aroused such hostility in French clerical circles that he was forced—or at least believed he was forced—to escape to England in the dead of winter. In 1660, however, Charles, as monarch, who never had any reason to doubt Hobbes's royalist convinctions, could afford to manifest indifference to questions concerning Hobbes's religiosity, or lack of it, though not to go so far as to permit further publication of Hobbes's political views.* Moreover, Charles himself, who was not known for his piety as a Protestant, the faith in which he was born, or for his devoutness as a Catholic, the faith in which he died, may have secretly shared some of Hobbes's opinions. In addition to believing that religion was subservient to politics, he apparently entertained "rather an odd idea" of God, holding that "to be wicked and to design mischief, is the only thing God hates."[3] Hobbes would hardly have disagreed with this very unorthodox and perhaps even heretical "odd idea." Clearly, the king's private convictions did not permit, much less require, him to treat Hobbes as an infidel or pariah.

Hobbes also had other friends in high places, as has been mentioned, and the immediate consequence, according to Aubrey, was that he had nothing to fear from the "witts at Court" who "were wont to bayte him." Adept at defending himself, Hobbes "would make his part good," and he apparently was in the presence of the king and his courtiers on more than one occasion, for Charles "would call him *the beare:* 'Here comes the beare to be bayted!' "† The king's tolerant good humor, however, did not guarantee the annual payment of Hobbes's £100 pension, as Hobbes began to discover as early as 1663. By that date the king was supporting at least six illegitimate children and an unknown but probably larger number of mistresses, leaving uncertain the future of the support he was providing Hobbes. Worried,

---

* Sorbière may have been the first to observe that monarchs had nothing to fear from Hobbes, whatever his true religious views, an insight that escaped many of Hobbes's contemporaries. "He has in his Grounds of Politicks, undoubtedly," Sorbière noted in 1663, "very much obliged the Crowned Heads; and if he had not fallen upon Points of Religion, or contented himself to write against the Presbyterians, and the pretended Bishops of his Country, I should have no Room to find any fault with him." *Journey*, 40.

† Aubrey may have learned from Sorbière that Hobbes was "bayted" at court: "I know not how it comes to pass," Sorbière commented, in connection with the remarks just quoted, "that Clergy are afraid of him, and so are the *Oxford* Mathematicians, and their Adherents; wherefore his Majesty was pleased to make a very good Comparison, when he told me he was like a Bear, whom they baited with Dogs to try him." *Journey*, 40.

Hobbes wrote Aubrey on September 7, "[T]her is nothing at this time so much in hand at the Court as cutting off of pensions, and the abridging of expenses. . . . And I begin to feare that my pension may cease as well as other mens."

Hobbes's fear, for once, was well founded. Sometime after 1670 he found it necessary to remind Charles that though pensions in general were again being paid from the king's privy purse, "yet your Majesty's Officers refuse to pay the pension of your petitioner without your Majesty's express command." In his undated petition to the king, Hobbes begged Charles, "(considering his extreme age, perpetual infirmity, frequent and long sickness, and the aptness of his enemies to take any occasion to report that your petitioner by some ill behavior hath forfeited your wonted favour)," to order payment of the pension, and the king may have done so.[4] But the full payment of the pension in arrears was never made, apparently, for Hobbes referred to the matter in his will.

Hobbes in his post-Restoration years, noted the ever-approving Aubrey, "was marvellous happy and ready in his replies, and that without rancor (except provoked)—but now I speake of his readinesses in replies as to witt and drollery . . . he did not care to give, neither was he adroit at, a present [i.e., quick] answer to a serious quaere." But Hobbes was not difficult to provoke, and as an old man he impressed more than one acquaintance, including the king himself, as being exceedingly opinionated, close-minded, and stubborn, at least in connection with topics on which he regarded himself as an authority. Charles apparently agreed with Sorbière that Hobbes was "very Dogmatical," and he may also have believed that Hobbes's dogmatism was the main reason for his exclusion from the Royal Society.[5] While a 1664 account of Hobbes that was communicated to Robert Boyle is not entirely free from suspicion of bias, the account originating with a colleague of Boyle's and fellow member of the Royal Society, it cannot be dismissed for that reason, since it agrees in substance with other reports. In a letter to Boyle, Robert Hooke, who encountered Hobbes and the third earl in the shop or workroom of an instrument maker, confided to Boyle, "[T]he character I had formerly receiv'd of him was very significant. I found him to lard and seale every asseveration with a round othe, to undervalue all other men's opinions and judgments, to defend to the utmost what he asserted though never soe absurd, to have an high conceipt of his own abilities & performances though never soe absurd & pitiful, & he would not be perswaided but that a common spectacle glass was as good an eye-glass for a 36 foot glass [i.e., telescope] as the best in the world, and pretended to see better than all the rest by holding his spectacle in his hand, which shuk as fast one way as his head did the other, which I confess made me bite my tongue. . . ."[6]

Hobbes's account of Hobbes's physical state is consistent with Aubrey's report, cited earlier, that Hobbes's palsy, which had begun in Paris sometime before 1650, became more pronounced in the years that followed. Despite the worsening palsy, and another illness about 1668 that rendered him, according to Aubrey, "very sick and like to die," Hobbes produced two political works of importance during the final period of his life, in addition to his mathematical papers, translations of Homer, and some miscellaneous writings. While the first and better known of these books, his study of the Civil War he entitled *Behemoth*, cannot be precisely dated, it probably was dictated to an amanuensis, or secretary, in 1668 or a year or two earlier. The second and much less familiar work, which Hobbes apparently never regarded as finished and which he did not want published, may have been written, again through an intermediary, as early as 1662, or as late as 1675, according to the latest available information.[7] *Behemoth*, as was mentioned earlier, was not officially published until 1682, three years after Hobbes's death, though printed editions had begun to appear in London in 1679. *A Dialogue*, first issued in 1681 bound with Hobbes's *The Art of Rhetoric*, was not published separately, at least in English, until 1971.[8] Both books enjoy the additional distinction of being cast in the form of a two-person discussion or dialogue, in *Behemoth* between an older "A" and a younger "B," and in *A Dialogue* between "Lawyer" and "Philosopher."*

In *Behemoth*, which Hobbes dedicated to his influential friend at court Sir Henry Bennet, baron of Arlington (1618–1685), Hobbes returned to themes he had discussed almost forty years earlier in *Thucydides*.[9] In Hobbes's view, the Civil War, like the Peloponnesian War, originated in corruption of thought, disobedience, and human weakness, not in economic or social grievances. The "disobedient," in fact, were "esteemed the best patriots," and since their number included those opposed to tax increases, King Charles I was unable

---

* In his *Examination et Emendatio Mathematicae Hodiernae* of 1660, Hobbes featured an earlier dialogue between "A" and "B," prompting Wallis to protest that A and B were respectively Thomas and Hobbes by which device "when Hobs hath occasion to assume what he cannot prove, Thomas, by a *Manifestum est* saves him the trouble of attempting a demonstration." Quoted in Macdonald and Hargreaves, *Hobbes: Bibliography*, 46. In *Behemoth*, Hobbes again is A and B, presumably because Hobbes preferred the question-and-answer style of presentation to a straightforward narrative or expository method of explicating the causes of the Civil War. The dialogue form may also have reflected Hobbes's experience and prowess in disputations when he was an Oxford undergraduate.

to raise an army large enough to win the war. Had Parliament given him adequate funds, Hobbes aruged, "he might have had soldiers enough in England. For there were very few of the common people that cared much for either of the causes, but would have taken any side for pay or plunder." As for the other, better sort of people, they were "corrupted" by "divers sorts" of "seducers," most of whom, Hobbes emphasized, reiterating a familiar theme, were ministers or university graduates. The former, of course, included religious spokesmen of all persuasions: Presbyterians, Anglicans, Papists, Independents, Anabaptists, Fifth Monarchy Men, Quakers, "Adamites, &c." They were joined in the "corruption" by those who as youths had read the Greek and Roman philosophers, in whose books "popular government was extolled by the glorious name of liberty, and monarchy disgraced by the name of tyranny. . . . And out of these men were chosen the greatest part of the House of Commons, or if they were not the greatest part, yet, by advantage of their eloquence, were always able to sway the rest."[10]

To this number of "seducers" and "corrupters," Hobbes added "the city of London and other great towns of trade," the merchants of which admired the "great prosperity of the Low Countries after they had revolted from their monarch" and believed that a similar change in England would produce similar results. There also were opportunists and adventurers who "longed for a war" as a way of becoming rich or replenishing their wealth that they had "wasted." Finally, once again, there were "the people in general [who] were so ignorant of their duty, as that not one perhaps of ten thousand knew what right any man had to command him, or what necessity there was of King or Commonwealth. . . . King, they thought, was but a title of the highest honour. . . ."[11] *Behemoth*, like *Leviathan*, was in large part given over to religion and the usurpation by popes and bishops of powers rightfully belonging to monarchs and other civil sovereigns. Since the book was written at about the time Hobbes was somewhat occupied in defending himself against charges of heresy, we hear, once again, that heresy, "a word which, when it is used without passion, signified a private opinion," can be declared only by general church councils basing themselves on "canonical Scriptures," or "by the high court of Parliament of this realm, with the assent of the clergy in their convocation." (Significantly, most of the long paragraph making this point is italicized.) Hence "if there arise any new error that hath not yet been declared heresy [by a church council of the type that issued the Nicene Creed, to the meaning of which Hobbes devoted an entire appendix in his Latin *Leviathan*] . . . it cannot be judged heresy without a Parliament. For how foul soever the error be, it cannot have been declared heresy neither in the Scriptures nor in the Councils; because it was never before heard of. And consequently there can be no error, unless it fall within the compass of blasphemy against God or treason against the King, for which a man can in equity be punished." "Besides," Hobbes reminded his Protestant readers, "who can tell what is declared by the Scripture, which every man is allowed to read and interpret to himself?" And what about Protestantism itself, which had been condemned as heresy by several church councils, "as they pretend, upon the authority of the Scriptures"?[12]

Having disposed of the issue of heresy, at least to his own satisfaction, Hobbes could focus once more on the "distempers of the state of England in the time of our late King Charles," among which were those caused by the pope and his Jesuit emissaries. Referring to the Gunpowder Plot as "the most horrid act that ever had been heard of before," Hobbes had B declare of the pope and papal authority, "[T]here was never such another cheat in the world, and I wonder that the Kings and States of Christendom never perceived it." Equally unperceived, according to Hobbes, was the great "distemper" caused by the Presbyterians with their belief that Scriptures could be read and understood by everyone. "For after the Bible was translated into English, every man, nay, every boy and wench, that could read English, thought they spoke with God Almighty, and understood what he said, when by a certain number of chapters a day they had read the Scriptures once or twice over." Because of this, Hobbes maintained, "reverence and obedience . . . was cast off"; and still another pernicious consequence was the multiplication of sects, a development that added to "the disturbance of the commonwealth."[13]

Hobbes's castigations of the Presbyterian clergy is of particular interest. As the son and grandson of Anglican ministers, he presumably was more familiar with the style and behavior of Church of England clerics, and one wonders whether he borrowed, consciously or unconsciously, from this experience. To begin with, A instructed B, the ministers "so framed their countenance and gesture at their entrance into the pulpit, and their pronunciation . . . and used the Scripture phrase . . . as that no tragedian in the world could have acted the part of a right godly man better than these did; . . . [nor could anyone] suspect any ambitious plot in them to raise sedition against the state. . . ." Second, they went further than the bishops in condemning "Romish religion," in order to cast "suspicion on the bishops, as men not yet well purged from idolatry." Third, they pretended their prayers were *"extempore,* . . . dictated by the spirit of God within them"* instead of carefully rehearsed beforehand, thereby promoting "a dislike of the *common-prayer-book,* which is a set form,

premeditated, that men might see to what they were to say *Amen.*"
Fourth, they never, "or but lightly," inveighed "against the lucrative
vices of men of trade or handicraft; such as are feigning, lying, coz-
ening, hypocrisy, or other uncharitableness . . . which was a great
ease to the generality of citizens and the inhabitants of market-towns,
and no little profit to themselves." Fifth, "by preaching up an opinion
that men were to be assured of their salvation by the testimony of
their own private spirit, meaning the Holy Ghost dwelling within
them* . . . [they] made no doubt but that [people] had all that was
necessary, how fraudulently and spitefully soever they behaved
themselves to their neighbours that were not reckoned amongst the
Saints, and sometimes to those also." Sixth, they condemned "with
great ernestness and severity . . . two sins, carnal lusts and vain
swearing; . . . the common people were thereby inclined to believe,
that nothing else was sin, but that which was forbidden in the third
and seventh commandments. . . ." As a result, men and women believed
that the "delight" they "took in the sight of one another's form, though
they checked the proceeding thereof so that it never grew up to be a
design, was nevertheless a sin." Such preaching "brought young men
into desperation and to think themselves damned, because they could
not (which no man can, and is contrary to the constitution of nature)
behold a delightful object without delight. And by this means they
became confessors to such as were thus troubled in conscience. . . ."
Finally, the ministers spoke against "oppression": "you may reckon
this among their artifices, to make the people believe they were
oppressed by the King, or perhaps by the bishops, or both. . . ."[14]

Since many of these ministers had been educated in the universities, Hobbes could express only despair "of any lasting peace amongst
ourselves, till the Universities here shall bend and direct their studies
to the settling of it, that is, to the teaching of absolute obedience to
the laws of the King."[15] Indeed, the universities were iniquitous from
the beginning, A instructed B, because they had been established, in
the main, for "the advancement of [the pope's] own authority" in
those countries where they were founded. "There they learned to dispute for him, and with unintelligible distinctions to blind men's eyes,

---

*Hobbes's view is reminiscent of the incident involving his father, a man named Brooke,
and a "Mr. Wisedome," reported in Chapter 1, pp. 24–25. On May 27, 1589, Thomas
Hobbes senior, appearing as a witness against Brooke, testified that Brooke had taken
exception to Wisedome's assertion, in a sermon, that his "brethrene are the salt of the
earth and the light of the world." Brooke, apparently, had also stated that at least some
ministers "were not chosen of God nor of the holy ghost." We do not know whether
Hobbes's father shared this opinion, or what role, if any, he played in shaping his son's
view.

whilst they encroached upon the rights of kings." Castigating the
Schoolmen who dominated the universities, among whom Peter
Lombard and "John Scot of Duns" would have to be judged "two of
the most egregious blockheads in the world," Hobbes intimated that
university teachers were little more than papal agents whose principal function was "to make good all the articles of faith, which the
Popes from time to time should command to be believed."[16] While
Hobbes did not specifically include Aristotle among the "blockheads," he did not hesitate to declare that "none of the ancient philosophers' writings are comparable to those of Aristotle, for their
aptness to puzzle and entangle men with words, and to breed disputation, which must at last be ended in the determination of the Church
of Rome."[17] In proportion as the church was benefited by the confu-
sions of Aristotle's logic, physics, and metaphysics, the Commonwealth was "much hurt" by Aristotle's politics, together with the
teachings of Cicero, for both eloquently advocated "democratical
principles"; people "from the love of their eloquence fell in love with
their politics, and that more and more, till it grew into the rebellion
we now talk of, without any other advantage to the Roman Church
but that it was a weakening to us, whom, since we broke out of their
net in the time of Henry VIII, they have continually endeavoured to
recover."[18]

Again and again in *Behemoth*, Hobbes stressed, as he had so often
before, that the principal duty or obligation of the citizen "is compre-
hended wholly in obedience to the laws of the commonwealth,"
including those that pertained to religion. Since the truths of religion
cannot be established with absolute certainty by any man, "because
men can never by their own wisdom come to the knowledge of what
God hath spoken and commanded to be observed, nor be obliged to
obey the laws whose author they know not,they are to acquiesce in
some human authority or other," which authority was not "a stranger"
(by which Hobbes chiefly meant, presumably, the pope and Presbyterian clergy), but the king and Parliament. Indeed, the argument
was so self-evident that B could only "wonder at people that have
never spoken with God Almighty, nor knowing one more than another
what he hath said, when the laws and the preacher disagree, should
so keenly follow the minister (for the most part an ignorant, though
a ready-tongued, scholar), rather than the laws, that were made by
the King with the consent of the Peers and Commons of the land."[19]

Though he was almost eighty years old when he wrote *Behemoth*,
Hobbes's wit, far from having been dulled or tempered by age, was
no less sharp than it had been earlier. *Behemoth*, in fact, may well be
the wittiest of his books, and even when he was not witty, Hobbes

was more successful than any other political writer of his day in stuffing a great deal of meaning into a relatively few words. In castigating the universities, Hobbes observed, "The *Universities* have been to the nation, as the wooden horse was to the Trojans."[20] Apropos of noting the conditions that make for obedience and disobedience, Hobbes commented drily that a man "reads that covetousness is the root of all evil; but he thinks, and sometimes finds, it is the root of his estate."[21] Mocking the pretensions to righteousness of the clery, Hobbes had A say, "I confess, that for aught I have observed in history, and other writings of the heathens, Greek and Latin, that those heathens were not at all behind us in point of virtue and moral duties, notwithstanding that we have had much preaching, and they none at all. I confess also, that considering what harm may proceed from a liberty that men have, upon every Sunday and oftener, to harangue all the people of a nation at one time, whilst the state is ignorant of what they will say . . . I have thought much preaching an inconvenience."[22] Charging the Presbyterian clergy with responsibility for the murder of the king and the deaths of "near 100,000 persons" in the Civil War, Hobbes posed the question, "Had it not been much better that those seditious ministers, which were not perhaps 1000, had been all killed before they had preached? It had been (I confess) a great massacre; but the killing of 100,000 is a greater."[23]

While in *Behemoth* Hobbes was unsparing of the papacy, the Presbyterian clergy, and the universities, no class or interest in English society was held entirely blameless. One cause of Strafford's impeachment was "that the Lords, most of them, following the principles of warlike and savage natures, envied his greatness, but yet † were not of themselves willing to condemn him of treason. They were awed to it by the clamour of common people that came to Westminister, crying out, *'Justice, Justice against the Earl of Strafford!'* "[24] Asked whether the city of London had been able to "swallow" the charges against King Charles I levied by Parliament, A replied to B, "Yes; and more too, if need be. London, you know, has a great belly, but no palate nor taste of right and wrong."[25] Again: ". . . there can hardly arise a long or dangerous rebellion, that has not some such over-

---

*While we do not know how Hobbes arrived at the figure of 100,000 killed in the Civil War, that number of deaths is confirmed by Asa Briggs in *A Social History of England* (New York: Viking, 1984), 141. One of every 58 persons in England, Scotland, and Wales died during the four years of the war; by comparison, in the United States Civil War, the most costly in human lives of any American war except the Second World War, the fatalities on both sides totaled 215,000, or one death for every 144 persons.

† The section of this sentence beginning with "following" was printed for the first time by Tönnies.

grown city, with an army or two in its belly to foment it . . . because
the grievances are but taxes, to which citizens, that is, merchants,
whose profession is their private gain, are naturally mortal enemies;
their own glory being to grow excessively rich by the wisdom of buy-
ing and selling."[26]

Acerbic as always, Hobbes in *Behemoth* advanced no illusions
about the impulses and motivations of human nature, quite apart
from those involved in the causes of the Civil War. "It happens many
times," he advised, not for the first time, "that men live honestly for
fear, who, if they had power, would live according to their own opinions. . . ."[27] Observing, once again, that the game is not always to the
strong, or the swift, but often to the merely crafty, he reminded his
readers, "A fool may win from a better gamester, by the advantage of
false dice, and packing of cards."[28] Toward the end of *Behemoth* Hobbes
may have been the first political philosopher, or social scientist, to
formulate a principle that became, almost three centuries later, the
basis of what the distinguished sociologist Robert Merton was to call
the "self-fulfilling prophecy": nothing, Hobbes wrote, "so well directs
men in their deliberations, as the foresight of the sequels of their
actions; prophecy being many times the principal cause of the event
foretold."[29] Certainly, Hobbes, in the course of his long life, had often
acted in accordance with his own "foresight" and "prophecy," but
not always, of course, wisely.

Behemoth had been written because Hobbes felt passionately about
the causes and consequences of the Civil War and also because, as he
put it in his "Epistle Dedicatory," there "can be nothing more
instructive towards loyalty and justice than will be the memory, while
it lasts, of that war."[30] Hobbes's *A Dialogue between a Philosopher and
a Student of the Common Laws of England,* on the other hand, is without passion, much less well written than *Behemoth,* and unfinished.
Perhaps Hobbes would not have written it at all had he not been
urged to do so by Aubrey. According to the latter, one of whose intentions may have been to divert Hobbes from his mathematical controversies with John Wallis, "In 1664 I sayd to him 'Me thinkes 'tis pitty
that you that have such a cleare reason and working head did never
take into consideration the learning of the lawes'; and I endeavoured
to perswade him to it. But he answered that he was not like to have
life enough left to goe through with such a long and difficult taske. I
then presented him the lord chancellor Bacon's Elements of the Lawe
(a thin quarto), in order therunto and to drawe him on . . . and the
next time I came to him he shewed me therein two cleare paralog-
ismes in the 2nd page . . . which I am heartily sory are now out of my
remembrance. I desponded, for his reasons, that he should make any

tentamen [i.e., attempt] towards this designe; but afterwards, it seemes, in the countrey he writt his treatise *De Legibus* (unprinted). . . ." Aubrey also quoted from a letter of Hobbes, dated August 18, 1679, in which Hobbes referred to *De Legibus* as "imperfect" and refused permission to print it to his publisher, William Crooke, and to another London bookseller who had offered to publish it, a Mr. Horne.

Aubrey's report suggests that *A Dialogue* was written some years after 1664, rather than as early as 1662, as some scholars believe. Much of the final decade of Hobbes's life was spent at Hardwick and Chatsworth, that is, "in the countrey" where, if Aubrey can be trusted, "he writt his treatise." Though Aubrey referred to *A Dialogue* as *De Legibus* and alluded to it as "unprinted," leading some to suggest "there is a question whether the 'treatise de legibus' is this *Dialogue*,"[31] his catalogue of Hobbes's works leaves no doubt the two titles referred to the same book. In his listing of manuscripts left by Hobbes, Aubrey included "A dialogue concerning the common lawes." There was no mention by him of any book or manuscript entitled *De Legibus*.

Whatever the composition date of the unfinished *A Dialogue*, Hobbes's intention in writing it is clear. As he had earlier attached major responsibility for the Civil War to the doctrines expounded in the pulpits and universities, and sought to establish the supremacy of the sovereign power in matters of religion and statecraft, so he now blamed the judges and lawyers and turned his attention to sovereign supremacy in law. But in arguing that sovereignty in legal affairs resided in the king and in laws made pursuant to his wishes, rather than in laws administered by an independent judiciary, Hobbes was addressing himself, as he had not done in his other books, to a single individual, the foremost defender in his time of the common law and integrity of courts, Sir Edward Coke (1552–1634). With Coke, who had been dead at least thirty years when Hobbes wrote *A Dialogue*, as with Bramhall earlier, Hobbes inevitably was to have the last word, but he apparently was less satisfied with his rebuttal of Coke than he had been with his refutation of Bramhall, and probably never intended it to be published.[32]

The exchange between "Philosopher" and "Lawyer" in *A Dialogue* is an exchange, in a sense, between Hobbes and the dead Coke or, rather, to improve the sense, between Bacon and Hobbes, speaking through Philosopher, and Coke (Lawyer, however, occasionally represents Hobbes as well). Coke, perhaps the greatest lawyer of his time, had been Bacon's arch-rival, and the more successful claimant, for the high positions of attorney general and chief justice (successively, of the Courts of Common Pleas and King's Bench), and while we can only speculate about Hobbes's motivations in writing *A Dia-*

logue so many years after the deaths of both Bacon and Coke, we can hardly doubt that it was "to some extent a polemic against Coke" that reflected Hobbes's having "appointed himself the heir" of Bacon's concept of law; in effect, "Hobbes's controversy with the dead Coke is the continuation of Bacon's."[33]

Coke makes his initial appearance in *A Dialogue* in its second page, where he is referred to as "the renowned lawyer Sir Edward Coke," but though "renowened," he has already been found wanting. Philosopher, in his first very Hobbesian exchange with Lawyer, observes "that the great masters of the *mathematics* do not so often err as the great professors of the law." Coke's error, it seems, is his belief that "reason is the soul of the law," whereas, insists Philosopher, reason is largely irrelevant. In the course of his study "of the statutes from Magna Charta down to this present time," he was not concerned with the question "which of them was more or less rational," says Philosopher: "I read them not to dispute, but to obey them, and saw in all of them sufficient reason for my obedience. . . ."[34] Authority that commands obedience and not reason or wisdom, in short, is "the soul of the law," and therefore Coke is wrong to believe that "the reason of a judge, or of all the judges together without a King, is that *summa ratio*, and the very law: which I deny, because none can make a law but he that hath the legislative power . . . for all the laws of England have been made by the kings of England, consulting with the nobility and commons in parliament. . . ."[35]

Philosopher's reference to kings' "consulting" with Parliament in the making of laws has led some students of Hobbes to believe that the Hobbes of *A Dialogue* is less absolutist than the Hobbes of *Leviathan* because in the later work Hobbes emphasizes that peace and justice in England require a measure of collaboration between king and Parliament.[36] Here and there in *A Dialogue*, Philosopher appears to be saying as much, but a careful examination of his words, and of the contexts in which they are said, suggest there was little if any shift in Hobbes's thought during the preceding twenty or more years. Thus, in discussing with Lawyer the king's power to raise an army, Philosopher maintains, "[I]t is the King that makes the laws, whosoever pens them; and in this, that the King cannot make his laws effectual, nor defend his people against their enemies, without a power to levy soldiers; and consequently, that he may lawfully, as oft as he shall really think it necessary to raise an army, (which in some occasions may be very great) I say, raise it, and money to maintain it." When Lawyer responds with the statement that before and during the Civil War "the people were of another mind," questioning the king's right to "take from us what he pleases, upon pretence of a

necessity whereof he makes himself the judge," Philosopher answers,
"The people reason ill. They do not know in what condition we were,
in the time of the Conqueror, when it was a shame to be an Englishman; who if he grumbled at the base offices he was put to by his
Norman masters, received no other answer than this, *thou art but an
Englishman.* Nor can the people, nor any man that humours their
disobedience, produce any example of a King that ever raised any
excessive sums, either by himself or by the consent of his Parliament,
but when they had great need thereof. . . . The greatest complaint by
them made against the unthriftiness of their Kings, was for the
enriching now and then a favourite, which to the wealth of the kingdom was inconsiderable, and the complaint but envy."[37]

Philosopher appears to take the position that the "base" situation in which Englishmen found themselves under William the Conqueror was not wholly unlike that of the state of nature, from which
perspective they have had little to complain about, in reality, since
the time of the Conqueror, succeeding English kings being rarely given
to "unthriftiness." But in any case, Philosopher continues, kings should
not be dependent upon Parliaments for the right to levy taxes in behalf
of raising armies, regardless of what statutes and even kings themselves may declare, for, he asks rhetorically, how shall I avoid being
enslaved by a foreign invader, "or how shall I avoid the destruction
that may arise from the cruelty of factions in a civil war, unless the
King, to whom alone, you say, belongeth the right of levying and dis-
posing of the militia by which only it can be prevented, have ready
money, upon all occasions, to arm and pay as many soldiers, as for
the present defence, or the peace of the people, shall be necessary?
. . . Tell me not of a Parliament, when there is no Parliament sitting,
or perhaps none in being, which may often happen. And when there
is a Parliament, if the speaking and leading men should have a design
to put down monarchy, as they had in the Parliament which began
to sit the third of November, 1640, shall the King, who is to answer to
God Almighty for the safety of the people, and to that end is intrusted
with the power to levy and dispose of the soldiery, be disabled to
perform his office, by virtue of these acts of Parliament which you
have cited? If this be reason, it is reason also that the people be abandoned, or left at liberty to kill one another, even to the last man.
. . ."[38] In short, the alternative to the king's power to rule with or
without consent of Parliament is a return to the state of nature.

Though Lawyer repeatedly presses Philosopher to assent to the
proposition that the king as "sole legislator" should consult with Parliament, Philosopher continues to assert that the king, and the king
alone, has power to decide whether to abide by or disregard parlia-

mentary advice. The king, Philosopher insists, "is so far bound to their assents, as he shall judge conducing to the good and safety of his people. For example, if the Lords and Commons should advise him to restore thos laws spiritual which in Queen Mary's time were in force, I think the King were by the law of reason obliged, without the help of any other law of God, to neglect such advice." Once again, Lawyer maintains that the king "sinneth against God" if he refuses to consult Parliament, but he adds the significant, and Hobbesian, qualification that even sinning against God, the king "cannot be compelled to any thing by his subjects by arms and force." To this, Philosopher can only respond succinctly, "We are agreed upon that already."[39]

Philosopher is no less agreed that "the King should be supreme judge," and he disputes Coke's stress on the role of lawyers and judges in the making of law. Though Coke in his *Institutes of Law* "often takes occasion to magnify the learning of the lawyers, whom he perpetually termeth the sages of the Parliament, or of the King's council . . . I say, that the King's reason, when it is publicly upon advice and deliberation declared, is that *anima legis;* and that *summa ratio* and that equity, which all agreed to be the law of reason, is all that is or ever was law in England, since it became Christian, besides the Bible."[40]

Between the lines of these and other observations of Philosopher, one has no difficulty detecting in Hobbes a certain animus toward lawyers that may have originated, at least in part, in the innumerable and, for long periods of time, unending lawsuits in which the Devonshires and, on occasion, Hobbes himself had been involved, beginning with those Christian had initiated with respect to the debts of her dead husband, the second earl. In his *Institiutes* Coke had advanced six "causes" of the vast increase in litigation during the first part of the seventeenth century, "causes" of which Hobbes did not think much. The "causes," as listed by Lawyer, were the following: "1. Peace. 2. Plenty. 3. The dissolution of religious houses and dispersing of their lands among so many several persons. 4. The multitude of informers. 5. The number of concealers. 6. The multitude of attorneys."[41] "I see," the comment of Philosopher began, "Sir Edward Coke has no mind to lay any fault upon the men of his own profession, and that he assigns for causes of the mischiefs, such things as would be mischief and wickedness to amend," such as "peace" and "plenty." Among such faults, Philosopher alleged, "the covetousness of lawyers [which] was not so great in ancient time, which was full of trouble, as they have been in time of peace; wherein men have leisure to study fraud, and get employment from such men as can encourage to contention. And how ample a field they have to exercise this mystery in, is manifest from this, that they have a power to scan and construe every word in a statute, charter, feoffment [i.e., a grant of land in fee], lease, or other deed, evidence, or testimony."[42] In the seventeenth century, as in the twentieth, if Philosopher is to be believed, few transactions were possible without lawyers.

In *A Dialogue* Hobbes's censure of Coke did not overlook the latter's treatment of heresy in his *Institutes*. Coke, according to Lawyer, had regarded heresy as a crime that "ranketh before murder." Hobbes, of course, had personal as well as intellectual reasons to dispute the judgment that heresy in and of itself was a crime punishable by death, and he may well have felt relief that Coke was not alive to represent this point of view in Parliament. "The principal thing to be considered," Philosopher began the discussion, "which is the heresy itself, he leaveth out. . . . I say, heresy is a singularity of doctrine or opinion contrary to the doctrine of another man, or men. . . ."[43] The fourteen pages devoted to the topic lend support to the speculation that *A Dialogue* was written during the time when Hobbes was somewhat occupied in defending himself against charges he was an atheist or heretic, that is, toward the end of the 1660s or early 1670s. At that time, and, indeed, even now in the Catholic church, his view that heresy was essentially a difference of opinion about a religious issue was, to say the least, a novel concept.

As was noted earlier, *A Dialogue* may not have been published while Hobbes was still alive because he did not wish to engage in new controversies during his last years; in April 1673, by which time he had survived the sixth and greatest outbreak of the plague in the course of his lifetime, and was coping as best he could with the infirmities of age already mentioned, Hobbes was eighty-five years old.* While we have no evidence that extreme old age had any mellowing effect on his opinions—in his last publication, his *Decameron Physiologicum* of 1678, he was still disputing Wallis's geometry—we should perhaps attach some importance to a gift of books Hobbes presented to Oxford University. Though he believed to the end of his life that the universities bore a heavy responsibility for the "late troubles," in 1674, according to the records of Hertford College, Oxford, "Thomas Hobbes Malmesburiensis olim ex aula Magd. donavit snipsius opera latina 3 vol." These three Latin volumes, presumably Hobbes's *Opera Philo-*

---

* An estimated 68,596 Londoners, or about 15 percent of the city's population, perished in the great plague of 1664–65. Hobbes may also have witnessed the great fire of London in 1666, in which only six persons died but which destroyed 436 acres of buildings, including 13,200 houses, 86 churches (among them St. Paul's), the guild hall, and the royal exchange. *Encyclopaedia Britannica*, 13th ed., X, 401.

sophica Omnia of 1668, may have been intended as a peace offering, or as a good will gesture by an "old boy," but the salubrious effect, if any, of Hobbes's gift was short-lived. For in 1674 Hobbes once again found himself involved in controversy with an eminent Oxford academician and cleric, the formidable and forbidding John Fell (1625–1686), dean of Christ Church, self-appointed guardian of Oxford's morals and manners, and "the most zealous man of his time for the Church of England."[44] Fell, who now is chiefly remembered for the lines addressed to him by Tom Browne,* had strongly disapproved of Hobbes since the publication of *De Cive*, and he regarded *Leviathan* as "monstrosissimus" and "publico damno notissimus." Fell himself, apparently, wrote nothing about either Hobbes or his books, but as the financial sponsor of the Latin version of Anthony à Wood's *History and Antiquities of the University of Oxford*, he insisted on his right to edit and if necessary delete portions of Wood's manuscript that he regarded as false, improper, or misleading. Among these deletions were lengthy complimentary references to Hobbes by Cosimo de' Medici and Sorbière, which Fell replaced with negative assertions, including those already quoted with regard to *Leviathan*. Struck out by Fell was Wood's mention that Cosimo during his visit to England "went more than once to visit this great philosopher, in whose company he seemed much to delight. And because he would retain the memory of such a noted person and express his veneration for him, did carry with him (besides what his retinue did) most of his works and picture: all which are at this time reserved as rarities in the library and closet of the said duke, than which none in the Christian world ('tis thought) goes beyond." Fell even went so far as to remove the passage "King Charles II loved him and his facetious company and after the restauration allowed him 100li. per annum out of the exc[h]ecquer. To sum up all, he is excellently well skilled in the Latin and Greek, a great critick and poet, and above all a philosopher and mathematician."[45]

Wood, who was dismayed by these changes, notified Aubrey, at

---

*Browne, about to be expelled from the university, was offered a pardon by Fell provided he was able to render a sight translation of Martial's thirty-third epigram:

> Non amo te, Sabidi, nec possum dicere quare;
> Hoc tantum possume, dicere, non amo te.

Browne's translation was

> I do not love you, Dr. Fell,
> But why I cannot tell,
> But this I know full well,
> I do not love you, Dr. Fell.

Encyclopaedia Britannica, 13th ed., X, 24.

that time a close friend and collaborator, and Aubrey, needless to remark, informed Hobbes, who, in Aubrey's words, "taking it ill, was resolved to vindicate himselfe in an epistle to the author." Hobbes's Latin "epistle," dated April 20, 1674, which Hobbes wanted Wood to include in his *History*, was shown to Fell, Wood being careful, as he himself put it, "to let him see that he would do nothing underhand against him." Fell's reaction to the "epistle," according to Aubrey, was "to read it over carelessly, and not without scorne, and when he had done bid Mr. Wood 'tell Mr. Hobbes that he was an old man, had one foote in the grave, that he should mind his latter end and not trouble the world any more with his papers, etc.'—or to that effect."[46]

Hobbes was no more inclined to follow Fell's advice then he had earlier been inclined to oblige Wallis by abandoning interest in geometry. Subsequently meeting with the king in St. James's Park, adjoining "pall-mall," and informing him of the treatment he had received from Fell—Aubrey implied the meeting was by chance— Hobbes asked for and was given permission to vindicate himself, the "king seeming to be troubled at the dealing of the deane." Permission to publish his "epistle," however, was granted Hobbes "conditionally that he should touch nobody but him who had abused him neither that he should reflect upon the Universitie." By July the "epistle" was printed, and not long afterward, "divers copies" having been sent to Oxford "coffee houses and stationers' shops, a copie forthwith came to the deane's hands, who upon the reading of it fretted and fumed, sent for the author [Wood] of the History and chid him telling withall that 'he had corresponded with his enemie.' "[47] Reminded by Wood that he had previously been shown the "epistle," Fell, "recollecting himselfe," told Wood that "Hobbes should suddenly heare more of him,' " adding, according to Wood, that "he would have the printer [of the "epistle"] called to account for printing such a notorious libell." Fell's reply to Hobbes, which was appended to Wood's *History*, did not provke Hobbes to a further exchange, but " 'tis supposed," Aubrey suggested, "that it might be the cause why Mr. Hobbes was not afterwards so indulgent, or spared the lesse to speake his opinion, concerning the Universities and how much their doctrine and method had contributed to the late troubles."[48] What Aubrey intended to convey by this curious passage, which implies that Hobbes had somehow been "indulgent" of universities prior to his difficulties with Fell, is not at all clear.

If Hobbes indeed "had one foote in the grave" in 1674, Fell, and only Fell, was aware of the fact. Hobbes's translation of Homer, *The Travels of Ulysses*, first published in 1673, was reissued in 1674, 1675 (two editions), and 1676, in addition to two mathematical works, his

Principia et Problemata of 1674, and *Decameron Physiologicum* of 1678, his last book. At least one posthumous publication, the *Historia Ecclesiastica* (1688), a verse history, in Latin, of religious history "From Moses to the Time of Martin Luther" (as the title of the English version put it in 1722), was probably written in 1671. While many critics share Dryden's view of Hobbes's rendering of Homer—namely, that "Mr. Hobbes in the preface to his own bold translation of the *Iliad* (studying poetry as he did mathematics, when it was too late,) Mr. Hobbes, I say, begins the praise of Homer where he should have ended it"[49]—Hobbes's translation and his writing three other books when he was well beyond his eightieth birthday testify to a mental and physical vigor in old age that would be unusual at any time in history but that was unique in the late seventeenth century. Moreover, it was not entirely by accident that Hobbes lived more than twice as long as most men and women of his era.

Early in life, apparently, perhaps reflecting, once again, the influence of Bacon, Hobbes seems to have been aware of the importance of diet and exercise. In the first edition of the *Essays* (1597), Bacon urged, in his "Of Regiment of Health," that while "Strength of Nature in youth, passeth over many Excesses," one should "Discerne of the comming on of Yeares, and thinke not, to doe the same Things till; For Age will not be Defied. . . . Examine thy Customes, of Diet, Sleepe, Exercise, Apparell, and the like; And trie in any Thing, thou shalt judge hurtful, to discontinue it by little and little. . . . To be free minded, and cheerfully disposed, at Houres of Meat, and of Sleep, and of Exercise, is one of the best Precepts of Long Lasting. . . . I commend rather, some Diet, for certaine Seasons, then frequent Use of *Physicke*. . . . *Celsus* could never have spoken it as a *Physician*, had he not been a Wise Man withall; when he giveth it, for one of the great precepts of Health and Lasting; That a Man doe vary, and enterchange Contraries; But with an inclination to the more benigne Extreme: Use Fasting, and full Eating, but rather full Eating; Watching and Sleep, but rather Sleep; Sitting, and Exercise, but rather Exercise; and the like. So shall Nature be Cherished, and yet taught Masteries." According to Aubrey, Hobbes "even in his youth" avoided excesses "as to wine and women" and "seldome used any physique." From the age of sixty "his dyet, etc., was very moderate and regular . . . he dranke no wine, his stomach grew weak, and he did eate most fish, especially whitings, for he sayd he digested fish better than flesh." In addition to a daily walk, usually in the morning following breakfast, Hobbes "did twice or thrice a yeare play at tennis (at about 75 he did it); then went to bed there and was well rubbed. This he did believe would make him live two or three yeares the longer. In the countrey, for want of a tennis-court, he would walke up-hill and downe-hill in the parke, till he was in a great sweat, and then give the servant some money to rubbe him." No doubt this regimen owed something to Hobbes's belief, communicated to Aubrey, that "old men were drowned inwardly, by their owne moysture; e.g. first, the feet swell; then, the legges; then, the belly; etc."

"Moysture," if Aubrey can be trusted, had much to do with Hobbes's interest in music when he was an old man. "He had alwayes bookes of prick-song lyeing on his table:—e.g. of H. Lawes' etc.," Aubrey reports, "*Songs*—which at night, when he was abed, and the dores made fast, and was sure nobody heard him, he sang aloud (not that he had a very good voice) but for his health's sake: he did beleeve it did his lunges good, and conduced much to prolong his life." In Aubrey's other version of this report, Hobbes is said to have believed that singing prick songs "would make him live two or three yeares longer."

We do not know Hobbes's favorite prick songs, defined as music "sung from notes written or 'pricked' as distinguished from that sung from memory or by ear," in short, songs or other vocal music that had been written and published.[50] But we do know that Hobbes's preferred composer of such songs was Sir Henry Lawes (1596–1662), another Wiltshireman and the foremost songwriter of his day, for whose attention the leading poets of the time wrote verses in the hope he would put them to music. Hobbes in 1652 attended musicales at Lawes's house in London,[51] where he may have joined in the singing of "Phyllis, Why Should We Delay," the lyrics of which express a worldly viewpoint wholly in sympathy with Hobbes's own sentiments.* Perhaps he was more familiar, however, with the better-known and still popular "Gather Ye Rosebuds While Ye May," the musical

---

*The words of "Phillis, Why Should We Delay" are as follows:

I

Phillis, why should we delay
Pleasures shorter than the day?
Could we, which we never can,
Stretch our lives beyond their span,
Beauty like a shadow flies
And our youth before us dies.

II

Or would youth and beauty stay,
Love has wings and will away;
Love has swifter wings than time,
Change in love too oft do's chime;
Gods, that never change their state,
Vary of their love and hate.

(lyrics are continued on page 226)

version of Robert Herrick's poem, composed by Henry Lawes's older brother William (1582–1645), killed in 1645 by a stray bullet while fighting with the royalists at the siege of Chester.[52]

Hobbes's fear of "moysture," though not his resorting to prick song, is confirmed by Kennet. In his old age that was passed at Hardwick and Chatsworth, Kennet wrote in 1708, Hobbes's "profess'd Rule of Health was to dedicate the Morning to his Health, and the Afternoon to his Studies. And therefore, at his first rising he walk'd out and climb'd any Hill within his reach; or if the Weather was not dry, he fatigued himself within Doors, by some Exercise or other to be in a Sweat; recommending that Practice upon his Opinion, that an old Man had more Moisture than Heat, and therefore by such Motion, Heat was to be acquired, Moisture expell'd."[53]

Kennet also provides the fullest account extant of Hobbes's life during his last years with the Devonshires, an account corroborated in certain though not all particulars by Aubrey. Hobbes's daily routine, according to Kennet, was to exercise before taking "a comfortable breakfast" (Aubrey describes his breakfast as "bread and butter"), following which he "went around the Lodgings to wait upon the Earl, the Countess, and the Children, and any considerable Strangers, paying some short Adresses to all of them. He kept these Rounds till about 12 a Clock, when he had a little Dinner provided for him, which he eat always by himself without Ceremony" (Aubrey has Hobbes sitting to dinner "exactly by eleven, for he could not now stay till his lord's howre—scil. about two: that his stomach could not beare"). Retiring to his study after dinner, Hobbes, writes Kennet, "with 10 or 12 Pipes of Tobacco laid by him . . . fell to smoaking, and thinking, and writing for several Hours" (Aubrey reports that Hobbes "tooke a pipe of tobacco, and then threw himselfe immediately on his bed, with his band off, and slept (tooke a nap of about halfe an howre). In the afternoon he penned his morning thoughts").[54]

At "the Mention of his Name," continues Kennet's memoir, the third earl and his family would say, "He was a Humorist, and that no body could account for him," but this is at variance with another

---

III
Phillis, to this true we owe
All the love betwixt us now;
Let not you and I inquire
What has been our past desire;
On what shepherds you have smil'd,
Or what nymphs I have beguil'd.

Reliquary of English Song, collected and edited by Frank Hunter Potter (New York/London: G. Schirmer, 1943; first published 1915), I, 58–59.

of Kennet's recollections stating that Hobbes, far from being a "Humorist," would, when he had company, "Discourse till he was press'd or contradicted, and then he had the Infirmities of being short and peevish, and referring to his Writings for better Satisfaction. His Friends who had the Liberty of introducing Strangers to Him, made these Terms with them before their Admission, That they should not dispute with the old Man, nor contradict him."[55] Aubrey and Kennet agree that Hobbes made use of few books; Aubrey recalls never seeing "above halfe a dozen about him in his chamber. Homer and Virgil . . . sometimes Xenophon, or some probable historie, and Greek Testament, or so." Neither Aubrey or Kennet mentions that Hobbes had access to the Devonshire library, which by 1679 was many times larger than the library that had awaited him more than seventy years earlier.

Hobbes's "short and peevish" manner when contradicted may have reflected, at least in part, his declining health. According to the two most complete accounts of his final days, one of them originating with James Wheldon, a servant of the Devonshires who was Hobbes's amanuensis and executor, and the other with Justinian Morse, the third earl's secretary at the time, Hobbes fell ill with "the strangury," or acute pain and difficulty in urinating, possibly caused by an ulcer or tumor of the bladder, about the middle of October 1679. In a lengthy letter to Wood dated January 9, 1679 [i.e., 1680], Morse reported that Hobbes at first had "made use of some medicines by the advice of a Chirurgion, but finding little benefitt he asked the Chir: whether he thought his distemper cureable, to which being answer'd it would be very difficult to make a perfect cure, and the best that could be expected was ease for the present, hereupon Mr Hobbs brake out into an expression to this effect; That then he should be glad to finde a hole to creepe out of the world at, this I have from the Chirurgions own mouth . . . for Mr Hobbs has seemed to be more affraid of the paines he thought he should endure before he dyed then of death. But that of his being 90 years seeking a hole is a mistake."*[56]

The "hole," however, was not to be used for almost two months. Several weeks after the attack of "strangury," the third earl, his family, and his household, who usually spent the winters at Hardwick, traversed the ten miles from Chatsworth to Hardwick in a number of

---

*Wood had written in his diary of December 10 that Hobbes "on his death bed he should say that he was 91 years finding out a hole to go out of this world, and at length found it." Wood's diary earlier referred to the death of "Mr. Thomas Hobbs the mathematician" as occurring on "August 21 or 22, 1667," which was either a printer's error or, more likely, a reference to another Thomas Hobbes. Clark, ed., *Life and Times*, II, 471–72. The reference in error, or to a different Thomas Hobbes, is in II, 116.

coaches. Provision was made for the ill and failing Hobbes to remain, as comfortably as possible, at Chatsworth, but Hobbes strongly objected. Wheldon states in his letter to Aubrey that Hobbes "would not be left behind; and therefore with a feather bed laid into the coach, upon which he stay warme clad, he was conveyed safely, and was in appearance as well after that little journey as before it." Kennet, much less kindly disposed toward Hobbes, maintains that Hobbes's insistence on being moved reflected his timidity and wish to be "free from Danger: He could not endure to be left in an empty House; whenever the Earl removed, he would go along with him. . . ."[57]

Whether because of complications attending the "strangury," or the strains of the move, or more probably both, "seven or eight days after," according to Wheldon (Morse says "a day or two aftr"), "his whole right side was taken with the dead palsy, and at the same time he was made speechlesse. He lived after this seven days, taking very little nourishment, slept well, and by intervalls endeavoured to speake, but could not. In the whole time of his sicknesse he was free from fever. He seemed therefore to dye rather for want of the fuell of life (which was spent in him) and meer weaknesse and decay, then by the power of his disease, which was thought to be onely an effect of his age and weaknesse." Further details come from Morse, who thought that the "palsy," or stroke, deprived Hobbes of "reason and sense too, for when I saw him, which was about two days before he dyed I did not perceive he knew any body, though he looked about. . . ."[58]

Wheldon wrote nothing about Hobbes's dying as a professed Christian, thereby indirectly adding substance to claims that Hobbes lived and died an atheist, whereas Morse, who once witnessed Hobbes taking the sacrament, appears uncertain about the significance of this and other reported occasions upon which Hobbes displayed some interest in religion when he was close to death. Following his stroke or, as Morse puts it, "Being soe suddenly seized he did not take the Sacrament, nor seeme to desire the company of any Minister, which in charity may be imputed to his want of understanding, but as I am informed by my Lords Chaplaine (a worthy Gent) he had severall times lately received the Sacrament of him, and from others in his absense (as I hear) and I did once see him receive it and received it my selfe with him, and then he tooke it with seemeing devotion, and in humble, and reverend posture, and I cannot learn that he ever refused it."[59] Aubrey does not identify his source in stating that Hobbes "recieved the sacrament of Dr. [John] Pierson [bishop of Chester], and in his confession to Dr. John Cosins, at . . . [left blank], on his (as he thought) death-bed, declared that he liked the religion of the church of England best of all other."* Aubrey's opinion, that Hobbes "was a Christian 'tis cleare," was shared by, among others, Sir Robert Southwell, clerk of the Privy Council under Charles II, who in a letter of December 13, 1679, wrote, "Mr. Hobbes is lately dead, in all the forms of a very good Christian."[60] But not everyone, as will shortly be seen, held a similar view, then or in later years.

On Saturday, December 5, 1679, two days after his death at Hardwick, his body "was put into a woollen shroud and coffin, which was covered with a white sheet, and upon that a black herse cloth, and so carryed upon men's shoulders, a little mile to church. The company, consisting of the family and neighbours that came to his funerall, and attended him to his grave, were very handsomely entertained with wine, burned and raw, cake, biscuit, etc. He was buried in the parish church of Hault Hucknall, close adjoining to the raile of the monument of the grandmother of the present earle of Devonshire [Anne Keighley, the wife of the first earl], with the service of the Church of England by the minister of the parish." Hobbes's gravesite, Wheldon added, eventually would be covered with a black stone, on which would be "a plain inscription of his name, the place of his birth, and the time of that and of his death." Morse confirms this report but the inscription, in Latin, on the black stone laid flat on the floor of the aisle, includes the additional information that Hobbes had served the Devonshires "Father and Son" for many years and that he had been "a just man whose learning was celebrated at home and abroad."† According to Kennet, Hobbes before his final illness had invited friends to submit possible epitaphs, among which his favorite tombstone inscription was "This is the true Philosopher's Stone," which would have had, Kennet continues, "as much Religion in it, as that which now remains."[61]

Hobbes's will, dated September 25, 1677, revealed that he had accumulated a considerable amount of money over the years. Since Hobbes had declared, in his *Autobiography* and elsewhere, that he had little interest in wealth, Aubrey and other friends were surprised

---

* Aubrey is referring latterly to Hobbes's near-fatal illness in 1647 when Dr. Cosin (1594–1672), later bishop of Durham, visited him in Paris and administered the sacrament. Hobbes in 1666 and occasionally thereafter called attention to this episode when he was charged with being an atheist and heretic. Relevant also is part of a letter he wrote on October 20, 1668, in which he declared, "Nor do I much wonder that a young woman of clear memory, hourely expecting death, should bee more devot than at other times. 'Twas my own case." *E.W.*, VII, 464.

† Hatchwell asserts (catalogue, inside cover) that the inscription chosen for the grave "was composed by Hobbes himself."

that, as Aubrey put it, "He dyed worth neer 1000*li.*, which (considering his charity) was more then I expected. . . ." To Elizabeth Alaby, who may have been Hobbes's *"delictum juventutis"* (as reported by Kennet), Hobbes left £200; Elizabeth, an orphan who probably was nine or ten years old in 1679, was placed in Wheldon's care. Hobbes apparently hoped that she would eventually be married to one of Wheldon's sons "provided they like one another, and that he was not a spendthrift."[62] Mary Tirell and Elenor Harding, the two daughters of his deceased brother, Edmund, were each left £40, with the further stipulation that if Elizabeth Alaby died before reaching the age of sixteen, the bequest to her was to be divided between Mary and Elenor. As an afterthought to the will, added after his signature and those of two witnesses, Hobbes provided £10 to one Mary Dell, not otherwise identified. To the eldest of Edmund's five grandchildren, who was named for his great-uncle, Hobbes had earlier given "a peece of land, which may and doth, I think, content him"; to the other four grandchildren Hobbes bequeathed the £100 promised to him, and soon after his death paid, by the third earl, "as a furtherance to bind them apprentices."* For reasons not known, Hobbes left nothing to the children or grandchildren of his sister, Anne Hobbes Lawrence, and his will also did not provide for Elenor Harding's children or grandchildren. Though in death, as in life, his name was linked with his birthplace, Malmesbury—on the black marble stone atop his grave it is "Thomae Hobbes Malmesburiensis"—Hobbes did not provide funds for the "free schoole" he and Aubrey had talked of establishing years before, or for any other memorial to himself.

Wheldon, to whom he left the remainder of his money "and goods whatsoever," including a "warm Coat" Hobbes had had made shortly before he died, was also to be given the unspecified amount in arrears of Hobbes's pension from the king, "or as much of it as it pleases his majestie." While we do not know whether this money was ever paid, we have evidence that Wheldon, with or without it, was the principal beneficiary of Hobbes's will, presumably because he had served as Hobbes's amanuensis, personal servant, and Elizabeth Alaby's guardian and because he was to continue in the role of Elizabeth's guardian. Between 1662 and 1679 Wheldon received £400 from Hobbes

---

*The "Pedigree of Hobbes," as given by Aubrey, records two grandnephews named Thomas Hobbes, one of them the grandson of Anne Hobbes Lawrence, and the other Edmund Hobbes's grandson, a beneficiary of the will, identified by Aubrey as a Malmesbury tanner "aetat. 27, December last. His estate, 30 *li.* per annum." According to the "Pedigree," Edmund Hobbes had at least eleven grandchildren by his son, Francis, and his two daughters Mary and Elenor, which fact, if true, makes for uncertainty as to which four grandchildren (besides Thomas) Hobbes referred to in his will.

in the form of gifts and payments for services, and in 1680, in keeping with the will, he was given another £600, a very substantial sum for those days.[63] Indeed, Hobbes and perhaps Wheldon were affluent and even relatively wealthy individuals as measured by the income levels of their times. Hobbes's salary during his final years was £80 per annum (Wheldon was paid £6, later £10, by the Devonshires), an amount equal to the estimated annual family income in 1688 of "Naval officers," and greater than the annual family incomes of "Eminent clergymen," "Shopkeepers and tradesmen," "Military officers," and "Persons in liberal arts and sciences." Hobbes's income, in fact, was more than that of "persons in the law," and almost a third that of "Gentle-men."[64]

Hobbes's wealth, however much it may have surprised Aubrey and others, is not difficult to account for. In addition to his salary and irregular pension from the king, Hobbes enjoyed a substantial income from his books. At the time of his death, Aubrey reports, William Crooke, his publisher, "had 500 *li.* of his in his hands." The dedica-tions of the books also produced income; for dedicating *De Corpore* to the third earl, for instance, Hobbes received a gift of £40, in accord-ance with the custom of the times. With his living quarters and board provided, and a clothing allowance as well, Hobbes had few expenses, and with no dependents other than Elizabeth Alaby (who arrived on the scene late in his life), he had little cause to spend money during most of the years between 1608 and 1679. Had he been paid the legacy left him by the second earl, and the full amount of the pension bestowed upon him by Charles II, the value of his estate at the end might have astonished Aubrey and not merely surprised him.

Hobbes's death on December 4, 1679, unlike his birth, was not attended by rumors of the landing of an armada or any other event apt to induce premature labor in pregnant women and strike fear in the breasts of their newborn infants. By contrast with 1588, the year 1679, which witnessed the signing of at least three European peace treaties, two of them involving Sweden and one France, was a reason-ably calm and quiet year. But in one respect, perhaps, the final months of 1679 were different from those of most years. The Oxford weather of November and December, if Wood can be belived, was unique in that "frostie weather for a weeke in the middle of November" was succeeded by "hot, soultry weather for a weeke suddenly after, the air thick and moist and the sun not appearing for a weke togeather in the latter end. Unless it were the 2nd of Dec., wee had not the sun appeared in eight dayes, but air verie moyst and sometimes soultry. Which caused colds and feavers and odde distempers, of which sev-erall die. And for this reason, because the weather before that time, viz. about the middle of Nov., was verie cold, severall old men march off."[65]

Had Hobbes escaped the "stranguery" and subsequent stroke, would he, considering his age and condition, have been carried off by the "colds and feavers and odde distempers"? No one can answer such a question, of course, but we can be certain that if Hobbes had been taking his customary morning walk on or about November 15, he would have needed that "warm Coat."

TEN

HOBBES IN HIS TIME AND OURS

O N OCTOBER 12, 1979, the mayor of Malmesbury, the Reverend A. H. Bird, was host to a small gathering of townspeople and their guests honoring the three hundredth anniversary of Hobbes's death. The menu for the "Thomas Hobbes Tercentenary Dinner," which may or may not have reflected Hobbes's own tastes, featured watercress soup, "Roast Haunch of Fallow Deer, Grand-Veneur," spinach tartlets, and "Evelyn Salad," among other dishes, and at the outset the diners were served sherry. Following the dinner, the gathering was addressed by Christopher Hill, formerly master of Balliol College, Oxford, and a foremost authority on the English revolution and seventeenth-century English history, who was introduced by Councillor T. B. C. Winch, chairman of the dinner. At the close of Hill's address, a bust of Hobbes, commissioned by the town council and executed by Theodora Heal, was unveiled.

The back of the printed program for the dinner carried the verses in celebration of Hobbes written three centuries earlier by John Sheffield, "Duke of Buckingham" [sic], and the novelist Aphra Behn. Sheffield's tribute to Hobbes declared,

> While in dark Ignorance we lay afraid
> of fancies, Ghosts, and every empty Shade;
> Great Hobs appeared, and by plain Reason's Light
> Put such fantastick Forms to shameful Flight.

Behn, striking a different note in praise of Hobbes, had proclaimed,

> Is he then dead at last, whom vain report,
> So often deign'd immortal in meer sport?
> Whom we on earth so long alive did see,
> We thought he here had Immortality.

Not far from Malmesbury, Oxford University in the final months of 1979 sponsored a series of lectures on Hobbes accompanied by a display of his works, and Hertford College, into which Magdalen Hall had been absorbed, hosted a small party "for members of the local philosophical community to contemplate Hobbes' portrait and study the books that he left to the college."[1] On Sunday, December 9, Hobbes was remembered at evensong in the parish church of Hault Hucknall, where he was buried. "Despite the general view that he was an atheist," the Reverend Charles Brinkworth, the local minister observed, "there is considerable evidence that he remained a faithful member of the Church of England and we will be remembering him accordingly."[2]

It was not always so. Malmesbury did not notice, let alone commemorate, the one hundredth or two hundredth anniversaries of its most famous citizen's birth and death; even today the bust of Hobbes that was placed in the council room is the only visible reminder that Hobbes was born and spent the first fifteen years of his life in the town. On July 21, 1683, Hobbes's *De Cive* and *Leviathan* were two of the more than two dozen books publicly burned in an Oxford college quadrangle, to the accompaniment, according to Wood, of "severall hums" sung by the 250 "scholars of all degrees and qualities" present.[3] Earlier, while Hobbes was still living, one Daniel Scargill, a fellow of Corpus Christi College, Cambridge, had been expelled from the university for "being a Hobbist and atheist"; in the course of recanting his views, Scargill had "attributed his moral ruin to Hobbes's principles."[4] As late as 1968, a distinguished citizen of Malmesbury, who may not have been present at the "Tercentenary Dinner," was able to declare that Hobbes, though "greatly venerated in all Socialist countries . . . is apparently almost forgotten in this land. At recent visits of Russian and German parties to Malmesbury they were horrified to find he was so little known here." The Russians, presumably, were interested in Hobbes because his principles "were what might be called socialistic in these days, with a dash of Atheism."[5]

The view of Hobbes as a socialist would appear to be eccentric or, worse, silly until we recall even serious scholars charging that "Hobbes's theories lead to the all-powerful, all-embracing State such as existed before the war in National-Socialist Germany and now exists behind the Iron Curtain. . . ."[6] Since the publication of *De Cive*, Hobbes has been regarded as an atheist by many lay persons and scholars alike, and this belief, which is both more damaging and more creditable than other allegations, has no doubt been partly responsible for Hobbes's relative obscurity until the late nineteenth century. In 1649, and again in 1703, all of his works were placed on the Vatican's *Index*

Librorum Prohibitorum, and they remain on it today. But even in non-Catholic countries Hobbes's books received little attention for more than two hundred years. Excluding two English editions of Hobbes's collected works, the first in 1750 and the second, edited by Molesworth, in 1838–45, *Leviathan* in English was not published between the first edition of 1651 (or possibly 1680, in the case of the third, or "ornaments," issue of the first edition) and 1881.[7] In the United States, *Leviathan* did not make an appearance until 1885, and on that occasion it did so as a reprint of the London edition the same year.[8] By 1900 five further editions had appeared, and in the present century *Leviathan* and other books by Hobbes, notably the English versions of *De Cive* and *Behemoth*, have become readily available in numerous hardcover and paperback editions. Since 1911 *Leviathan* has been published in Italian (1911–12), Spanish (1940), Czechoslovak (1941), Polish (1954), Russian (1964–65), German (1966, with an earlier edition, translated from the Latin version, in 1794–95), and Japanese (1974), though not yet, so far as is known, in Chinese.[9]

Clearly, Hobbes is more congenial to twentieth-century minds, for reasons to be explored in due course, than he was to those of the seventeenth, eighteenth, or nineteenth centuries. The accessibility of his major works and the widespread interest in their major themes, however, have not made easier an understanding of Hobbes, much less facilitated a broad agreement on the meaning and importance of his principles. *Leviathan*, his most discussed book, has been hailed as "the greatest, perhaps the sole, masterpiece of political philosophy written in the English language" (Michael Oakshott),[10] and "as the world's greatest store of political wisdom" (R. G. Collingwood).[11] But *Leviathan*, on equal authority, has also been called "a fantastic monster, such as is sometimes cast up, with other strange births, in political, as in marine, convulsions . . . an isolated phenomenon in English thought, without ancestry or posterity; crude, academic, and wrong" (H. R. Trevor-Roper).[12] Moreover, Hobbes himself has not fared better than his best-known book.[13] "Thomas Hobbes," T. S. Eliot wrote in 1927, "was one of those extraordinary little upstarts whom the chaotic motions of the Renaissance tossed into an eminence which they hardly deserved and have never lost."[14]

Eliot believed that "Hobbes was undoubtedly an atheist and could hardly have been unconscious of the fact,"[15] and this view, too, is widely maintained, though it is not without its critics.[16] Such statements, scattered through Hobbes's writings, as "Fear of Power invisable feign'd by the mind, or imagined from Tales publicly allowed, is Religion; not allowed, is Superstition," and "To say that God hath spoken to a man in a Dream, is nor more than to say, he Dreamt that

God spake to him,"[17] have led one student of Hobbes to conclude that "if he was not an atheist, he was certainly an agnostic," and another to wonder whether Hobbes's "whole treatment of 'the true religion' is not a colossal piece of irony."[18] That Hobbes was not religious in a formal sense seems clear from his writings on the subject, in one of which he identified as "the natural Seed of Religion" the four essentials of "Opinion of Ghosts, Ignorance of Second Causes, Devotion towards what men fear, and taking of things Casual for Prognosticks."[19]

But he nowhere declared, or implied, he was wholly without religious conviction, and while some students of Hobbes maintain he refrained from doing so because of the manifest dangers in those days of proclaiming oneself an atheist or agnostic, a contributing factor of importance may have been his awareness that religion, insofar as it was firmly under state control, has its uses in the suppression of that lawless and savage behavior which, deeply rooted in human nature, was in most men always and everywhere a threat to peace and stability. Whatever his own reservations about religion, Hobbes had no wish to undermine the faith of others, especially those whose civil obedience and compliance with the law were anchored to religious belief.

There also is at least circumstantial evidence that Hobbes personally, insofar as any label can be applied to him, was a qualified deist, that is, one who believed that the universe had been set in motion by a creative force, or "first cause," which could be regarded as God or God-like, but that the natural and physical laws of the universe were not governed by this God or God-like entity. "And forasmuch as God Almighty is *incomprehensible,*" he wrote in *Human Nature,* "it followeth, that we can have *no* conception or *image* of the *Deity* . . . excepting only this, that *there is a God:* for the effects we acknowledge naturally, do include a power of their producing, before they were produced; and that power presupposeth something existent that hath such power: and the thing so existing with power to produce, if it were not eternal, must needs have been produced by somewhat before it, and that again by something else before that, till we come to an eternal, that is to say, the first power of all powers, and first cause of all causes: and this is it which all men conceive by the name of GOD. . . . "[20] Hobbes, in other words, almost certainly did not believe in a personal God, or in heaven and hell, or in the scriptural version of human history, and he must have doubted that Jesus Christ was of divine origin, though he was careful not to say so. His affirmations of religious faith, moreover, which struck many of his contemporaries and later readers as lacking in sincerity, failed to convince, and in the seventeenth century, if not in the twentieth, perceived reservations about established Christian doctrines, or a failure to proclaim them with fervor and enthusiasm, were more than enough to arouse suspicion of atheism or heresy.

Hobbes's awareness of the uses of religion and his qualified deism are apparent in a "Fragment on the Relation between Virtue and Religion," found among his papers and "probably by him," though not in his hand (see Appendix 3). In the "Fragment," Hobbes argued that "virtue & religion are essentially the same" because virtuous acts require "a governing principle, from whence such acts and habits must proceed." The actions of animals, Hobbes insisted, may appear virtuous, but they cannot be deemed such, because "brutes" are ignorant of "the conducting principle" based on religion. Both religion and virtue relate to "prudence," Hobbes emphasized, because "who can doubt that prudence obliges a man to be religious as well as virtuous? Who can doubt but that prudence obliges a man to acquit himself in his offices to God, as well as to the world? . . . because that if there were no God, neither were there any prudence in being virtuous. For whatsoever may be argued for the practice of virtue and for the support of it in the world upon a political account; as either from its private conveniences to particular persons, or from its public usefulness to the ends of Government; set aside religion and all are but wood without weight." Without religion, in other words, virtue and prudence itself, and by extension politics and "the ends of government," rest on shaky foundations.

Had Hobbes totally dismissed religion, or been universally viewed as hostile to religious faith, he would have had even more enemies, like Wallis and Ward, and fewer friends, some of them close, who were ministers or priests. According to Aubrey, these friends included, in the Church of England, William Chillingworth; George Eglionby (or Aglionby), dean of Canterbury; Jasper Mayne, Newcastle's chaplain; and perhaps others. Despite his pronounced antagonism to the papacy, Hobbes, as has been noted, was treated with affection and respect by Mersenne and Gassendi, and he enjoyed cordial relations with such prominent English Catholics as Digby and, at court, Arlington (who was a secret Catholic). We may doubt that had these Catholic friends, in particular, regarded Hobbes as an outright atheist, the interest in science and mathematics they shared with him would have been sufficient, especially in the case of Mersenne and Gassendi, to sustain a continuing friendship.*

---

* Mersenne, if not also Gassendi, may have entertained hopes of persuading Hobbes to become a Catholic. When Hobbes fell ill in Paris in 1647 and was believed to be dying, Robertson reported, he was visited by Mersenne, who broached the subject of conversion. "Father," Hobbes is supposed to have responded, "I have debated all that with

To a certain cast of religious mind, moreover, or to a religious temper that was worldly and sophisticated, the uses to which Hobbes himself put religion were hardly anathema. For Hobbes, unlike official representatives of the religions battling throughout Europe, was indifferent to the question of which religion was superior in dogma, ritual, or scriptural truth. To such a question, Hobbes's answer was as simple as it was brief: let the sovereign decide—an answer that was as compatible with one religion, a critic correctly perceived, as with another. For the possible consequences of establishing a sovereign who was also a secular pope or archbishop would have been, had that sovereign been a Catholic in 1651, that "we ought to have embraced Romish idolatry. If a Jew had been general of the Army, and would have been bidden him (Hobbes) be circumcised, he would have done it. If a Turk had been turned up Trump and bidden Mr. Hobbes go to Mecca and worship at Mahomet's tomb, he would have done it; if a Persian had proved uppermost and have bidden him worship at Haly's shrine and say Haly was a greater prophet than Christ, he would have done it."[21] Hobbes's emphasis on the subordination of religion to the civil authority could not have been wholly without appeal to Catholic kings confronting Protestant dissenters, or to Protestant rulers confronting Catholic recusants, and it may have contributed to his acceptance, despite doctrinal differences, by friends who adhered to more-orthodox religious views. Whatever else Hobbes was, as all but his most obtuse critics were aware, he was an upholder of long-established institutions, not a destroyer of them.

While his attitude toward the Catholic church would appear to be an exception, his strictures may have been motivated, at least in part, by a wish to undermine papal authority, viewed in England as a subversive influence, rather than by a desire to refute Catholic belief as such. Like William Tyndale (1492?–1536), Hobbes was convinced that "it is the bloody doctrine of the Pope which causeth disobedience, rebellion, and insurrection," and that "all men without exception are under the temporal sword."[22] Hobbes also insisted, with Tyndale, "The King is, in this world, without law; and may at his lust do right or wrong, and shall give accounts but to God only,"[23] a belief that ruled out sovereign accountability to popes, archbishops, and congregations. Here as elsewhere in Hobbes's thought, we are reminded

---

myself long ago, and I have no mind to discuss it now; you can entertain me better. When did you last see Gassendi?" *Hobbes*, 63–64. Aubrey's version is rather different: "When Mr. T. Hobbes was sick in France, the Divines came to him, and tormented him (both Roman Catholic, Church of England, and Geneva). Sayd he to them, Let me alone, or els I will detect all your Cheates from Aaron to yourselves." Whichever story is true, would Mersenne and the other "Divines" have made an effort to convert Hobbes if they had believed him to be a convinced atheist?

he had certain nostalgic affinities with an earlier age when it was widely accepted that monarchs "may not be resisted, do they never so evil, they must be reserved unto the wrath of God."[24] Indeed, Hobbes himself could well have said, as did Elizabeth, "I see many over-bold with God Almighty, making too many subtle scannings of his blessed will, as lawyers do with human testaments."*

But Hobbes's writings on religion, like his writings on other topics, are not without their ambiguities, inconsistencies, and contradictions, as most commentators have observed, one of whom has argued that "it is most reasonable to see Hobbes's philosophy of religion as an unsuccessful venture—unsuccessful either as construction or destruction."[25] As has already been noted, Hobbes's discussion of religion lends itself to a dismaying variety of interpretations, some of them mutually exclusive. No doubt some part of this confusion derives from Hobbes's tendency, in accordance with "prudence," to qualify his remarks and occasionally equivocate in discussions of politics and religion, though not in arguments about mathematics and science, where the penalties for imprudence were much less severe. Often inclined to hedge his bets in taking a controversial position, Hobbes when pressed on a point was apt to deny he had said what he was thought to have said, or meant what he was thought to have meant.

But thus far no one has suggested that our problems in understanding Hobbes may reflect, in addition to factors previously mentioned, the expression in his writing of certain ambivalences rooted in his childhood and early years. The son and grandson of clergymen, Hobbes must have been brought up in a religious household, but it was a religious household presided over by an undistinguished and impecunious curate (not vicar, as Aubrey, and other writers following Aubrey, maintained), who, after years of contention with his parishioners and acrimonious disputes with neighboring clergy, was excommunicated and, in effect, required to leave Malmesbury. One result of the curate's disgrace, we can infer from Aubrey, was that his family was forced into dependence upon the earnings of Hobbes's brother, Edmund, who was about two years older, and probably to accept assistance from Uncle Francis; the expenses of Hobbes's Oxford

---

*Quoted in Thompson, *Universities*, 15. Long before *De Cive* and *Leviathan*, Shakespeare observed in *Troilus and Cressida:*

> Take but degree away, untune that string,
> And, hark, what discord follows!

Quoted in Rowse, *England*, 43. A homily often read in church (in lieu of a sermon), which Hobbes may have heard as a boy in Malmesbury, admonished, "Take away kings, rulers, princes, magistrates, judges, and such states of God's order . . . no man shall sleep in his own house or bed unkilled, no man shall keep his wife, children and possessions in quietness. . . ."

education, according to Aubrey, were borne by Francis Hobbes. While we do not know the fate of Hobbes's mother, we can speculate that her life could not have been easy after the disappearance of her husband, even assuming that the early marriage of her daughter, Anne, obviated a need for continuing support. But Mrs. Hobbes may not have been a contented wife before her husband was lost to her. If we can trust Aubrey's report that the Reverend Thomas Hobbes was "a good fellow," and believe that the Brokenborough "common alehouse goer" of 1590 was Hobbes's father, we can imagine that a fair amount of his time and money was spent in local taverns, an activity that cannot have been entirely acceptable to his spouse, as it is not acceptable to other husbands' wives anywhere in the world. Perhaps, too, the elder Hobbes was given to outbursts of temper—Aubrey described him as "choleric"—and even to occasional acts of violence, as in the assault on Jeane, at home. If so, we can understand better why his son all of his life feared and avoided physical dangers or confrontations and, unlike many of his contemporaries, apparently displayed no interest in "blood" sports.

Hobbes, to be sure, never discussed with anyone, so far as we know, his feelings about his father, but he would have been a most unusual son to have grown into manhood without developing at least some negative sentiments about his father's failings and their consequences. Hobbes's experience of his clerical father, in short, may have contributed significantly to his ambivalence about religion, which was marked by a rejection of orthodox Christian doctrines, and to his unyielding insistance that religion breeds discord and controversy and therefore should be firmly under the control of secular sovereign power.* Perhaps, too, his willingness to become involved in controversies with religious authority figures, such as Bramhall (and, at a further remove, the pope), and to dispute the Puritans and Presbyterians, owed something to negative feelings about his father, who was, after all, the first religious authority figure to play a significant role in his life. Even Hobbes's interest in mathematics and science, and especially his conviction that the truths of geometry were superior to other kinds of knowledge, may have been, in some sense, a reaction to his father's Anglicanism and, by extension, to religion in general.

The Reverend Thomas Hobbes may also have influenced his son in other respects. Almost all students of Hobbes have taken notice of

---

id a conscious or unconscious memory of his father, together with events leading to the Civil War, play a role in Hobbes's choosing as the title-page inscription of *Behemoth* this quotation from Lucretius: "So many evils can religion bring about" ("Tantum religio potuit suadere malorum")? We can only speculate about the answer.

his "insecurity" and "timidity"; reports have come down to us that he was afraid of the dark and kept a candle burning at night and that he would not be left alone in an empty house (allegedly the reason he was carried on a bed from Chatsworth to Hardwick shortly before he died).[26] Kennet insisted that Hobbes "was a great Coward, his whole Life was govern'd by his Fears,"[27] and the novelist Rose Macaulay has suggested he was "womanish."[28] But these comments reflect, at best, half-truths, for as Isaac Disraeli perceptively observed, Hobbes may have been "more practically timorous" than other men, but "no man was more speculatively bold."[29] Hobbes's "excessive timidity," in Disraeli's words, was often accompanied by an aggressive, argumentative style of expression that was experienced by his readers as provocative and by his critics, even when it did not add insult to injury, as inflammatory. Hobbes apparently welcomed controversies of all sorts and enjoyed using adversary language whether or not there was any occasion for it. In his *Autobiography*, as was noted earlier, he had frequent recourse to battlefield similes and images, though he was a man who would go to almost any extreme to avoid battlefields.

Such verbal belligerence supports the hypothesis that Hobbes, however much he may have disliked his "choleric" father and what his father represented, partially identified with him. His intellectual wars may also have served as an outlet for feelings of anger and disappointment that had their origins in childhood but that Hobbes as a child, in what may well have been an authoritarian household typical of the time, could not express. While we cannot know, of course, in what familial atmosphere Hobbes spent his early years, the hypothesis is not inconsistent with Aubrey's report that Hobbes as a boy "was playsome enough" but "even then [had] a contemplative melancholinesse." Also relevant, perhaps, is the circumstance that Hobbes never married or apparently ever entertained any serious thought of marrying, as did Aubrey, and establishing a family of his own.

Of greater significance, in this context, may be Hobbes's wording in *Leviathan* of the famous phrase that declares that life in the state of nature is "solitary, poor, nasty, brutish, and short." Why, we may wonder, did he list "solitary" first? A "short" life, some would argue, is a far greater calamity, and others might wish to insist that "nasty" or "brutish" conditions are worse evils. The answer surely cannot be that Hobbes was influenced by purely literary and stylistic considerations, for the phrase does not lose anything if the words are rearranged, as they often are in popular recall. Equally memorable, and quotable, would be "poor, brutish, solitary, nasty, and short," or even "short, nasty, solitary, brutish, and poor." Clearly, Hobbes's motivation in beginning the phrase with "solitary" must have been other than simple ease or harmony of expression.

The word "solitude," moreover, had made at least two earlier appearances in Hobbes's writings. "I must more plainly say," Hobbes wrote in *De Cive*, "that to man by nature . . . that is, as soon as he is born, solitude is an enemy. . . ."[30] In *De Corpore* Hobbes maintained that "all such calamities as may be avoided by human industry, arise from war, but chiefly from civil war; for from this proceed slaughter, solitude, and the want of all things."[31] These references to "solitude," and the priority of "solitary" in *Leviathan*, are hardly contradictory of reports that Hobbes personally could not abide being alone, and we can therefore surmise that he regarded the "solitary" condition not just as a foremost evil in the state of nature and in war but also as a particularly unhappy circumstance in his own life. While most children and even many young adults experience the desertion or death of a parent as a withdrawal of love and support, or in some instances as rejection, and as a result often become depressed and anxious, Hobbes's fear and intolerance of "solitude" in his mature years appear inexplicable until we remember his father's disappearance and, perhaps as a consequence, his youthful "contemplative melancholinesse."

Indeed, the traumas of his childhood may have established the basis of something more significant than his pessimistic view of human nature and rejection of formal religion. In Hobbes's writings there is a curious inconsistency about authority that occasionally was present in his relations with authority figures. On the one hand, he was foremost among seventeenth-century English political philosophers in his willingness, as he put it in a Latin "Epistle Dedicatory," to "exalt in civil power"; in a century that witnessed the rise of the social contract and the first, faint stirrings of parliamentary supremacy, Hobbes's absolutism appears almost medieval. But he also wrote against and in defiance of authority, not merely the authority of Catholic popes and cardinals, and Protestant archbishops and bishops, but the authority of royalists and parliamentarians, courts and judges, universities and professors, mathematicians and scientists, Gresham College (the Royal Society), and philosophers ranging from Aristotle to Descartes.

Clarendon insisted that Hobbes also demonstrated an "extreme malignity to the Nobility," and though he overstated the case, basing his remarks on a misinterpretation of certain passages in *Leviathan*, Clarendon succeeded in calling our attention to scattered hints and nuances in Hobbes's writings suggesting that he was not wholly without envy of the rich, or wholly without resentment of the wellborn, whose birth alone assured them a high place in society. But in seeming contradiction of such sentiments, Hobbes could be, and often was, deferential to the point of being obsequious to those who represented power and authority. Here and there in his letters, especially in those to Newcastle and Clifton, and in some of his book dedications, Hobbes's fervid declarations of affection and respect seem almost, or at least slightly, insincere, no matter how much allowance we make for the hyperbole typical of the period. His books, moreover, with few exceptions were dedicated to those in ascendant positions: the second and third earls of Devonshire, Charles II, Newcastle, Arlington, Henry Lord Pierrepont (Viscount Newark), even Duke Cosimo de' Medici. Unlike Bacon, who dedicated the first edition of his *Essays* to his brother Anthony, and Aubrey, some of whose works were dedicated to close personal friends, Hobbes never dedicated a book to a family member or relative, and he rarely honored anyone who was not a benefactor.

One possible explanation is that Hobbes, who, we have argued, was insecure as a child, never lost the sense that life is fraught with uncertainty and hazard and for that reason best experienced in the company of those who can offer shelter and protection. While no one would deny that Hobbes lived through an age of tumult and turmoil, not all Englishmen of the seventeenth century were as anxious and fearful as he or had a similar need to attach themselves to influential persons. The dukes, earls, and viscounts of his dedications, Charles II above all, related to Hobbes as protectors, and however much he may have doubted, in secret, their intelligence or competence, or envied their privileges, he was careful to devote time, energy, and even occasional literary efforts (such as *De Mirabilibus Pecci* and his essay on horsemanship for Newcastle) to their cultivation. Indeed, except for a brief time, Hobbes was never far from the sumptuous shelter, in a literal sense, provided by the Devonshires, and he was never indifferent to the security they afforded. Surely, this attachment of almost seventy years, during which England's most controversial thinker was supported by one of England's most privileged families, is unique, not merely in the annals of British aristocracy but also in intellectual history.*

Whether unique or not, it may help us understand still other facets of Hobbes's political theory, namely, his view of the state as a

---

* The benefits to Hobbes of his association with three Devonshire generations are more apparent than the benefits to them. Clearly, Hobbes was a man of great charm and wit, as well as intelligence, and he may have had other unrecorded gifts that appealed to Cavendishes of all ages. Unfortunately, the Devonshire histories so far published do not explore the family's side of the connection.

"Mortal God" and his conception of sovereign power, so long as peace and order are preserved, as absolute. For if the Devonshire attachment reflected Hobbes's need for security and protection, his "Mortal God" and sovereign, however rationalized in terms of human nature and the state of nature, may have been, in theoretical terms, the political expression of a similar need—or, in other words, the Devonshires writ large. In fact, Hobbes's idealized polity, as he implied in discussions of the family and relations between parents, children, and servants, is, on a smaller scale, not unlike an orderly and secure household in which the father or, in his absence, the mother wields unquestioned authority, and the obedient children and servants know their place and do as they are told. The arrangement is not one-sided, of course, as it is not one-sided in Hobbes's ideal state; in return for their compliance, the children and servants are protected from war and violence, and sleep securely in their beds at night. Citizens in Hobbes's political society enjoy the same benefits, and in addition the fruits of culture, science, and knowledge in general. In both family and society, as is obvious by now, whoever rules chooses the religion, interprets its sacred writings, prescribes its rituals, and enforces its commandments.

If life at Hardwick and Chatsworth fulfilled all or most conditions that Hobbes regarded as ideal—by his own account, the years he spent in the service of the second earl were the happiest of his life—Hobbes may well have had it in mind when, sometime between 1608 and the publication of *Thucydides* in 1629, he began to give substance and shape to his political philosophy.[32] The principal features of this philosophy were in place, we have argued, long before the outbreak of the Civil War, and the war and its aftermath must have impressed Hobbes as more than ample confirmation of his theories about human nature and its role in political affairs. But Hobbes claimed that he was writing not just for seventeenth-century England but for all societies at all times. As he stated in his reply to Bramhall in 1668, "I will say this much [of my works], that neither he, if he had lived, nor I, if I would, could extinguish the light which is set up in the world by the greatest part of them." Like all political theorists, Hobbes believed that the "light" that he had created would shine forever. Nothing, of course, except possibly death, is forever, but that observation does not preclude an inquiry into Hobbes's relevance to our time and condition. Indeed, the question of Hobbes's importance in a century that, in some respects, has not been dissimilar to his own can hardly be put aside.

The twentieth century, as it draws to a close, would appear to confirm Hobbes's pessimism, as it has confirmed the pessimism of

Freud. Its unending horrors, which so far have included two world wars and innumerable lesser wars, the Holocaust, and a multitude of massacres, pogroms, and genocidal crusades—perhaps as many as one hundred million persons have died violently—could be understood to mean that Hobbes was right about the state of nature, because the world as a whole, and certain nations, such as Germany under Hitler, the Soviet Union under Stalin, and Cambodia under Pol Pot, to mention a few of many examples, can be recognized as states of nature. Hobbes probably would also have regarded nuclear weapons not as a means of ensuring peace between the great powers but as promising still another bloody episode in the interminable war of "every man, against every man."

But if we grant that much, though not all, of recent history tends to confirm Hobbes's, and Freud's, view of human nature, we do not by that admission necessarily endorse Hobbes's conclusion that any government was preferable to the state of nature and no government, and that authoritarian government was best of all. For Hobbes's solution, unlike Freud's, would substitute for man's thralldom to his baser instincts a worse enslavement by the state. In such a condition, man would perhaps, be safe and materially secure, but he would not be free or independent. No doubt Hobbesian government would promote all those benefits of civilization that, Hobbes argued in *Leviathan*, did not flourish in the state of nature: "Industry ... Culture ... Knowledge ... Arts ... Letters." But the benefits would be unlike those that exist in a free society: industry with regimentation, culture with indoctrination, knowledge with thought control, arts and letters with censorship. Given the strengths and persistence of the passions Hobbes complained of, we can imagine that in the Hobbesian state, where these passions were suppressed, man would be safe and secure in his bed at night, but that his dreams would be nightmares.

These features of Hobbes's thought, however, do not suggest that he was a precursor of Hitler, as some have insisted, or that he was an intellectual forerunner of fascism. Nor was he, as others have maintained, an ancestor of Bentham and therefore a founding father of the welfare state. Least of all was he a Marxist (insofar as anyone who lived before Marx could have been a Marxist); Hobbes nowhere declared that politics is a function of economics or that power follows property, and his infrequent statements expressing sympathy for the poor do not make him a socialist, no more than Machiavelli's view that force and fraud were "praiseworthy," in war,[33] a view Hobbes to some extent shared, makes Machiavelli a warmonger or militarist.

Hobbes and Hobbesian thought, unhappily for those prone to categorize, are resistant to labels, all of which oversimplify and distort reality. But if Hobbes can be designated something more than a Hobbesian, which is one way of dealing with his complexity, perhaps he can be designated, or labeled, to repeat what was written earlier, a "radical in the service of reaction."* Hobbes's iconoclasm, defiance of religion and politics in seventeenth-century England, and refusal to accept the established wisdom of his day reflected a radical disposition, but it was a disposition in favor of an absolutism that was moving off the stage of history and that in England was to disappear forever not long after his demise. Though his rejection of divine right offended royalists, his insistence that peace, order, and self-preservation required the monarch to be all-powerful was intended to establish absolutism on a new and much more solid foundation, namely, on necessity. Indeed, under divine right the absolute powers Hobbes claimed for sovereignty were not exercised by any English king of the seventeenth century, and the inferior status to which he reduced Parliament was not willingly accepted by any English Parliament of the seventeenth century. Not even Elizabeth ruled as Hobbes demanded that a sovereign rule; Henry VIII was, perhaps, the last English king to qualify, or almost qualify, as a Hobbesian monarch. Hobbes's radicalism, in short, faced backward, not forward.

If one allows for differences of time, place, and context, certain themes and attitudes in Hobbes suggest he was an exemplar of what in recent years has come to be called in the United States the "radical right" or, in Richard Hofstadter's phrasing, "pseudo-conservatism."[34] Hobbes, too, could be shrill, angry, and suspicious when he faced opposition, and inclined to question the motives as well as the arguments of those who disagreed with him. In blaming the universities and the clergy for the unrest that culminated in the Civil War, and in discounting economic and social issues, Hobbes was articulating, in effect, his own version of the "devil" or "conspiracy" theory of politics, which holds that the difficulties and problems including defeat in war, that a nation experiences have been brought about by the machinations of evil men in high places. The ends or goals of policy, which were civic peace and stability, Hobbes believed, justified almost any means; like the American "radical right," Hobbes attached supreme importance to law and order.† Permissiveness and a lack of

---

*T. S. Eliot, in his defense of Bramhall, called Hobbes "a revolutionary in thought and a timid conservative in action; and his theory of government is congenial to that type of person who is conservative from prudence but revolutionary in his dreams. . . . In Hobbes there are symptoms of the same mentality as Nietzsche: his belief in violence is a confession of weakness." "Bramhall," 317. One is wise not to follow Eliot so far, or, if one insists on following him, to do so with caution.

† Aubrey recalled Hobbes saying "that if it were not for the gallowes, some men are of so cruell a nature as to take a delight in killing men more than I should to kill a bird." No advocate today of capital punishment has been able to improve on that argument.

discipline at home, school, and in society, Hobbes maintained, were among the significant causes of the unrest that afflicted England, and he favored the taking of strong measures to eradicate them. Finally, Hobbes had no more faith than today's "radical right" adherents in the intelligence and capacity of average citizens, and there can be little question that had he been alive in 1688–89, he would have regarded the Glorious Revolution as no less inglorious than its predecessor.

Given his convictions about human nature and the state of nature, Hobbes could hardly have been expected to believe that men who were not able to govern themselves would be able, by assembling, to govern others. But these convictions also may tell us something important about Hobbes himself. Hobbes could be, and often was, arrogant and supercilious, as has been noted by many commentators, but arrogance can mask a low estimate of oneself and serve as a defense against feelings of unworthiness. While we do not know enough about Hobbes to be certain he harbored such feelings, we have his own reference, in his *Autobiography*, to "the little worm that is myself," and his statement, not long before his death, invoking the "worm" image or perhaps "The Devil's Arse of Peak," that "he should be glad to finde a hole to creepe out of the world at." Hobbes's identifying himself as a "worm," and his alluding to a "hole," may signify much or little; we can be sure only that the lowly worm is not among the noblest of earth's creatures. Although such evidence is too flimsy to establish that Hobbes suffered from self-doubt, the possibility exists that he did so and that those qualities he did not like in others, which collectively formed his conception of human nature, were qualities he perceived and disliked in himself. In *Leviathan* he had suggested that "whosoever looketh into himself, and considereth what he doth . . . shall thereby read and know . . . the thoughts, and Passions of all other men." Perhaps, then, the mirror that Hobbes held up to his fellow Englishmen and the world, and in which they were supposed to see reflected fear, envy, greed, ambition, and competitiveness, was the mirror in which Hobbes had first seen himself.

Those who do not trust themselves do not trust others, and those whose own instincts and impulses make them apprehensive, are apt to call for more religion, which Hobbes did not, or for more authority, which he did. Persons made anxious by a threatened loss of control have always turned to the external supports and reinforcements of church or state, and Hobbes, perhaps, was no exception. Like Freud, whose theory of instincts or drives Hobbes would have found congenial but who rejected both church and state as remedial agencies in favor of the superego or conscience, Hobbes did not believe that most persons were capable of either self-control or self-government. But unlike Freud, who toward the end of his life—by which time Hitler had been in power more than six years and had begun the Second World War—despaired of any solution, Hobbes, we may suppose, was too anxious, too insecure, and too fearful to abandon faith in the "Mortal God" even had he, in the very different political and intellectual climate of 1679, wanted to.

Faced with the choice between the superego and the superstate, that is, between social control from within or social control from without, democrats will always choose the former. Democrats, however, are not found everywhere in the world, not even everywhere in the democracies of Western Europe and North America. Those who believe, or hope, that Hobbes was as mistaken about politics as he was about mathematics would wish there were more democrats and more democracies, but more of both would not, in the long run, prove that Hobbes was wrong. Hobbes's importance in the future and the future of democracy depend upon whether democrats can solve problems, including the problem of war, for which Hobbes's prescription was absolutism. Unfortunately, there is little evidence, three hundred years after Hobbes, that these problems are being solved by democrats, and therefore little confidence in some quarters that democrats can prove Hobbes wrong. Indeed, few major events, or trends, or movements of men anywhere, as the twentieth century draws to a close, prove that Hobbes was wrong.

APPENDIX I

The Disputed Authorship of *Horae Subsecivae* and Hobbes's Annotations

IN 1934 THE LATE LEO STRAUSS, then at the University of Berlin, discovered a manuscript in the Chatsworth Library entitled *Essayes,* the author of which signed himself "W. Cavendish." A longer version of this manuscript, with several additional essays but without the attribution to "W. Cavendish," was published in 1620 as *Horae Subsecivae: Observations and Discourses* with a preface disclaiming authorship by "Ed. Blount." Strauss believed that both the *Essayes* and *Horae Subsecivae* had been composed between 1612 and 1620 and that the former, in the style of Bacon's essays, had been "written in Hobbes's hand." Had this been true or had it been established that the *Essayes* were the work of Hobbes's pupil, the future second earl, the *Essayes* could have been regarded as "a source for Hobbes's early thought," or at least as a reflection, through Hobbes's influence on William Cavendish, of Hobbes's thinking at the time. Strauss may not have been aware that in 1708 White Kennet, who was close to the Devonshires, stated that Gilbert Cavendish, elder son of the first earl, who had died sometime before 1618, was the author of *Horae Subsecivae.* (The book has also been attributed to Grey Brydges, the fifth baron Chandos [ca. 1580–1621]).

More recently, the argument has been made that *Horae Subsecivae* was written before 1610 by William Cavendish, the future second earl, and revised by him following an eight-month visit to Italy in 1614–15; the evidence for this view is the inclusion in the published version of material based on travel, including an essay entitled "Discourse on Rome"—material missing from the Chatsworth manuscript. Another essay, the "Discourse of Lawes," makes reference to the "different Constitutions, & *Lawes,* in our two late Plantations, of *Virginia,* & the *Bermudas";* settlement in the Bermudas was not begun until 1612, and the Somer Islands Company did not become a distinct corporation until 1615.[1]

Clearly, *Horae Subsecivae* must have originated with one of the Caven-dishes, but which Cavendish? Gilbert Cavendish, about whom nothing is known other than that he died early, may also have traveled to Italy and other coun-tries and been acquainted with the Virginia and Somer Islands companies. Perhaps, then, the work was begun by Gilbert and completed by William after Gilbert's death, with or without Hobbes's assistance. In any event, the manuscript of *Horae Subsecivae* was not written by Hobbes and therefore cannot be treated as an early account of his thought.[2]

The Chatsworth copy of *Horae Subsecivae*, however, has been annotated on the page margins by someone whose handwriting appears to be identical to that of Hobbes.* The style of the annotations, moreover, is similar to that of Hobbes; some of the comments, not all of which are legible, are sharp, pithy, and acerbic—in a word, Hobbesian. While they do not throw much light on Hobbes's early or late thinking—and we have no way of asertaining when he annotated the book—they have a certain interest in and of them-selves. The more important of these annotations follow:

	TEXT OF *Horae Subsecivae*	HOBBES'S ANNOTATIONS
page 1	For not onely hee that speakes of himselfe more good then is true, but hee also that sayes more then he is sure will bee beleeved, justly deserves the name of *Arrogant*.	arrogance is [unreadable] with-out reason or judgment
3	Honour found out *Cincinnatus* digging in his Garden and made him Dictator.	offices should use men not men offices
4	An *Arrogant* person, if he joyne in the performance of any laud-able action, with men of modest natures, deales with them in the sharing of the praise. . . .	The Virtuous parts with his owne for peace the arrogant will have part of yours wrongfully if yt lie in his poure or no peace
	Ambition	
13	Ambition was the first tempta-tion by which the Divell wrought upon our first Parents, to encite them to a desire of knowing good and evill equally with God.	adams posterity might of all other beasts beware of this we payd so deare for yt

---

* No differences are discernible between the script of letters, manuscripts, and miscel-laneous papers known to have been written by Hobbes and that of the annotations. The identification of handwriting, however, is not an exact science, and the possibility that the annotations were in fact made by someone else cannot absolutely be ruled out.

Text of *Horae Subsecivae*	Hobbes's Annotations
page 18 . . . the nature of *Ambition* is to commiserate ourselves, for that wee seemingly want or desire: for when wee see another man possessed of that, that our endevours aspired unto, presently *Envy* breaks forth. . . .	if one humer in man have so many strange effects what is he upon many if the like nature infect hym
21 [Ambitious men] will endevor to take [from others] and adde as much to themselves in the opinion of the world, as either industry or art can devise. Which kind of contention is pernicious to all well-ordered Commonwealths.	but seldom looked into
22 Some of this sort, that think themselves most cunning in their trade, will not plainly professe Ambition, but maske, or shadow with other colours, whereby they hope they may more safely passe undetected, undiscovered.	amongst fools
28 Our first thoughts should be to make our selves worthy to receive dignity and employment. . . .	The second that we should not seeke for places but let places seeke us

Of Detraction

| 54   [Detractors] are the very moths, that corrupt and canker in every Commonwealth; how they worke, and weare, and eate into every mans good name, experience witnesseth. | a state suffers in nothinge more then in slanderous reports |
| 59   The *Separatists,* or *Sanctified,* as they terme themselves . . . talke of Ecclesiasticall functions, Ceremonie, and Government, with that disdaine and reproch. . . . | the Impure Puritan |

Of Death

| 133   Many men without the knowledge of Religion, have excellently expressed their contempt of Death. . . . | in a desperate way |

TEXT OF *Horae Subsecivae*	HOBBES'S ANNOTATIONS
page 134 There be few lingring diseases or sudden paines, that be not more sensible and painful then Death, and the recoverie fro them, is as a short reprieve.	if we live let us live for the lord if we dye let us dy for the lord

Of Country Life

| 166–67 . . . the state oftentimes . . . fix their greatest places upon men low, and meanely descended . . . (which) cannot but be interpreted as disgrace, and must reflect upon the ill education, and weakenesse of knowledge in our Gentry, and Nobilitie. . . . | the new way of scoullinge [?] fond fathers want of order in universities and the dissolute examples and liberty of Inns of Courts, which the base bentchers umbes [?] and laughes |

Of Religion

| 185–86 For certainly the prosperitie, and decayes of States, do very much depend upon good, and religious, governments: morally good, I dare say. . . . | a certayne truth |

Of Reading History

| 193 And it is certain, that where neither Affection, nor Flattery, nor Feare beare sway, you shall finde perfectly delineated the image of truth. . . . | which are in few historyes |

| 220–21 And though Philosophy be an Art that aymes onely at this scope, yet all the precepts therein, will not so soone teach a man fortitude, and constancie of minde, severitie, and militarie discipline, temperance and all other vertues, as will the examples of Mutius Scaevola, the Decii, Manlius, Fabritius, and other such noble *Romane* Citizens. | things acted according to precept exceed the precept |

Appendix II

Hobbes on "Hereditary Right"

ALTHOUGH THE MANUSCRIPT recording this discussion, catalogued as D. 5. in the Devonshire Collection of Hobbes's manuscripts and papers at Chatsworth, is undated, the attribution is to the fourth earl (first duke) of Devonshire (1640–1707), suggesting that the probable date of this "formal disputation," in the catalogue's words, was sometime after the fourth earl reached his maturity in 1660 (he was not made a duke until 1694). The first paragraph, however, is in the handwriting of the third earl (1617–1684), while Hobbes's answer, beginning "Here again you mistake me," is in the hand of a servant or amanuensis. The third and fourth earls, both heirs by right of descent, would have had more than an academic interest in Hobbes's views on the subject of "hereditary right." Since this document, entitled "Questions relative to the hereditary right, Mr. Hobbes," has not been published in its entirety, it here is reprinted in full:

"If you allow that a king does not hold his title by divine institution, as indeed tis absurd to say he does, then I suppose you will admit that his title to Govern arises from his protecting those that are governed. My next question therefore is this, If a Successour to a Crown, be for some reason or other which is notorious, incapable to protect the people, if the Government should devolve upon him, is not the Prince in possession obliged to put him by, upon the request of his subjects?

"Here again you mistake me. I deny not but a King holds his Title by Divine Right. But I deny that any Heir apparent does so. Nor did I mention the word *Institution;* nor do I know what you mean. But I will show you what I mean by Example. If a Constable lay hands upon me for misdemeanor, I ask him by what right he meddles with me more than I with him. He will answer me, *Jure Regio* by the right of the King. He need not say, because you are a Thief. For perhaps I might truly say as much of him. Therefore that which is said to be done *Jure Devine* in a King is said to be done by Warrant or commission from God; but that I had no commission. Law and right differ. Law is a command. But Right is a Liberty or privilege from a Law to some certain person though it oblige others. Institution is no more than Enthroning, Proclaiming, Anointing, Crowning etc. Which of all humane, and done *Jure Regio*. But tis not so of Heirs apparent. For God [word inked out] is not Heir [one or more words inked out] to any King. Nor has any inheritance to give.

"You say the Right of a King depends upon his protecting of the people. I confess that as the King ought to protect [two words inked out, perhaps the second word is "all"] his people, so the people ought to obey the King. For it is impossible for the best King in the world to protect his people, except his subjects furnish him with so much money as he shall judge sufficient to do it.

"To your next question, whether the King in possession [word inked out] be obliged to put by his next Heir in case of notorious incapacity to protect them. I answer that if the incapacity proceed from want of money, I see no reason, though he can, why he should do it. But if it proceed from want of natural reason the King in possession may do it, but is not obliged thereunto. Therefore I will speak of that subject no more till we have such a weak king. But in case the King in possession may lawfully disinherit his diseased Heir and will not; you have not yet answered me to the question, Who shall force him for I suppose the sound King living cannot be lawfully deposed by any person or persons that are his Subjects; because the King dying is *ipso facto* dissolved; and then the people is a Multitude of lawless men relapsed into a condition of war of every man against every man. Which by making a King [word inked out] they intended to avoid."

Appendix III

"Fragment on the Relation between Virtue and Religion"

THE "FRAGMENT," here published for the first time, is catalogued as D. 4. in the Devonshire Collections, Chatsworth. The catalogue reference carries the notation "Found among Hobbes's papers and probably by him. In a hand not certainly identified, but not unlike that of the First Duke of Devonshire." The full text is as follows:

"That virtue & religion are essentially the same; & that they never separate in the subjects; insomuch, that where the one is wanting, the other can be but vainly pretended to.

"Whereas therefore (1) some may pretend to be virtuous without religion, I affirm of such, that they have no virtue. And the reason is this—because virtue consists not in base acts & habits, but in a governing principle, from whence such acts and habits must proceed. Virtue is the product and operation of prudence, whereby a man directs all his actions to prosper and similar ends: & therefore although we cannot but allow that many actions of brutes carry in them all the resemblances of virtue, yet we do not allow those brutes to have virtue itself, because they have not the conducting principle: Now who can doubt but that prudence obliges a man to be religious as well as virtuous? Who can doubt but that prudence obliges a man to acquit himself in his offices to God, as well as to the world? Nay who can doubt but that prudence obliges a man to direct all his virtuous actions to the ends of religion, that is, to the honour of God? because that if there were no God, neither were there any prudence in being virtuous. For whatsoever may be argued for the practice of virtue and for the support of it in the world upon a political account; as either from its private conveniences to particular persons, or from its public usefulness to the ends of Government; set aside religion and all are but wood without weight. The apostle himself allows that. Let us eat & drink were a juster conclusion: so that if there be no honour due unto God, virtue is but a serious folly; & it were wiser to be loose than to be restrained. Since therefore it is impossible but that the same prudence which obliges a man to the offices of virtue should equally oblige him to the offices of religion; it is likewise impossible for a man to be virtuous in any proportion farther than he is religious too, so that whosoever shall make light of God and religion and yet please himself in the meantime that he is either temperate, or chaste, or just, or Liberal or grateful; such a man for all this has no more virtue to boast of than the beast of the field. It were happy for him if he had no more sin to answer for than they, but that cannot be, because the beasts want prudence by nature, but he wants it only by choice. As for those who pretend to be religious, and yet in the meantime are careless of virtue (of which kind we may meet with greater numbers than of the former) of such I affirm that they have no religion. There are too many that fancy themselves religious because they have been consecrated to God by a solemn office; because they can boast of a pure Faith; because they can argue against corruptions, and Superstition, because they attest the Sabbath and the Sanctuary, and at their leisure attend the ritual offices of Religion; although in the meantime they neglect the moral, the renewing of the mind and the discipline of the affections; and live as loose as would give offense to an indifferent Infidel. Now that such men have no Religion is apparent from this—That whereever Religion is it is accepted of God, be it but weak and infirm, so long as it is founded in tenderness, & humility of spirit (as all religion must be founded) God never rejects it—not the smoaking flax, nor the braised reed. But on the contrary when men found the opinion of their being religious in outward formalities, without the serious reformation of manners, God rejects such worshippers with scorn & disclaims all the honours they pretend to do him . . ."

(unfinished)

NOTES

PREFACE

1. Quoted in Charles Edward Mallet, *A History of the University of Oxford* (London: Methuen, 1924), II, 398. Mallet does not identify the source of the observation.
2. The title of Aubrey's work, which appeared in two volumes, was *Letters Written by Eminent Persons . . . and Lives of Eminent Men by John Aubrey, Esq. . . .* Both volumes, which were based on Aubrey's manuscripts in the Bodleian Library and Ashmolean Museum, were edited by Dr. Phillip Bliss and the Reverend John Walker. In 1898, a revised and corrected version of *Brief Lives*, in two volumes, appeared as *"Brief Lives," Chiefly of Contemporaries, Set Down by John Aubrey, between the Years 1669 & 1696* (Oxford: Clarendon Press), edited by Andrew Clark. More-recent editions include Oliver Lawson Dick, ed., *Aubrey's Brief Lives* (Ann Arbor: University of Michigan Press, 1957; first published London: Secker and Warburg, 1949). The Clark edition, despite omissions caused by, to quote Anthony Powell, "squeamishness," is regarded as the definitive one, and all references to *Brief Lives* are to this edition.
3. *Encyclopaedia Britannica*, 13th ed. II, 891. The best biography of Aubrey, and one that is indispensable to an understanding of his life and times, is Anthony Powell, *John Aubrey and His Friends*, new and rev. ed. (London: Heinemann, 1963; first published 1948). See also the lengthy "The Life and Times of John Aubrey," in Dick, ed., *Aubrey's Brief Lives*, xiii–cvi.
4. George Croom Robertson, *Hobbes* (Edinburgh and London: William Blackwood, 1910), v–vi. Hobbes's political theory, Robertson later commented, "is explicable mainly from his personal disposition, timorous and worldly, out of all sympathy with the aspirations of his time" (57).

O N E MALMESBURY

1. All quotations from Hobbes's *Autobiography* are from the translation by Benjamin Farrington in *Rationalist Annual* (1958), 22–31.
2. Garrett Mattingly, *The Defeat of the Spanish Armada* (London: Cape, 1956); Michael Lewis, *The Spanish Armada* (London: Batsford, 1960).
3. While we cannot know how many, or the degree to which, English citizens were truly fearful, the opinion of one historian of the Armada is that "the English did not panic at so formidable a threat, though . . . they had every reason to be scared." Lewis, *Armada*, 86.
4. Quoted from Mattingly, *Defeat*, 160. The following account of the prophecies and predictions related to 1588 is based on this work, pp. 159–68.
5. *Ibid.*, 165.
6. W. Aldis Wright, ed., *Bacon's Essays and Colors of Good and Evil*, with notes and glossarial index (London and New York: Macmillan, 1890), 151.
7. Repeated searches of Wiltshire and Gloucestershire county records offices, diocesan archives, Malmesbury (borough council) minute books, and other possible sources of information have failed to produce any information whatsoever about the Middleton (Mydleton or Myddleton were alternative spellings) family mentioned by Aubrey. Unfortunately, records of marriages, baptisms, and deaths in Malmesbury and vicinity are not complete for the late sixteenth and early seventeenth centuries, with the sorry result that we do not know where Hobbes's parents were born or

when and where they married, died, and were buried. We do not even know his mother's given name. One is tempted to speculate, however, that the Alice Courtnell who married a Thomas Hobbes on May 3, 1578, in the parish of St. Martin, Salisbury, may have been Hobbes's mother. One of Hobbes's grandnieces was named Alice (or "Alce," as Alice often was spelled in those days), and Salisbury is not far from Malmesbury. But Alice or "Alce," of course, like Thomas and even Hobbes itself, were common names in seventeenth-century England. (The marriage referred to is recorded in "Marriages at Salisbury, Parish of St. Martin, 1559–1812," Wiltshire Parish Register, vol. 9, 12.)

8. Major General Sir Richard H. Luce, The History of the Abbey and Town of Malmesbury (Malmesbury: Friends of Malmesbury Abbey, 1979), 87.

9. Wiltshire County records, under the heading "Inquisitions Post Mortem" of James Stumpe, who died September 26, 1602, list "2 closes of pasture in tenure of Thomas Hobbes next Stanbridge . . . a close of 7 acres called Ales Heath in tenure of Edmund Hobbis." Wiltshire Notes and Queries (Devizes, 1917), VIII, 533–34. Presumably, the grandnephew Thomas Hobbes was not the "Thomas Hobbes of Westport" who suffered a "presentment" in 1631 "for disturbing the congregation by playing." Hobbes had at least three grandnephews named Thomas and one great-grandnephew. R. B. Pugh and E. Crittall, History of Wiltshire (London: Oxford University Press, 1956), III, 39 n. 81.

10. As late as 1820, distant relatives by marriage of Edmund Hobbes apparently were still active in Malmesbury. His grandson Thomas Hobbes, who was born in 1652, through his wife, Anne Player, was probably related to a Player who attended a Malmesbury meeting in October 1820 to decide whether the common should be "ploughed up and turned into agricultural holdings. The moving spirits seem to have been Messrs. Hanks, Robins, and Player." Luce, History, 194. I have been informed by Mr. George Truell of Crowthorne, Berkshire, whose wife is a direct descendant of grandson Thomas Hobbes, that his father-in-law, Major Adrian Wrigley Fosbroke-Hobbes (1896–1935), amassed a considerable number of notes on the Hobbes "family-tree," which have not been "consolidated." According to Mr. Truell, Major Fosbroke-Hobbes, who had three daughters, was the last descendant of Edmund Hobbes to bear the family name. I am indebted to Mr. Truell for this information.

11. Hobbes himself was not always accurate, and his memory as he grew older was fallible. He once told Aubrey that Sir Henry Knyvett of Malmesbury, who had been a high sheriff and a member of Parliament for Malmesbury, had "died of a feaver" shortly after he returned from "some command at the Invasion of 1588"; in fact, Knyvett lived until 1598. Luce, History, 84. See also 81–83.

12. Many years later Hobbes made use of the same card-playing expression, this time as a double-edged metaphor, in comparing the exercise of sovereignty in law to the playing of a trump card, "save that, in matter of government, when nothing else is turned up, clubs are trumps." A Dialogue between a Philosopher and a Student of the Common Laws of England (1681), in E.W., IV, 122.

13. Maurice Ashley, England in the Seventeenth Century (1603–1714) (London: Penguin Books, 1956; first published 1952).

14. Wallace Notestein, The English People on the Eve of Colonization, 1603–1630 (New York: Harper Torchbooks, 1962; first published 1954), 69.

15. J. P. Cooper, ed., The Decline of Spain and the Thirty Years War, vol. 4 of The New Cambridge Modern History (Cambridge: Cambridge University Press, 1970), 535.

16. Brasenose College Register, 1509–1909 (Oxford, 1909), 72. See also Alumni Oxonienses, 1500–1714 (Oxford; 1891). The latter refers, on p. 721, to Hobbes senior as "vicar of Westport and of Charlton, Wilts; father of the next [i.e., the subject of this study]."

17. Oxford University Archives, Subscription Register, 1581–1615 (S.P. / 38 / Register Ab.). I am grateful to Robin Peedell, assistant librarian of Brasenose College, Oxford, for showing me this material related to the senior Hobbes's apparently brief attendance at Oxford.

18. Bernulf Hodge, A History of Malmesbury (Malmesbury: Friends of Malmesbury Abbey, 1976; first published 1968), 18.

19. Peter Jowitt, "Thomas Hobbes: Philosopher," in Malmesbury: 1100 Years a Borough (1100th Anniversary Committee, n.d).

20. Hodge, History, 19.

21. Peter Laslett, The World We Have Lost (London: Methuen, University Paperbacks, 1979; first published 1965), 78.

22. Salisbury Consistory Court, Deposition Book 10, 49.

23. Delecta Book, 1588–1599, archdeacon of Wiltshire.

24. Act Book of Office 1601–1604 / 5, archdeacon of Wiltshire.

25. Quoted in Luce, History, 80.

26. Deposition Book 21, 21–22; 25–26.

27. A. H. Dodd, Life in Elizabethan England (London: Batsford, 1967; first published 1961), 78. In other words, there were not enough trained and competent clergymen to serve all the parishes which were entitled to one.

28. Deposition Book 22b, 19–20; 30–31.
29. *Ibid.*, 48a–49.
30. The "perfect English town," Godfrey Smith has suggested, "will have a curving High Street and stone houses. It will be small enough to command a prospect of farms and fields around its entire perimeter but large enough to have its own library. It will be refreshed by trout streams and at least one pub that sells Wadsworth Six X on draught, while its church will boast a row of vicars running back in an unbroken line for six or seven hundred years. Such are the blessings of our sleepy town of Malmesbury. Birthplace of Thomas Hobbes and resting place of Saxon kings. . . ." Godfrey Smith, "In Praise of Malmesbury," *Sunday Times* (London), March 23, 1980. Smith's opinion was shared by, among others, Sir John Betjeman, the late poet laureate, who once referred to Malmesbury as "the Queen of winding hilltop towns . . . of great and intimate beauty, clustering around its Benedictine Abbey, whose porch is like a Romanesque manuscript rendered into stone." Quoted in 1980 by Malmesbury's mayor, the Reverend Arthur H. Bird, in *Malmesbury Town Official Guide* (1980). William Cobbett's less elegant tribute, in the early 1820s, was as follows: "It is a nice town, with a fine situation and a most pleasant place to live in." Quoted in *Malmesbury: 1100 Years a Borough* (1980). More than 160 years later, and despite many changes, Malmesbury still is a nice town.
31. Quoted in Luce, *History*, 3.
32. Ibid., 7. See also Stan Hudson, *A Hill Top Town* (Malmesbury: Hudson, 1977; reprinted 1978), 43, 48–50.
33. Quoted in Luce, *History*, 20.
34. Quoted ibid.
35. Ibid., 70–71.
36. Lucy Toulmin Smith, ed., *The Itinerary of John Leland in or about the Years 1535–1543*, pts. 1–2 (London, 1907), 132.
37. If, indeed, 1,000 persons lived in and around Malmesbury in 1548, Malmesbury was one of the more populous towns in England. As late as 1688 the mean size of a city or town probably was "only a little over 1,000 . . . (there were) 10 cities of about 18,000 people, 30 cities (or 'great towns' as King is careful to say) of about 2,500 and then 100 of about 1,300 inhabitants. . . . The majority of the town-dwelling population outside London . . . lived in 250 places of some 900 people and 400 further places of something over 650." Quoted from D. V. Glass, "Two Papers on Gregory King," in Laslett, *World*, 57–58. Sometime after 1690 King made a study of English society in 1688, the results of which were summarized by him in a table. According to Laslett, "King's calculation was made on extensive and probably fairly reliable evidence, and was the only one ever worked out by a contemporary for a European society in wholly pre-industrial times" (31).
38. Hodge, *History*, 22–23.
39. Richard Muir, *The English Village* (London: Thames and Hudson, 1980), 118.
40. These games were still played in the early part of this century. See Hudson, *Hill Top Town*, 131–32.
41. Richmond Lattimore, introd. to *Euripides I: Four Tragedies* (Chicago: University of Chicago Press, 1961; first published 1955), v. The plot summary of *Medea* that follows is based on "The Introduction to the *Medea*" and the translation of the play by Rex Warner, 55–108.
42. Edith Hamilton, *The Greek Way* (New York: Avon, Discus Books, 1973; first published 1930), 204.
43. Quoted ibid., 205.
44. Pt. 2, chap. 30.
45. Pt. 2, chap. 8. In *De Cive*, the reference to Pelias and his daughters is found in chap. 12.
46. *E.W.*, IV., 268–69, In *A Dictionary of Quotations in Most Frequent Use Taken Chiefly from the Latin and French*, 5th ed. (London, 1809), the Latin statement quoted is attributed to Ovid.
47. Quoted in Oliver Lawson Dick, ed., *Aubrey's Brief Lives* (Ann Arbor: University of Michigan Press, 1957; first published 1949), xxii.

T W O OXFORD

1. Charles Edward Mallet, *A History of the University of Oxford* (London: Methuen, 1924), II, 398.
2. *E.W.*, III, 669.
3. As Robertson noted, "The universities seemed to (Hobbes) mere hotbeds of political sedition, instituted by Rome in the Middle Ages to support Papal encroachment on the civil power, and still preserving, in whatever changed conditions of modern national life, their cold ecclesiastical spirit." George Croom Robertson, *Hobbes* (Edinburgh and London: William Blackwood, 1910), 4–5. Still, in 1609, one year after Hobbes's departure from Oxford, a student was disciplined for defending the proposition quoted; whether or not he was a Papist, he was not the only university student to hold such a view.
4. *E.W.*, VI, 347.
5. In Oxford University's history the names of Hart Hall, Magdalen Hall, and Hertford College are intertwined. Hertford College, formerly Hart Hall, was dissolved in 1805.

Magdalen Hall was re-created as Hertford College in 1874, and Hertford College survives still. Magdalen College, meanwhile, continues as one of Oxford's most prestigious and wealthiest colleges.

6. Mallet, *History*, II, 289. The period covered is 1603–21.

7. Students as young as ten, and as old as twenty-one, matriculated at Oxford during the reigns of Elizabeth and James I, but rarely were they younger or older than that. In 1581, one entering student was nine, 5 were ten, 18 were eleven, 47 were fourteen, 74 were fifteen, 95 were sixteen, 111 were seventeen, 129 were eighteen, 105 were nineteen, and 32 were twenty-one. Mallet, *History*, II, 140.

8. "Settlement of Religion," in G. R. Elton, ed., *The Tudor Constitution: Documents and Commentary* (Cambridge: Cambridge University Press, 1962; first published 1960), 389.

9. *Encyclopaedia Britannica*, 13th ed., XXII, 258–62.

10. Quoted in R. B. Wernham and J. C. Walker, eds., *England under Elizabeth (1558–1603)* (London: Longmans, Green, 1932), 164.

11. Charlotte J. Smith, "Intellectual and Social Life at Oxford in 1600" (Ph.D. diss., University of Chicago, 1914).

12. Mark H. Curtis, *Oxford and Cambridge in Transition, 1558–1642* (Oxford: Oxford University Press, 1965; first published 1959), 229. The Laudian statutes enjoining strict religious orthodoxy derived their name from William Laud (1573–1645), who became chancellor of Oxford in 1629 and archbishop of Canterbury four years later. Vehemently opposed to Puritanism and Noncomformity, Laud was widely regarded as sympathetic to "Popery," and in 1642 he was impeached by the Long Parliament. Despite a pardon from Charles I, Laud was executed on Tower Hill on January 10, 1645.

13. Smith, "Life," 15.

14. Curtis, *Oxford and Cambridge*, 88. See also Craig R. Thompson, *Universities in Tudor England* (Washington: Folger Shakespeare Library, 1959), 21–22; Mallet, *History*, 186–89.

15. Quoted in Thompson, *Universities*, 15. See also Maurice Ashley, *England in the Seventeenth Century (1603–1714)* (London: Penguin Books, 1956; first published 1952), 157; Wallace Notestein, *The English People on the Eve of Colonization, 1603–1630* (New York: Harper Torchbooks, 1962; first published 1954), 130–45.

16. Smith, "Life," 23.

17. In 1603 the city of Oxford asked the university to contribute money for the relief of sufferers. A song written during an earlier epidemic featured *Death* warning the university community:

Thinke you that I dare not come to Schooles,
Where all the cunning Clerks be most;
Take not I away both Clerks and fooles?
And am I not in every coast?
Assure your selves no creature can
Make death afraid of any man,
O know my coming where or when.

Quoted in Mallet, *History*, II 110.

18. Smith "Life," 23–24.

19. Ibid., 24.

20. Apparently, they behaved well in the presence of the king, but there were some difficulties before his arrival. On the morning of August 27, "Schollers were uncivill at St. Marie's . . . (where) they satt at the Sermon hard by the Vicechancellor with the Hatts on." As a consequence, more than one hundred were "sent to Prison," presumably after James departed on the thirtieth. From "The Preparations at Oxford in August 1605," in *De Rebus Anglicanis Opuscula Varia*, bk. 1, 626–47. See also Mallet, *History*, II, 230–34.

21. "Preparations at Oxford," 646. Perhaps the disputations and speeches were shorter in 1605 than they had been in 1566 when Elizabeth paid her first visit to Oxford. On that occasion the queen "was welcomed by Leicester and others, who made speeches in Latin and Greek. She was lodged at Christ Church and before retiring listened to more Latin speeches, and a Te Deum in the cathedral. Sunday she remained at home, perhaps too many Latin speeches had discouraged her. Monday she attended an English play and Tuesday morning she was present at a disputation at St. Mary's on Natural and Moral Philosophy. Wednesday there were disputations on Civil Law, with an English play in the evening. Thursday there were disputations in 'Physick' and Divinity, and the Queen made a Latin speech. On Friday Convocation was held and degrees were conferred. At a great dinner following gloves were given to the Queen and all her followers. After a farewell oration the cavalcade left. It is interesting to note that when Elizabeth revisited Oxford in 1592, she said she would not listen to such long speeches." Smith, "Life," 27.

22. Robertson, *Hobbes*, 9. See also Sir Leslie Stephen, *Hobbes* (London: Macmillan, 1904). Stephen, too, doubted that as a student Hobbes's "eyes had been open to the evils which he afterwards recognised" (5).

23. Mallet, *History*, II, 398.

24. The English version of *De Cive*, in Hobbes's own translation, was published at London in 1651 under the title *Philosophical Rudiments Concerning Government and Society*.

25. Dedicatory epistle to the (third) earl of Devonshire, *De Corpore* (1655).

THREE HARDWICK AND CHATSWORTH

1. Quoted in Mark Girouard, *Hardwick Hall* (London: National Trust, 1976), 9. I am indebted to this immensely interesting book for much that precedes and follows this quotation with reference to Bess of Hardwick and Hardwick Hall. See also Francis Bickley, *The Cavendish Family* (London: Constable, 1911).

2. See Girouard, *Hardwick Hall*, 11. Arabella Stuart, born in 1575, was the only child of the marriage. Orphaned at an early age, Arabella became Bess's ward. Arabella's chances of succeeding Elizabeth were never great, and they vanished entirely when Elizabeth, on her deathbed, named James VI of Scotland, subsequently James I, as her successor. Though Arabella was treated kindly by the king and his wife, she continued to be involved in intrigue, and following her secret marriage to another claimant to the throne, she was imprisoned in the Tower, where she died in 1615.

3. Girouard, *Hardwick Hall*, 9.

4. Quoted in Lindsay Boynton, ed., *The Hardwick Hall Inventories of 1601*. (London: Furniture History Society, 1971), 2.

5. Girouard, *Hardwick Hall*, 40.

6. Quoted in John Pearson, *Stags and Serpents: The Story of the House of Cavendish and the Dukes of Devonshire* (London: Macmillan, 1983), 34.

7. Bickley, *Cavendish Family*, 41.

8. Lawrence Stone, *Crisis of the Aristocracy*, quoted in Pearson, *Stags and Serpents*, 34.

9. Pearson, *Stags and Serpents*, 35. According to Bickley, *Cavendish Family*, 41, King James persuaded William's father "who had lately taken a second wife and seemed to grudge money to the son of his first, to establish the young couple becomingly." The earl's first wife was Anne Keighley, by whom he had three sons and three daughters. His second wife, by whom he had one son, John, who died in 1616, was Elizabeth Wortley, a widow. Other accounts of the Cavendishes make no mention of this second wife, but her existence is confirmed by a legal document of 1639, signed by both Hobbes and the third earl of Devonshire, referring to the first earl's widow as the "Rt. Hon. Elizabeth Countess Dowager." Elizabeth must have survived her husband, who died in 1625 or 1626, by some years.

10. The modern equivalent in pounds or dollars of these amounts is difficult to estimate, since opinions vary considerably on the contemporary values of seventeenth-century money. One suggestion, made in 1973, is that the 1604 pound should be multiplied by 100 in order to arrive at its true value. (A. L. Rowse, *Shakespeare the Man* [London: Paladin Books, 1976; first published 1973], 181.)

Another proposal, of 1976, is that 1608 money units should be multiplied by at least 20 (Girouard, *Hardwick Hall*, 13); still another, put forward in 1960, is that money of the late sixteenth century should be multiplied 15 to 20 times, which would make the pound of that era worth, in terms of 1960 exchange rates, between $42 and $56 (Virginia A. La Mar, *Travel and Roads in England* [Washington: Folger Shakespeare Library, 1979; first published 1960], 5). Eight years earlier, the pound was estimated to be worth "at least ten times what it is today" (Maurice Ashley, *England in the Seventeenth Century (1603–1714)* [London: Penguin Books, 1956; first published 1952], 17). With the exchange rate for the pound fluctuating, in early 1985, around $1.12, or less than half what it was worth in 1973, we can reasonably calculate that the 1600 pound was approximately equivalent to at least $100, thus suggesting that in 1608–12 the first earl might have spent roughly $116,300 on Hardwick improvements. What Hobbes made of this expenditure, undertaken at a time when much of England, including Malmesbury, was experiencing a severe rise in prices and a fall in wages that meant near starvation for vast numbers of the poor, is impossible to say. Surely, he was aware that the sixfold price increase between 1510 and 1610 had produced conditions in which, as in Lincolnshire, "there are many thousands in these parts who have sold all they have even to their bed straw, and cannot get work to earn any money. Dog's flesh is a dainty dish, and found upon search in many houses, also such horse flesh as hath lain long in a deke (ditch) for hounds. And the other day one stole a sheep who for mere hunger tore out a leg and did eat it raw." Sir William Pelham, quoted in Charles Wilson, *England's Apprenticeship, 1603–1763* (London: Longman, 1979; first published 1965), 119.

11. Girouard, *Hardwick Hall*, 38, 65–71.

12. *An Answer to a Book Published by Dr. Bramhall* (1682, written in 1668), in *E.W.*, IV, 294, *A Dialogue between a Philosopher and a Student of the Common Laws of England* (1681, probably written about 1675), *E.W.*, VI, 126.

13. Gunpowder Plot was the name given to a conspiracy organized by Catholic fanatics, mainly Jesuits, to blow up James I and Parliament on November 5, 1605. The conspirators, numbering in all about thirty persons, of whom Fawkes was one of the leaders, hoped that their efforts would inspire a general insurrection and a return to Catholic orthodoxy. The plot, however, was discovered in time, and in the end more than half the conspirators, including Fawkes, were killed or executed.

14. W. Aldis Wright, *Bacon's Essays and Colours of Good and Evil* (London: Macmillan, 1890), xiv–xx. Wright's identification of the first essay is derived from "internal evidence, based on a comparison of it with the rest," and this comparison leads him to name the other two essays as Hobbes's translations. He cautiously adds, however, "This of course is mere conjecture, but it seems a reasonable one" (xx).

15. Catherine Drinker Bowen, *Francis Bacon: The Temper of a Man* (Boston: Atlantic–Little, Brown, 1963), 210.

16. Quoted ibid., 35.

17. Quoted in Douglas Bush, *British Literature in the Earlier Seventeenth Century, 1600–1660* (Oxford: Oxford University Press, 1945), 237.

18. Bacon, letter to Burghley, quoted in *Encyclopaedia Britannica*, 13th ed., III, 136, from J. Spedding, *The Life and Letters of Lord Bacon* (1681), I, 108–9.

19. Quoted in the *New Encyclopaedia Britannica* (1974), II, 564.

20. Bush, *British Literature*, 286–87.

21. Quoted in Bowen, *Francis Bacon*, 10. In *Thomae Hobbesii Angli Malmesburiensis Philosophi Vita*, published by "R.B." (Richard Blackbourne, M.D., a friend of Aubrey) in 1681, Hobbes stated, "Causam omnium rerum quaerendam esse in diversitate motuum" ("The cause of all things resides in the diversity of motion") (xxi). Hobbes apparently made this "discovery" shortly after 1636.

22. Bacon's death, Aubrey recalled Hobbes's having told him, was due to "an experiment: viz., as he [Bacon] was taking the aire in a coach . . . towards High-gate, snow lay on the ground, and it came into my lord's thoughts, why flesh might not be preserved in snow, as in salt . . . [Bacon] went into a poore woman's howse . . . and bought a hen, and made the woman exenterate it, and then stuffed the bodie with snow, and my lord did help to doe it himselfe. The snow so chilled him, that he immediately fell so extremely ill, that he could not returne to his lodgings . . . they putt him into a good bed warmed with a panne, but it was a damp bed that had not been layn-in [since] about a yeare before, which gave him such a cold that in 2 or 3 dayes, as I remember he [Hobbes] told me, he dyed of suffocation." This account is confirmed by Bacon himself, who in a letter dictated a day or two before his death wrote to a friend, "I was likely to have had the fortune of Caius Pli-

nius the elder, who lost his life by trying an experiment about the burning of the mountain Vesuvius. For I was also desirous to try an experiment or two, touching the conservation and induration of bodies. As for the experiment itself, it succeeded excellently well. But . . . I was taken with such a fit of casting as I knew not whether it were the [kidney] stone or some surfeit or cold, or indeed a touch of them all three. . . . I know how unfit it is for me to write to your Lordship with any other hand than mine own; but in troth my fingers are so disjointed with this fit of sickness that I cannot steadily hold a pen." Quoted in Bowen, *Francis Bacon*, 225–26.

23. Quoted from the 1678 edition in English and Latin, the first appearance of the *Peak* in English. The translation into English, according to the title page, was "by a Person of Quality." His or her identity is unknown.

24. White Kennet, *A Sermon Preach'd at the Funeral of the Right Noble William Duke of Devonshire . . . With Some Memoirs of the Family of Cavendish* (London, 1708), 108–9.

25. Ibid., 116.

26. *Report on the MSS and Papers of Thomas Hobbes (1588–1679) in the Devonshire Collections, Chatsworth, Bakewell, Derbyshire* (London: Royal Commission on Historical Manuscripts, 1977). According to the *Report*, "Epigrams in Imitation of Martial," catalogued as F.I., carry the signature of the third earl, who did not succeed to the title until 1628. The "fact that the writer signs himself *Cavendish*, not *Devonshire*, indicates a date previous to 1628," at which time, as the *Report* notes, the third earl was eleven years old. But would a boy of eleven or younger, unless unusually precocious, have been interested in the epigrams?

27. Noel Malcolm, "Hobbes, Sandys, and the Virginia Company," *Historical Journal*, 24 (1981), 297–321.

28. Bickley, *Cavendish Family*, 40.

29. *E.W.*, III, 81.

30. Malcolm "Hobbes," 301.

31. The quoted statement from *Leviathan* is in *E.W.*, III, 114; the later quotation is from Malcolm, "Hobbes," 318.

32. Malcolm, "Hobbes," 318.

33. Quoted from Pomfret, *Life of the Countess of Devonshire*, 25, in Bickley, *Cavendish Family*, 43.

34. Bickley, *Cavendish Family*, 43.

F O U R   THUCYDIDES

1. Quoted in Ferdinand Tönnies, "Hobbes-Analekten—I," *Archiv für Geschichte der Philosophie*, 17 (1903), 291–92.

2. Edith Hamilton, *The Greek Way* (New York: Avon-Discus Books, 1973; first published 1930), 139.

3. Ibid., 136–37. See also Bertrand de Jouvenal, "Introduction," in David Grene, ed., *Thucydides: The Peloponnesian War: The Thomas Hobbes Translation* (Ann Arbor: University of Michigan Press, 1959), v–xiv.

4. Bk. 8, chap. 97.

5. John H. Finley, Jr., *Thucydides* (Ann Arbor: University of Michigan Press, Ann Arbor Paperbacks, 1967), 300–301. See also idem, *Three Essays on Thucydides* (Cambridge: Harvard University Press, 1967), 22–23, 143–44, 150, 155, 161.

6. Finley, *Thucydides*, 303–4.

7. "Of the Life and History of Thucydides," *E.W.*, VIII, xvi–xvii.

8. John V. A. Fine, *The Ancient Greeks: A Critical History* (Cambridge: Belknap Press / Harvard University Press, 1983), 472–73.

9. Finley, *Three Essays*, 143–44, 155.

10. M. I. Finley, "Introduction," in Warner, trans., *Thucydides * History*, 9.

11. Finley, *Thucydides*, 311; Hobbes, *E.W.*, VIII, xiv–xx.

12. Warner, trans., *Thucydides * History*, 242; Hobbes, *E.W.*, III, 29.

13. *E.W.* VIII, xxix–xxx.

14. Quoted in Sir Leslie Stephen, *Hobbes* (London: Macmillan, 1904), 10.

15. *E.W.*, VIII, xxi.

16. See Grene, ed., *Thucydides*, 166: "Normally there was no *eisphora*, or general tax, paid by Athenian citizens, and the allies made their regular contributions themselves at fixed times of year through their representatives instead of, as in this instance, being dunned by special Athenian collection agents."

17. Quoting Hobbes's references to Cleon, Robertson puzzlingly commented "For Cleon might safely be written there the name of Eliot or Pym." George Croom Robertson, *Hobbes* (Edinburgh and London: William Blackwood, 1910), 24. If by "safely" he meant "justifiably," Robertson was going against the judgment of most contemporaries of Eliot and Pym, including such an establishment figure as Edward Hyde, earl of Clarendon.

18. As Notestein observes, "Had the [first Stuarts] only been willing to give some small degree of toleration to the Puritans, who by the end of Elizabeth's reign had become modest in their requests, it might have prevented that great fissure in English life which revealed itself in the Civil Wars and was evident for two centuries afterward." Wallace Notestein, *The English People on the Eve of Colonization, 1603–1630* (New York: Harper Torchbooks, 1962; first published 1954), 156.

19. Preston King, *The Ideology of Order* (New York: Barnes & Noble, n.d.; first published 1974), 60–64; J. P. Cooper, ed., *The Decline of Spain and the Thirty Years War*, vol. 4 of *The New Cambridge Modern History* (Cambridge: Cambridge University Press, 1970), 259–61; Conrad Russell, *Parliaments and English Politics, 1621–1629* (Oxford: Clarendon Press, 1979); idem, *The Crisis of Parliaments* (Oxford: Oxford University Press, 1971); Alan G. R. Smith, "Crown, Parliament and Finance: The Great Contract of 1610," in Peter Clark, Alan G. T. Smith, and Nicholas Tyacke, eds., *The English Commonwealth, 1547–1640: Essays in Politics and Society* (New York: Barnes & Noble, 1979).

21. Quoted in *Encyclopaedia Britannica*, 13th ed. XXII, 680.

21. Robertson, *Hobbes*, 24.

22. Quoted in G. R. de Beer, "Some Letters of Thomas Hobbes," *Notes and Records of the Royal Society*, 7 (1950), 195–206. The letter, undated, also appears in *E.W.*, VII, 451.

23. University of Nottingham, Manuscript Department Catalogue No. C 561. By "Geneva print" Hobbes probably meant the strict Calvinism for which Geneva at that time was known.

24. Ibid.

25. Ibid., No. C 560.

26. Ibid., No. C 541.

27. Ibid., No. C 562.

28. Ibid., No. C 566.

29. Historical Manuscripts Commission, "Additional Manuscripts of Sir Hervey Juckes Lloyd Bruce," in *Reports on Manuscripts in Various Collections*, vol. 7 (London, 1914), 401.

30. Ibid., 416.

31. Quoted in a personal communication from W. Middlebrook, dean of the School of Education, Trent Polytechnic, Nottingham. Professor Middlebrook is an authority on the Clifton Family and the hall and village that carry the Clifton name.

32. University of Nottingham, Manuscript Department Catalogue No. C 539.

33. Communication from W. Middlebrook.

34. Stephen, *Hobbes*, 16.

F I V E IN MOTION AND ON MOTION

1. *E.W.*, IV, 18.

2. "Dedication" of *Humane Nature* to the earl of Newcastle, May 9, 1640, *E.W.*, IV.

3. *E.W.*, IV, 7–8.

4. Richard Peters, *Hobbes* (London: Penguin Books, 1967; first published 1956), 23.

5. John Laird, *Hobbes* (London: Ernest Benn, 1934), 36. Laird, to be sure, refers to the *Short Tract* as "important evidence of Hobbes's philosophical development."

6. Ferdinand Tönnies, "Contributions à l'histoire de la pensée de Hobbes," *Archives de*

Philosophie, 12 (1936), 79.

7. All quotations from the *Short Tract* are taken from Tönnies's edition of *The Elements of Law*, 152–67.

8. Geoffrey Keynes, *The Life of William Harvey* (London: Oxford University Press, 1966), 386. *De Corpore*, an early version of which may have been written in 1645, apparently also included Hobbes's reflections on Thomas White's *De Mundo Dialogi Tres* (Paris, 1642). White (1593–1676), a Catholic priest who was a friend of Hobbes, according to Wood, despite many disagreements, devoted most of his work to what he termed "a long meditation" on Galileo's *De Mundo Dialogi*. Hobbes's extended commentary on White's *De Mundo* has recently been published as *Thomas Hobbes: Thomas White's "De Mundo" Examined*, trans. from the Latin by Harold Whitmore Jones (Bradford, Eng.: Bradford University Press, in association with Crosby Lockwood Staples [London], 1976).

9. R. T. Petersson, *Sir Kenelm Digby: The Ornament of England* (London: Cape, 1956), 121.

10. *Encyclopaedia Britannica*, 13th ed. VIII, 261–62; Petersson, *Digby; Memoirs of Sir Kenelm Digby* (London, 1827); Historical Manuscripts Commission, *Report on the Manuscripts of Allan George Finch*, vol. 1 (London, 1913), 61.

11. Kurt Weber, *Lucius Cary: Second Viscount Falkland* (New York: Columbia University Press, 1940), 74–156. According to Weber, "less certainty" attaches to the inclusion in the Falkland "circle" of Cowley, John Selden, Sir Kenelm Digby, and, contrary to what most scholars of the period believe, Hobbes himself.

12. See Frithiof Brandt, *Thomas Hobbes' Mechanical Conception of Nature* (Copenhagen: Levin & Munksgaard, 1928), 145, 391–92.

13. Mydorge (1585–1647) was "a friend of Descartes, a patron of letters, and the author of a considerable work on conic sections. . . . His greatest service to science is that from 1627 he assisted his friend Descartes in the cutting of optical glasses in many different forms. . . . Cavendish took a great interest in Mydorge. He is even said to have tried to induce Mydorge 'par des promesses magnifiques d'un establissement considerable' to come to England to the court of Charles I." Brandt, quoting from Baillet and *Biographie universelle*, ibid., 390–91.

14. Letter dated January 26, 1634.

15. Quoted in Geoffrey Trease, *Portrait of a Cavalier: William Cavendish, First Duke of Newcastle* (New York: Taplinger, 1979), 74.

16. *E.W.*, VII, 468.

17. Trease, *Portrait*, 159.

18. Hobbes, like many another English traveler in the seventeenth century, made as much use as possible of rivers and canals in moving from one place to another. Water routes, by contrast with roads, were without potholes and ruts, washed-out bridges, highwaymen, and other gross inconveniences. Byfleet on the river Wey, which connects with the Thames at Weybridge, two miles to the north, may have been a convenient overnight stopping point for travelers by water from Gravesend who were bound for destinations west or north of London; Gravesend on the Thames, was a short distance overland from Dover, the most-used Channel port. From Byfleet, much if not all of the remaining travel to Oxford, which was near Welbeck, could have been accomplished by riverboat. But neither the Thames nor the Wey may have been navigable at all times, and Hobbes's protracted stay in Byfleet may have been due, at least in part, to low water levels or other problems affecting travel on the rivers. (For much of this information I am indebted to A. Rogers of the Information Centre, Weybridge Library, Weybridge, Surrey.)

19. Historical Manuscripts Commission, *The Manuscripts of His Grace the Duke of Portland, Preserved at Weybeck Abbey*, vol. 2 (London, 1893), 129. The date of the letter is October 16, 1636.

20. Ibid., 130. The outbreak of the plague in 1636, its fourth major appearance since 1603, took 10,400 lives in London alone. In the following year another 3,082 Londoners died, as did 3,597 residents of Newcastle (of a total city population of 20,000). *Encyclopaedia Britannica*, 13th ed., XXI, 694–96.

21. Mildred Campbell, *The English Yeoman* (New York: Augustus M. Kelley, 1968; first published 1942), appendix 3.

22. The "Proceedings" is listed as D. 6 among Hobbes manuscripts and papers in the Devonshire Collections at Chatsworth. Written in the hand of one Halleby, a Chatsworth steward or overseer at the time, the document is also signed by him. The Hobbesian flavor of the "Proceedings" is nowhere more apparent than in a reference to the "diverse causes" of the third earl's suspicions of his mother, suspicions "(which are not necessary to be here mentioned; because every man may lawfully seeke to secure himself upon his owne suspitions, whether they be well or ill grounded)." In short, as Hobbes frequently observed, men will believe what they wish to believe, whether true or false, and act accordingly.

23. Trease, *Portrait*, 166. I have also drawn from John Pearson, *Stags and Serpents: The Story of the House of Cavendish and the Dukes of Devonshire* (London: Macmillan, 1983), 38–41; Francis Bickley, *The Cavendish Family* (London: Constable, 1911), 74–79; introd. to *The Life of the Duke of Newcastle and Other Writings by Margaret, Duchess of Newcastle*

(London: Dent, n.d.); *Encyclopaedia Britannica*, 13th ed., XIX, 470–71.

24. *The Common Reader*, 1st ser. (London: Hogarth Press, 1925), 98.

25. Quoted in introd. to *Life of the Duke of Newcastle*, xviii.

26. Quoted in Bickley, *Cavendish Family*, 79.

27. S. Arthur Strong, ed., *A Catalogue of Letters and Other Historical Documents Exhibited in the Library at Welbeck* (London, 1903).

28. *Life of the Duke of Newcastle*, 153, 154, 161, 163.

29. Pt. 1, chap. 9.

30. *E.W.*, III, 46.

31. Letter of December 25, 1636. See below, n. 32.

32. Strong, ed., *Catalogue*, vii. The *Catalogue* reproduces Hobbes's essay and its opening page in Hobbes's hand. Hobbes's only other known reference to some finer points of horsemanship was in connection with a horse purchased in France by Newcastle, Hobbes acting as Newcastle's agent, a horse in which the earl was disappointed. "I told

Mr. Benjamin and Monsieur de Prè," Hobbes wrote Newcastle from Paris on August 25, 1635, "—who is Monsieur Benjamin's eldest sonne, and teaches under his father—of the faults your Lordship found in the horse. For the opening his mouth, they confess it, and say that when he was young and first began to be dressed he put out his head too much, which they that dressed him endeavoring to amend, for want of skill, did by a great bitte convert into this other fault of gaping. For his feete they obstinately deny that he has any fault in them at all, and do suppose that the journey may have hurt him, or his wearinesse made it seeme so. That he has no other ayre but corvettes, is a thing your Lordship was made acquainted with before. The greatest fault is his price, which price adding the forty pounds you gave me, is a very good reason why he should hence forward be called *Le Superbe*." *Manuscripts of . . . the Duke of Portland*, 126.

33. Quoted in Trease, *Portrait*, 88.

S I X THE FIRST TO FLEE

1. *E.W.*, III, 113.

2. See Richard Peters, *Hobbes* (London: Penguin Books, 1967; first published 1956), 26–27; John Laird, *Hobbes* (New York: Russell & Russell, 1968; first published 1934), 10–11. As Laird puts it, "This action is commonly regarded as an instance of prodigious poltroonery; and perhaps it was."

3. *The Elements of Law* was published for the first time in the form of two essays: *Of Human Nature* and *De Corpore Politico*. According to Tönnies, subsequent editions, including that of Molesworth (*E.W.*, IV), especially editions of *Of Human Nature*, contained "a great many errors and some omissions." He therefore decided to publish a version of *The Elements* based on the manuscript copy of Hardwick, portions of which are in Hobbes's own hand. Hobbes's manuscripts at Chatsworth, however, among which is the one Tönnies consulted, include three copies of *The Elements*. The first, (catalogued as A. 2A.), incorrectly entitled HOBBES LEVIATHAN—ORIGINAL MS, lacks the "Dedication" but "appears to be in Hobbes's own hand." The second (A. 2B.) has a "Dedication" that is "in Hobbes's own hand" and some marginal notes also in his hand. The third (A. 2C.), "In the hand of an unidentified amanuensis," is incomplete, the last page of the "Dedication" missing. Presumably, the Tönnies edition of *The Elements*, to which all the following references are made, was based on the first copy.

4. *De Cive*, as Hobbes conceived the work originally, was to be the third book of a three-part treatise devoted to body, man, and citizen. But because England "some few years before the civil wars did rage, was boiling hot with questions concerning the rights of dominion and the obedience due from subjects," he had decided to write and publish *De Cive* first. He did not explain why, that being true, he had not written his book in English, as he had *The Elements*, or why it was not translated and published in England until 1651. Whatever the reasons, *De Cive*'s success on the Continent—several editions had appeared by 1650—led the poet Edmund Waller, an admirer of the book, to offer to translate it, but the offer was withdrawn when Waller, shown a few pages of Hobbes's own translation as a kind of example, concluded that Hobbes was far better qualified to render the book into English. *De Cive*, translated by Hobbes himself, appeared in England in 1651 as *Philosophical Rudiments concerning Government and Society*, a title that Hobbes may or may not have chosen. All references that follow are to the English edition as published in *E.W.*, II. The more recent *De Cive: The English Version*, ed. Howard Warrender (Oxford: Oxford University Press, 1983), appeared too late to be used in the present work.

5. As Goldsmith remarks, "The Elements of Law . . . is the first version of his later political works. . . . *The Elements of Law* must be regarded as the first draught of *De Cive* and *Leviathan*. . . . *De Cive* is a revised, expanded Latin version of *The Elements of Law*. . . ." M. M. Goldsmith, introd. to *Thomas Hobbes:*

The Elements of Law Natural and Politic, ed. F. Tönnies, 2d ed. (London: Frank Cass, 1969), v–vii. The revisions noted by Goldsmith are not, in the present author's opinion, significant.

6. *The Elements*, 41–42.
7. Ibid., 45, 50.
8. Ibid., 42–43.
9. Ibid., 50–51.
10. Ibid., 55–56.
11. Ibid., 61.
12. Ibid., 98. The last sentence is repeated in *Leviathan* in a slightly different context: ". . . for no man can obey two Masters" (pt. 2, chap. 20).
13. Introd. to *A Brief View and Survey of the Dangerous and Pernicious Errors to Church and State in Mr. Hobbes's Book, Entitled Leviathan* (Oxford, 1676).
14. *The Elements*, 103–4.
15. Ibid., 145.
16. Ibid., 145–46.
17. M[onsieur] Graverol, "Memoirs for the Life of M. Samuel Sorbière," in Sorbière, *A Voyage to England, Containing Many Things relating to the State of Learning, Religion, and Other Curiosities of That Kingdom* (London, 1709), xi.
18. Translated from the letter, in Latin, as published in Ferdinand Tönnies, "Siebzehn Briefe des Thomas Hobbes an Samuel Sorbière," *Archiv für Geschichte der Philosophie*, 3 (1889), 194.
19. According to Mintz, the illness was typhus, but he supplies no corroboration for this. Samuel I. Mintz, *The Hunting of Leviathan* (Cambridge: Cambridge University Press, 1969), 19.
20. *E.W.*, II, 9.
21. Ibid., 26.
22. Ibid.
23. Ibid., 6.
24. Ibid., 127.
25. *The Elements*, 94.
26. *E.W.*, II, 67.
27. Ibid., 156–57.
28. *Encyclopaedia Britannica*, 13th ed., xviii, 148. Robert Merton, however, regards Mersenne as a "statesman of science" and, borrowing a phrase from Robert Boyle, "one of the great 'philosophical merchants,' . . . a transmitter of scientific knowledge and an evoker of scientific excellence. It may be enough to say that he conveyed many of Galileo's observations to France (often before Galileo got around to publishing them); that he needled Descartes into putting some of his salient ideas into print; that he wrote brilliantly perceptive accounts of the necessity for *both* specialization and collaboration in science. . . ." Merton, *On the Shoulders of Giants* (New York: Harcourt, Brace & World, Harbinger Books, 1965), 74–75. See also Martha Ornstein, *The Role of Scientific Societies in the Seventeenth Century* (Chicago: University of Chicago Press, 1928), 139–44. Among his own writings, Mersenne's most important work was a book in Latin on the theory of music and musical instruments, *Harmonicorum Libri* (Paris, 1636). A French edition appeared a year later.

29. Mersenne, *Questions théologiques, physiques, morales, et mathématiques* (Paris, 1634).
30. *Encyclopaedia Britannica*, 13th ed., XI, 503.
31. Quentin Skinner, "Thomas Hobbes and His Disciples in France and England," *Comparative Studies in Society and History*, 8 (1966), 155. See also P. H. Hardacre, "The Royalists in Exile during the Puritan Revolution," *Huntington Library Quarterly*, 16 (1953), 353–70; Philip A. Knachel, *England and the Fronde* (Ithaca: Cornell University Press, published for the Folger Shakespeare Library, 1967).
32. "Of one other friend and warm admirer we know little. This was Du Verdus, a noble of Languedoc." Sir Leslie Stephen, *Hobbes* (London: Macmillan, 1904), 36.
33. Paul Tannery, *Mémoires scientifiques*, vol. 10 (Paris: Gauthier-Villars, 1930), 464–65. See also René Pintard, *Le Libertinage érudit dans la première moitié du XVIIe siècle* (Paris: Boivin, 1943), 356.
34. George Croom Robertson, *Hobbes* (Edinburgh and London: William Blackwood, 1910), 236.
35. Laird, *Hobbes*, 256.
36. Georges Ascoli, who compared the Du Verdus translation with Sorbière's earlier one, concluded that Du Verdus relied heavily on Sorbière. Ascoli, *La Grande-Bretagne devant l'opinion française au XVIIIe siècle*, 2 vols. (Paris: J. Gamber, 1930). The "authoritative edition" in French, according to Stephen, is Sorbière's. François Tricaud, Hobbes's most recent French translator and the first and only one to complete the translation into French of *Leviathan* (in 1971), believes that Du Verdus learned English for the express purpose of doing the translation. Tricaud, trans., *Thomas Hobbes: Léviathan: Traité de la matière, de la forme et du pouvoir de la république ecclésiastique et civile* (Paris: Editions Sirey, 1971). The Tricaud edition is also annotated and presents, for the first time, a comparison between the English and Latin *Leviathan*s. Perhaps in gratitude to Du Verdus for this French *De Cive*, Hobbes dedicated to him his *Examinatio et Emendatio Mathematicae Hodiernae* in 1660.
37. Tannnery, *Mémoires*, X, 465.
38. Ibid.
39. Areas of agreement and disagreement are dealt with by Frithiof Brandt, *Thomas Hobbes' Mechanical Conception of Nature* (Copenhagen: Levin & Munksgaard, 1928), 172–79; Peters, *Hobbes*, 28; Miriam M. Reik, *The Golden Lands of Thomas Hobbes* (Detroit:

Wayne State University Press, 1977), 76–79; Laird, *Hobbes*, 92–102.

40. *Encyclopaedia Britannica*, 13th ed., VIII, 81.

41. Descartes's *Meditations* and Hobbes's "Objections," together with those of Gassendi and others, may be found in *The Philosophical Works of Descartes*, rendered into English by Elizabeth S. Haldane and G. R. T. Ross, 2 vols. (Cambridge: Cambridge University Press, 1981; first published 1911). The quoted material is from II, 61.

42. Ibid., 67.

43. Ibid.

44. Letter from Charles Cavendish to John Pell, August 2, 1648, in Helen Hervey, "Hobbes and Descartes in the Light of Some Unpublished Letters of the Correspondence between Sir Charles Cavendish and Dr. John Pell," *Osiris*, 10 (1952), 84. Pell (1611–1685), an Oxford-educated mathematician and philosopher, during the Civil War held successive chairs in both disciplines at the Universities of Amsterdam and Breda. He also served, after

1645, as Cromwell's representative to the Swiss Protestant cantons.

45. See Skinner, "Hobbes," 153.

46. T. R. Harrison et al., eds. *Principles of Internal Medicine*, 4th ed. (New York: McGraw-Hill, 1962), 1864–66.

47. Guy Patin, *Lettres*, vol. 2 (Paris, 1846), 593–94. Patin, apparently, was familiar with Sorbière's translation into French of *De Cive*.

48. John Evelyn (1620–1706), the English diarist, may have been one of Hobbes's last visitors in Paris. On September 7, 1651, he recorded in his *Diary*, he and Hobbes, from a window in the latter's house, watched Louis XIV and a vast entourage ride past on their way to the parlement. Unfortunately, Evelyn's *Diary*, unlike that of Pepys, rarely included gossip and usually was sparing of details, with the result that we have no account of his visit to Hobbes other than the brief report above. *Diary of John Evelyn*, vol. 2 (London: Bickers, 1879), 26–28.

SEVEN "LEVIATHAN"

1. See John Pearson, *Stags and Serpents: The Story of the House of Cavendish and the Dukes of Devonshire* (London: Macmillan, 1983), 45.

2. George Croom Robertson, "Some Newly Discovered Letters of Hobbes," *Mind*, 15 (1890), 440–47.

3. Quoted in Francis Bickley, *The Cavendish Family* (London: Constable, 1911), 58–59. The exact date of the letter is not given. Robert Payne, who filled a variety of roles in the earl's household, was a confidant and frequent correspondent of Hobbes. According to Bickley, if Hobbes had not been absent in France, "he would probably have tutored a third heir of the Devonshires."

4. Quoted in Oliver Lawson Dick, ed., *Aubrey's Brief Lives* (Ann Arbor: University of Michigan Press, 1957; first published 1949), lxxxvii–lxxxviii.

5. Ibid., lxxxvii.

6. Sir Edward Nicholas in a letter to William Edgeman, quoted in Miriam M. Reik, *The Golden Lands of Thomas Hobbes* (Detroit: Wayne State University Press, 1977), 86.

7. The rumor, first printed in John Dowel, *The Leviathan Heretical* (London, 1683), 137, was totally without substance. No biographer of Cromwell, including Antonia Fraser, the author of the recent study *Cromwell: The Lord Protector* (New York: Knopf, 1973), has ever found any evidence to support the allegation. (Personal communication from Ms. Fraser.)

8. In 1842 W. Whewell asserted, "In the common editions (of *Leviathan*), the face has a manifest resemblance to Cromwell ... in these, the engraving is well executed and finished. But in the copy belonging to Trin-

ity College Library, the face appears to be intended for Charles the First. The engraving of this copy is very much worse than the other. ..." Quoted in A. R. Waller, ed., "Note," in *Thomas Hobbes: Leviathan; or, The Matter, Forme & Power of a Commonwealth, Ecclesiasticall and Civil* (Cambridge: Cambridge University Press, 1904), v. The statement was quoted from W. Whewell's lecture on Hobbes, included in his *Lectures on the History of Moral Philosophy* (London, 1842), 21.

9. Hugh Macdonald and Mary Hargreaves, *Thomas Hobbes: A Bibliography* (London: Bibliographical Society, 1952). Macdonald and Hargreaves list a second Latin edition of Hobbes's work, also dated 1668, that was printed in Amsterdam and sold by a London bookseller. They do not mention the 1676 Latin edition published in London.

10. Ibid., 28. The attribution to Holland is based on evidence that the "bear" ornament is found "only in books printed in Holland between 1617 and 1670." The first page of the "Introduction" is headed by the engraved drawing of two winged figures and Saint Christopher, with the initials "C.C." in the central portion. Saint Christopher and the initials are believed to represent the Amsterdam printer Christoffel Cunradus (or Conradus), who was active at the time *Leviathan* was first published.

11. Ibid., 29.

12. Ibid. See also C. B. Macpherson, ed., *Hobbes: Leviathan* (Baltimore: Penguin Books, 1968), 68; Waller, ed., *Hobbes: Leviathan*, viii. The early publishing history of the Latin *Leviathan* is also complicated. The editions of 1670

and 1676 are identical except for type differences between the first and last two pages of the 1670 edition and the corresponding pages of the 1676 edition. The 1678 edition appears to have been an exact reprint of the 1670 edition. See "Introduction," in François Tricaud, trans., *Thomas Hobbes: Léviathan* (Paris: Editions Sirey, 1971), xviii.

13. Keith Brown, "The Artist of the *Leviathan* Title-Page," *British Library Journal*, 4, no. 9 (1978), 24–36. I am greatly indebted to this unique, careful study of the drawing and engraving of the *Leviathan* title page.

14. Ibid., 28.

15. Ibid., 29.

16. Ibid.

17. Ibid.

18. "Introduction" to *Leviathan*. The composition of Leviathan's body also points toward Hollar as the artist. In Prague, Hollar took "a close interest" in Mannerist artists, one of whose favorite devices was the "composition of figures whose outlines are made up of, often symbolically significant, smaller figures." Hollar himself is known to have experimented with such devices. Brown, "Artist," 34.

19. Brown, "Artist," 34.

20. Zbigniew Lubiénski, *Die Grundlagen des ethisch-politischen Systems von Hobbes* (Munich: Ernest Reinhardt, 1932), 254–70. Lubiénski is supported in this by F. C. Hood, *The Divine Politics of Thomas Hobbes: An Interpretation of "Leviathan"* (Oxford: Clarendon Press, 1964). Arguments for and against the priority of certain passages in Latin are discussed at length in Tricaud, trans., *Hobbes: Léviathan*, xix–xxvi.

21. Pt. 2, chap. 21.

22. Pt. 2, chap. 29.

23. Ticaud, trans., *Hobbes: Léviathan*, xxvi.

24. Macdonald and Hargreaves, *Hobbes: Bibliography*, xvi.

25. John Laird, *Hobbes* (New York: Russell & Russell, 1968; first published 1934), 33.

26. George Croom Robertson, *Hobbes* (Edinburgh and London: William Blackwood, 1910), 196–97.

27. Samuel I. Mintz, *The Hunting of Leviathan* (Cambridge: Cambridge University Press, 1969; first published 1962), 14.

28. Richard Peters, *Hobbes* (London: Penguin Books, 1967; first published 1956), 226.

29. Pt. 4, chap. 47. This reference and all subsequent references in this chapter to *Leviathan* are to the first ("head") edition, folio, of 1651, a copy of which is in the writer's possession. These references are followed by corresponding citations in Molesworth.

30. Ibid.; *E.W.*, III, 699. Hobbes's fulminations at religion were directed mainly at the Roman Catholic church, but he was capable of firing sharply pointed barbs at Protestantism. Thus, following one savage casti-

gation of the Catholic clergy, in the course of which he observed that "Ignorance" and "Fraudulent intention" had led to revolts against the Catholic church in France, Holland, and England, he concluded, "I may attribute all the changes of Religion in the world, to one and the same cause; and that is, unpleasing Priests; and those not onely amongst Catholiques, but even in that Church that hath presumed most of Reformation." Pt. 1, chap. 12; *E.W.*, III, 109.

31. "Introduction"; *E.W.*, III, x.

32. Ibid.; *E.W.*, III, xi.

33. Ibid.; Ibid.

34. Ibid; *E.W.*, III, xi–xii.

35. Ibid; *E.W.*, III, xii.

36. Pt. 1, chap. 1; *E.W.*, III, 1.

37. Ibid; *E.W.*, III, 3.

38. Pt. 1, chap. 2; *E.W.*, III, 10.

39. Pt. 1, chap. 3; *E.W.*, III, 17.

40. Pt. 1, chap. 4; *E.W.*, III, 25.

41. Pt. 1, chap. 6; *E.W.*, III, 38–51.

42. Pt. 1, chap. 11; *E.W.*, III, 85–93.

43. Ibid.

44. Pt. 1, chap. 13; *E.W.*, III, 110–116.

45. Ibid.

46. Ibid.

47. Pt. 1, chap. 17; *E.W.*, III, 153–59.

48. Pt. 2, chap. 18; *E.W.*, III, 159–70.

49. Pt. 2, chap. 21; *E.W.*, III, 196–209.

50. Ibid.

51. *A Brief View and Survey of the Dangerous and Pernicious Errors to Church and State in Mr. Hobbes's Book, Entitled Leviathan* (Oxford, 1676), 181.

52. Leo Strauss, *The Political Philosophy of Hobbes: Its Basis and Genesis*, trans. Elsa M. Sinclair (Oxford: Clarendon Press, 1936), 120–21.

53. C. B. Macpherson, *The Political Theory of Possessive Individualism* (Oxford: Oxford University Press Paperbacks, 1979; first published 1962), 48.

54. Macpherson, ed., *Hobbes: Leviathan*, 48–53. Literature arguing for or against these interpretations by Strauss, Macpherson, and others is too extensive to be explored here, and it is also to one side of our major concern, which is less with what Hobbes thought than with why he thought it. The most useful confrontation of the interpretations mentioned is C. B. Macpherson, "Hobbes's Bourgeois Man," and Keith Thomas, "The Social Origins of Hobbes's Political Thought," in K. C. Brown, ed., *Hobbes Studies* (Cambridge: Harvard University Press, 1965), 169–83, 185–236.

55. Pt. 2, chap. 30; *E.W.*, III, 340.

56. According to Strauss (*Political Philosophy*, 121), in the Latin version of *Leviathan* "Hobbes left out the phrases which were hostile to the aristocracy."

57. Pt. 2, chap. 30; *E.W.*, III, 322–43. In our own time a similar position has been taken by

Hannah Arendt and others favoring world-wide population control.

58. Pt. 2, chap. 31; *E.W.*, III, 357–58.

59. Pt. 3, chap. 37; *E.W.*, III, 435.
60. Pt. 4, chap. 44; *E.W.* III, 609–10.
61. Pt. 4, chap. 45; *E.W.* III, 660–63.

EIGHT DISQUISITIONS AND DISPUTATIONS

1. John Chandos, ed., *In God's Name: Examples of Preaching in England, 1534–1662.* (Indianapolis and New York: Bobbs-Merrill, 1971), 554.
2. According to Bowle, Bramhall regarded his controversy with Hobbes as a "sportive occupation." John Bowle, *Hobbes and His Critics* (London: Frank Cass, 1969; first published 1951), 28.
3. Quoted in John Laird, *Hobbes* (New York: Russell & Russell, 1968; first published 1934), 34.
4. *E.W.*, IV, 235–36.
5. Ibid., V, 23–24.
6. Ibid., 25–26.
7. The two editions are listed as nos. 48 and 49 in Hugh Macdonald and Mary Hargreaves, *Thomas Hobbes: A Bibliography* (London: Bibliographical Society, 1952), 37–38. Whereas the printers and dates of the second and third editions of *Leviathan* remain doubtful, there is no question that the second edition of *Of Libertie and Necessitie* was published in London in 1654 by the same printer who had published the first edition. The Macdonald and Hargreaves ordering of the two editions, however, has been challenged by the British bookseller and authority on Hobbes Richard Hatchwell, whose August 1979 catalogue of a collection of books by and about Hobbes, a collection subsequently bought in total by the Japanese, is itself a bibliography. Hatchwell argues the priority of the second edition of 1654 on the grounds that it is "better printed ... with better punctuation, capital letters, and text." He does not, though, discuss the significance of the change of date. Hatchwell's opinion was apparently shared by Molesworth, who noted, following the 1652 date in his edition of Hobbes's *English Works*, "In the first edition of 1654 this date is 1646." *E.W.*, IV, 278. Whatever the correct order of the two editions, the assumption that Hobbes must have known of the second edition, whichever it was, is not affected.
8. The Hobbes-Bramhall controversy about free will is discussed at length in Sir Leslie Stephen, *Hobbes* (London: Macmillan, 1904), 157–72; Laird, *Hobbes*, 189–96; Richard Peters, *Hobbes* (London: Penguin Books, 1967; first published 1956), 167–77; Samuel I. Mintz, *The Hunting of Leviathan* (Cambridge: Cambridge University Press, 1969; first published 1962), 110–33. In the opinion of T. S. Eliot, John Bowle, and other critics of Hobbes, Bramhall had much the better

argument. See Eliot's "John Bramhall," in *Selected Essays* (New York: Harcourt, Brace & World, 1964; first published 1932), 311–19; Bowle, *Hobbes*, 114–33.
9. *E.W.*, IV, 282.
10. Ibid., V, 26–27.
11. George Croom Robertson, *Hobbes* (Edinburgh and London: William Blackwood, 1910), 191.
12. Ibid., 193–94. See also Laird, *Hobbes*, 21–22.
13. *E.W.*, IV, 281.
14. Ibid., 408.
15. Quoted in Bowle, *Hobbes*, 117.
16. Quoted ibid., 120. So far as is known, Bramhall's *Catching of the Leviathan*, in which only the third and final chapter dealt with Hobbes's politics, was last published in 1677, when it appeared in the second Dublin edition of his *Collected Works*.
17. Quoted in Bowle, *Hobbes*, 121.
18. Quoted ibid., 124–25.
19. Quoted ibid., 129.
20. Quoted ibid., 130.
21. All quotations from *A Brief View* are taken from the first edition, on large paper, "Printed at the THEATER," Oxford University, 1676. Of this issue of the first edition, 1,050 copies were printed; another issue, on small paper, was also published at this time. A second impression, in a printing of 1,250 copies, appeared the same year. On the verso of the title page is the legend "IMPRIMATUR / RAD. BATHURST / Vice-Can. Oxon." and the date "July 1, 1676." Presumably, "RAD. BATHURST" was Dr. Ralph Bathurst (1620–1704), sometime dean of Wells Cathedral, whose Latin verses in praise of Hobbes appeared at the beginning of Hobbes's *Humane Nature* (1650).
22. *Brief View*, 11.
23. Ibid., 14.
24. Ibid., 20–21.
25. Ibid., 21.
26. Ibid., 24.
27. Ibid., 28.
28. Ibid., 31. For reasons not clear, this passage is quoted incorrectly in Bowle, *Hobbes*, 165.
29. Ibid., 29.
30. Ibid., 42.
31. Ibid., 45.
32. Ibid., 56–57.
33. Ibid., 54.
34. Ibid., 54–55.
35. *Leviathan*, pt. 2, chap. 19.
36. *Brief View*, 85.
37. Ibid.
38. Ibid., 319.

39. Ibid., 322.
40. Ibid., 4.
41. Ibid., 298.
42. Of the many accounts of this warfare, the most comprehensive, and the ones to which I am most indebted, are those of Robertson, *Hobbes*, 167–85; Laird, *Hobbes*, 102–9; and Miriam M. Reik, *The Golden Lands of Thomas Hobbes* (Detroit: Wayne State University Press, 1977), 167–79.
43. *E.W.*, VII, 281.
44. Ibid., 349.
45. Ibid., 352–53.
46. Ibid., 352.
47. Ibid., 387.
48. Quoted in Macdonald and Hargreaves, *Hobbes: Bibliography*, 44.
49. Quoted ibid., 48.
50. *E.W.*, IV, 440.
51. Ibid., 416. Wallis's accusation appeared in his *Hobbiani Puncti Dispunctio* (1657). His language drew a rejoinder from Hobbes's physician friend Henry Stubbe (1631–1676), who at one time was occupied in translating *Leviathan* into Latin. In an extract of a letter, the recipient and date of which are unknown, Stubbe called Wallis a "puny

professor" who, as "The Doctor (Sir Reverence)," might have used a "cleanlier expression than that of a *shitten piece.*" *E.W.*, VII, 426–27. According to Aubrey, Stubbe in July 1676 drowned "riding between Bath and Bristol."
52. *E.W.*, VII, 7.
53. Ibid., 14.
54. Ibid., 127.
55. Ibid., 122.
56. G. R. de Beer, "Some Letters of Thomas Hobbes," *Notes and Records of the Royal Society*, 7 (1950), 197; review (anon.) of Robertson's *Hobbes*, in *Quarterly Review*, May 1887, p. 439.
57. Quoted in Martha Ornstein, *The Role of Scientific Societies in the Seventeenth Century* (Chicago: University of Chicago Press, 1928), 108–9.
58. Quoted from Huygens, *Oeuvres complètes*, II, 296, and Scott, *Mathematical Work of Wallis*, 170–71, in Reik, *Golden Lands*, 178–79.
59. Ibid.
60. Quoted from Boyle's preface to his *Examen* (1662), ibid., 180.
61. See Reik, *Golden Lands*, 176.
62. *E.W.*, IV, 436–37.

N I N E   THE BEAR IN WINTER

1. Joseph Grove, *Lives of the Cavendishes* (London, 1764), 4.
2. The artist must have been Samuel Cooper (1609–1672), generally regarded as the greatest miniaturist in the history of art. According to Antonia Fraser, a crayoned portrait of Charles made by Cooper was "for the benefit of the new coinage." Fraser, *Royal Charles: Charles II and the Restoration* (New York: Delta, 1980), 193. Cooper also painted Hobbes, Aubrey reported, in a portrait requested by Charles that subsequently hung in his "closet" (i.e., private room); this may or may not be the unfinished sketch of Hobbes that was in the collection of James II and is now in the Cleveland Museum of Art. Cooper's portraits in miniature of the king's family, including several of his mistresses and illegitimate children, were much admired, and he painted, in addition, Elizabeth Pepys, the wife of the diarist, and Aubrey himself.
3. Quoted in Gilbert Burnet (later bishop of Salisbury), *History of My Own Time* (1683), in Fraser, *Royal Charles*, 257.
4. *E.W.*, VII, 471–72.
5. Samuel Sorbière, *A Journey to England*, (London, 1709), 40.
6. Manuscripts Related to Gresham College, Extract of Letter from Mr. Hooke to Robert Boyle, Esq., about the Year 1664, Additional Manuscripts, British Museum, 6, 193.
7. *A Dialogue between a Philosopher and a Stu-*

dent of the Common Laws of England, ed. and with an introd. by Joseph Cropsey (Chicago: University of Chicago Press, 1971). If Aubrey was correct, however, *A Dialogue* was not begun until sometime after 1664. See below, pp. 216–17.
8. Ibid. The three earlier English publications of *A Dialogue* were in the 1750 edition of Hobbes's *Moral and Political Works;* Francis Maseres, ed., *Select Tracts Relating to the Civil Wars in England . . .* (London, 1815); and in *E.W.*, VI.
9. All references to *Behemoth* are to Ferdinand Tönnies, ed., *Behemoth; or, The Long Parliament*, by Thomas Hobbes, 2d ed., with a new introd. by M. M. Goldsmith (London: Frank Cass, 1969). Tönnies's edition of *Behemoth*, first published in 1889, was based on a manuscript copy Tönnies discovered in St. John's College, Oxford, believed by Tönnies to be the original draft. According to him, the first and subsequent editions of *Behemoth*, including that of Molesworth, contained errors, corrections, and deletions, many of which related to "statements of opinion too strong to be known" when the book first was published. Tönnies deciphered these corrections and restored the deletions wherever possible, marking the changes he had made with asterisks and parentheses. One of his changes was in the title, which originally had been *Behemoth; or, The Long Parliament.* In the early editions of the book, "The Long

Parliament," which Hobbes had regarded as an abomination, was omitted from the title, presumably as a concession to the sensibilities of Parliaments that succeeded it. Unfortunately, Tönnies modernized the language of *Behemoth*, with the result, as Goldsmith notes (p. viii), that while the book is more easily read, "it loses a bit of its seventeenth-century character." Goldsmith, who consulted the St. John's manuscript, also establishes that Tönnies occasionally relied on Molesworth's text in reproducing a word or phrase, thereby, in certain instances, repeating errors Molesworth had made.

10. Ibid., 2–3.
11. Ibid., 3–4.
12. Ibid., 9–10.
13. Ibid., 20–22.
14. Ibid., 24–26.
15. Ibid., 56.
16. Ibid., 40–41.
17. Ibid., 41–42.
18. Ibid., 43–44.
19. Ibid., 46, 50.
20. Ibid., 41.
21. Ibid., 54.
22. Ibid., 63–64.
23. Ibid., 95.
24. Ibid., 69.
25. Ibid., 104.
26. Ibid., 126.
27. Ibid., 47.
28. Ibid., 38.
29. Ibid., 188; Robert K. Merton, "The Self-Fulfilling Prophecy," *Antioch Review*, Summer 1948, pp. 193–210, reprinted in Merton, *Social Theory and Social Structure*, rev. and enl. ed. (Glencoe, Ill.: Free Press, 1957), 421–38.
30. Tönnies, ed., *Behemoth*, v.
31. Cropsey, ed., *Dialogue*, 5–6.
32. According to Cropsey, whose lengthy introduction to his 1971 edition of *A Dialogue* is the most comprehensive analysis of that document that has been made thus far, the absence of any protest by Aubrey and others when *A Dialogue* was published in 1681 constitutes "evidence against the view that this is a work desired by Hobbes to be suppressed" (p. 7). He may be correct about Hobbes, but Aubrey's failure to protest publication does not prove his point. So far as is known, Aubrey also did not object to the republication in 1683 of the English translation of *De Mirabilibus Pecci*, a work of which Hobbes in his later life was ashamed and which he wished he had never written. The earlier English version, published in 1678, when Hobbes was still alive, carried the notice "This Latine Poem, writ by the famous Mr. Thomas Hobs of Malmesbury . . . is now translated into English, although without the knowledge of Mr. Hobs." Quoted in Macdonald and Hargreaves, *Hobbes: Bibliography*, 6.

33. Cropsey, ed., *Dialogue*, 11–12.
34. *E.W.*, VI, 3.
35. Ibid., 5.
36. See Cropsey, ed., *Dialogue*, 14.
37. *E.W.*, VI, 11.
38. Ibid., 13.
39. Ibid., 22–23.
40. Ibid., 15.
41. Ibid., 44.
42. Ibid., 45.
43. Ibid., 96–97.
44. Quoted from Anthony à Wood's *Athenae Oxonienses and Fasti*, in *Encyclopaedia Britannica*, 13th ed., X, 240.
45. Andrew Clark, ed., *Life and Times of Anthony Wood* (London, 1891–1900), II, 291.
46. Ibid., 293.
47. Wood altered the latter part of this sentence in Aubrey's account, making it read, "fumed at it as a most famous libell; and soon after meeting the author of the History, chid him." Ibid. Wood (1632–1695), not easily discouraged by Fell or anyone else, continued to collect information about Hobbes and other Oxford alumni, which he published in his two-volume *Athenae Oxonienses* in 1691–92. By that time Fell was dead, but Wood, who was suspected of being a Catholic or at least sympathetic to Catholicism, was in difficulty with other Oxford University authorities. In July 1693 his *Athenae Oxonienses* was condemned for having libeled Clarendon, as a result of which Wood was fined and banished from the university until he recanted, and the second volume of the *Athenae* was publicly burned. A contributing factor in Wood's disgrace may have been Wood's referring to Fell's reply to Hobbes as "scurrulous," and several Oxford dignitaries are known to have objected to the inclusion in *Athenae* of another Hobbes biography that had an account of the Fell-Hobbes controversy. The conclusion should not be drawn, however, that Wood was, like Aubrey, an unreserved admirer of Hobbes, for as will be seen in the final chapter, he was not. *Encyclopaedia Britannica*, 13th ed., X, 788–89. See also Allan Pritchard, "The Last Days of Hobbes: Evidence of the Wood Manuscripts," *Bodleian Library Record*, 10 (1980), 178–87.
48. Clark, ed., *Life and Times*, 293–94.
49. Quoted from Dryden's preface to the *Fables* (1700), in Macdonald and Hargreaves, *Hobbes: Bibliography*, 58.
50. *Oxford English Dictionary*. *Grove's Dictionary of Music and Musicians* (Philadelphia: Theodore Presser, 1927; first published 1907), III, 813, distinguishing prick songs from those "performed extemporaneously," explains that the word "prick" is derived from the word "as used to express the point or dot forming the head of the note. . . . The term 'pricking of musick bookes' was formerly

employed to express the writing of them."

51. Geoffrey Trease, *Portrait of a Cavalier: William Cavendish of Newcastle* (New York: Taplinger, 1979), 170. Trease's reference to this event, however, is somewhat ambiguous: "She (Margaret, Duchesse of Newcastle) drove with her sisters in Hyde Park, attended a musical evening at Henry Lawes's house, ran into Hobbes and asked him to dinner."

52. *Grove's Dictionary of Music and Musicians*, II, 656. *Choice Psalmes Put into Musick for Three Voices . . . Composed by Henry and William Lawes* was published in 1648, but Henry Lawes's *Ayres and Dialogues, For One, Two, and Three Voyces*, first issued in 1653, probably was one of the books of prick song, perhaps in a later edition, to which Aubrey referred.

53. White Kennet, *A Sermon Preach'd at the Funeral of the Right Noble William Duke of Devonshire* (London, 1708), 107. "Hobbes's belief that diet and exercise prolong life, with respect to which he was, like Bacon, centuries ahead of his time, apparently was not shared by most of his friends. But few of them went to the extreme of John Hall of Durham, twenty-nine years old when he died

in 1656. Hall, poet, essayist, and pamphleteer, "greatly objected to any form of exercise," and "being inclined to pursinesse & fatnesse, rather than he would use any great motion, thought fitter to prevent it by frequent swallowing down of pebble-stones, which proved effectuall." Quoted in Robert K. Merton, *On the Shoulders of Giants* (New York: Harcourt, Brace & World, 1965), 77.

54. Kennet, *Sermon*, 107–8.

55. Ibid., 109.

56. Quoted in Pritchard, "Last Days of Hobbes," 183.

57. Kennet, *Sermon*, 115.

58. Quoted in Pritchard, "Last Days of Hobbes," 183–84.

59. Quoted ibid.

60. Quoted ibid., 184.

61. Kennet, *Sermon*, 116–17.

62. Reik, *Golden Lands*, 225.

63. Ibid.

64. Based on Gregory King, *Natural and Political Observations and Conclusions upon the State and Condition of England* (1696), printed as an appendix to George Chalmer's *Estimate of the Comparative Strength of Great Britain . . .* (London, 1804).

65. Clark, ed., *Life and Times*, II, 471.

T E N   HOBBES IN HIS TIME AND OURS

1. Geoffrey Warnock, principal of Hertford College, in *The Times* (London), December 4, 1979.

2. Quoted ibid.

3. Andrew Clark, ed., *Life and Times of Anthony Wood* (London, 1891–1900), II, 63–64. Hobbes's books were in good company: Stephen Junius Brutus's *Vindiciae Contra Tyrannos* (Brutus is believed to have been the pseudonym of the French Huguenot Hubert Languet), "John Milton's pieces in defense of the king's murder," and works by John Knox were also committed to the flames. Wood, who apparently approved of the bonfire, states that Wallis was not present. "Hobs his *Leviathan*," he wrote (I, 472), "hath corrupted the gentry of the nation, hath infused ill principles into them, atheisme."

4. Sir Leslie Stephen, *Hobbes* (London: Macmillan, 1904), 60–61.

5. Bernulf Hodge, *A History of Malmesbury* (Malmesbury: Friends of Malmesbury Abbey, 1976; first published 1968), 17–19. Hodge noted, however, that though Hobbes "is apparently classed as a form of Karl Marx abroad . . . in actual fact he was far from that in real life."

6. Maurice Ashley, *England in the Seventeenth Century (1603–1714)* (London: Penguin Books, 1956; first published in 1952), 114.

7. The 1881 edition was edited by J. Thornton and published by Oxford University Press.

8. The book, published in New York by E. P. Dutton, contained an introduction by Henry Morley.

9. Publications and dates are based on listings in the Library of Congress's *National Union Catalog: Pre-1956 Imprints*.

10. Michael Oakeshott, *Hobbes on Civil Association* (Oxford: Basil Blackwell, 1975), 3.

11. Quoted in Thomas A. Spragens, Jr., *The Politics of Motion: The World of Thomas Hobbes* (London: Croom Helm, 1973), 19.

12. H. R. Trevor-Roper, *Men and Events* (New York: Harper & Row, 1957), 236.

13. Of the many evaluations of Hobbes as a scientist and philosopher, as opposed to political theorist, the most incisive is that of Frithiof Brandt: "Hobbes was a transitional figure. He was born when scholasticism prevailed, he was one of the pioneers of the mechanical conception of nature, but he developed into a scholastic mechanicist. He never forgot the deductive logic he had learnt as a young man at Oxford. He always remained an adherent of deduction. And when the members of the Royal Society adopted the experimental method of research, Bacon's method, Hobbes could no longer keep abreast of them." Because of this backwardness, Brandt maintains, Hobbes when he died "was almost a forgotten figure in natural science." Brandt, *Thomas Hobbes' Mechanical Conception of Nature* (Copen-

hagen: Levin & Munksgaard, 1928), 378.

14. T. S. Eliot, "John Bramhall," in *Selected Essays* (New York: Harcourt, Brace & World, 1964; first published 1932), 312. Hobbes's theory of government, Eliot continued (313), "has no philosophic basis: it is merely a collection of discrete opinions, prejudices, and genuine reflections upon experience which are given a spurious unity by a shadowy metaphysic."

15. Ibid., 314.

16. The belief that Hobbes was an atheist or was close to being one has been held by Leo Strauss, John Bowle, Basil Willey, H. R. Trevor-Roper, A. D. Lindsay, and Sterling P. Lamprecht, among others. The contrary view, that he was not an atheist or was writing about religion in the context of a theism or an earlier tradition of religious thought, has been put forward by Howard Warrender, Michael Oakeshott, Keith Brown, Willis B. Glover, M. M. Goldsmith, and Samuel I. Mintz, among others; F. C. Hood, however, is almost alone in arguing that Hobbes was an orthodox Christian.

17. Quoted in *The Last Sayings, or Dying Legacy of Mr. Thomas Hobbs of Malmesbury Who Departed This Life on Thursday, Decemb. 4. 1679* (London, 1680).

18. John Bowle, *Hobbes and His Critics* (London: Frank Cass, 1969; first published 1951), 42; Richard S. Peters, "Thomas Hobbes," in *The Encyclopedia of Philosophy* (New York: Macmillan, 1967), IV, 45. Peters, in *Hobbes* (London: Penguin Books, 1967; first published 1956), 227, 229, 237, and 238, repeatedly makes use of the word "irony" to describe Hobbes's attitude toward religion.

19. Quoted in *Last Sayings*.

20. *Humane Nature* (1650), *E.W.*, IV, 59–60.

21. John Whitehall, quoted by Bowle, *Hobbes*, 180.

22. Quoted from Tyndale's *The Obedience of a Christian Man* (1528), in Craig R. Thompson, *Universities in Tudor England* (Washington: Folger Shakespeare Library, 1959), 22.

23. Quoted Ibid.

24. Quoted Ibid.

25. Ronald Hepburn, "Hobbes and the Knowledge of God," in Maurice Cranston and Richard S. Peters, eds., *Hobbes and Rousseau: A Collection of Critical Essays* (Garden City, N.Y.: Anchor Books, 1972), 88.

26. Peters (*Hobbes*, 26–27) related Hobbes's "fear" to a "desire for esteem [that] expressed itself in the flattering delusion that men were taking note of him and planning

his decease" and to "an exaggerated sense of his own importance." Hobbes, he argued (26, 28, 35), all of his life suffered from a "feeling of insecurity," had "the angry, aggressive style of an insecure man," and in *Leviathan* vented "the over-confident appeal of an insecure, angry, and intellectually arrogant theoretician." A French view, in 1697, was that while Hobbes's reported fear of ghosts ("fantomes") and demons ("demons") was discounted by his friends, "they do not deny that he did not wish to live by himself; they content themselves with the suggestion that this was because he was afraid of assassins" ("Mais il semble qu'ils ne nient pas qu'il n'osait demeurer seul; ils se contentent d'insinuer que c'était à cause qu'il craignait les assassins"). *Dictionaire historique et critique de Pierre Bayle* (Paris, 1820; first published 1697), VIII, 168.

27. White Kennet, *A Sermon Preach'd at the Funeral of the Right Noble William Duke of Devonshire . . .* (London, 1708), 113.

28. John Laird, *Hobbes* (New York: Russell & Russell, 1968; first published 1934), 3.

29. Isaac Disraeli, *Calamities and Quarrels of Authors*, new ed. (London: Frederick Warne, n.d.; *Calamities of Authors* first published 1812–13, *Quarrels of Authors* 1814), 454.

30. *E.W.*, II, 2n.

31. Ibid., 8.

32. A most improbable coincidence is that the third earl of Devonshire, as painted by Van Dyck, bears a marked resemblance to the face of the "Mortal God" on the engraved title page of the first edition of *Leviathan*, which, as we noted earlier, is believed by some to have depicted Charles II or Cromwell (see above, pp. 154–60). Similarities between the portrait and the engraving can be seen in the mustaches (in the engraving, however, the mustache is fuller), the part and curl of the hair over the forehead, the fall of hair on the shoulders, and the shadowing below the lower lip. Though the third earl, who was thirty-four in 1651, was in Paris during the early years of Hobbes's extended sojourn there between 1640 and 1651, no evidence for his having modeled, as it were, for Hollar, assuming Hollar was the engraver, has ever come to light.

33. *Discourses*, bk. 3, chap. 40.

34. The "radical right" is portrayed in Daniel Bell et al., *The New American Right* (New York: Criterion Books, 1955). See especially Hofstadter's article, "The Pseudo-conservative Revolt."

Appendix I

1. Noel Malcolm, "Hobbes, Sandys, and the Virginia Company," *Historical Journal*, 24 (June 1981), 320–21.

2. The disputed authorship of the manuscript, and the book itself, is also discussed in Friedrich O. Wolf, *Die Neue Wissenschaft des*

Thomas Hobbes ... Mit Hobbes Essayes (Stuttgart-Bad Cannstatt: Frommann-Holzboog, 1969), 133–34. The manuscript itself is reprinted on pp. 135–67. See also James Jay Hamilton, "Hobbes's Study and the Hardwick Library," *Journal of the History of Philosophy*, 16 (1978), 451–52; and Malcolm, "Hobbes."

Select Bibliography

Ashley, Maurice. *England in the Seventeenth Century (1603–1714)*. London: Penguin Books, 1956; first published 1952.

———. *Charles II*. London: Panther Books, 1973; first published 1971.

Aubrey, John. *"Brief Lives," Chiefly of Contemporaries, Set Down by John Aubrey, between the Years 1669 and 1696*. Edited by Andrew Clark. 2 vols. Oxford: Clarendon Press, 1898.

Bickley, Francis. *The Cavendish Family*. London: Constable, 1911.

Botwinick, Aryeh. *Hobbes and Modernity: Five Exercises in Political Philosophical Exegesis*. Lanham, Md.: University Press of America, 1983.

Bowen, Catherine Drinker. *Francis Bacon: The Temper of a Man*. Boston: Atlantic–Little, Brown, 1963.

Bowle, John. *Hobbes and His Critics: A Study in Seventeenth Century Constitutionalism*. London: Frank Cass, 1969; first published 1951.

Boynton, Lindsay, ed. *The Hardwick Hall Inventories of 1601*. London: Furniture History Society, 1971.

Brandt, Frithiof. *Thomas Hobbes' Mechanical Conception of Nature*. Copenhagen: Levin & Munksgaard, 1928.

Bridenbaugh, Carl. *Vexed and Troubled Englishmen, 1590–1642*. New York: Oxford University Press, 1968.

Brown, Keith C., ed. *Hobbes Studies*. Cambridge: Harvard University Press, 1965.

Catlin, George E. G. *Thomas Hobbes as Philosopher, Publicist and Man of Letters*. Oxford: Basil Blackwell, 1922.

Clarendon, Edward, Earl of. *A Brief View and Survey of the Dangerous and Pernicious Errors to Church and State, in Mr. Hobbes Book Entitled Leviathan*. Oxford, 1676.

Clark, G. N. *The Seventeenth Century*. London: Oxford Paperbacks, 1960; first published 1929.

Coleman, Frank M. *Hobbes and America: Exploring the Constitutional Foundations*. Toronto: University of Toronto Press, 1977.

Collins, A. *Historical Collections of the Noble Families of Cavendish*. London, 1752.

Coltman, Irene. *Private Men and Public Causes: Philosophy and Politics in the English Civil War*. London: Faber and Faber, 1962.

Cooper, J. P., ed. *The Decline of Spain and the Thirty Years War*. Vol. 4 of *The New Cambridge Modern History*. Cambridge: Cambridge University Press, 1970.

Cranston, Maurice, and Richard S. Peters, eds. *Hobbes and Rousseau: A Collection of Critical Essays*. Modern Studies in Philosophy. Garden City, N.Y.: Anchor Books, 1972.

Curtis, Mark H. *Oxford and Cambridge in Transition, 1558–1642*. Oxford: Clarendon Press, 1959.

De Beer, G. R. "Some Letters of Thomas Hobbes." *Notes and Records of the Royal Society*, 7 (1950), 195–206.

Devonshire, Duchess of. *The House: A Portrait of Chatsworth*. London: Macmillan, 1982.

Dewey, John. "The Motivation of Hobbes's Political Philosophy." In *Studies in the History of Ideas*. Vol. 9. New York: Columbia University Press, 1918.

Dick, Oliver Lawson, ed. *Aubrey's Brief Lives*. Foreword by Edmund Wilson. Ann Arbor: University of Michigan Press, 1957; first published 1949.

Disraeli, Isaac. *Calamities and Quarrels of Authors*. New ed. London: Frederick Warne, n.d.; first published 1812–14.

Dodd, A. H. *Life in Elizabethan England*. London: Batsford, 1967; first published 1961.

Eliot, T. S. "John Bramhall." In *Selected Essays: 1917–1932*. New York: Harcourt, Brace & World, 1964; first published 1932.

Ellenby, Jean. *The Stuart Household*. Over, Cambridge: Dinosaur Publications, 1981.
Elton, G. R., ed. *The Tudor Constitution: Documents and Commentary*. Cambridge: Cambridge University Press, 1962; first published 1960.
Fraser, Antonia. *Cromwell, The Lord Protector*. New York: Knopf, 1973.
———. *Royal Charles: Charles II and the Restoration*. New York: Delta, 1980; first published 1979.
———. *The Weaker Vessel*. New York: Knopf, 1984.
Girouard, Mark. *Hardwick Hall*. London: National Trust, 1976.
Goldsmith, M. M. *Hobbes's Science of Politics*. New York: Columbia University Press, 1966.
———. Introduction to *Thomas Hobbes: The Elements of Law Natural and Politic*. Edited by Ferdinand Tönnies. 2d ed. London: Frank Cass, 1969.
Grove, Joseph. *Lives of the Cavendishes*. London, 1764.
Goulding, R. W. *Margaret (Lucas) Duchess of Newcastle*. Lincoln, 1925.
Hargreaves-Mawdsley, W. N. *Oxford in the Age of John Locke*. Norman: University of Oklahoma Press, 1973.
Harrison, Molly, and O. M. Royston. *How They Lived: 1485–1700*. Oxford: Basil Blackwell, 1965; first published 1963.
Hartley, Harold, ed. *The Royal Society: Its Origins and Founders*. London: Royal Society, 1960.
Hervey, Helen. "Hobbes and Descartes in the Light of Some Unpublished Letters of the Correspondence between Sir Charles Cavendish and Dr. John Pell." *Osiris*, 10 (1952), 67–90.
Hill, Christopher. *The Century of Revolution, 1603–1714*. New York: W. W. Norton, 1966; first published 1961.
———. *The Experience of Defeat: Milton and Some Contemporaries*. New York: Viking, 1984.
———. *Puritanism and Revolution*. London: Secker and Warburg, 1958.
Hill Christopher, and Edmund Dell, eds. *The Good Old Cause: The English Revolution of 1640–1660*. 2d ed. New York: Augustus M. Kelley, 1969; first published 1949.
Hobbes, Thomas. *The English Works of Thomas Hobbes of Malmesbury*. Edited by Sir William Molesworth. 11 vols. London: Bohn, 1839–45.
———. *De Cive: The English Version*. Edited by Howard Warrender. Oxford: Oxford University Press, 1983.
Hood, F. C. *The Divine Politics of Thomas Hobbes: An Interpretation of "Leviathan."* Oxford: Clarendon Press, 1964.
Kennet, White. *A Sermon Preach'd at the Funeral of the Right Noble William Duke of Devonshire . . . with Some Memoirs of the Family of Cavendish*. London, 1708.
Kenyon, J. P. *The Stuart Constitution: Documents and Commentary*. Cambridge: Cambridge University Press, 1966.
———. *Stuart England*. London: Penguin Books, 1978.
———. *The Stuarts*. London: Fontana / Collins, 1978; first published 1958.
Knachel, Philip A. *England and the Fronde: The Impact of the English Civil War and Revolution on France*. Ithaca, N.Y.: Folger Shakespeare Library and Cornell University Press, 1967.
King, Preston. *The Ideology of Order*. New York: Barnes & Noble, 1974; first published 1974.
Laird, John. *Hobbes*. New York: Russell & Russell, 1968; first published 1934.
La Mar, Virginia A. *Travel and Roads in England*. Washington: Folger Shakespeare Library, 1979; first published 1960.
Lamont, William, and Sybil Oldfield. *Politics, Religion and Literature in the Seventeenth Century*. London: Dent, 1975.
Lamprecht, Sterling. "Hobbes and Hobbism." *American Political Science Review*, 34 (1940), 31–53.
Laslett, Peter. *The World We Have Lost*. London: Methuen, 1979; first published 1965.
Luce, Major General Sir Richard H. *The History of the Abbey and Town of Malmesbury*. Malmesbury: Friends of Malmesbury Abbey, 1979.
Macdonald, Hugh, and Mary Hargreaves. *Thomas Hobbes: A Bibliography*. London: Bibliographical Society, 1952.
McNeilly, F. S. *The Anatomy of Leviathan*. London: Macmillan, 1958.
Macpherson, C. B. *The Political Theory of Possessive Individualism: Hobbes to Locke*. Oxford: Clarendon Press, 1962.
Malcolm, Noel. "Hobbes, Sandys, and the Virginia Company." *Historical Journal*, 24 (1981), 297–321.
Mallet, Charles Edward. *A History of the University of Oxford*. Vol. 2, *The Sixteenth and Seventeenth Centuries*. London: Methuen, 1924. Reprint. New York: Barnes & Noble, 1958.
The Manuscripts of His Grace the Duke of Portland, Preserved at Welbeck Abbey. Historical Manuscripts Commission, 13th Report, Appendix, pt. 2. London, 1893.
Marriott, J. A. R. *Life and Times of Lucius Cary, Viscount Falkland*. 2d ed. London, 1908.
Marwil, Jonathan L. *The Trials and Counsel of Francis Bacon in 1621*. Detroit: Wayne State University Press, 1976.
Merton, Robert K. *On the Shoulders of Giants*. New York: Harcourt, Brace & World, Harbinger Books, 1965.

Mintz, Samuel I. *The Hunting of Leviathan: Seventeenth-Century Reactions to the Materialism and Moral Philosophy of Thomas Hobbes.* Cambridge: Cambridge University Press, 1969.

Notestein, Wallace. *The English People on the Eve of Colonization, 1603–1630.* New York: Harper Torchbooks, 1962; first published 1954.

Oakeshott, Michael. *Hobbes on Civil Association.* Oxford: Basil Blackwell, 1975; first published 1946.

Ornstein, Martha. *The Role of Scientific Societies in the Seventeenth Century.* Chicago: University of Chicago Press, 1928.

Pearson, John. *Stags and Serpents: The Story of the House of Cavendish and the Dukes of Devonshire.* London: Macmillan, 1983.

Peters, Richard. *Hobbes.* London: Penguin Books, 1967; first published 1956.

Plamenatz, John. *The English Utilitarians.* Oxford: Basil Blackwell, 1949.

Powell, Anthony. *John Aubrey and His Friends.* New and rev. ed. London: Heinemann, 1963; first published 1948.

Raphael, D. D. *Hobbes: Morals and Politics.* London: Allen and Unwin, 1977.

Reik, Miriam M. *The Golden Lands of Thomas Hobbes.* Detroit: Wayne State University Press, 1977.

Robertson, George Croom. *Hobbes.* Edinburgh and London: William Blackwood 1910. Reprint. St. Clair Shores, Mich.: Scholarly Press, 1979.

Ross, Ralph, Herbert W. Schneider, and Theodore Waldman, eds. *Thomas Hobbes in His Time.* Minneapolis: University of Minnesota Press, 1974.

Rowse, A. L. *The England of Elizabeth.* Madison: University of Wisconsin Press, 1978; first published 1950.

Saintsbury, George. *A History of English Prose Rhythm.* London: Macmillan, 1922.

Scott, A. F. *The Stuart Age.* New York: Crowell, 1975.

Skinner, Quentin. "The Context of Hobbes's Theory of Political Obligation." In *Hobbes and Rousseau,* edited by M. Cranston and R. S. Peters. Garden City, N.Y.: Anchor Books, 1972.

Singer, S. W. *The Table-Talk of John Selden.* 2d ed. London: John Russell Smith, 1856.

Sorbière, Samuel. *A Voyage to England, Containing Many Things relating to the State of Learning, Religion, and Other Curiosities of That Kingdom.* London, 1709.

Spragens, Thomas A., Jr. *The Politics of Motion: The World of Thomas Hobbes.* London: Croom Helm, 1973.

Stephen, Sir Leslie. *Hobbes.* English Men of Letters Series. London: Macmillan, 1904.

Strauss, Leo. *The Political Philosophy of Hobbes: Its Basis and Genesis.* Translated by Elsa M. Sinclair. Oxford: Clarendon Press, 1936.

Thompson, Craig R. *Universities in Tudor England.* Washington: Folger Shakespeare Library, 1959.

———. *The English Church in the Sixteenth Century.* Washington: Folger Library, 1979; first published 1958.

———. *Schools in Tudor England.* Washington: Folger Library, 1979; first published 1958.

Tönnies, Ferdinand. "Contributions à l'histoire de la pensée de Hobbes." *Archives de Philosophie,* 12 (1936), 73–98.

———. "Hobbes-Analekten." *Archiv für Geschichte der Philosophie,* 17 (1903), 291–317; 19 (1906), 153–75.

———. "Siebzehn Briefe des Thomas Hobbes an Samuel Sobière, nebst Briefen Sorbière's, Mersenne's." *Archiv für Geschichte der Philosophie,* 3 (1889), 194–200.

———. *Thomas Hobbes: Der Mann und der Denker.* Osterwieck / Harz and Leipzig: U. W. Zickfeldt, 1912.

Trease, Geoffrey. *Portrait of a Cavalier: William Cavendish, First Duke of Newcastle.* New York: Taplinger, 1979.

Trevor-Roper, Hugh. *Edward Hyde, Earl of Clarendon.* Oxford: Clarendon Press, 1975.

Warrender, Howard. *The Political Philosophy of Hobbes: His Theory of Obligation.* Oxford: Clarendon Press, 1957.

———. "A Reply to Mr. Plamenatz." In *Hobbes Studies,* edited by Keith Brown. Cambridge: Harvard University Press, 1965.

Watkins, J. W. N. "Philosophy and Politics in Hobbes." *Philosophical Quarterly,* 5 (1955), 125–46.

———. *Hobbes's System of Ideas: A Study in the Political Significance of Philosophical Theories.* Rev. ed. London: Hutchinson University Library, 1973.

Weber, Kurt. *Lucius Cary: Second Viscount Falkland.* New York: Columbia University Press, 1940.

Wernham, R. B., and J. C. Walker, eds. *England under Elizabeth.* London: Longmans, Green, 1932.

Whitlock, Ralph. *The Folklore of Wiltshire.* Totowa, N.J.: Rowman and Littlefield, 1976.

Willey, Basil. *The Seventeenth Century Background.* Garden City, N.Y.: Anchor Books, 1953; first published 1934.

Wilson, Charles. *England's Apprenticeship, 1603–1763.* London: Longman, 1979; first published 1965.

Wood, Anthony à. *Athenae Oxonienses.* Edited by Philip Bliss. 4 vols. London, 1813–20.

INDEX